CONTEMPORARY ART
FROM CRESCENT MOON PUBLISHING

The Art of Andy Goldsworthy: Complete Works: Special Edition
by William Malpas

The Art of Andy Goldsworthy
by William Malpas

Andy Goldsworthy: Touching Nature
by William Malpas

Richard Long: The Art of Walking
by William Malpas

The Art of Richard Long: Complete Works
by William Malpas

Constantin Brancusi: Sculpting the Essence of Things
by James Pearson

Alison Wilding: The Embrace of Sculpture
by Susan Quinnell

Eric Gill: Nuptials of God
by Anthony Hoyland

The Erotic Object: Sexuality in Sculpture From Prehistory to the Present Day
by Susan Quinnell

Minimal Art and Artists in the 1960s and After
by Laura Garrard

Land Art: A Complete Guide to Landscape, Environmental, Earthworks, Nature, Sculpture and Installation Art
by William Malpas

Andy Goldsworthy In Close-Up
by William Malpas

Richard Long In Close-Up
by William Malpas

Land Art In Close-Up
by William Malpas

Colourfield Painting: Minimal, Cool, Hard Edge, Serial and Post-Painterly Abstract Art From the Sixties to the Present
by Stuart Morris

Mark Rothko: The Art of Transcendence
by Julia Davis

Jasper Johns: Painting By Numbers
by L.M. Poole

Brice Marden
by Laura Garrard

Frank Stella: American Abstract Artist: Special Edition
by James Pearson

Maurice Sendak and the Art of Children's Book Illustration
by L.M. Poole

Sacred Gardens: The Garden in Myth, Religion and Art
by Jeremy Robinson

Sex in Art: Pornography and Pleasure in Painting and Sculpture
by Cassidy Hughes

Land Art In the U.S.A.

Land Art In the U.S.A.

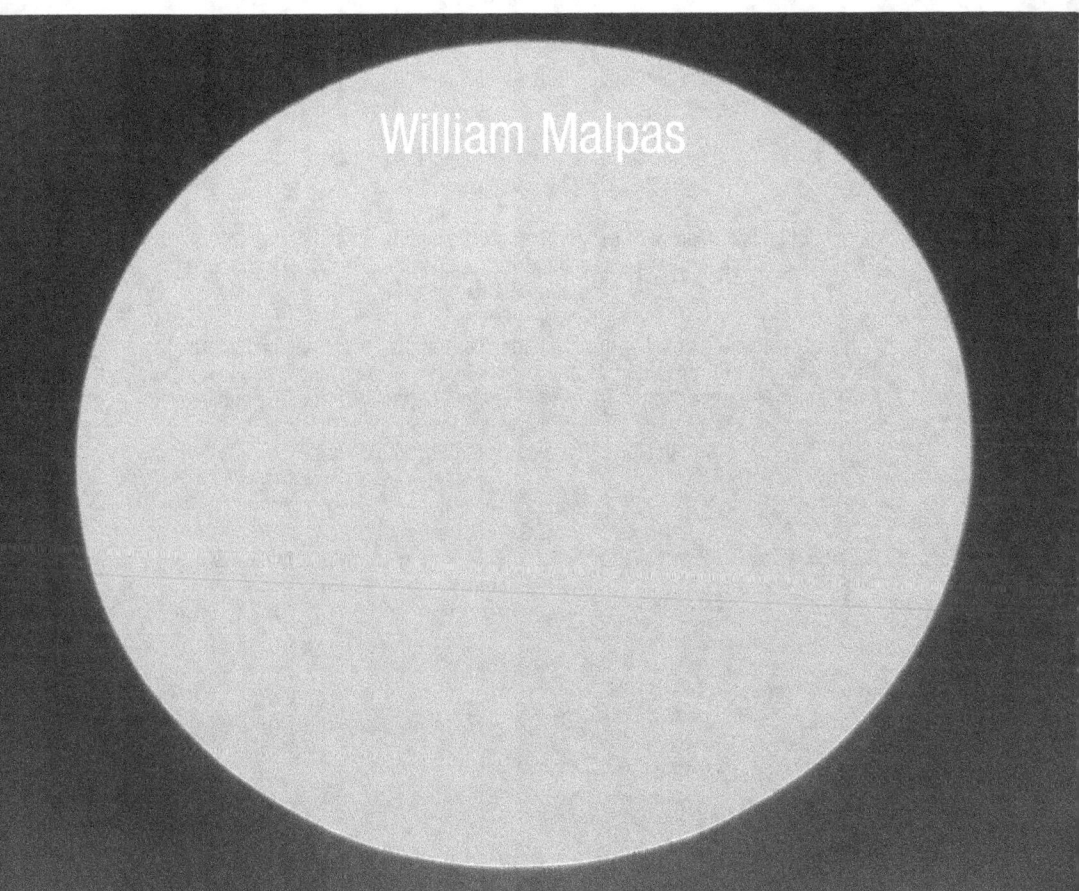

William Malpas

Crescent Moon Publishing

CRESCENT MOON PUBLISHING
P.O. Box 393,
Maidstone,
Kent, ME14 5XU,
United Kingdom

First published 2008. © William Malpas 2008.

Printed and bound in Great Britain.
Set in Helvetica Neue Condensed 9 on 14pt.
Designed by Radiance Graphics.

British Library Cataloguing in Publication data

Malpas, William
Land Art In the U.S.A, (Sculptors Series)
1. Earthworks (Art) 2. Installations (Art) 3. Environment (Art) 4. Sculpture, Modern –
21st Century
I. Title

709'.040476

ISBN-13 9781861712400

Contents

PART THREE: EUROPEAN LAND ARTISTS IN AMERICA

Acknowledgements

Thanks to Richard Long; Peter Redgrove; Andy Goldsworthy; Chris Drury; Viking Press, London; Penguin, London; Thames & Hudson, London; Anthony d'Offay Gallery, London; Henry Moore Centre for Sculpture, Leeds.

Thanks to the authors quoted and their publishers.
Illustrations © the artists.
Thanks to the copyright holders of the illustrations:
Musée d'Art Moderne de la Ville de Paris. Tate Modern, London. Royal Mail Group. John Weber Gallery, New York. Chinati Foundation, Texas. Lisson Gallery, London. Howard Lipman, Connecticut.
Alice Aycock. Donna Dennis. Patricia Johanson. Nancy Holt. Carl Andre. Ana Mendieta. James Turrell. Christo. Walter de Maria. Robert Morris. Michael Heizer. Robert Morris. Frank Stella. Gordon Matta-Clark. Jackie Winsor. Eva Hesse. Barbara Bloom. Dan Flavin. Judy Chicago. Charles Ross. Herbert Bayer. Hans Haacke. Jasper Johns. Robert Irwin. Richard Serra. Jeff Koons. Bruce Nauman. Richard Long. Hamish Fulton. Andy Goldsworthy. Chris Drury. Lawrence Weiner. Donald Judd. Dennis Oppenheim. David Nash. Jan Kounellis.

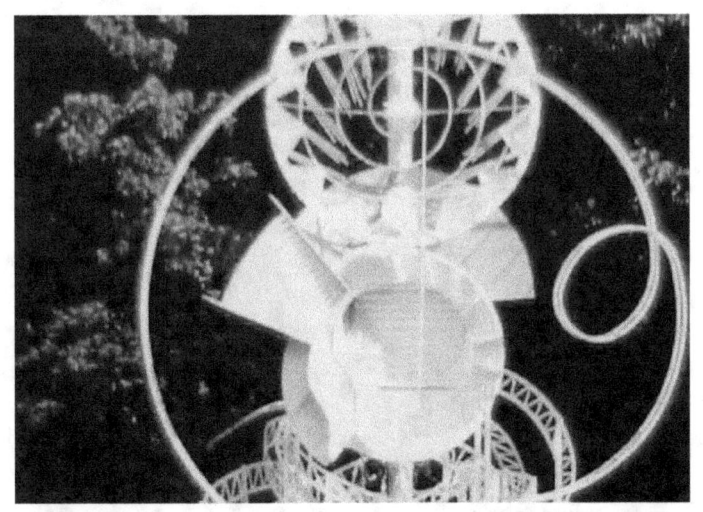

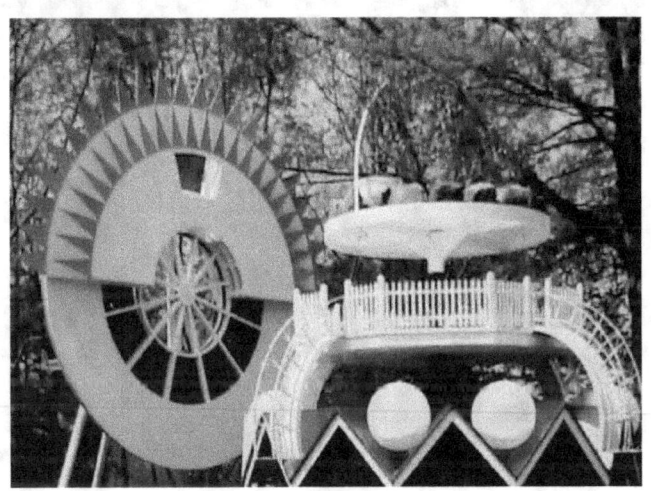

Alice Aycock

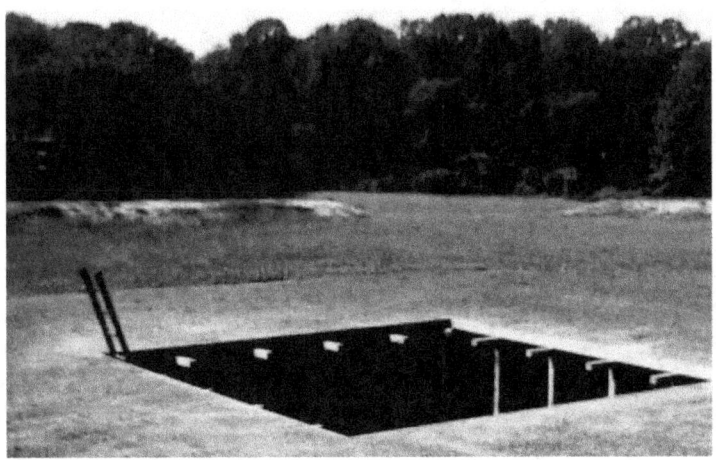

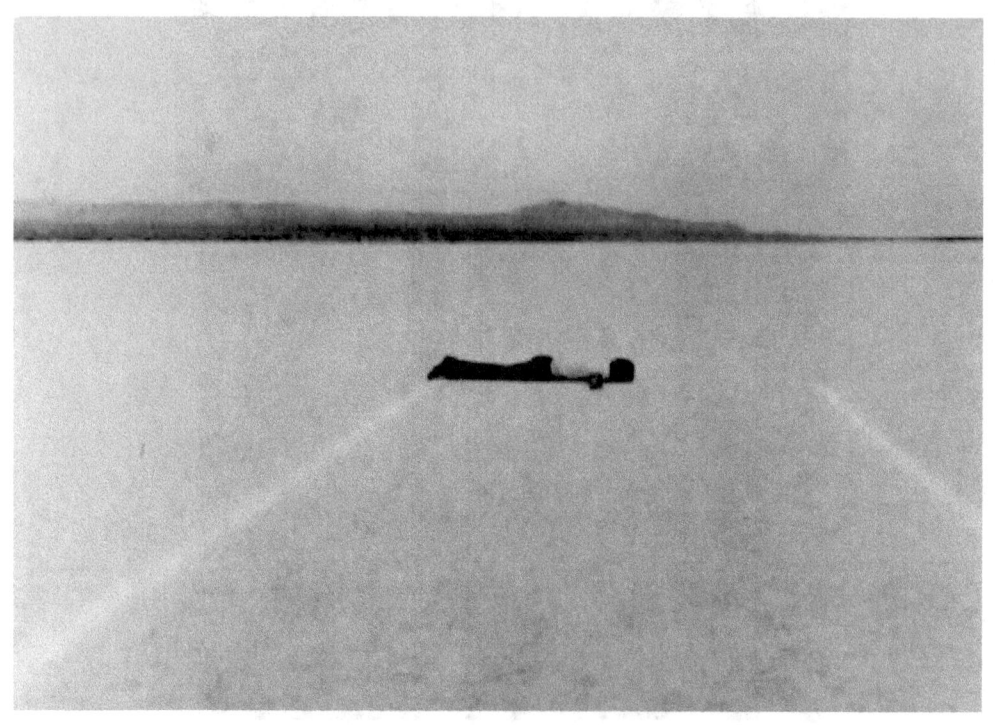

Walter de Maria at work in the American desert

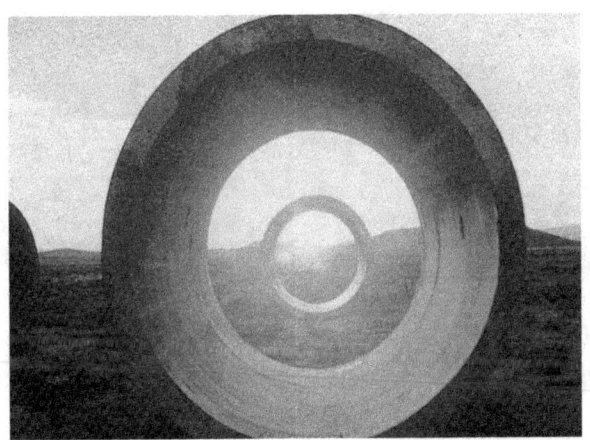

Nancy Holt, Sun Tunnels, 1976

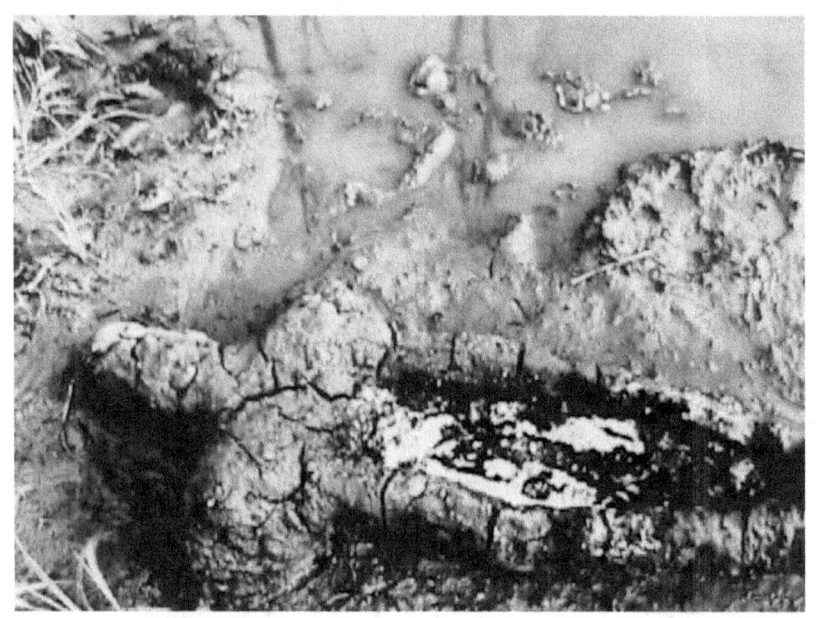

Ana Mendieta, Silueta Series, 1979

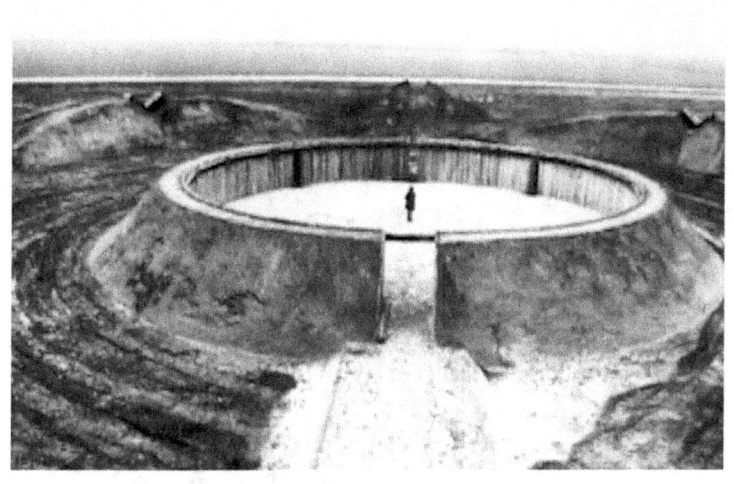

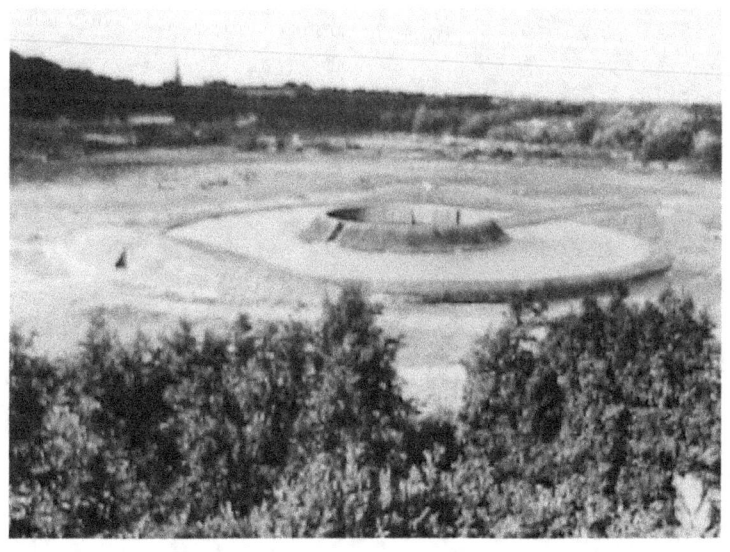

Robert Morris, Observatory, 1971

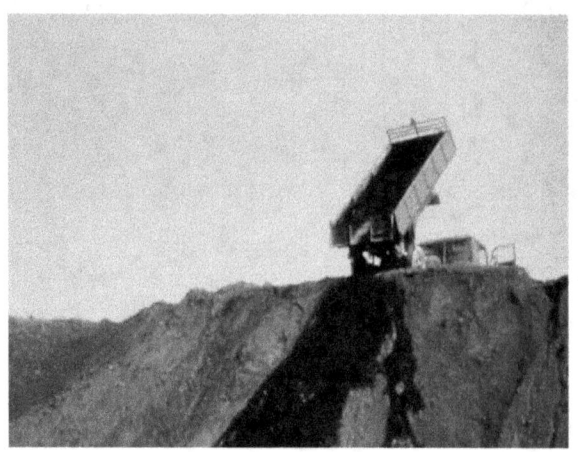

Robert Smithson, Ashphalt Rundown

PART ONE

LAND ART IN AMERICA

1

Introduction

Most land artists have their favourite motifs, practices, materials and styles, instantly recognizable: Robert Smithson with his giant spiral earthworks; Michael Heizer carving up the Nevada desert; Dennis Oppenheim's Conceptual borderlands and con-centric circles; Walter de Maria's lightning fields; Nancy Holt's celestial observatories; Christo's vast wrapped structures; the Roden Crater and 'skyspaces' of James Turrell; Hans Haacke's steam, fog and ice ephemeralities; Alice Aycock's underground labyrinths of nightmares and childhood memories; Richard Long's stone circles and rows; and Andy Goldsworthy's serpents, arches, walls, snowballs, body prints, splashes, cairns and holes.

The term 'land art' is used here as a shorthand to refer to many kinds of art, including landscape art, earth art, earthworks, nature art, green or ecological art, and installations. Land art was part of modernism and, in particular, 1960s art, the time of late Henry Moore, Robert Morris, Yves Klein, Tony Smith and Phillip King. It was the 1960-70s era of what Rosalind Krauss called 'expanded field' sculpture, the High Renaissance of land art.1 Krauss's 'expanded field' sculptors included Robert Irwin, Michael Heizer, Richard Serra, Walter de Maria, Sol LeWitt, Bruce Nauman, Alice Aycock, Mary Miss, Dennis Oppenheim, Nancy Holt, George Trakis, Richard Long, Hamish Fulton, Christo and Joel Shapiro.

I have concentrated on some of the more well-known American land artists, such as Robert Smithson, Walter de Maria, Michael Heizer, Robert Morris, Nancy Holt, Alice Aycock, Mary Miss, Carl Andre, Dennis Oppenheim, and James Turrell.

There are, of course, many more artists working with place, site, landscape and the environment. They include Robert Adzema, Vijali, Ana Mendieta, Jan Norman, Jane Balsgaard, Jussi Heikkilä, Tom Van Sant, Sherry Wiggins, Charles Jencks, Roger Ackling, Gordon Matta-Clark, Kazuo Shiraga, Bonnie Sherk, Charles Simonds, Isamu Noguchi, Richard Serra, Tony Smith, Daniel Buren, Gutzon Borglum, Jørn Rønnau, Helge Røed, Lars Vilks, Andy Lipkis, Nils Udo, Giuliano Mauri, Bror Westman, Debbie Duffin, Gloria Carlos, Phyllidia Barlow, Richard Fleischner, Michelangelo Pistoletto, Hiroshi Teshigahara, Vong Phaephanit, Alighiero Boetti, Herman de Vries, Joseph Beuys, Betty Beaumont, Betsy Damon, Andy Lipkins, Keith Arnatt, Herbert Bayer, Ant Farm, Newton Harrison, Helen Myer Harrison, Charles Ross, Peter Erskine, Juan Geuer, Jody Pinto, John Baldessari, Donna Henes, Phyllis Yampolsky, William Furlong, Art & Language, Peter Fend, Christian Philip Müller, Cildo Meireles, Harriet Feigenbaum, Ian Hamilton Finlay, Meg Webster, Jan Dibbets, Toshikatsu Endo, Mark

Dion, Guo-Qiang Cai, Peter Hutchinson, Lothar Baumgarten, Maya Lin, Douglas Huebler, Bruce McLean, Avital Geva, Barry Flanagan, Mierle Laderman Ukeles, Viet Ngo, Mel Chin, Agnes Denes, William Jackson Maxwell, Constance DeJong, Doris Bloom, Reiko Goto, Michelle Oka Doner, Buster Simpson, Martha Schwartz, Peter Richards, Douglas Hollis, Patrick Zentz, Othello Anderson, Fern Shaffer, Lynne Hull, Patricia Johanson, Karen McCoy, Dominique Mazeaud and Alan Sonfist. What is written here about the more well-known land artists also applies to the other artists cited above, plus many others.

Performance art, live art, body art and action art has many links with land, environmental, nature and installation art. In performance art, the field is vast. There isn't space in this study to consider them all (there are plenty of other studies). There are artists who talk to dead hares in their arms (Joseph Beuys), artists who carry out weird post-Catholic rituals or cut up sheep carcasses (Hermann Nitsch), artists who perform nude with film, video and installations (Carolee Schneemann), artists who draw on their bodies (while naked, of course), artists who sat in rooms and menstruated (Catherine Elwes), sculptors who stood and sang in suits (Gilbert & George), artists who replayed the physical martyrdom of saints (Ron Athey), groups who threw paint and food over each other while singing vaudeville songs (the Kipper Kids), artists who painted gallery floors with their long hair (Janine Antoni), artists who examined their genitals and masturbated before an audience (Annie Sprinkle), artists who had themselves bound and gagged in a gallery, holding a pig's heart (Tania Bruguera), artists who (while naked, of course) masturbate with cuddly toys (Mike Kelly), artists who meditate, chant, sing and play music (Caryle Reedy), groups who burn US flags and protest against war while naked on Brooklyn Bridge (Yayoi Kusama), artists who re-enact car crashes at a happening (Jim Dine and Judy Tersch), artists who douse themselves in water (Nam June Paik), artists who shoot guns at paint-filled balloons (Niki de Sant Phalle), artists who burn books (John Latham), groups who stage a protest 'blood bath' in a New York street (Guerrilla Art Action Group), artists who sat on horses in galleries (Jannis Kounellis), performers who locked themselves in rooms for six days while covered in paint (Stuart Brisley), artists who hung themselves upside-down in galleries (Jill Orr), creative couples who walk and bump into each other for an hour (while naked, of course), artists who scrubbed cow bones (Marina Abramovic), artists who stand against trees (nude, of course), covered in mud and plants (Ana Mendieta), artists who set themselves on fire (Tomas Ruller), or ignite gunpowder charges (Roman Signer), groups who sit naked in healing baths (Cai Guo Qiang), performers who have their clothes cut off by the audience (Yoko Ono), artists who signed semi-nude women as 'living sculptures' (Piero Manzoni), artists who hid under wooden ramps in galleries and masturbated while speaking to visitors (Vito Acconci), artists who hung between bridges (Dennis Oppenheim), and artists who crucified themselves on the roof of a Volkeswagen (Chris Burden),

Some of the key writers on land art include Rosalind Krauss, Lucy Lippard, Michael Fried, Kenneth Baker, John Beardsley, Lawrence Alloway, John Coplans, Diane Waldman, Harold Rosenberg, Stephanie Ross, Robert Hobbs, David Bourdon, Mel Gooding, Germano Celant, Alan Sonfist, Baile Oakes, Jeffrey Kastner, Andrew Causey, and Gilles Tiberghien.

Key land art shows include *Earth Art* (Andrew Dickson White Museum of Art, Cornell University, 1969), which showed Dibbets, Long, Smithson, Oppenheim and Morris, *Land Art* (Hanover, 1970), *Earthworks* (Dwan Gallery, 1968), *The New Sculpture, 1965-75* (Whitney, 1990), *Qu'est-ce que la sculpture moderne?* (Paris, 1986), *Virginia Dwan, Art Minimal, Art Conceptuel, Earthworks* (Paris, 1991), *Earthworks* (Seattle, 1979), *Conceptual Art, Arte Povera, Land Art* (Turin, 1971), and many of the Documenta exhibitions at Kassel. At *Earth, Air, Fire, Water* (Boston, 1971), Haacke, Christo, Smithson, Oppenheim, Long, Sonfist, Huebler, Hutchinson, Warhol and Heizer showed works.

Some of the best places to see land art *in situ* is in sculpture parks and gardens. In the US, these include Grounds For Sculpture in New Jersey, Rockerfeller Estate, New York, the Storm King Art Center, New York, Empire State Plaza Art Collection, Albany, New York, Abington Art Center Sculpture Garden, Pennsylvania, Hirshhorn Museum and Sculpture Garden, Washington, DC, Des Moines Art Center, Iowa, Walker Art Center, Minneapolis, Laumeier Sculpture Park, St Louis, Sheldon Sculpture Garden, University of Nebraska, Lincoln, Florida International University, Miami, Chinati Foundation, Marfa, Texas, Oakland Museum, California, Franklin D. Murphy Sculpture Garden, UCLA, L.A., Los Angeles County Museum of Art and the Museum of Outdoor Arts, Colorado.

Any visit to land and environmental art displays in the United States would take in many of the above sites, with Donald Judd's transformation of the army base at Marfa being near the top of the list. Further essential sites include Michael Heizer's *Double Negative* in the Nevada desert, Walter de Maria's *Lightning Field* in Quemado,

New Mexico, James Turrell's volcano transformation, *Roden Crater,* near Flagstaff, Arizona, Robert Smithson's *Spiral Jetty* in the Great Salt Lakes and Nancy Holt's *Sun Tunnels* in Lucin, Utah.

And to reach some of these land artworks one has to be a little adventurous: *Sun Tunnels* is approached down a 4-mile dirt track; Heizer's *Double Negative* is 5 miles from the Overton airport in Nevada; and *Spiral Jetty* is 15 miles from the Golden Spike National Historic site.

Although it may appear that land artists tour the whole globe making art, they actually stick to a small number of countries (tending towards the Northern hemisphere, and the Western world). For instance, there are few major land artists who have made significant work in Africa, or large parts of South America, or mainland China, or Russia. There are few Western land artworks in Egypt, for instance (perhaps because the competition is pretty fierce there from some of the most wonderful structures humans have ever made – the tombs, temples, cities and pyramids of ancient Egyptians. Of course, there are also social, political, cultural and ideological reasons for the lack of major land art in Islamic and Middle Eastern territories. And even more after 9/11, the Gulf War, and the Iraq war).

Europe's a favourite location, but not Eastern Europe. Favourite places tend to be America and Europe, obviously, and Japan, and occasionally Australia. Occasionally also India (if it's India, it's usually the scenic parts to the North, in Nepal or the Himalayas). But even in America, birthplace and chief centre of land art, artworks tend to be clustered around the East (New York, Washington, DC, Chicago), the South-West (New Mexico, Arizona), the Mid-West (Colorado), or California.

For some critics, the worst kind of land art is that which avoids political or 'important' or problematic issues, such as AIDS, poverty, 'Third World' debt, globalization, colonialism, war, terrorism, and so on. It romanticizies the natural world. It's conservative. It's nostalgic (for a vanished agricultural, working class past that never existed in the first place). It's escapist. It's self-indulgent. It's élitist. It's repetitive and lacks imagination. It lacks formal experimentation. It over-simplifies its subjects. For the nay-sayers, land art is a romantic retreat into escapist, nostalgic fantasies about nature, with nothing to say about the anxieties, problems and challenges of living in the contemporary, 21st century world. It's hippy, tree hugger art which panders to the middle class's nostalgia for nature, seen from the perspective of neurotic city dwellers who hanker for the peace and quiet of the countryside. It's an art that flatters and assuages the bourgeoisie's liberal guilt over wrecking the natural world with its ceaseless, massive consumption and pollution. It doesn't seem to say much about the late capitalist world, the technological, post-industrial, consumer society.

2

The Alchemy of Matter:
Land Art Aesthetics

SPIRIT OF PLACE: LAND ART, NATURE POETRY AND NATURE MYSTICISM

For the land artist, the whole planet can be an artist's studio. The land artist ranges over the whole globe. A desert, a beach, a field, a hill, a valley, a forest becomes a studio, a place of creative activity. The landscape itself is crucial in land art. That's obvious. Or is it? This means the very texture and colour and shape and dampness and springiness and strength and size of moss, for instance. Or a stone. Or a crevice in a rock wall. The way the light falls on a clump of grass, the little bits of dead, yellowish grass on top of the newer, green grass. Pine cones, closed-up. Flowers turning sunward in the late afternoon.

These are the things land artists deal with in making art. These are the actualities that artists employ when they create artworks. To fully appreciate land art, then, one has to look really closely, to grasp the details, as well as the overall conception and the grand design. This is true of small sculptures, as well as the larger earthworks. Then there are the many layers of human history to consider, the social uses of the land, ranging from industrial and agricultural usage to the private, intimate experiences of individuals.

For David Nash, land art is 'close-up', not distanced:

> The term "landscape" is like "portrait". It is an expression of a distancing: here I am and there it is. But what has been happening in the last twenty years or so is that artists have been getting right in there. Saying no, it is not out there. It is here. We want to make our images with what is here – here. That is why it is called land art rather than landscape art, "scape" denoting distancing.[1]

For David Nash, land art is about getting as close as possible to nature: the land artist does not paint nature like the painter, at a distance, with a paintbrush or watercolour block in front of her or him. The sketchpad or easel is a wall, a veil, a barrier between artist and world. The land artist, rather, dives in, 'gets right in there', as Nash says. The land artist does not use oil or pastel or ink to 'represent' nature. Rather, she or he works directly with nature, getting her or his fingers dirty with mud, snow, animal waste, stone, ferns and wood.

Land art gains much of its power (its meaning, its value, its presence) from particular places. Many land artists, for instance, work away from urban areas. Some, like Michael Heizer and Walter de Maria, work in what are regarded as 'exotic' locations – deserts and mountains. The 'glamour' of the locations aids the sculptures. Some land art is overpowered by the Romantic settings.

Land art is very much the product of the privileged, relatively wealthy First World, a world in which the Northern hemisphere is superior to the Southern; American, Eurocentric ethics are dominant; bourgeois/ 'imperialist' politics predominate; and the racial 'colour' of the art is not black, brown, red or yellow, but definitely white. Though 'post-colonial', land art is distinctly not 'politically correct' when it comes to issues of ethnicity or economy (although there is a strain of land art that engages with political, financial and ecological issues).

THE LAND ART SUBLIME: LAND ART AND ROMANTICISM

Land art and land artists seem to have much in common with Romantic art and Romantic artists. The marks of late 18th / early 19th century European Romanticism include: exalting nature; going to extremes; the cult of solitude; the predominance of subjectivity; rebellion; the artist as outsider; infinity; the sublime, and so on. Contemporary artists (such as Mark Rothko, Robert Smithson, David Inshaw, Anish Kapoor, James Turrell and Thérèse Oulton) express some of the elements of Romanticism cited above.

Land art in its grander moments echoes the gestures of High Romanticism – the Blakean, Whitmanesque, Goethean, Turnerian gestures – which have become so familiar in Western art. 'The Romantics' awe in the face of nature is hard to revive in a culture as estranged from nature as ours' remarked Robert Hughes, 'but, enfolded in distance and immensity, such works of land-art [by Michael Heizer and Walter de Maria] are saturated in nostalgia for it'.1

The 'Land Art Sublime' (pace Robert Rosenblum's coining of the term 'Abstract Sublime' to describe Barnett Newman's and Mark Rothko's paintings) might include the snow and stone circles made in the wildernesses of Scotland, Nepal and Peru of Richard Long; Christo's islands surrounded with pink polypropylene; the stone circles of Nancy Holt; and of course Robert Smithson's Spiral Jetty. The sheer scale of some of the works of land artists is of itself visceral and erotic (Walter de Maria's Lightning Field, Christo's Running Fence, Viet Ngo's Lemna System).2

Land art in the USA is bound up with notions of Romanticism. For Robert Rosenblum, the Abstract Expressionists (in particular Mark Rothko) were the last in a long line of Romantic artists. Speaking of his book *Modern Painting and the Northern Romantic Tradition*, Rosenblum said

> were I to write a supplementary chapter to it – I stopped with Rothko and Abstract Expressionism – I would probably include earthworks of the late 1960s and 1970s. Those seem in some way to be the last gasp of that tradition of trying to find some sort of connection with the Great Beyond or the Void. (1988, 7)

Certainly the works of Smithson, Heizer, de Maria, Turrell *et al*, are part of this Romantic tradition. The Romantic ethics of taking things to extremes, of going to the infinite and the eternal, are very much to the fore in land art, which is an art which quite definitely sustains Romantic myths and tenets.

There is a macho posturing to some land art theory (some of it no doubt unintentional) in which the relationship with nature is seen as 'fundamental', 'raw', 'violent' and 'intense'. American earthwork artists speak of working in nature as difficult, dirty, uncompromising and exhausting. In America the poetic reference is Walt Whitman, as well as Thoreau, Longfellow, Twain, Melville and Emerson.

The land artist has a special, fetishistic relation with her/ his materials: they are not simply bits of matter to be wielded in a particular way. They are treated with respect. Wolfgang Laib dusts the Earth with pollen, to form an enormous square layer of brilliant yellow. The delicacy – and potency – of the sculpture is immediately apparent. This is the sort of sculpture that exerts a synæsthetic power over the gallery goer: the pollen affects not only the visual sense with its incandescent hues, but also affects smell, taste and touch. Another of Laib's installations was *The Passageway* (1988-93), made up of huge panels of beeswax. 'I believe that the impossible, the invisible and visions can become reality if one really wants to make the effort' said Laib.[3] Anya Gallaccio made large installations using flowers: thousands of red roses in *Red On Green* (1992), 101 sunflowers in *Preserve Sunflower* (1991) and 1,600 zinnias in *Untitled* (1992). Gallaccio's flowerpieces emphasized beauty and decay, sensuality and death.

Goldsworthy, Laib and Chris Drury collect leaves, berries, pollen, honey and other natural elements and weave sensuous artifacts that are ephemeral and intricate. Dennis Oppenheim worked with snow and circles in his *Annual Rings*, a series of concentric circles that straddled the Canadian/ American border, and with burning circles onto grass in his *Branded Mountain*. In fact, Oppenheim was the first land artist to work with snow on a grand scale.

LAND ART AND GARDENS

'Land art' is a term that includes a wide variety of artistic forms, like the term 'garden'. Gardens are not a single form with a single set of characteristics. Gardens can be so various that some critics have suggested that the word 'garden' is as broad and vague as words such as 'art'.[1] It's a term so general it's practically useless.

Gardens can be very small or very big; they can be flat or terraced; they can be circular, square, or narrow; they can be organized around a 'natural' plan or a strict geometric plan; they can be 'wild' or 'tamed'; they can be enclosed or open; they can contain lakes, ponds, streams, fountains, statues, trees, statues, lawns, shrubs, rocks, walls, fences, benches, flowers, stones, follies, ruins, grottoes, temples, paths and many kinds of environmental art.

A traditional Japanese (Zen Buddhist) garden, with its stones and sand raked into patterns, is quite different from, say, a suburban yard in Iowa. Gardens can be vast displays of state and regal power, such as the gardens at Versailles or Hadrian's Villa, or modest attempts at cultivating food in a yard. Gardens have been made for many reasons: in the pursuit of decoration, finance, medicine, religion, contemplation, play, sport and food. Sculptor Isamu Noguchi thought of gardens as

> sculpturing of space: a beginning, and a groping to another level of sculptural experience and use: a total sculpture space experience beyond individual sculptures. A man may enter such a space: it is in scale with him; it is real. (1968)

For some critics, the most interesting aspect of land art is its connection with gardening and landscape design.[2] But for the chief land artist – Robert Smithson – art degenerates as it approaches gardening.[3]

If there can be 'found art', can there be 'found gardens'? Perhaps an artist, working in the Conceptual and environmental art mode, could simply claim any piece of land as their 'found garden', just as artists such as Marcel Duchamp, Kurt Schwitters and Robert Rauschenberg took found objects and exhibited them as art (and Gordon Matta-Clark bought tiny pieces of land and it became an artwork). When does a garden start becoming a garden? How many objects are required to make a garden? Is a single blade of grass a garden? Are two plants on a window ledge a garden? Or five plants, or ten plants, clustered together in pots? Is an overgrown path a garden? Or an allotment dedicated to growing tomatoes and potatoes? Is a couple of yards of grass behind an abandoned gas station a garden? Is a municipal park, consisting only of children's swings and slides on grass, a garden? Is a farmer's field a garden? Or a farm?

And when does a garden stop being a garden? Is a garden of a hundred years ago that can barely be seen amidst piles of refuse still a garden? How much of the human touch is required to make a piece of land a garden? If sand raked into a pattern can be a garden for the Japanese Zen Buddhist, is any piece of raked sand a garden? Are the patterns made in the sand by the receding tide a garden? Is the sea making gardens with every tide? Or the wind, or erosion, or earthquakes or other natural forces? Does a garden have to have the 'human' touch to make it a true garden?

Environmental or land or garden art can include American earthworks (such as those by James Turrell and Mel Chin); ephemeral interventions in the environment (such as those by Andy Goldsworthy, Hans Haacke and Michael Singer); architectural installations (such as those by Alice Aycock, Mary Miss and Nancy Holt); land art as performance art (Richard Long, Hamish Fulton, Christo), even if the artist is the only audience; land art that involves landscaping and garden art (such as Alan Sonfist, Patricia Johanson, Robert Irwin and Ian Hamilton Finlay); and sculpture or art parks. There are 'video gardens', too, such as Matthew McCaslin's *Bloomer* installation: 12 TV monitors played tapes of flowers blooming in time-lapse. The TV sets were arranged in groups like plants, with the cables tangled on the floor (St Louis Art Museum).

'TRUE CAPITALIST ART'?: THE COST OF LAND ART

Not all of land art, but much of land art is very expensive. That is, it is costly moving tons of earth around. Taking a motorbike out into the desert and drawing lines with it is one thing (as Michael Heizer had done in *Circular Surface Displacement* [1968], North of Las Vegas), but making a 40 mile 18 foot high fence (Christo) is another. Much of land art requires patrons, sponsors, co-ordination with galleries, lawyers, public administrators, helpers and industry. The costliness of land art may explain why much of it is American.[1] Land art requires investment with no immediate return. Patrons are crucial to land art. In American earthworks the key patrons were the Dia Art Foundation, Robert C. Scull and Virginia Dwan, director of the Dwan Gallery between 1966 and 1971.

Richard Long perhaps spoke for many British sculptors when he writes of his aversion to American earthwork art:

> In the sixties there was a feeling that art need not be a production line of more objects to fill the world. My interest was in a more thoughtful view of art and nature, making art both visible and invisible, using ideas, walking, stones, tracks, water, time, etc, in a flexible way... It was the anti-thesis of so-called American "Land Art," where an artist needed money to be an artist, to buy real estate to claim possession of the land, and to wield machinery. True capitalist art.[2]

Although Long (and others) may despise the amounts of money spent by the American earthwork artists, isn't he also part of '[t]rue capitalist art'? Doesn't he also live off his art? Doesn't he just wander around the planet on his sacred 'walks', putting a few stones into a pile, and taking a photo of his efforts? Isn't Richard Long (and British artists such as David Nash, Shirazeh Houshiary, Rachel Whiteread, Richard Wentworth, Bill Woodrow, Hamish Fulton and Richard Deacon) also a part of the 'capitalist' art world?[3] Don't Long's artworks sell for lots of money, a lot more money than the materials cost? Isn't Long being hypocritical when he criticizes the bombastic aspects of American land art when he himself benefits from the hugely over-priced art gallery system, where even mundane art it seems (such as artists' prints) are sold for 'silly prices'?

It's easy to view the Christos' wrapped buildings or Walter de Maria's $500,000 *Vertical Earth Kilometer* as expensive, pointless art. This sort of land art may be '[t]rue capitalist art', an art of excessive cost and excessive waste, but then, art has been full of idiot amounts of money for ages. What about Christo's wrappings? They cost a bomb, for sure, but, as Christo says, he pays for it himself, with money made from selling smaller works. Christo's *Running Fence* cost $2.5 million; *The Umbrellas* in Japan and California, cost $26,000,000. Christo says his art 'has to do with things that are very simple'.[4] This definition can also apply to other land artists; they, too, transform ordinary things.

When these transformations of the ordinary cost so much, and require 200 rock climbers, as Christo's covering of the Reichstag in Berlin needed, then commentators wonder about the 'importance' of such artistic productions. There is something right and homely about Andy Goldsworthy and his couple of stonewallers building a wall in the Northern wildernesses of Britain. They toil away in true grimy, stalwart, Eric Gill-like craftsman style. But there's something cynical and obscene, perhaps, about Michael Heizer or Walter de Maria carving great gashes in the American desert, or Christo making artworks that cost 26 million dollars yet only last for two weeks. Surely that money would be better spent on a hospital? Or on feeding needy groups or countries? Surely artworks that cost millions of dollars but only 'benefit' a (relatively) tiny amount of people are wasteful? Isn't famine relief a better alternative? Perhaps one could make famine relief/ earthquake relief/ medical supply/ housing, and other 'charity' and 'aid' projects, an art event? Perhaps if Christo spent $26 million on providing food for the needy instead of wrapping a building in Berlin in a bit of plastic, people would not be so angry? When artists spend such vast amounts of money on art, it's no wonder people find this obscene. But then, if spending millions of dollars on art were outlawed, we'd have no Hollywood, no movie industry, no television. These are the hypocrisies and ambiguities that surround art. How can one 'justify' a $26,000,000 Christo wrapping? Or a typical Hollywood feature film (cost: $45 million, with a typical advertizing budget of $5-15 million)?

LAND ART AND PHOTOGRAPHY

In land art photography, the viewer is not offered a *range* of viewpoints of a work, although land artists clearly take more than one shot of each work they make. No artist takes just *one* photo out of a 36 exposure 35mm film, or one frame out of a twelve shot 120mm format film, or one image out of 100s available on a digital camera. No, an artist, like an photographer, takes a range of shots, at different, bracketed exposures, from different viewpoints (much as the trendy advertising film director of today shoots twelve hours of footage for just one thirty second advert).[1]

Each land artist, then, must select this or that viewpoint, behind this bush or next to that tree. The land artist is therefore also a photographer, selecting views, reframing their works, making choices about lighting, angles, lenses, film stock, etc.

Land artists will make decisions about exactly *when* to photograph their work. Some works are ephemeral, and last only moments, so the photograph must be taken immediately (but even when a work lasts only a few seconds or minutes, there are still choices about which moment to select). Other works, such as Robert Smithson's *Amarillo Ramp* or Nancy Holt's *Star-Crossed* (1981), last longer.

The land artist as photographer can therefore wait for a certain combination of sunlight and clouds. This is particularly crucial in cloudy places, where lighting can vary so dramatically over a few minutes. As anyone who has been in Dartmoor or the the Andes will know, the sunlight can burst through the clouds at one moment, then a moment later there'll be dark, sombre clouds, looking as if it's going to rain. A moment later, it *will* rain, and afterwards, facing away from the sun, one might see a rainbow. Much of the world's weather is this changeable, so every land art photograph is a highly selective and subjective view of a particular place.

Another critical aspect of photographing land art is not only deciding what to *include*, but choosing what to *exclude* from the composition. Visiting a land artwork in the flesh, one can see it from all sorts of angles, with all sorts of backgrounds, in all sorts of conditions. Knowing a land artwork only from a photograph, one knows only *that* particular viewpoint, and no others. The land artist will take great care in framing the images, to show the artwork from the best vantage points. Many aspects of the surroundings might be elided from the final published photographs – an apartment block, a row of cars, trash, people, power lines, and so on.

Land artists must also oversee the journey of the films they've shot from development through printing to framing. As anyone who has taken a photo will know, all manner of details can affect how one reads a photograph: how it is printed, light, dark, soft, hard, cropped, full frame, more red, more blue, burnt in, dodged, touched up, glossy or matt paper, and so on. The size of the photo affects it very much, as does the frame. Go into any framer's shop and one'll see a plethora of different types of frame. All these things the viewer might take in at one glance in a gallery, but the artist has to make decisions all the time about all these matters, and many more. Land artists/ sculptors, then, must be accomplished photographers. Their work must be high standard, for it is exhibited in 'high art' locations, such as the city gallery, or glossy coffee table art books.

In land art, the commentary, the written records, the obsessive documentation, is just as important as the artwork itself. Often, it *is* the artwork. The land artist's life becomes part of the artwork. Andy Goldsworthy said '[m]y art will always be a reflection of my way of life.'2 Brilliant late 1960s sculptor Eva Hesse spoke in Romantic, emotional terms of her art, employing words such as 'essence' and 'soul'. She spoke of wanting to emphasize 'soul or presence or whatever you want to call it.' These words of Hesse's could apply, with some minor revisions, tto land artist's art: 'I think art is a total thing. A total person giving a contribution. It is an essence, a soul... In my soul art and life are inseparable.'3

Jan Dibbets said that documenting the work wasn't important: 'I've done lots of works without taking photographs'.4 But most land artists record their activities (e.g.: 'walk this morning; made a snow sculpture; it wasn't successful; back home for lunch'). Ultimately, *any* activity can be land art. Going to the shops can be a piece of art. One might drop a stone on the path as one goes, or perhaps not. Either way, you've just made a work of art. Is, then, walking to Gilmor's corner store for a pint of milk and a pack of cigarettes a fully accomplished and thoroughly authentic work of art? Where does authenticity end and artifice begin? Or, rather, where does life end and art begin? Clearly, they are a continuum in land art.

Richard Long says that '[n]ot all walking is art'. That is, a walk becomes art when it is conceived as art. The conception of the walk, made before the walk, is crucial, even if there is no 'reason' at all for the walk. 'A walk, and place, can be chosen for any reason'.5 Long also says, though, that '[a]nything an artist makes, is art', but adds '[n]ot everyone is an artist.'6

The relation between outdoor and indoor works, between stone cairns in some remote zone and a stone cairn in a Western gallery, is resolved simply in land art by being regarded by the artist as a continuum. One can see how for the land artist both indoor and outdoor works are one, i.e., part of the same thing. But the viewer might see them as separate, because the viewer (usually) can't see many land art outdoor pieces. 7

The viewer only knows land art outdoor pieces from photos. So it's always an odd relationship with land artworks for the viewer. For the artist, it's great, because the big photos and writings relate to her/ his own experiences, of working outdoors. S/he knows the work inside out: *s/he lived it.* The viewer, though, gets a different experience: s/he sees odd phrases, titles, dates, measurements. Odd snippets of info. Or photos. So people love land art not because they love the photographs, or the writing. They love it, perhaps, because of *what it suggests*. Land art persuades people to look outwards, away from cities, towards the landscape, towards stones and water and all the rest of it. Perhaps that's why people love land art, and nature poetry, and all things to do with nature, from gardening to walking the dog to vacations in wildernesses. As Hamish Fulton put it, 'I walk on the land to be woven into nature' (1995).

The outdoor work itself isn't present in land art's text pieces or photos. The work isn't 'in' the gallery. No, the work is *elsewhere*, and it is to that *elsewhere place* that people want to go. Land art creates *desire* in people, as the paintings of J.M.W. Turner or the poetry of Aleksandr Blok creates desire – for travel, for other places. Richard Long spoke in a Santa Fe interview of feeling refreshed and renewed after a good walk: that's the experience, perhaps, that viewers wish to gain from land art, from all art. Land art, then, whether by Aycock, Shiraga, Drury or Christo, is part of a postmodern trend in self-reflexivity, the *mise-en-âbyme* commentary so familiar now. Art about (the artist's) life.

It's about reality. Land artists like what they see to be real, to be the object in and of itself (the 'thing-in-itself' of Existentialism, or Rainer Maria Rilke's *Kunstding*, 'thing of art'). They dislike illusionism. For land artists, their sculpture doesn't symbolize or represent nature, it *is* nature, a part of nature. As the painter Jasper Johns remarked: 'I find it more interesting to use a real fork as painting than it is to use painting as a real fork.' Similarly, one can see how, for Turrell, Johanson, Pierce, Michelle Stuart and other land artists, it's much more interesting to use a stone as a stone rather than as a representation of something else. Robert Smithson's definition of an earthwork is pertinent here: 'instead of putting a work of art on some land, some land is put into a work of art'.[8]

INSIDE — OUTSIDE

Sometimes it's odd to see land art in a gallery, because the mound of soil, the cairn of stones, the slate circle, demands the viewer to look outwards, to nature, to the wildernesses from whence this art comes. Richard Long's stone circles are familiar now, having been seen in art galleries and museums, but one is always aware of the place of their origin, and how odd they look.[1] Those sticks and stones are tiny parts of nature, bits extracted, chopped up, re-arranged, as all art is nature chopped up and reformed according to the artist's æsthetics. Land art creates an ambiguous continuity with the world of nature that exists outside the gallery. Sometimes this ambiguity works against the art on show in the gallery space.

Land art sites, in the first wave of land art (late 1960s/ early 1970s – land art's 'golden age'), tended to be wildernesses, deserts, post-industrial spaces, waste grounds, quarries and dumps. One of the reasons for going far from the gallery, the city and the pretty countryside spots was because land artists wanted to avoid the 'pastoral' and the 'picturesque' at all costs.2 Land artists, asserted Dennis Oppenheim, wished to go beyond the picturesque (while British land artists, such as Richard Long, had some relationship with the picturesque [ibid.]).

David Nash discussed this indoor/ outdoor problem in a 1978 interview:

> An object made indoors diminishes in scale and stature when placed outside. The reverse happens when an object made outside is brought inside, it seems to grow in stature and presence. It brings the outside in with it. The object outside has to contend with unlimited space, uneven ground and the weather. The sculpture I show inside is meant to be seen inside, it relates to the limited space, the peculiar scale, and the still air.3

The indoor-outdoor dialectic much concerned Robert Smithson, who said 'I don't think you're freer artistically in the desert than you are inside a room'.4 In fact, Smithson said he 'liked the artificial limits that the gallery presents'.5

One of the problems land art must address is the age-old relation between the 'real world' and art, between objects as they are in the everyday world, and objects as they are represented in art. Land art makes the viewer look again at the natural world: not just at the beauty of it, but at the multitudinous variety of forms in nature. Land art/ sculpture is a poetry of natural forms, in which notions of 'representation' are sidestepped, because it uses things 'as themselves' (the use of photography, though, sees a swift return of confusions over the politics of representation). An object such as the snowball in Andy Goldsworthy's *Snowballs in Summer* (1989 and 2000) is not plastic masquerading as a snowball, but a real snowball. Similarly, the twigs and stalks and needles and pebbles folded into the snowballs are real.

What's amazing is the actuality of nature: the variety of forms; the way the branches twist, for instance. Land artists would have the viewer look closely at nature again. By using 'real' objects, land artists aim to demolish notions of representation and mediation. Instead of a picture of snow, one has snow itself; rather than paint pebbles, or sculpt them in bronze, land artists use real pebbles.

Of course, there are problems with using objects as objects – Marcel Duchamp with his readymades confronted this problem. The problem is partly one of context: for, placed in a museum, so obviously as items to be studied, the natural forms become art. The objects may not be on pedestals, but they are perceived as art objects. If you're looking at land art in a book or a gallery, one is already anchored in a gallery/ art/ æsthetic mode of viewing.

Ephemeral, land art aims for an eternity in one place: the soul. As Lawrence Weiner, the American Conceptual/ Process artist who exhibited 'statements' (texts on a wall), said: '[o]nce you know about a work of mine, you own it. There's no way I can climb into somebody's head and remove it.'[6] Thus, much of land art exists in that socio-cultural space which is actually inside people's heads. Thus, anyone can 'own' land art: simply by thinking about it. Once thought about, land art, Conceptual art or Process art is 'possessed' by the viewer, in Weiner's system. Indeed, some Conceptual art requires the existence of the viewer to make the work work at all. The viewer brings the work alive.

Working inside was problematic for Goldsworthy, he confessed, because he was disconnected from the natural world outside, with its changes, its seasons, animals, people, history. The outside world was alive, while the gallery or public space could all too easily begin to feel dead after a while. 'I am not not sustained by working indoors. I have too much control inside, and after a while I am drained of reasons for being there'.[7]

CHANGES, CYCLES, SEASONS

Critical in land art is the concept and reality of change, for these works in wood, snow, ice, leaves, water, slate, grass and so on, do not stay around. They are not 'permanent', in the way that, say, bronze, marble, steel or stone can be. The soil in Walter de Maria's *Earth Room* dries out and alters; Robert Morris's steam works and Hans Haacke's balloons are blown away by the wind; Christo's plastic wraps stay on for two weeks. Joseph Beuys emphasized process, evolution, change: his sculpture, he said, was not 'fixed and finished. Processes continue in most of them: chemical reactions, fermentations, colour changes, decay, drying up. Everything is in a *state of change*.1 The notion of decay and entropy was an important element in Robert Smithson's earth art.2 It's the same for Richard Long: 'my work is partly about change or disappearance, invisibility... all these strange states of matter'.3

Some land artists enjoy the impermanence of (their) art, and exploit it. As politicians know, words such as 'permanent' are difficult to define, and even more difficult to maintain. Artists with a large vision of life know that nothing on Earth will be truly 'permanent'. After all, 'civilized' humanity is only 10,000 years old, or three million (depending on how one measures 'civilized'). And the planet itself will not last forever: millions more years, perhaps, but not forever.

Andy Goldsworthy said he is not against long-term art: '[t]hat art should be permanent or impermanent is not the issue. Transience in my work reflects what I find in nature and should not be confused with an attitude towards art generally. I have never been against the well-made or long-lasting.' *Domination* and *penetration*. These are familiar terms describing patriarchal actions or constructions or ideologies used by feminists. Is Goldsworthy, seemingly so delicate in his touches, dominating nature?

Yet, clearly, land artists (and not just the American earthwork artists – Heizer, de Maria, Smithson, Simonds, Christo, Aycock) do dominate nature. James Turrell's *Roden Crater* or Michael Heizer's gigantic *Double Negative* will clearly be around for a long time, unless someone or something destroys them. Andy Goldsworthy's stone pieces, too, may stay around for a while. There is a sense of gloating when Goldsworthy says '[f]ourteen years ago I made a line of stones in Morecambe Bay. It is still there, buried under the sand, unseen. All my work still exists, in some form.'

Daring not to change or affect nature, land artists do just that, all the time. They 'interact' with nature, but their 'interactions', however small scale, can't help changing nature. 'I like the idea of using the land without possessing it' said Richard Long, ever the idealist.4 Goldsworthy's aim is to 'touch' something in nature, the essence of nature itself, to understand it, and the identification of himself within nature.5 Thus, about the 'lake pieces', the stick and stalk sculptures he was commissioned to do in the Lake District in 1988, he remarked: 'I felt I really got through in the lake pieces. I had touched it, and understood it'.6

Some environmental/ action/ Conceptual artworks had a built-in impermanence, such as Allan Kaprow's *Fluids* (1967, Pasadena, California), large structures made from blocks of ice, which were left to melt. Barry Flanagan's *Hole in the Sea* (1969) was a cylinder embedded in a beach: Flanagan filmed the water covering the hole as the tide came in. Hans Haacke produced impermanent works, such as ice freezing around an element.[7] He wrote of an artwork which would be as majestic and as transient as birds gathering in the sky: 'I would like to lure 1000 seagulls to a certain spot (in the air) by some delicious food so as to construct an air sculpture from this combined mass.'

In "Natural Phenomena as Public Monuments" (1968), land artist Alan Sonfist suggested building 'museums of air' in cities, which would 'recapture the smells of earth, trees and vegetation at different seasons and at different historical times, so that people would be able to experience what has been lost' (1978). Sonfist also suggested monumentalizing the natural world with sounds: '[c]ontinuous loops of natural sounds at the natural level of volume can be placed on historic sites' (ibid.).

There are bronze and marble sculptures still looking remarkable from the Græco-Roman period, and stone figurines from the Palæolithic period. Michael Heizer's scars in remote deserts will endure, but not Robert Morris's steam works or Hans Haacke's *Grass Grows* (1969). Indeed, ephemerality, transiency and change are key components in land art. The bulk of some land artists' work is ephemeral. As Barry Flanagan writes:

> Truly sculpture is always going on. With proper physical circumstances and the visual invitation, one simply joins in and makes the work... there is a never-ending stream of materials and configurations to be seen, both natural and man-made, that have visual strength but not object or function apart from this. It is as if they existed for just this physical, visual purpose – to be seen.[8]

LIVING PLANTS

Many land artists have used living plants at some time or other. Some artists have installed trees upside-down (Vito Acconci) and plants upside-down in galleries (Michael Blazy, Henrik Håkansson, Sam Kunce). Some artists have trained plants to grow at odd angles (Hans Haacke, Cartsen Höller). Some artists have forced plants into vacu-formed moulds (Laura Stein) and rubber foam (Ingo Vetter, Annette Weisser). Some artists have lined rooms with cages of bay leaves to produce an aromatic environment (Guiseppe Penone). Some artists have planted seeds on their naked bodies (Teresa Murak). Some artists have planted clover fields in galleries (Nikolaj Recke) and made couches from grass (Daniel Spoerri). Some artists have built parks running up the sides of buildings (Vito Acconci); some have made enclosed indoor gardens (Knut Åsdam). Other artists have made portable orchards (the Harrisons); portable indoor vegetable gardens (N55); and crammed hothouses (Lothar Baumgarten). And some have let roses run riot over cars (Silvie Fleury). Herman de Vries is a close competitor with Andy Goldsworthy for the artist who's created the most works with living plants

Plenty of land artists and sculptors have used real flowers: Anya Gallaccio used roses (1992), sunflowers (1991) and zinnias (1992); Herman de Vries (who spread thousands of lavender flowers on a gallery floor in 1998); Wolfgang Laib with his pollen floor spreads; Richard Long, who pressed flowers flat in a field in *Brough of Birsay Circle* (1994); Jenny Holzer's *Black Garden*, a war memorial garden of very dark plants and flowers (1994); Gary Rieveschl, who planted *Heart Wave,* a line of 12,000 red tulips, in 1980; Daniel Buren also made a row of tulips, *11,000 Tulips* (1987, Holland); Peter Hutchinson, who planted 'thrown ropes' of flowers (1996); and Annette Wehrmann; Shelagh Wakely; Mark Dion; Meg Webster; Carsten Höller; Paula Hayes; Peter Fischl; David Weiss; Tobias Rehberger; Lothar Baumgarten; Brigitte Raabe; and Olaf Nicolai.

TREES IN LAND ART

Many sculptors and land artists have worked with trees: David Nash, Guiseppi Penone, William Jackson Maxwell, Robert Irwin, Jackie Winsor, Daniel Buren, Alan Sonfist, Harvey Fite, Peter Walker, Giuliano Mauri, Nils Udo, Luc Wolff, Maria Nordman, Sjoerd Buisman, Cosima von Bonin, Stefan Banz, Vito Acconci, Jørn Rønnau, Buster Simpson, Jan Dibbets, Helge Røed, Lars Vilks, Andy Lipkis, Herman de Vries and Mel Chin.

Using trees means working within a long and celebrated religious and cultural tradition.[1] For example, trees have since time immemorial been associated with spirits and religions. The Greeks believed that trees had spirits; there were the apples of immortality and trees of eternal life; Daphne turned into a tree when pursued by Zeus; Actaeon was turned into a stag in the forest when he spied Diana bathing nude; deities such as Athena, Artemis, Dionysus, Apollo, Orpheus and Cybele are associated with trees and woods.

Constantin Brancusi, more influential on land art than Picasso, Arp, Giacometti, Rodin, Matisse or Maillol, worked notions of shamanic flight into his *Birds in Space* sculptures, and most especially in his *Endless Column*, which is cited by many key sculptors (Judd, Andre, Morris) as an important inspiration. Brancusi's *Birds in Space* aimed to express the essence of flight, the moment when a quivering verticality is released from the chains of gravity and flies upward. One only has to look at David Nash's *Tripods*, Chris Drury's cairns of rocks, Barnett Newman's *Broken Obelisk*, or Donald Judd's ladders, to see how important Brancusi's sculptures were, with their shamanic, World Tree associations.

Planting trees has become a favourite with land and environmental artists: Alan Sonfist created various solid circles and rings of trees (*Circles of Life* [1986], *Circles of Time* [1987]); Mel Chin planted trees and plants on a landfill site in St Paul, MN (*Revival Field*); Joseph Beuys led the planting of oak trees a Documenta 7 in Kassel in 1982; Andy Lipkis planted trees in urban areas (such as L.A.), and organized fundraising marathon runs for trees (1979); Andy Goldsworthy has planted dwarf oak saplings in the Holocaust memorial in New York; Guiseppe Penone placed a long white crystal in tree trunks (*Light Traps*, 1994); Vito Acconci constructed a tower of trees (1996), one above the other, all of them upside-down; Robert Irwin installed nine plum trees in Seattle, Washington (1983), separated by blue screens; and Buster Simpson planted willow trees in drinking fountains (1993).

Daniel Buren constructed one of the most compelling of all treeworks: an olive tree standing atop a huge cube of soil in a gallery (*Untitled*, 1999), a truly spectacular (and enigmatic) work, with the tree and earth in proportion, quietly dominating the ornate room at Castello di Rivoli.

HOLES

Many land artists have dug holes, cracks, caverns, tunnels and underground labyrinths in the Earth. Maybe there's more to this than just the æsthetic dimension of creating new spaces. Andy Goldsworthy, for instance, has an anxious, ambivalent attitude towards holes in the ground which recalls the views of (usually male) philosophers on the negativity of holes and voids, which are associated with the sexual identity of women. These fears and ambiguities are found in much of Western culture: in Sigmund Freud's castration myth; in the belligerent misogynist theology of St Augustine, Tertullian, St Paul and Origen. In this view, women are vampires and loathed witches, sucking up masculine desire and energy. Another religious view sees women as Mother Goddesses, identified with nature, the seasons, vegetation and the powers of the Earth. One deity which some feminists and poets (such as Robert Graves and Peter Redgrove) have worshipped (though they would not use that term) is the 'Black Goddess', a divinity of darkness, night, the unknown and the supernatural.

STONE CIRCLES: LAND ART AND PREHISTORIC ART

The circle motif, one of the primæval symbols of eternity, cycles, time, rebirth, and so on, is employed throughout much of land art. Circles in land art are made from slate, timber, snow or by walking in a circle; they seem to be gentler, more eco-friendly kinds of 'sculpture'. The circle shape itself speaks of organic forms, and, in some religions, evokes the 'feminine' and the Goddess. Not a few sculptors and land artists have made the circle crucial to their works: British artists such as Alison Wilding, Richard Deacon, Stephen Cox, Anish Kapoor, and Peter Randall-Page, and US artists such as Robert Morris, Mary Miss, Robert Smithson and Dennis Oppenheim.

Land art based on circles includes Vijali's *World Wheel* (1987), Alan Sonfist's *Circles of Life* (1987) and *Pool of Virgin Earth* (1975), Adam Purple's *The Garden of Eden* (1975), Charles Jencks' *Snail Mound* (1992-94), Michael Heizer's *Circular Surface Planar Displacement Drawing* (1970), Stan Herd's *The Circle* (1992), and Mel

Chin's *Revival Field* (1993). Many of Nancy Holt's works are circular: *Annual Ring* (1981), *30 Below* (1980), and *Sun Tunnels* (1976).

Donald Judd produced two circular steel bands, 180 inches in diameter, as well as a concrete circular 'wall'. Robert Morris made gigantic circular works, such as his *Observatory* (1971), which was a huge earthwork recalling the megalithic structures of ancient times, such as Avebury stone circle. His *Labyrinth* (1974) was a maze-size sculpture, the kind of maze one finds in theme parks and country houses, except that Morris' *Labyrinth* used the ancient pattern of the Cretan labyrinth, itself a motif some see as distinctly feminine, speaking of Goddess mysteries. Herbert Bayer's *Mill Creek Canyon Earthworks* (1979-82) was a series of earthworks recalling ancient monuments. Robert Smithson's *Closed Mirror Square* was like an Aztec ziggurat, while his *Amarillo Ramp* recalled the massive embankments found at Neolithic earthworks in the British Isles such as Maiden Castle, or Iron Age hill forts such as British Camp on the Malvern Hills.[1]

Some artists have produced stone circles which look very much like Stonehenge, Britain's premier prehistoric site – such as Nancy Holt's monumental *Stone Enclosure: Rock Rings* or Alan Wood's *Ranchenge* (1983), a wooden Mid-West American version of Stonehenge. Vida Freeman's *Installation* (1981) in an L.A. gallery comprised white porcelain and stoneware stones with white pillars emerging from them. Michelle Stuart constructed cairns and circles in *Stone Alignments/ Solstice Cairns* (1979). Margaret Hicks fashioned three concentric circles from oak and sandstone in Texas (*Hicks Mandala*, 1975), intended for a 'Ritual of Giving'. David Harding cast his *Henge* (1972) from nine foot tall slabs of concrete, while Donna Myars' *Dream Stones* (1979) were cast and carved from cement. Michael McCafferty built his *Stone Circles* (1977) on a beach in Oregon, where they were flooded at high tide. Marlene Creates' interventions on prehistoric earthworks included laying rows of paper over them (*Paper Over the Turlough Hill Cairn*, 1981).

The spiral and snake employed by so many land artists down the ages (in ancient Peru, or on the doors of Neolithic tombs, or in the Mid-West of America) is associated with Goddess cults and with the energies of life. The circles and spirals of, Oppenheim and Smithson are also those of the Goddess, the ancient Earth Mother. In the eco-neo-pseudo-pagan view, the land artists, then, make marks upon Mother Earth, upon the surface or skin of the Goddess. Andy Goldsworthy inadvertently evoked phallic penetration when he said: 'I want to get under the surface... At its most successful, my 'touch' looks into the heart of nature' (WH). Land artists, then, penetrate or cut into nature. The Earth, which is regarded as female in this particular religious/ pagan worldview, is penetrated – by Michael Heizer gouging vast chunks out of the American desert, by Walter de Maria thrusting a kilometre-long brass rod into the Earth (this must be art's biggest phallus, surely?), and Goldsworthy, seemingly so gentle, has cut trenches into the earth, or smashed slabs of slate or pebbles or leaves, to make lines of broken, shattered material on the earth. He has torn leaves apart to form a line, and has smashed pebbles, making a line, like a fault line in continental structures (*Leaves Torn in Two*, 1986, *Broken Pebbles*, 1987). These are violent gestures, destroying the organic make-up of the natural forms he so adores. All land artists – all artists – must break up and reform materials, but these cracks and holes can look to the eco-friendly follower like scars on the body of the Earth.

Land artists often use circular forms, which hide the violence of their gestures. The spiral or circle is a 'kind', organic, even gentle shape, seemingly in tune with 'earth energies'. Circular structures (igloos, huts, stone circles, tombs, earthworks, pools) seem to be in harmony with nature, echoing the circle shapes of the planet itself, or suns, eyes, blood cells, orifices, orbits. The circular structures suggest primitive, archaic, more 'authentic' ethics, the 'back to nature' syndrome. There is, then, not only a mystical side to land art, to Smithson, Oppenheim, de Vries and Bayer, but also a nostalgic element (nostalgia is a key element in any religion). Looking *back* to the land, land artists also look *back* to a former, even ancient era which was, patently, better (to a golden age which is and was imaginary, which never existed). This is the hidden subtext in the writings of the land artists, this nostalgia for the better times of archaic cultures, when people lived 'in harmony' with the earth. This is, of course, a widespread nostalgia, not backed up by the evidence, which is that for ancient and prehistoric peoples life was as hard, if not harder, than it is now.

Many land artists have made mounds which recall prehistoric burial mounds (apart from the ones cited above) including Charles Jencks (*Snail Mound*, 1992-94), Judy Varga's *Geometry of Echoes Converge* (1980), Maya Lin's *Wave Field* (1995), Peter Walker's *Turf Mountain* (1993) and James Pierce (*Burial Mound*). These (Minimal) sculptures are ambivalently related to ancient monuments, however, as Samuel Wagstaff remarked of Tony Smith's works:

> They are related to early cultures intentionally or through sympathy – menhirs, earth mounds, cairns... [and] to this culture with equal sympathy – smoke-stacks, gas tanks, dump trucks, poured concrete ramps.[2]

Land artists, then, consciously or slyly invoke ancient, prehistoric monuments. Heizer, Smithson, Morris and Holt make references to ancient earthworks. (What separated Hans Haacke's earth mound from gardening? My *intent*, Haacke replied.) The famous *Serpent Mound* in Adams County, Ohio, dating from the 10th century AD, is an obvious ancestor of Andy Goldsworthy's *Lambton Earthwork* and landscaped art by Heizer, Bayer, Morris and others.

Some land artists work in megalith-rich landscapes (such as Richard Long in the South-West of Britain). There are over nine hundred stone circles in the British Isles. Long too makes connections with prehistoric art in terms of manufacture: the cave paintings at Lascaux, Long said, were made by people's hands on the rock. Long has made references to some of the key sacred/ religious/ prehistoric sites of Britain: to Silbury Hill, the largest humanmade mound in Europe, so the textbooks say; to the ithyphallic Cerne Giant in Dorset; to Glastonbury Tor, mecca for hippies, occultists and 'New Age' travellers; to Windmill Hill, and so on. Long even put a picture of himself with a rucksack in Africa right next to one of the famous ancient hill figures of England, the so-called 'Long Man of Wilmington', 231 foot tall, in Sussex. This is one of those prehistoric sites that some see as being an alien, or St Paul, or a Roman emperor, or King Harold. Richard Long ironically compared himself with another 'Long' Man.[3]

Locations such as *Serpent Mound* in Ohio or Silbury Hill and Glastonbury in the U.K. have long been revered by people as holy sites, 'places of power' as they are called. Land artists capitalize on the mystery of such places. One of Richard Long's works is a walk between two prime magical centres of Britain, Stonehenge and Glastonbury, both deeply associated with prehistoric astronomy, ancient priest-hoods, Arthurian legend, Merlin the Magician, the Age of Aquarius, ley lines, Druids, geomancy, and so on:

ON MIDSUMMER'S DAY
A WESTWARD WALK
FROM STONEHENGE AT SUNRISE
TO GLASTONBURY BY SUNSET
FORTY FIVE MILES FOLLOWING THE DAY[4]

The photograph that goes with this text is the sort of picture postcard view one finds in newsagents and heritage centres around the UK: Glastonbury Tor at sunset. Like St Paul's, the Tower of London, Big Ben, Buckingham Palace, Beefeaters, the changing of the guard, red buses and telephone boxes, this is one of the archetypal images of Britain.

Land artists' stone circles often recall prehistoric stone circles. While they may deny it verbally, Nancy Holt's *Stone Enclosure*, Robert Morris's *Observatory* and Richard Long's circle sculptures evoke the great circles of Europe: the Rollright Stones in Oxfordshire, Boscawen-Ûn in West Penwith, Cornwall, Little St Bernard Pass, the ones in Brittany, Stanton Drew in Somerset (a huge and little-known set of circles, and the nearest large circle to Richard Long's home in Bristol), and of course the mother of all stone circles, Avebury.

Some land artists maintain that their stone rings are subjective, private, individual works, quite different from the public, social art of the prehistoric stones circles. The ancient stone rings were made by a group of people, a society, constructed, perhaps, according to the plans of a priestly élite. Land art circles are (usually) the work of one person, but a major contemporary artist is no less a member of the cultural, æsthetic élite. Prehistoric stone circles may have been made for religious rituals, perhaps connected with the position of certain astronomical bodies or celestial alignments. The circles in stone, snow, dandelions, trees and concrete of land art are made for private consumption, for the artist alone, or for an onlooker who wanders into a gallery or a space then out again, back into the chaos of the city. Yet the ancient sacred sites and land art/ Postminimal earthworks have much in common, because art and religion join at so many points.

Land artists benefit from the allusions to ancient monuments, because the atmosphere and magic of prehistoric stones rubs off on their own work. In stressing the importance of megaliths, the land artists not-so-subtly imply a continuity between themselves and these prehistoric relics. The æsthetic continuity that's emphasized also implies religious affinities. Thus, the land artist is the postwar equivalent of the priests and hieratic sects who created Stonehenge, the lines in Peru, the Pyramids, and Australian aborigine 'songlines'. A spirituality is affirmed in land art, which only a few land artists actually speak about. But this religious feeling is definitely there, definitely a part of the discourse of American land artists such as Heizer, Turrell, Smithson, Morris and Holt.

MAZES

Mazes and labyrinths are favourite land art forms. Robert Smithson, Richard Fleischner and Alice Aycock created large earthwork mazes in the States in the late 1960s/ early 1970s. Andy Goldsworthy designed a maze (at Burham in 1988), and an earthwork which was a curving ramp, exactly like Smithson's *Armarillo Ramp*, though on a much smaller scale. Richard Fleischner created a *Sod Maze* in 1974, in the turf at Newport, Rhode Island, an enormous *Zig Zag* (1972) in grass (370 feet long) and a *Chain-Link Maze* (1978), 61 feet square. Michelangelo Pistoletto built an interior maze from large pieces of corrugated cardboard laid out across the whole gallery (*Labyrinth,* 1991). In *Monumental Ikebana* (1990) Hiroshi Teshigahara made a giant arched path from bamboo in a gallery space. For Vong Phaephanit's bamboo installation (*What Falls to the Ground Cannot Be Eaten*, 1991), a forest of bamboo sticks was hung from the ceiling of the London gallery, approached through a monumental black doorway.

The mazes of land artists can be seen as a part of the resurgence of interest in mazes which occurred in the 1980s (aligned, as ever, with green/ ecological/ occult/ New Age trends). Mazes were commissioned for country houses, zoos and theme parks. A maze became seen as one more feature for visitors to enjoy: apart from the country mansion or palace or museum interior and formal gardens, the public could visit a maze, and perhaps an adventure playground. Some mazes were set beside children's playgrounds, emphasizing the sense of play, rather than ritual. At country houses, the maze was part of the adventure playground, and was conceived as something of a gym or assault course: there were walkways and bridges over some of the passages in the brick maze, which were climbed via ropes and ladders.

LAND ART AND CONSTANTIN BRANCUSI

It was Constantin Brancusi's project to strip away the detritus that had accumulated around sculpture, Henry Moore said, and to offer the pure, simple shape. What Brancusi did was 'to concentrate on very simple shapes, to keep his sculpture, as it were, one-cylindered, to refine and polish a single shape to a degree almost too precious.'[1] This is what many contemporary sculptors have done, keeping their shapes simple and purified: Andy Goldsworthy, Stephen Cox, David Nash, Richard Serra, Donald Judd and Robert Smithson.

Quite a few artists (not all of them sculptors) have expressed admiration for Constantin Brancusi's photographs, the way he would set up his sculptures in his studio and photograph them at particular times of day, when the lighting was just right. Andy Goldsworthy said he admired how Brancusi created the conditions in his studio so that his work 'comes alive at a particular time of day as the light momentarily touches it'.[2] For Goldsworthy, Brancusi's works were at their best when they were arranged by the sculptor in his studio and photographed.[3] Somehow, it wasn't quite the same when they were displayed in modern art museums (such as the Pompidou Centre in Paris or the Museum of Modern Art in Gotham). The Brancusian ethics, of simplicity, purity, smoothness, interiority and organic form are found in the Minimal sculptors, as well as the Constructivist notion of working with materials in a 'natural' way, so that the material dictates the form one creates with it.

LIGHT AND SPACE

Light: one recalls the reported dying words of Romantic artists like Johann Wolfgang von Goethe, who called for 'more light!', or J.M.W. Turner, who said 'the sun is god'. Numerous sculptors, installation artists and land artists have worked with light and lighting: Douglas Wheeler, Hap Tivey, Susan Kaiser Vogel, Larry Bell, and James Turrell with his 'skyspaces', Robert Irwin's reworked gallery spaces, Dan Flavin and his fluorescent tubes, Bruce Nauman, who made very narrow corridors lit by green fluorescents, Maria Nordman's extensions to studio exteriors, Nancy Holt's *Sun*

Tunnels, Eric Orr's sound and light environments and DeWain Valentine's acrylic tubes hanging alone from gallery ceilings.

Eric Orr constructed a *Silence and the Ion Wind* installation (1980), a series of dark rooms culminating in the *Golden Room,* 'an allusive structure for an elusive experience', approached through an ion wind.[1] In *Wall Shadow, Sky Lights, Sound Tunnel, Zero Mass, Sunrise, Blood Shadow, The Stone Snake, Prime Matter* and *Blue Void,* Orr deployed sound, light, wind, sand, ice and shadow. In *Prime Matter* (1981) Orr created fog and flames from a twenty foot tall metal column (a larger version was constructed outside the Mitsui Fudosan Building in L.A. in 1991). Orr has fired xenon lasers up into the sky on top of skyscrapers in Long Beach, CA (a permanent installation, *Landmark Lumière,* 1991).

Many artists have taken gallery spaces and reworked them, adding walls or scrims, or curtains, or false ceilings, or doorways, or new windows. Often these light and sound spaces look like empty gallery rooms: Eric Orr (*Light Space,* 1985), Hap Tivey's *Sodium Exchange* (1976), Susan Kaiser Vogel's *Point Conception* (1980), DeWain Valentine's *Curved Wall Spectrum* (1974), Larry Bell's *Leaning Room II* (1988), Bruce Nauman's *Yellow Triangular Room* (1973), Douglas Wheeler's *All Gray Graduating Light* (1976), Maria Nordman's *6/ 21/ 79 One Day Only* (1979), James Turrell's *Second Meeting* (1988), and Robert Irwin's Kansas *Installation* (1979). The forerunners of these light spaces includes Yves Klein's *Le Vide.* Some artists made the reconstituted gallery interior one of their trademarks.

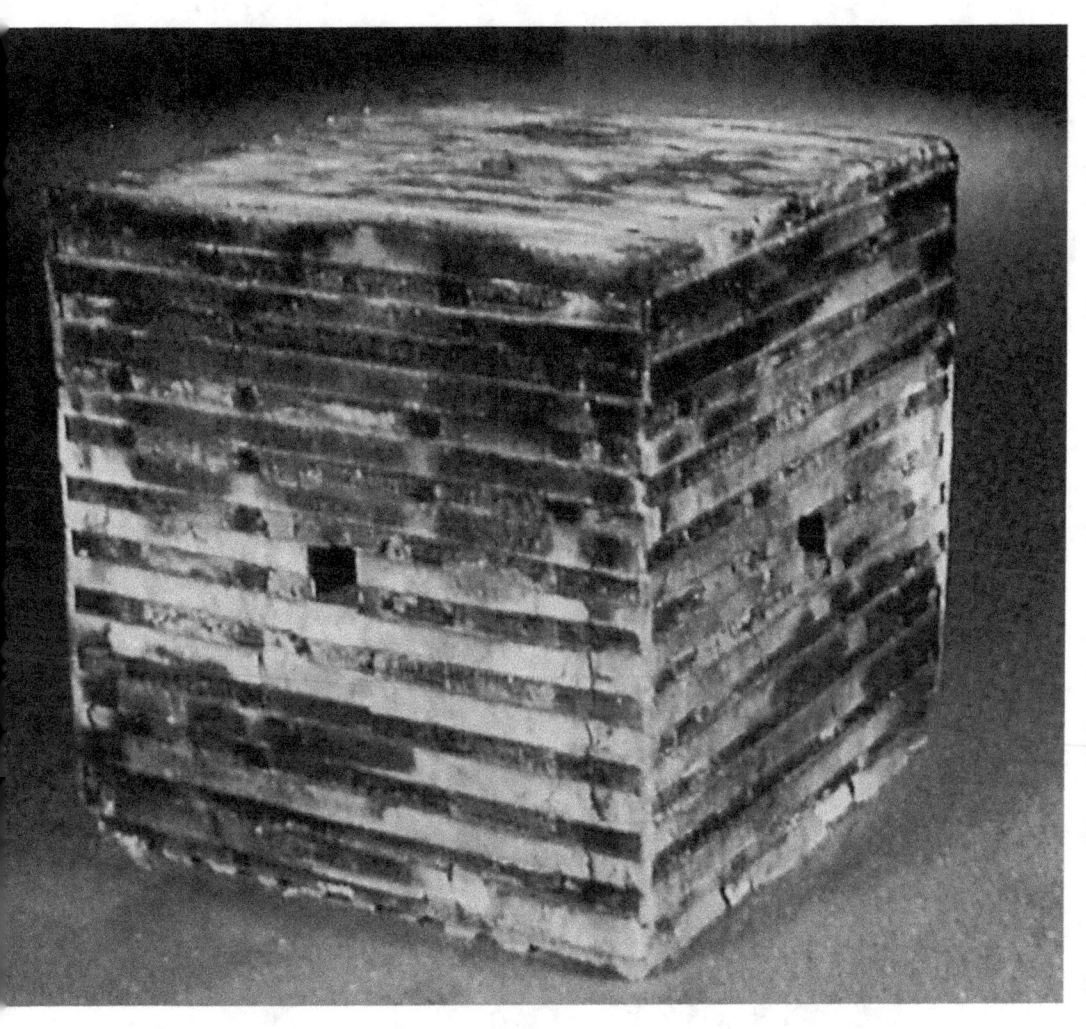

Jackie Winsor, Burnt Piece

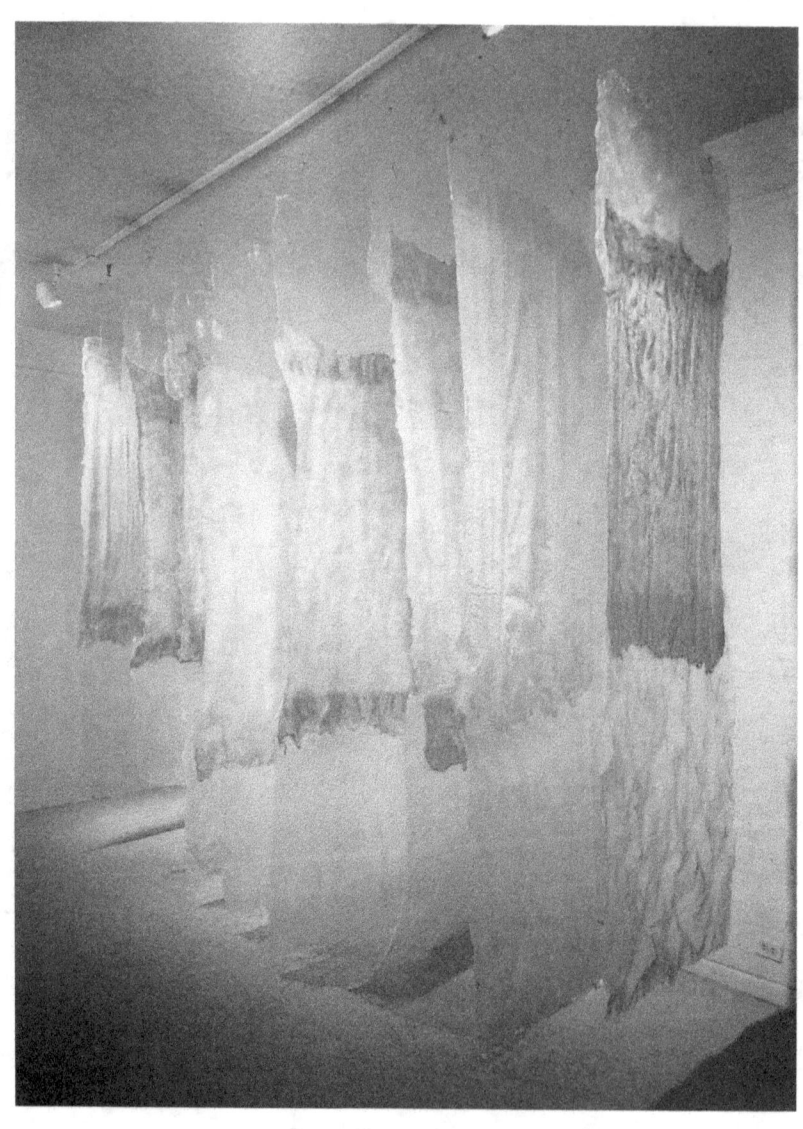

Eva Hesse, Contingent, 1969

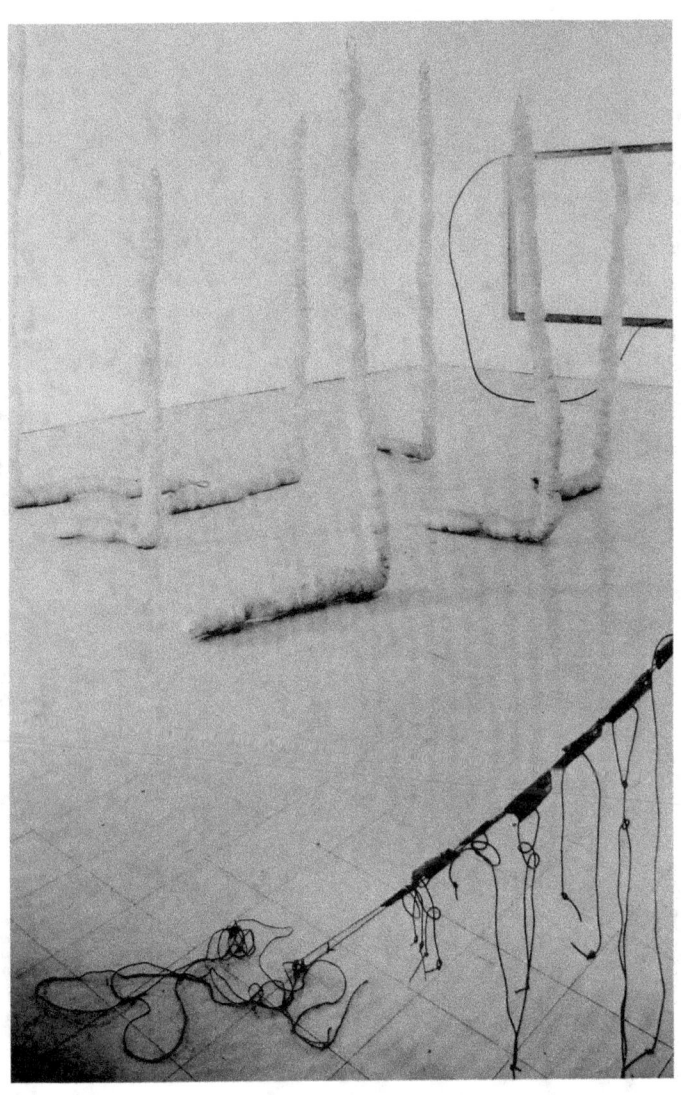

Eva Hesse, installation, 1970

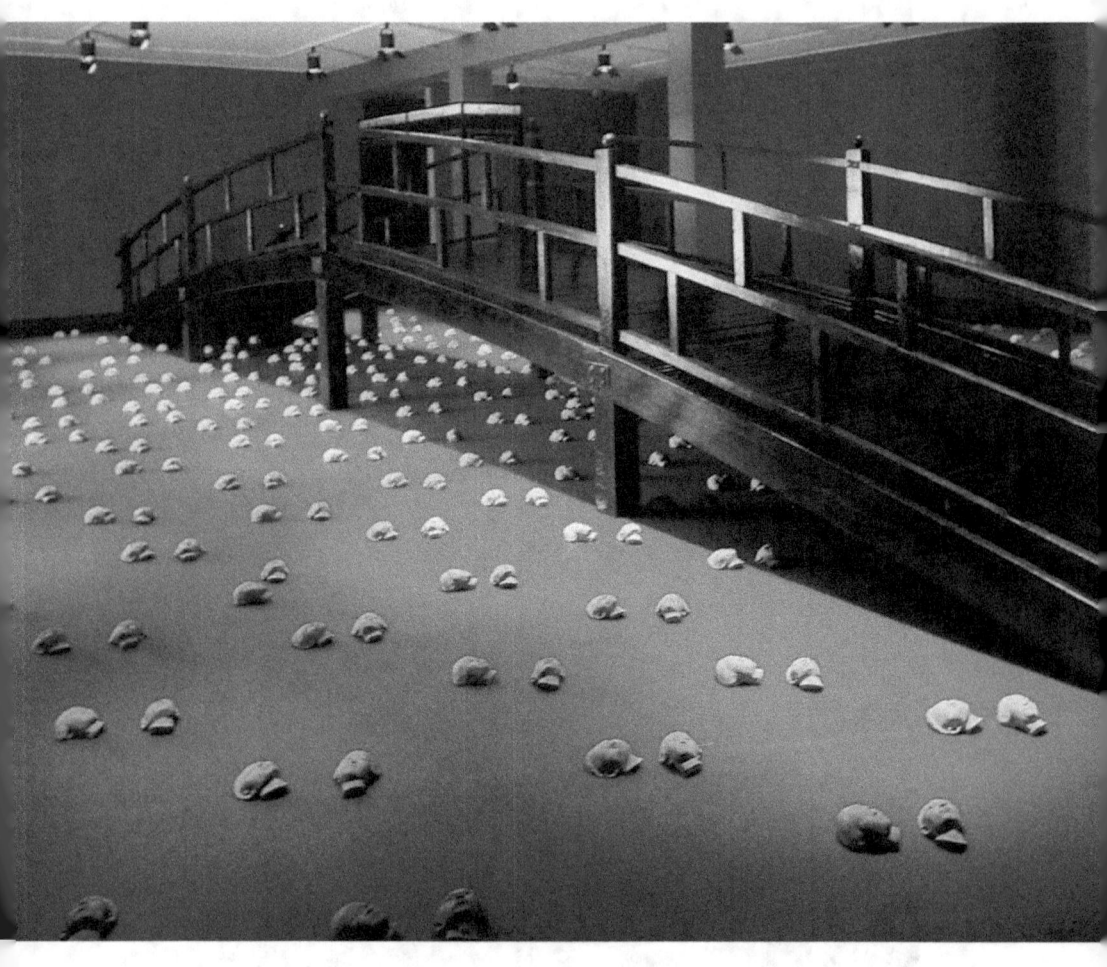

Barbara Bloom, Pictures From the Floating World, 1995

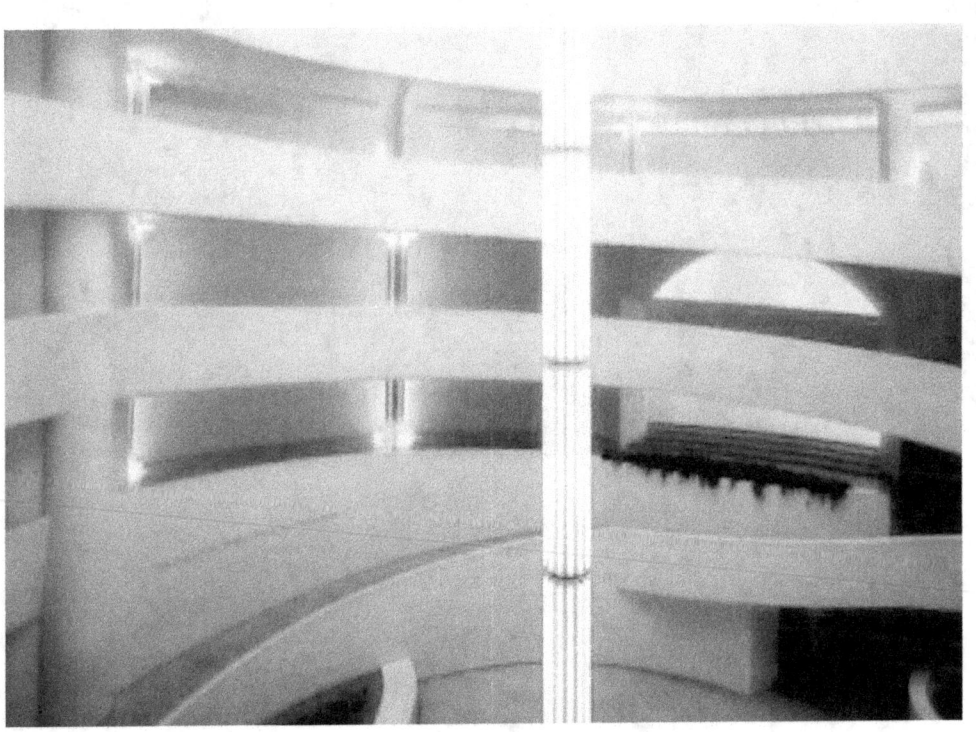

Dan Flavin, Untitled (To Tracy, To Celebrate the Love
of a Lifetime), 1992

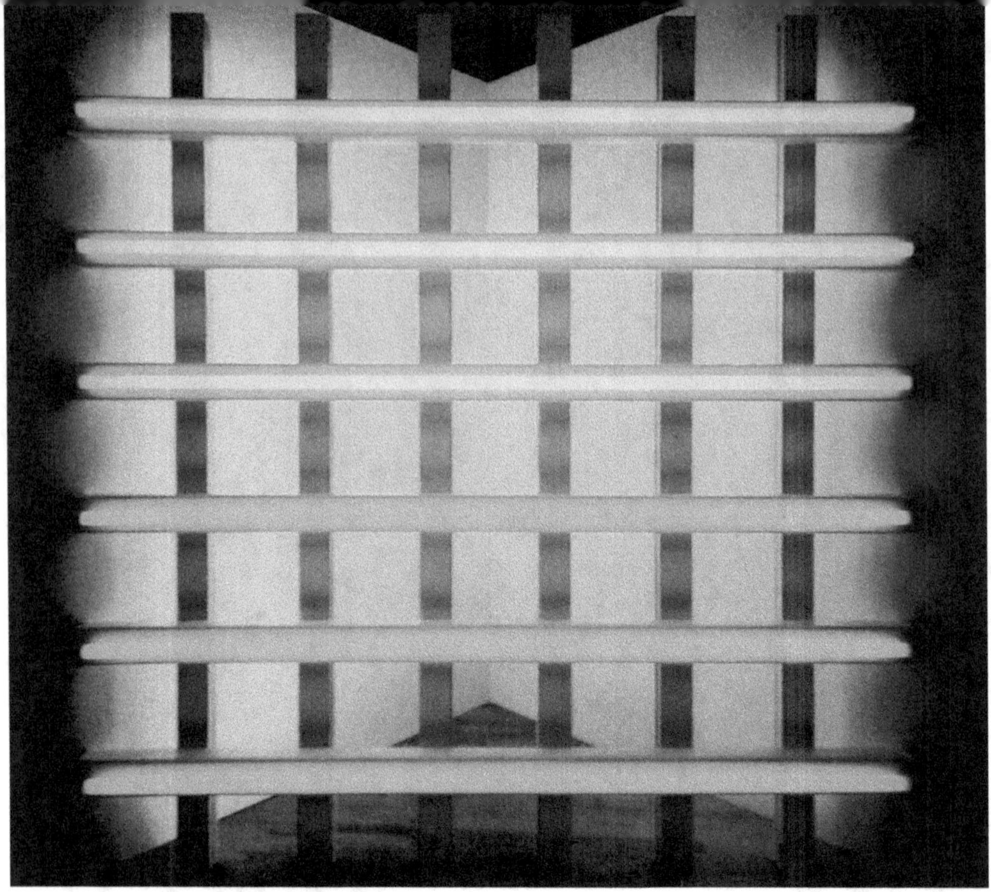

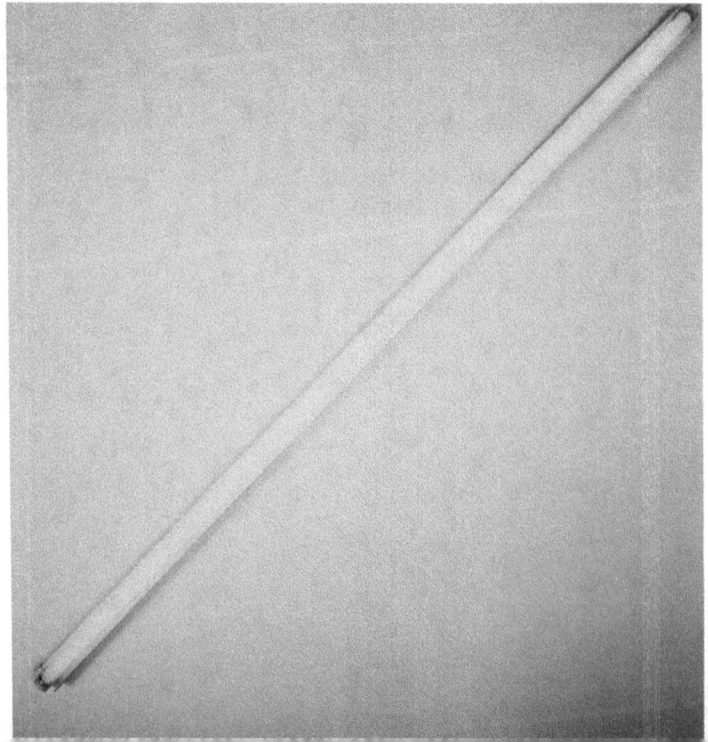

Dan Flavin

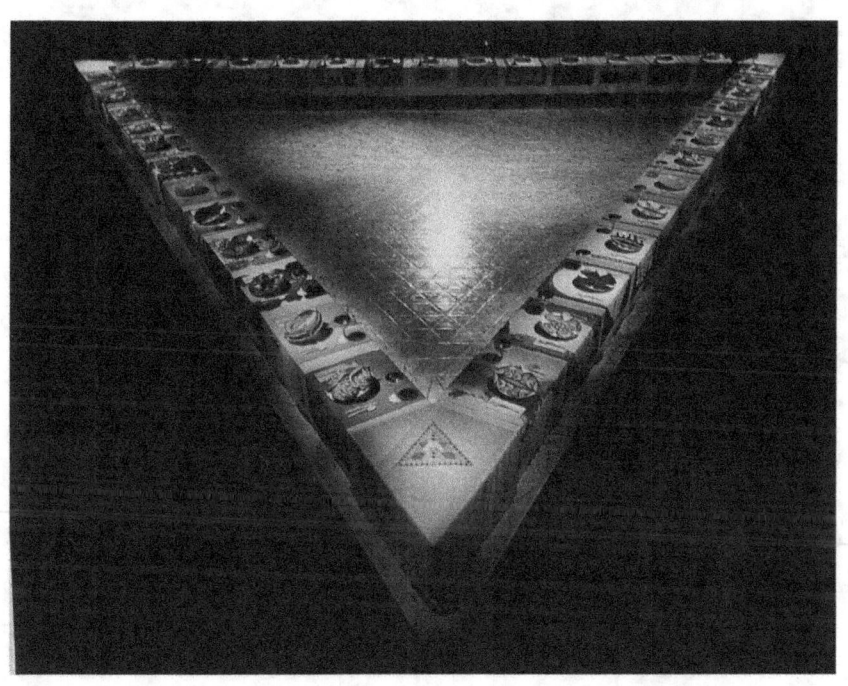

Judy Chicago

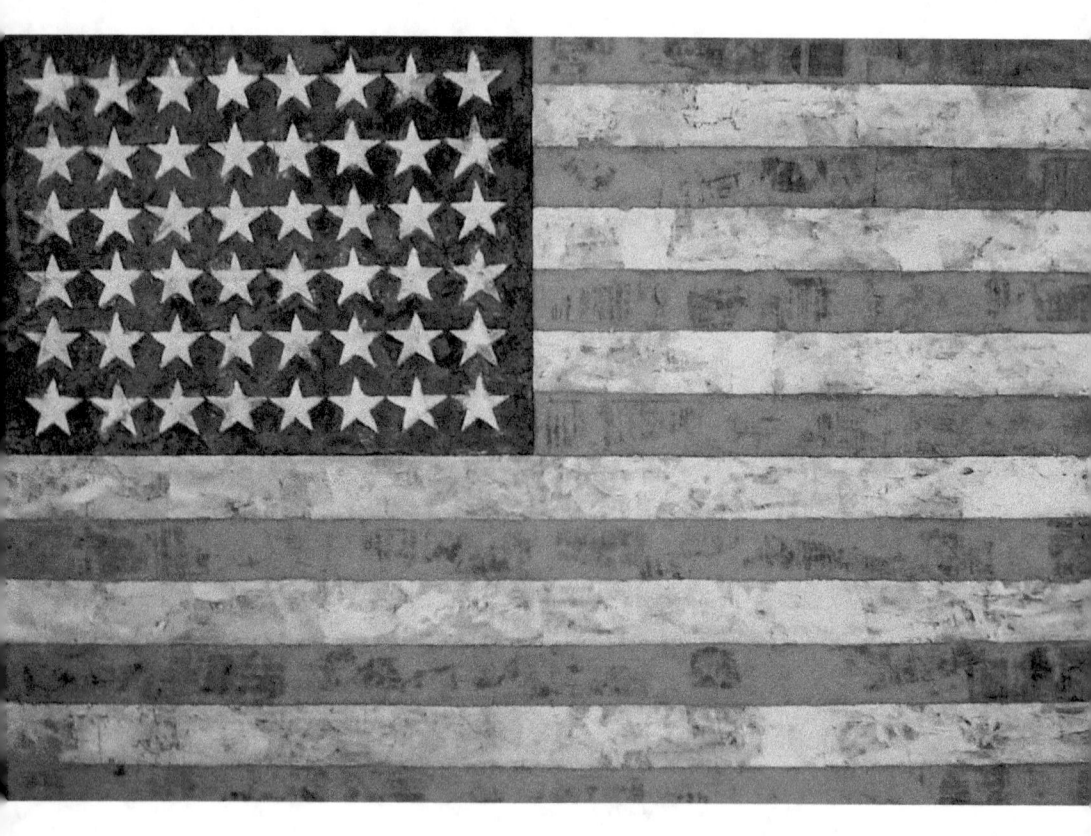

Jasper Johns, Flag, 1954-55

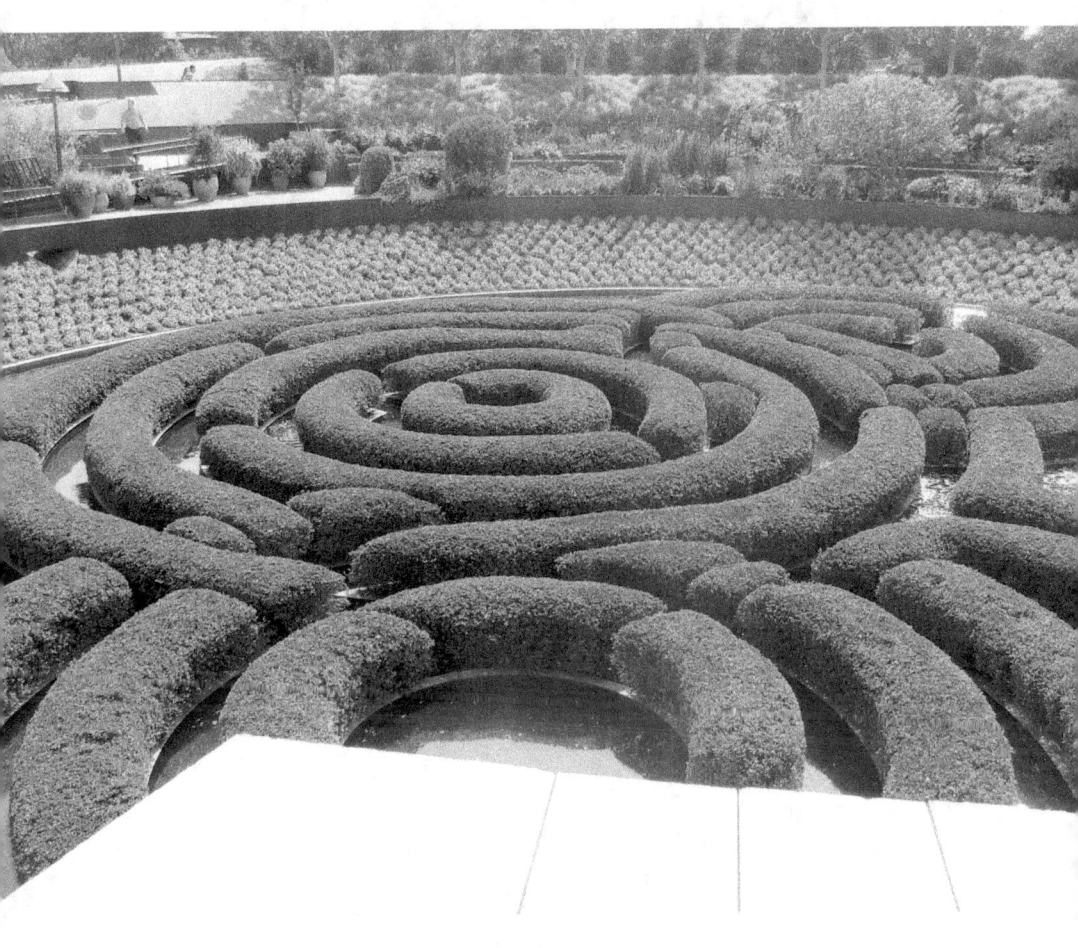

Robert Irwin's garden at the Getty in L.A.
()Photo: Cassidy Hughes)

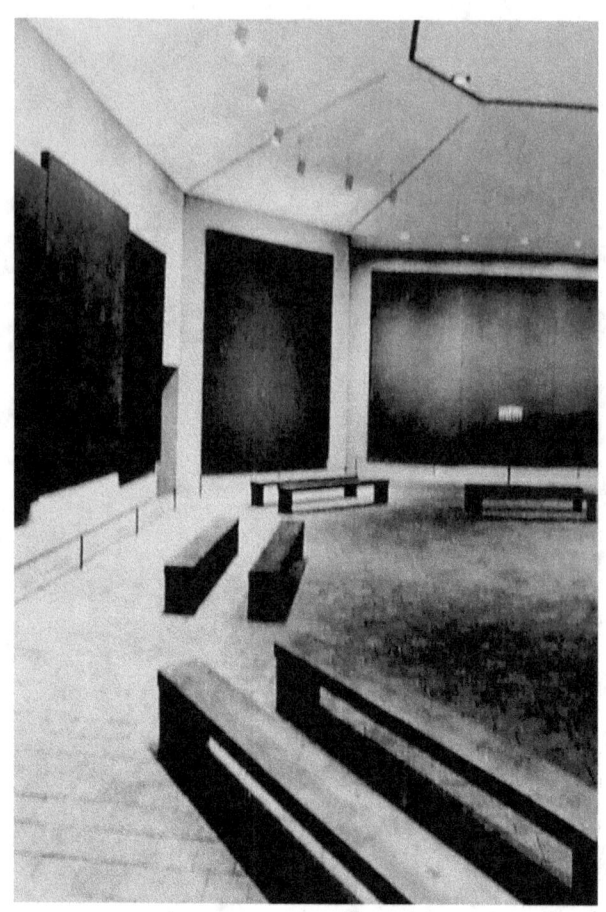

The Rothko Chapel in Houston, Texas

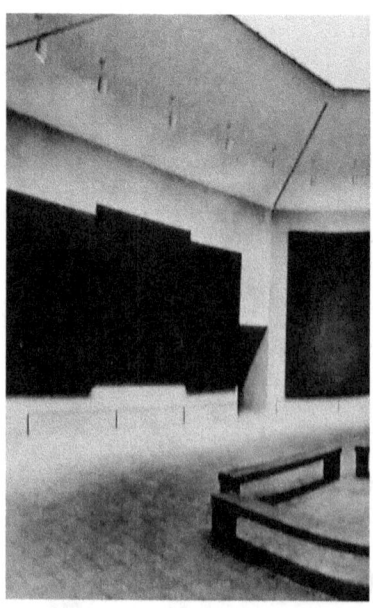

Agnes Martin, above, Sol LeWitt, below

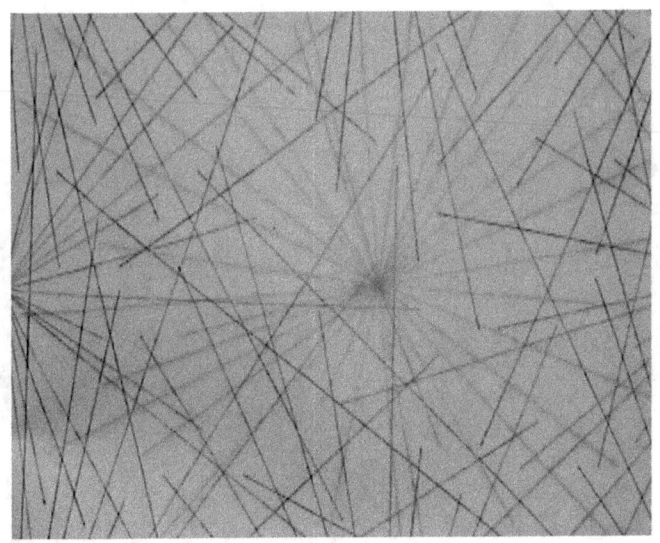

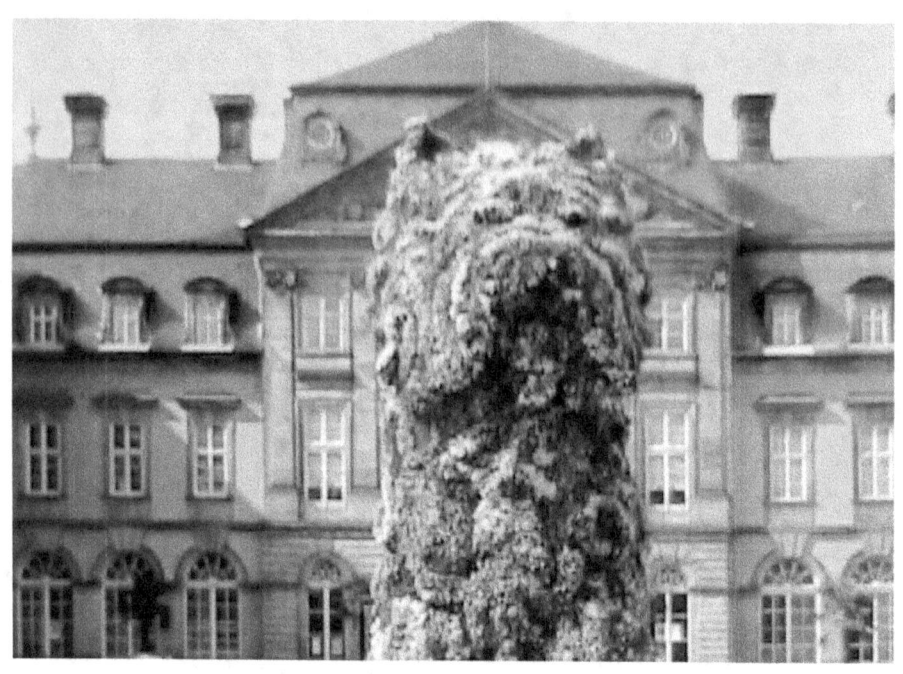

Jeff Koons

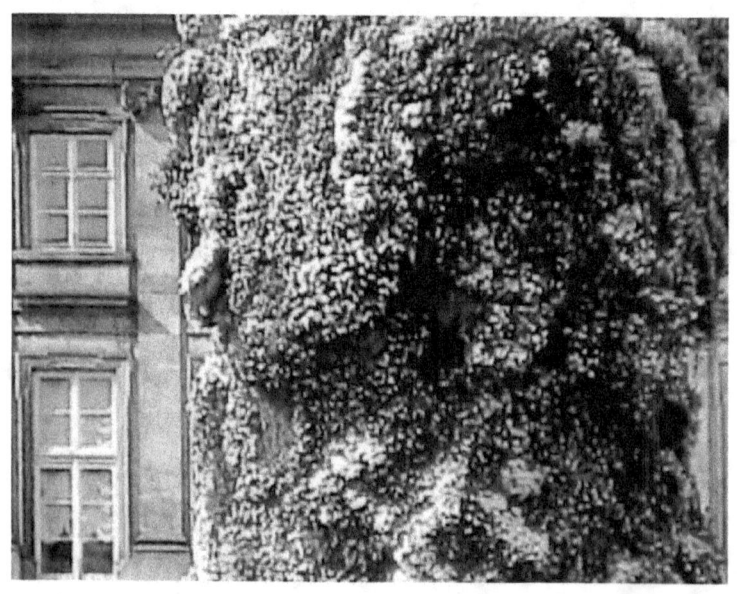

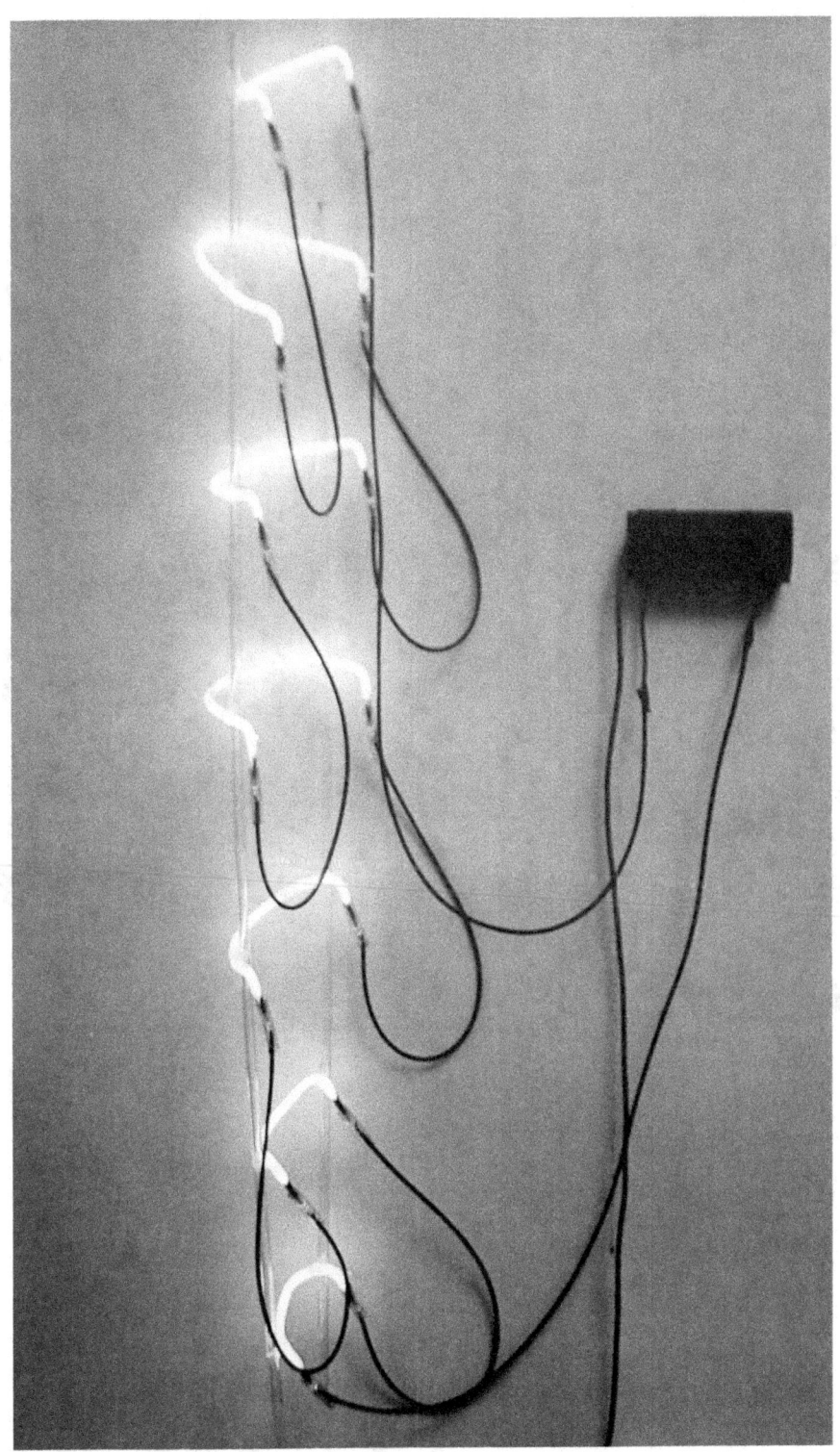

Bruce Nauman

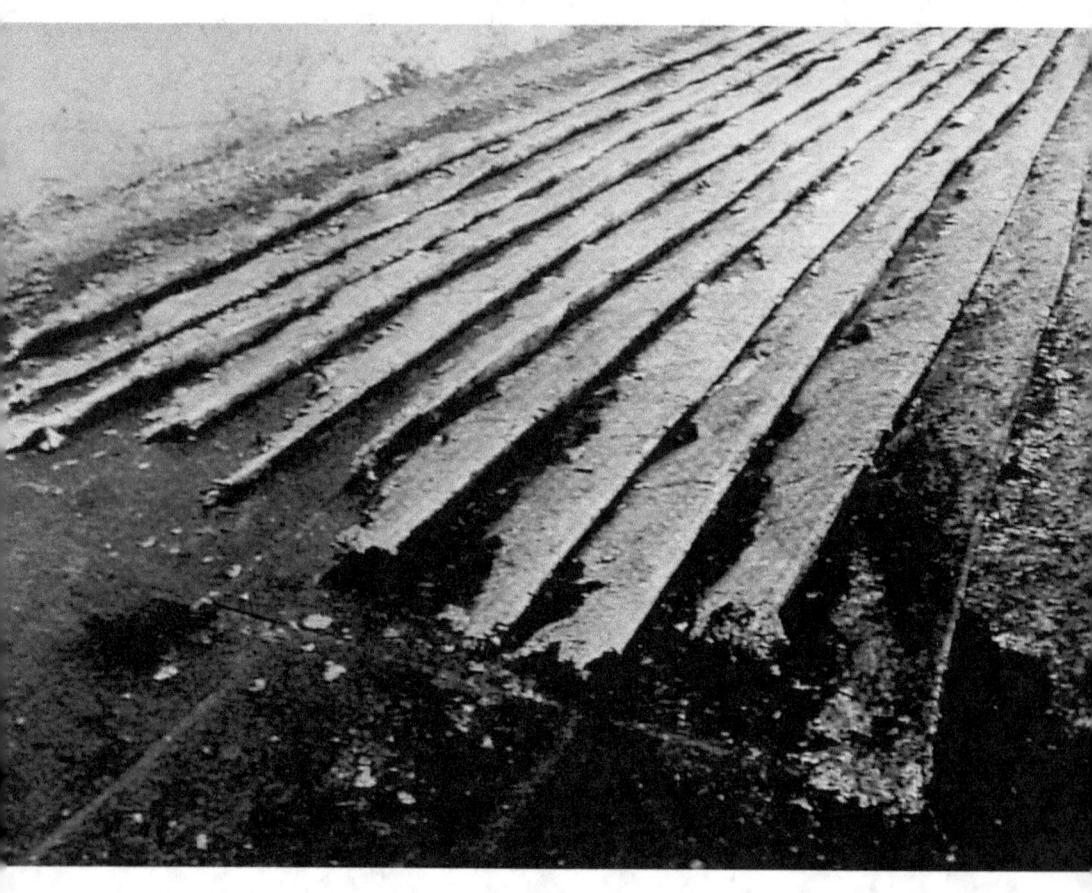

Richard Serra, Castings

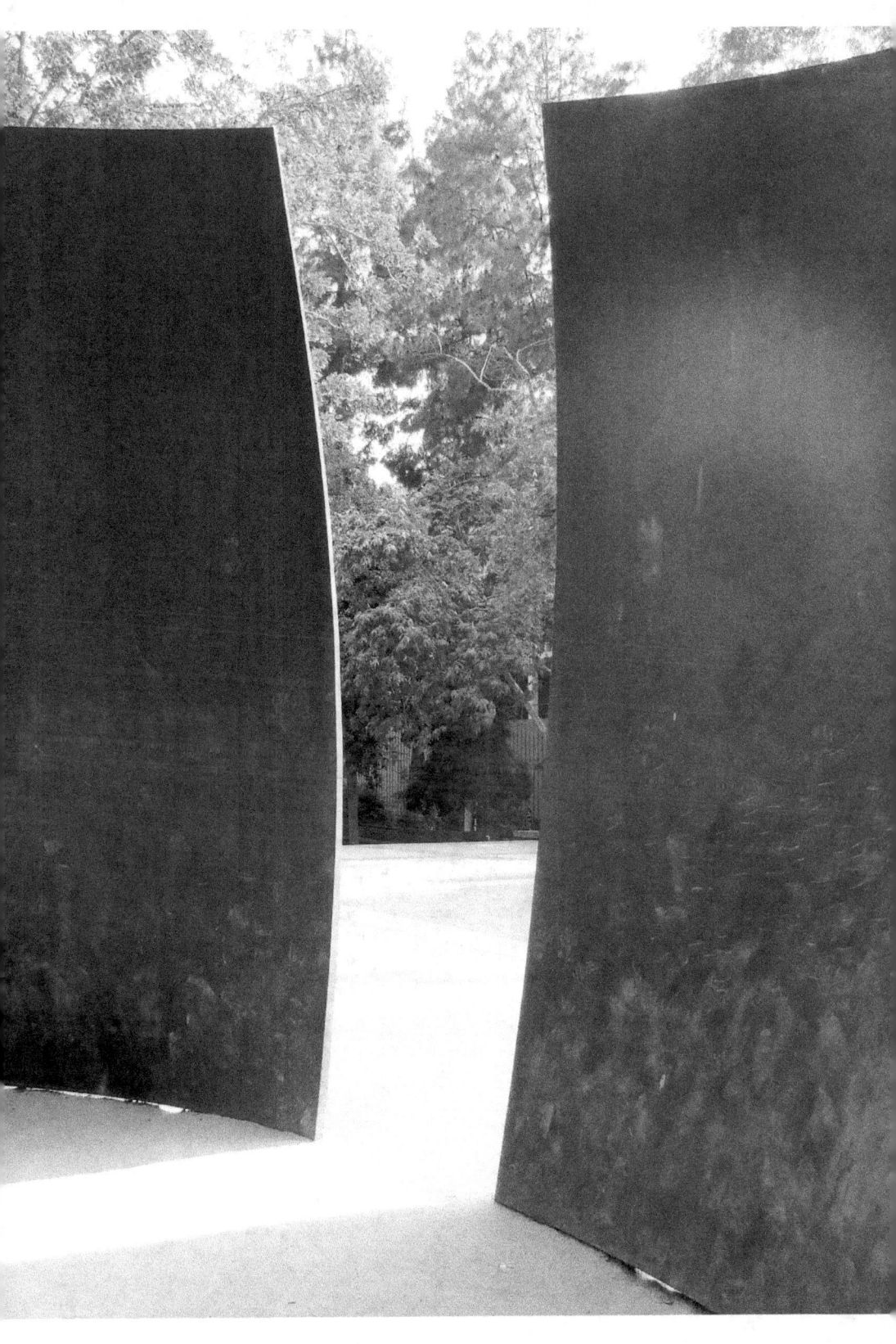

Richard Serra at USC in L.A. (Photo: William Malpas)

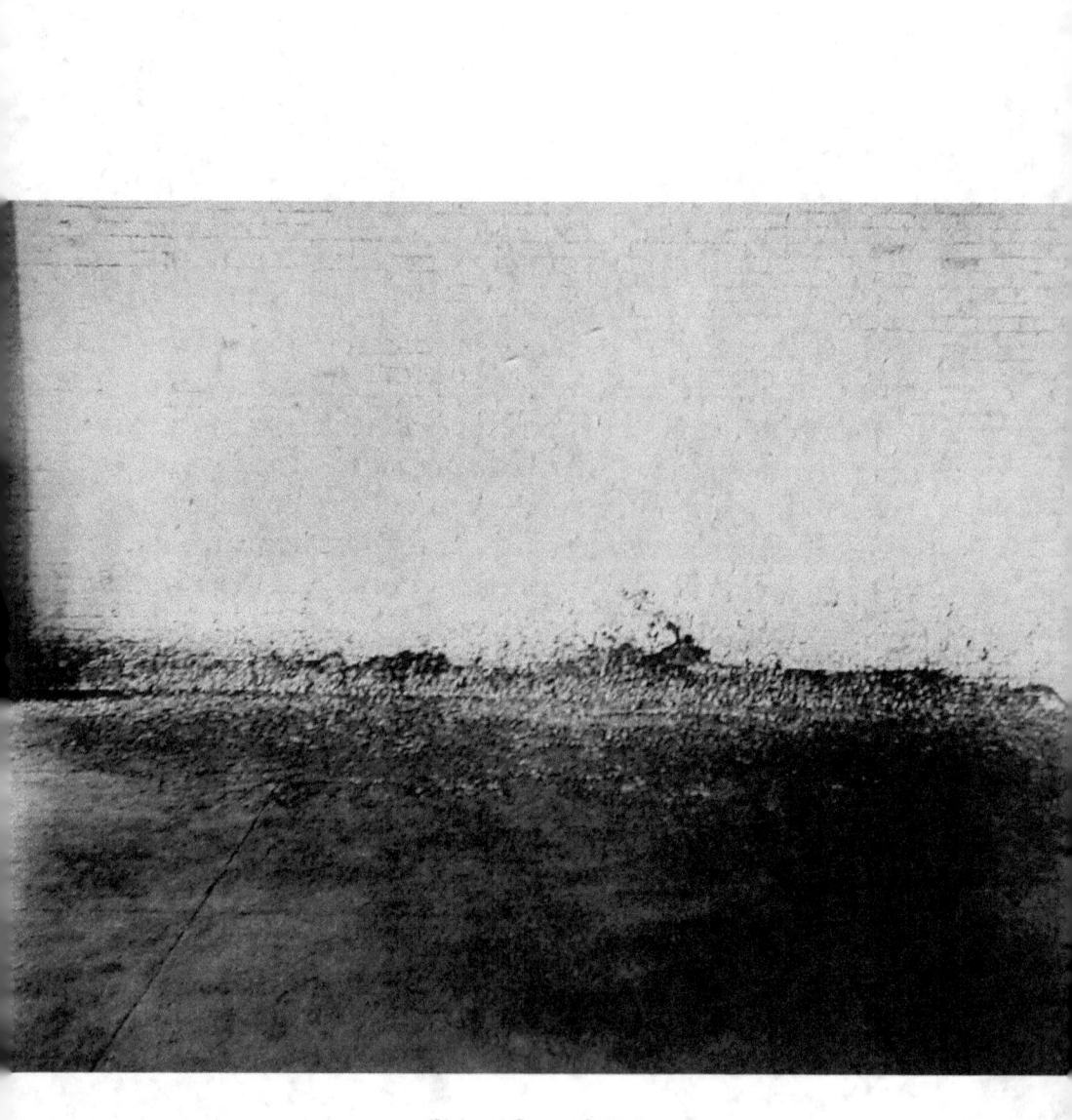

Richard Serra, Splashes

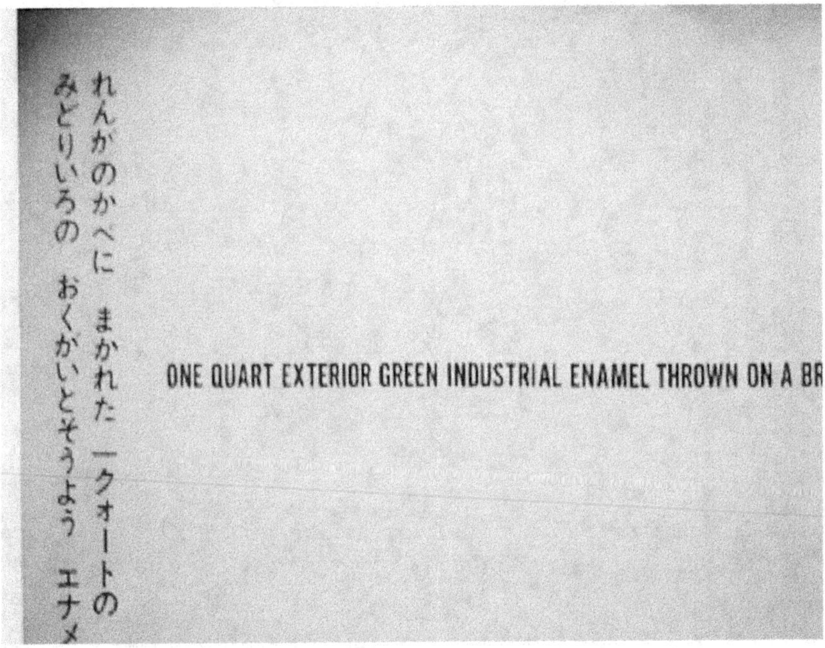

れんがのかべに まかれた 一クォートの

みどりいろの おくがいとそうよう エナメ

ONE QUART EXTERIOR GREEN INDUSTRIAL ENAMEL THROWN ON A BR

Lawrence Weiner

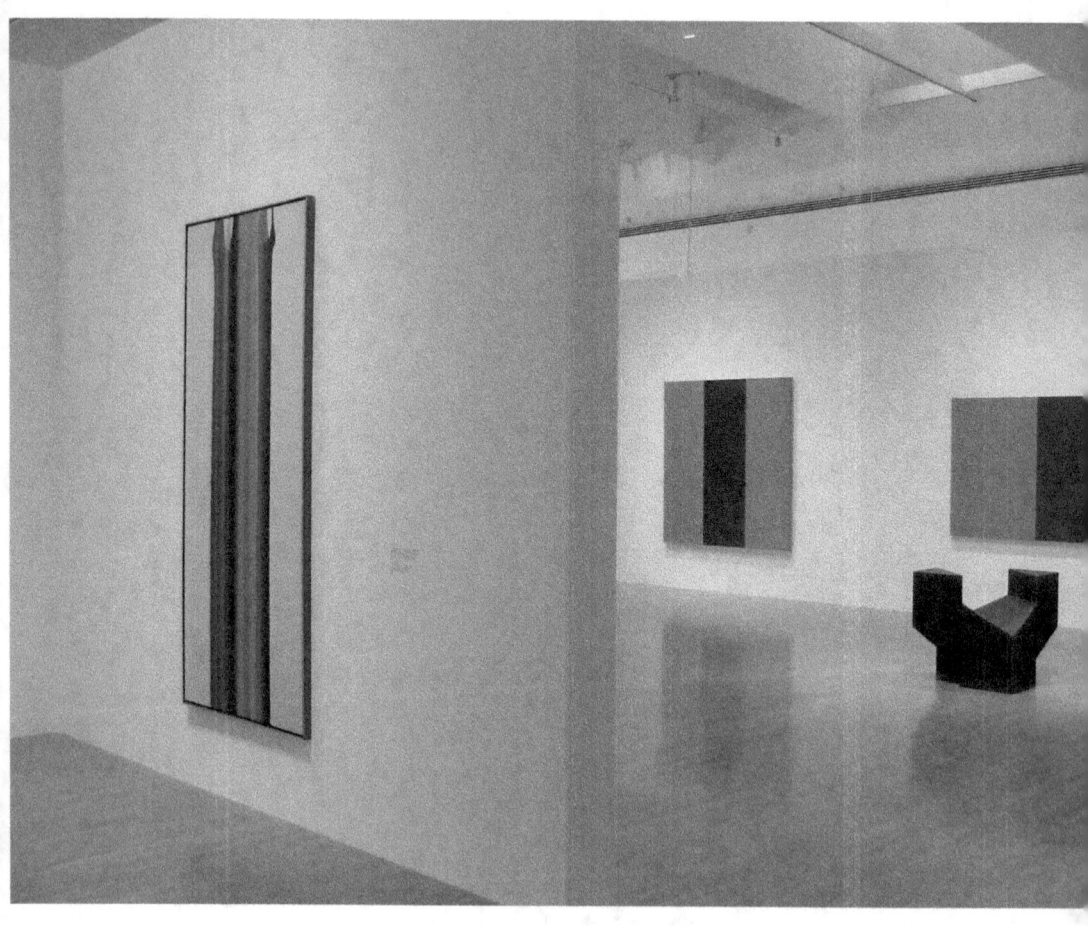

American art of the Sixties: Morris Louis and Brice Marden
at the Los Angeles County Museum of Art

3

Land Art and Art of the 1960s

THE PRESENCE OF THE OBJECT: LAND ART, MINIMAL ART AND 'OBJECTHOOD'

One can see the body written into, say, Andy Goldsworthy's delicate leaf sculptures, or Constantin Brancusi's extraordinary egg shapes, but not, perhaps, in the giganticism of Michael Heizer's *Double Negative*. Yet, even here, the human body is present – if only by the way it is violently dwarfed by the scale of Heizer's earthwork. Much of land art is vast. As Carl Andre said:

> I once described the change in sculpture in the 20th century as moving in its concerns from form to structure and now having a concern with place... I believe now you can make sculpture you can enter.[1]

In 1970, Heizer said that the old kind of sculpture had been replaced – 'destroyed, subverted, put down' (170). Kazuo Shiraga made works of art with his body, such as smearing mud on pieces of paper with his feet. His body-art was called 'the art of committing the whole self with the body'.[2] Minimal sculptures are not set on pedestals, like Renaissance or Greek sculpture; they sit on the floor, or lean against walls (as in Robert Morris's *Floor Piece*, or Carl Andre's *Cedar Piece*, 1959). The new sculptural space must have 'three, not two coordinates' said Robert Morris. 'The ground plane, not the wall, is the necessary support for the maximum awareness of the object'.[3] Minimal sculptures exist in the same space, on the same plane (the floor) as the viewer. They are, as Morris said, in an in-between cultural space, somewhere between being monuments and being ornaments, between being architecture and jewellry.[4]

MINIMAL ART, POSTMINIMAL ART AND LAND ART

The world of Minimal art was clean, calm, devoid of unruliness, violence, even ambiguity. Something like an airport: white, spotless, spacious. Or a new shopping mall. A row of pristine supermarket shelves, stacked high with new cans of fruit, the labels all turned face-out. Minimal art was an art for the 1960s, an era of commodification of a global scale, and the increasing affluence in the West after the austerity of the 1950s, where mass production created a uniformity to the appearances of so much of street, home, personal, medical, transport and educational furniture (especially in Europe and America). Minimal sculpture, Barbara Rose remarked, looks 'machine-made, industrial, standardized, materialized or stamped out as a whole'.[1]

Many land artworks appear to be 'simple', in that there doesn't seem to be much going on. But, as Donald Judd wrote in his influential "Specific Objects":

> it isn't necessary for a work to have a lot of things to look at, to compare, to analyze one by one, to contemplate. The thing as a whole, its qualities as a whole, is what is interesting.[2]

Some artists make a virtue of simplicity and ease: Jan Dibbets said he liked projects that anyone could do. For example, he chose four sites at random on a Netherlands map and went to each place and took a photo. It was '[q]uite stupid. Anybody can do that', Dibbets admitted. But Dibbets said he enjoyed searching for the places and photographing what was there. It was also silly for people to buy such works: 'it's stupid for other people to do it, or to buy it from me. What matters is the feeling'. And the feeling of the artist was something that couldn't be bought (1970).

LAND ART AND CONCEPTUAL ART

Land art is related to Conceptual art, and is a part of Conceptual art. Much of land art exists only in photographs, memories, words, various texts which are not the land art itself. Works that can be seen and those that are hidden or 'invisible' have the same importance for the artist. One of the hallmarks of the 'ideal Conceptual work', as Mel Bochner said, is 'an exact linguistic correlative, that is, it could be described and experienced in its data and it could be infinitely repeatable'.[1] Land art is often Conceptual art: Dennis Oppenheim's *Whirlpool Eye of Storm* (a jet trail in the sky), Hans Haacke's balloons floating over Central Park and Robert Morris's steam pieces exist now only as photographs, memories and criticism.

By contrast, James Turrell wanted to place the viewer right in the midst of his artworks, so they could experience directly the subject of his art (light, the sky, celestial events) for themselves. It was important for Turrell that his art wasn't a record or a photograph of something that happened elsewhere, that the viewer hadn't seen or couldn't see for themselves. Thus, at Roden Crater, Turrell constructed spaces that the spectator could enter physically, to experience light and the sky directly.

The pictorial or visual aspect of land art was over-emphasized by critics and viewers, Dennis Oppenheim argued in 1992. It was 'basically the *idea* of earthworks, the idea of the salt flats' that was important, not the visual element; '[t]he visual quotient is not as strenuous as you think'. Many land artworks were conceptual, mental, not visual or even physical. 'In other words,' said Oppenheim, talking about Smithson's *Spiral Jetty*, 'it's about the salt, submersions, the jetty, what is around the salt flats. In the end it's about mental configurations' (1992). This presents a problem, because most land artworks are known primarily in a visual form – in photographs. It'd be great if land artworks were visited or directly experienced, as Oppenheim and others intended, but they aren't. For Richard Serra, the 'focus of art for me is the experience of living through the pieces', but the actual work itself, the physical object, was not the whole point, or the whole pleasure, of making art: 'that experience may have very little to do with the physical facts of the work of art'.2

One of pluses of Conceptual art was that art could be just ideas, and the artist wouldn't have to carry around masses of materials. Dennis Oppenheim wrote:

> In 1968 and 1969 I lived in an apartment. I didn't need a studio. Everything that I had done as an artist was contained in one small case of slides. And it accounted for two of the most strenuous years of work in my whole life.3

Many sculptors have spoken of the importance of the *making* of the sculpture, its actual construction, with real (and sometimes organic, living) materials. As Barry Flanagan put it: '[m]y work isn't centred in experience. The making of it is itself the experience'.4 In some artists, the material employed also has a symbolic or added meaning, as in Joseph Beuys' *Fettecke* or 'fat corner', a sculpture with powerful autobiographical and semiotic associations. Beuys emphasized process, evolution, change: his sculpture, he said, was not 'fixed and finished. Processes continue in most of them: chemical reactions, fermentations, colour changes, decay, drying up. Everything is in a *state of change*'.5

Land art is meta-art, art about art, art that relies on other art to 'exist'. Land art exists for a brief moment, then becomes myth, gossip, photography, words (or more often, art criticism and journalism). Many of Richard Long's works are simply collections of words, printed in capitals, in Eric Gill's font, Gill Sans, on large pieces of paper. The text of one of Long's works can be printed here, and this text here will be very close to being a Richard Long artwork in itself (although he likes them printed much larger). Thus:

SPRING WALK

PRIMROSES AT 3 MILES

FROGSPAWN AT 18 MILES

A CROW NEST-BUILDING AT 29 MILES

A FARMER SOWING AT 34 MILES

LADYBIRDS AT 38 MILES

SQUIRRELS AT 57 MILES

LAMBS AT 62 MILES

STICKY BUDS AT 67 MILES

A TREE PLANTED AT 70 MILES

A BUTTERFLY AT 85 MILES

BLOSSOM AT 104 MILES

DAFFODILS AT 112 MILES

AVON ENGLAND 1991

That's a Richard Long artwork, and a real piece of land art. It seems as if Long has nothing much to 'say'. Well, he is a sculptor, so he wouldn't be so good at writing or speaking. Wrong. He's a land artist (though he dislikes the term 'land art' – artists often don't like being categorized this way or that), and land artists are always much concerned with writing and written texts. A Richard Long exhibition, for instance, features written texts on display, and photographs, as well as installation works and sculptures.

The texts of land artists also draw on poetry, on concrete or 'visual poetry', or typewriter art. Richard Long, for instance, prints his laconic texts in circles (*Full Moon Circle of Ground*, Dartmoor, 1983), in concentric circles (*Three Moors, Three Circles*, Liskeard to Porlock, 1982), in vertical lines, as in trendy style magazines (*The Isle of Wight as Six Walks*, 1982), and in curved swathes of text (*A Moved Line in Japan*, 1983).

Sixties Conceptual artist Lawrence Weiner produced text works, capital letters on a wall or in a book (Barbara Kruger, the Art & Language group and Michael Craig-Martin have also produced post-Conceptual wall works). Weiner's solution to making sculpture was that a sculpture on a plinth has to be 'translated' into language, so that people can understand it. Sculpture is language, and words are language, therefore, Weiner reckons, words can be sculpture:

> when you see a piece of wood lying on the ground with a piece of stone on top of it, you must translate that in your own head into language. What I try to do is present language itself as a key to what sculpture is about... It is a presentation of a piece of sculpture in language.[6]

Like John Baldessari and Sophie Calle, Weiner produces capital letters in short phrases which are about a viewer's relationship with an object. The words are a means or the expression of a relationship with something.

BILLOWING CLOUDS OF FERROUS OXIDE
SETTING APART A CORNER ON THE BOTTOM OF THE SEA

This is a typical Lawrence Weiner artwork.[7] Here's another:

THINGS PUSHED DOWN TO THE BOTTOM AND
PUSHED UP AGAIN

Richard Long commented that '[t]he discovery [Weiner] made that art does not necessarily have to be made, that was a great breakthrough'.8 Weiner is right, of course: words alone can be sculpture, for poets have long known that language is an *experience*, not simply abstractions or concepts. Language really does affect people – otherwise why would they spend so much time consuming language? That is, they consume 40 hours of broadcasting per week – that's over a day and a half spent consuming television and radio per week. So the words on a gallery wall of Weiner, Calle, Baldessari, Haacke and Fulton don't seem at first to be 'art'. They are not sensual and graspable in the physical realm, like a marble statue. Yet those words, whether photocopied on cheap paper or printed in high quality typography on deluxe paper, or painted onto the wall, are 'art', they are communication, language – even sculpture.

Postmodern/ post-Conceptual art ignites many important questions, such as: how does one know about the 'authenticity' or 'originality' of something when it is mediated by the mass media? How does one know something is 'the real thing', when all one knows of it is through images and sounds on radio, television, the internet and the press? Does it matter if the 'original' artwork is fake when the mediated product has such 'truth'? Is an artwork that consists of photographs that refer to an artwork, an idea, an experience that exists elsewhere (Lawrence Weiner's printed words 'wall statement' *Sometimes Found,* say) as 'authentic' as a bronze sculpture by Auguste Rodin? Is the artwork that is an 'idea' as sensual or compelling as one made out of marble or oil?

Laid over Richard Long's walks is the grid of the map: the maps in Conceptual art constitute a new landscape of the soul, as Robert Smithson wrote in 1968:

> A cartography of uninhabitable places seems to be developing – complete with decoy diagrams, abstract grid systems made of stone and tape (Carl Andre and Sol LeWitt), and electronic "mosaic" photomaps from NASA. (1968, 26)

Just about every land artist used maps in their work. Not just in the obvious sense of mapping (and finding) future sites for artworks, but as key elements in the artworks themselves. Robert Smithson made many mapworks, including map games, folded maps, aerial maps, and cut-up circular maps (*Untitled Circular Map*, *c.* 1968-70, *Entropic Pole*, 1967). Jan Dibbets chose places on a map at random, visited them and took a photograph. Dennis Oppenheim made maps a central ingredient in his 2-D Conceptual works, which combined maps, text, photos and sketches. Richard Long based many walks around maps, such as in a circle on a map, or a straight line. Chris Drury cut up and wove maps together (a development of his love of basket-weaving). Tom Van Sant collaged satellite maps. John Baldessari spelt out 'California' using maps in *The California Map Project* (1969). Charles Ross made star maps (1975-86). Jasper Johns painted a large map collage painting (1966-71). Nancy Holt buried poems (written for Carl Andre, John Perrault, Robert Smithson, Michael Heizer and Philip Leider) in remote locations, with a map marking the burial site (1969-71).

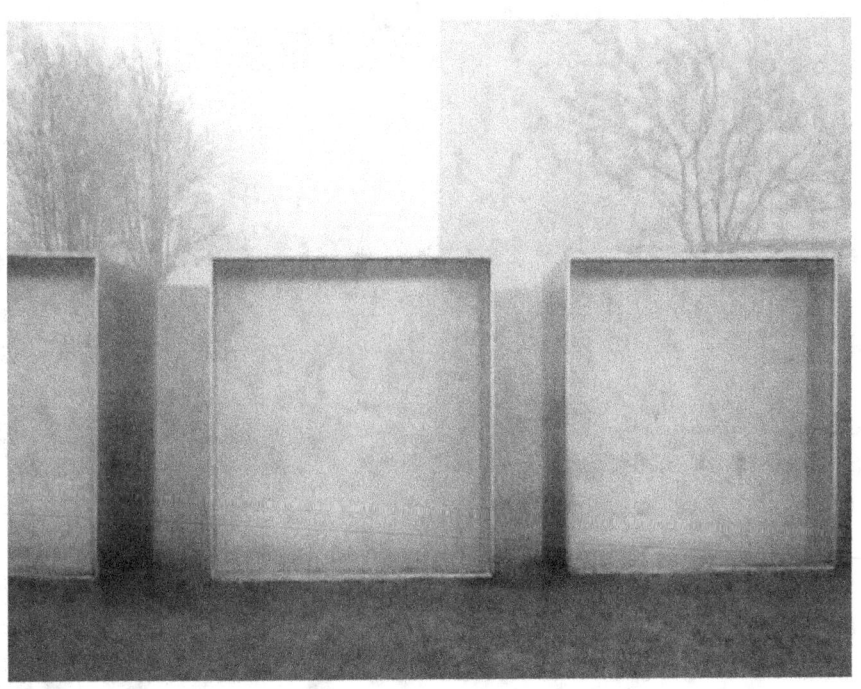

Donald Judd, Untitled, 1977

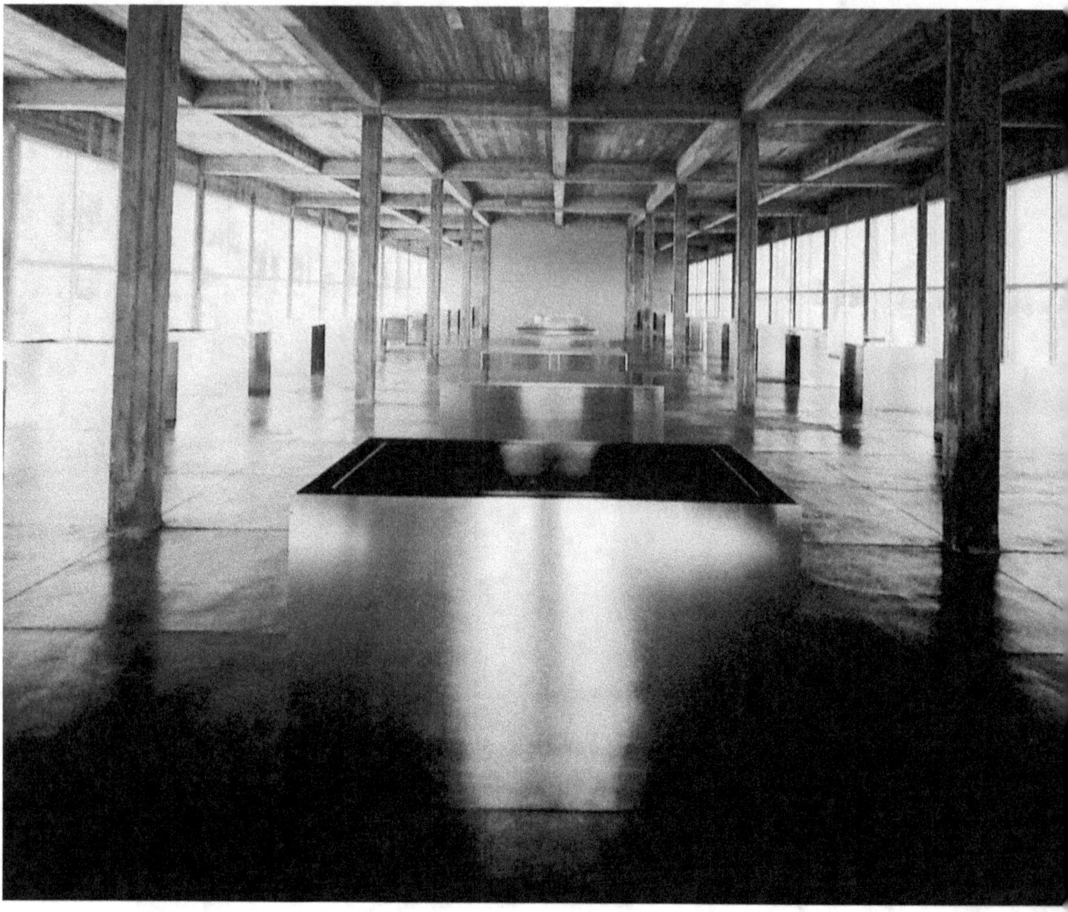

Donald Judd at Marfa, Texas

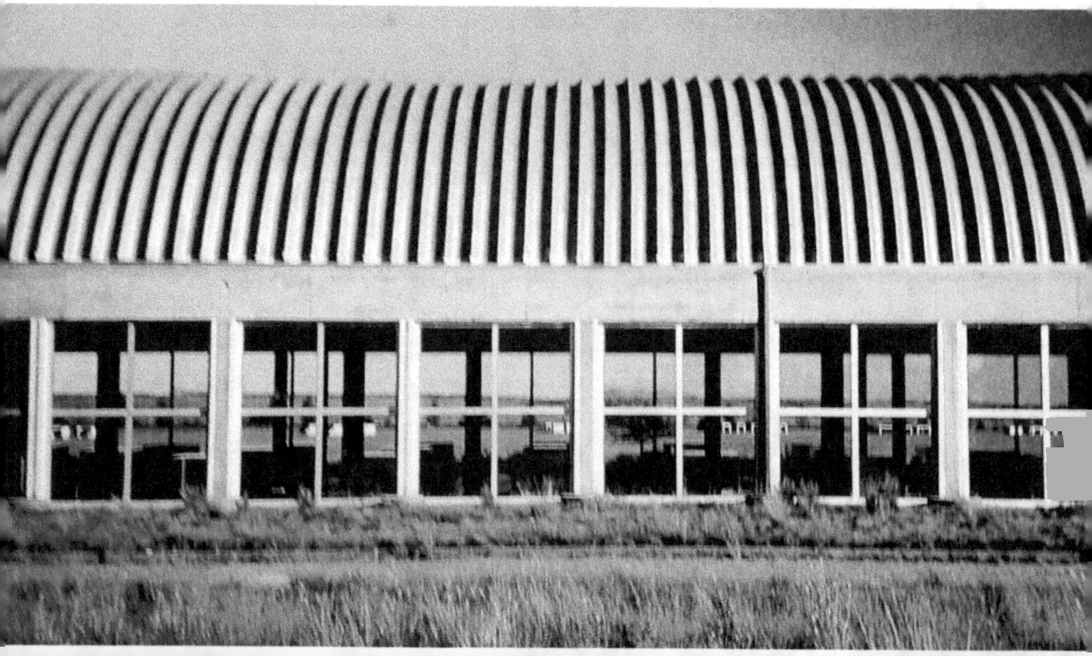

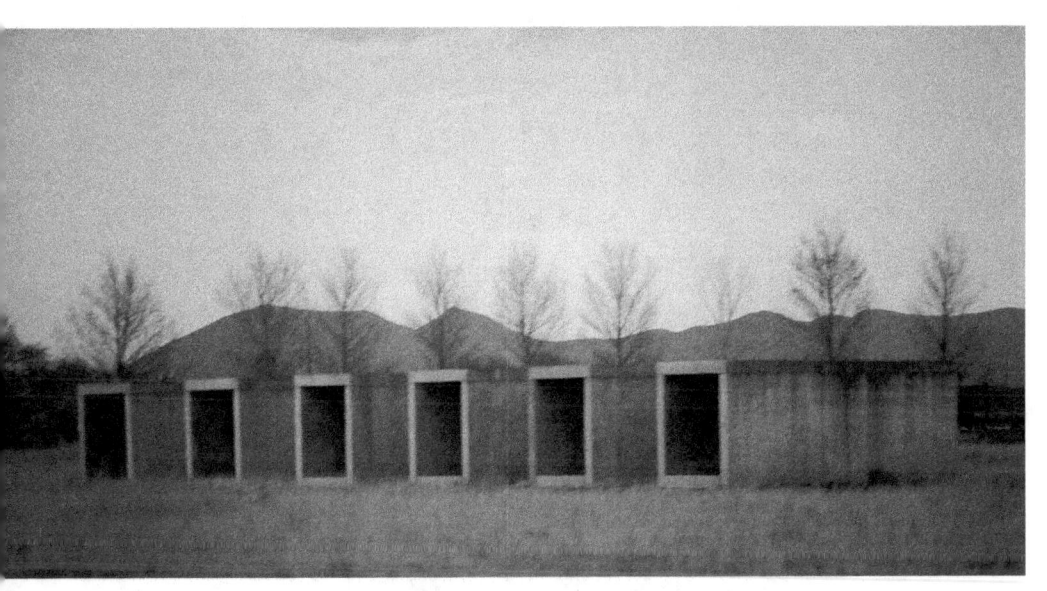

Donald Judd at Marfa, Texas

4

**Land Art, Gender, Sexuality
and the Body**

GENDER AND SCALE IN LAND ART

The awareness of scale is a function of the comparison made between that constant, one's body size, and the object. Space between the subject and the object is implied in such a comparison.

Robert Morris (1966, 21)

Contemporary artists, of all kinds, have made massive art. David Smith's *Wagon I* (1963-64, National Gallery of Scotland) and his *Cubi* sculptures are huge, heavy, chunky, truly colossal pieces which dominate their surroundings. Donald Judd wrote: '[t]his scale is one of the most important developments in twentieth century art' (1975, 200f). One of the largest earthwork projects, in the U.S. or anywhere else, is James Turrell's *Roden Crater Project,* a series of tunnels and chambers in an Arizonan extinct volcano, begun in 1974 and funded by the Dia Foundation. Turrell said:

> My art is made for one person. I like the solitary experience. Standing alone at night, perceiving the Roden Crater and the moon and stars, you really feel the vastness of the universe and yourself entering into it.[1]

'In sculpture, there's quite a concrete relationship between one's size as a person and/or mass as a person and the mass of a piece of sculpture' remarked Carl Andre (1970, 57). Richard Long's art is not monolithic in scale, usually: but his works can stretch over many miles, far longer than even Christo's fences (artists such as Christo made pieces that were 24 miles long). Even medium-sized pieces, such as Donald Judd's wooden boxes, are sometimes seen as monumental. A critic on *The New York Times* called Judd's 1977 installation at the Heiner Friedrich Gallery a 'majestic and finely measured presence'.[2]

Lucy Lippard described scale not just as something mathematical, optical, *seen*:

> Most discussions of scale consider it a strictly optical experience ...But a sense of scale is also a *sense* proper. Scale is *felt* and cannot be communicated either by photographic reproduction or by description.[3]

The bombastic, 'monumental', massive and brash 3-D art of modern sculpture was not made exclusively by male artists. Land artists Mary Miss, Nancy Holt, Sherry Wiggins, Donna Henes, Lynne Hull, Patricia Johanson, Alice Aycock and Agnes Denes have all made very large works. Other female architectural sculptors included Jackie

Ferrara, Donna Dennis and Elyn Zimmerman. For feminist critics, these women artists were drawn to shelter imagery: the origins of 'shelter sculpture', as Lucy Lippard called it, were in female biology and the female body.[4] Mary Miss created a 5 acre scale work in Illinois,[5] Patricia Johanson designed a large lagoon park in Dallas (1981-86), while Nancy Holt produced gigantic *Sun Tunnels*, 18 foot long pipes that were 9 feet high with many holes punched in the side, to let light in.[6] Nancy Holt's art, with its large, heavy landscaping gestures (such as her *Dark Star Park*), is comparable with the male earth artists. The globes and pools of water, though, are traditional 'feminine' volumes, here given a new, monumental turn. Helen Escobedo created some huge concrete and steel sculptures which 'attempt to fuse hard-edge geometric forms with nature's organic manifestations', as she put it. Works such as *Snake* (1980-81) rise impressively from the Earth, celebrating the flux and movement of organic forms. Beverly Pepper's large, curving mirrored slabs of wood buried in sandy beaches (*Sand Dunes*, 1985), large, curving mirrored slabs of wood buried in sandy beaches, might be seen as a type of 'Earth Mother art', art which worships and works with the Earth, rather than, as in so much of male land art, cutting or penetrating it, phallically (like Michael Heizer, Robert Smithson and Walter de Maria).

Many of the celebrated products of contemporary sculpture, however, have been made by male artists: Donald Judd's 'specific objects', blocks of aluminium and plexiglass that 'climb' gallery walls;[7] Tony Smith's monumental cubes with their *therenoce* (celebrating the primacy of presence, not effect);[8] Dan Flavin's mesmeric fluorescent tubes, a sculpture of light and space;[9] Sol LeWitt's Conceptual cubes and wall drawings like enormous graphs; Richard Serra's huge 'walls' or slabs of steel leaning together;[10] and Carl Andre's plates of steel, copper and zinc laid on the floor.[11]

One of the most exciting developments of contemporary sculpture and art is the installation, the taking over of a whole space or environment – the floor, walls and ceiling of a gallery, as in Rebecca Horn's *Ballet of the Woodpecker* (1986-87), a room full of mirrors, or Sylvia Stone's *Crystal Palace*. Many land artists' works are clearly related to the art installation: it is an art of environments, where the relatively small addition of a stack of stones forming a cairn sets alive the surrounding landscape. One sees the landscape in a new way: context is all-important.

LAND ART, SEXUALITY AND THE BODY

Much of sculpture in the modern era has been thoroughly traditional (conservative), and patriarchal, in its orientation and expression. Take Henry Moore, one of the most celebrated of Western sculptors. Moore's nudes, though, are no different from the conventional female nude, found in so much of 'high art' from the Renaissance onwards. Moore's polished wood surfaces, so softly rounded and enigmatic, seem so enchanting. But, despite his formal innovation, Moore is as sexist and reactionary a sculptor as Norman Rockwell is as a painter.

But when sexuality is addressed, contemporary (male) sculptors have rarely been ironic. Usually, the norms and dualities of male/ female, active/ passive, culture/ nature, good/ evil are exalted. The 'great' or celebrated names in contemporary sculpture – Alberto Giacometti, Henry Moore, David Smith, David Hare, Eduardo Chillida, Pablo Picasso, Isamu Noguchi, Claes Oldenberug, Mark Di Suvero, Jean Tinguely among many others – rarely tackled notions of sexuality in major works of sculpture. When Picasso incorporated eroticism, it was invariably heterosexist, as in his *Bust* (1932, estate of the artist) with its gigantic breasts, echoing the "Stone Venuses" of yore. The 'great' works of contemporary sculpture – in America, David Smith's *Cubi XXVII* (1965, Guggenheim Museum, New York), Claes Oldenburg's soft sculptures and giant blow-ups of everyday objects, Richard Serra's chunks of metal, and John Chamberlain's squashed cars (1961, Art Institute, Chicago) – seem to eschew issues of sexuality. Not much of mainstream or 'malestream' contemporary sculpture concerns itself with eroticism without pain or violence, and hardly ever feminism.

Some (land) artists have thrown or splashed material. In Andy Goldsworthy's 'throws' and 'splashes', the arcs or trajectories of the material become the artwork in itself. The curve of the thrown earth or sticks against the sky actually *is* the sculpture. Similarly, Bruce Nauman – who is, like Yves Klein, another celebrated Conceptual artist – photographed himself as a water fountain (1966). Richard Long threw mud against walls, either in a curtain of mud, or in a circle. Kazuo Shiraga wallowed in mud and threw mud-balls (*Making a Work With His Own Body*, 1955). Guo Qiang Cai created miniature explosions with gunpowder to evoke the mushroom clouds of nuclear explosions (1996). Bruce McLean's *Splash Sculpture* and *Mud Sculpture* (both 1968) are precursors of Goldsworthy's splashes and throws. Goldsworthy's throws offer plenty of ammunition to critics who dislike his work, because someone making splashes in a river with a stick or throwing sand or leaves in the air is the kind of art denigrated by the tabloid press in the UK.

WOMEN SCULPTORS AND LAND ARTISTS

Important contemporary women sculptors include Nancy Graves, Eva Hesse, Niki de Sant-Phalle, Rebecca Horn and Louise Nevelson, and women land artists such as Mary Miss, Nancy Holt, Sherry Wiggins, Donna Henes, Ana Mendieta, Vijali, Betsy Damon, Phyllis Yampolsky, Jody Pinto, Viet Ngo, Helen Mayer Harrison, Mel Chin, Karen McCoy, Meg Webster, Maya Lin, Martha Schwartz, Dominique Mazeaud, Lynne Hull, Doris Bloom, Patricia Johanson, Constance DeJong, Harriet Feigenbaum, Phyllidia Barlow, Debbie Duffin, Mierle Laderman Ukeles, Gloria Carlos, Agnes Denes and Alice Aycock.[1]

Eva Hesse, who died at the age of 34 in 1970, is especially interesting; her works repay many visits. Hesse was part of the group that included Carl Andre, Robert Ryman, Sol LeWitt and Mel Bochner. She worked in series, like other Process and Minimal artists. She called the repetitions 'sequels' and 'schemas'. Her artworks have an immediate, challenging impact. They hang from ceilings, in rows, made of rubber, latex, cloth, wire and fibreglass, evoking organic forms in ambivalent, sensual ways.[2] Pieces such as *Ingeminate* (1965, Saatchi, London) offer up a mysterious affirmation of life in the form of two coils of cord connected by a long piece of surgical hose. *Sans II* (1968, Saatchi, London), meanwhile, was a dozen rectangular 'compartments' made from fibreglass which hinted at some obscure systematization of flesh and organic form. Hesse wrote: '[i]f I can name the content... it's the total absurdity of life'.[3]

As Anna Chave noted, Hesse's forms resemble abstract 'breasts, clitorises, vaginas, fetuses, uteruses, fallopian tubes', articulating a new feminine sexual subjectivity, utilizing the female, not the male gaze.[4] Sometimes loosely hanging, finding their own form, at other times Hesse's sculptures were bound with wire, as if 'making psychic models', as Robert Smithson said.[5]

One aspect of 'feminist' or 'women's' art was (is) embodied by the figure of the

Goddess, the ancient and primæval Great Mother of all, celebrated then – and now – as Isis, Ishtar, Demeter, Kali, and so on. The Goddess embodying aspects of the 'feminine' – love, motherhood, purity, nobility, sacrifice, beauty, hunting, and so on. Since the 1960s, the Goddess has been variously interpreted as fact, experience, idea, æsthetic, cult, religion, pagan emblem and many other things by women artists and writers. There are a host of artists who pursue what one might call 'Goddess art', art that employs the figure of the Goddess as an embodiment of female being or experience: Ana Mendieta, Judy Chicago, Mary Beth Edelson, Miriam Schapiro, Niki de Sant-Phalle, Louis Bourgeois and Helen Chadwick. Mary Beth Edelson engaged in the resurgence of interest in the Goddess in her *Great Goddess* series (1975).

One might see Robert Smithson's spirals and circles as Goddess art, for the circles so clearly evoke Goddess themes such as time, cycles, (Moon) phases, dance, transformation, ritual, initiation, astronomy, and so on. The circle is also a profound shape for alchemists. As the *Rosarium Philosophorum* has it: 'make a round circle and you will have the stone of the philosophers'.[6] Richard Long created, in Ireland, an ancient maze form out of small stones set on grass (*Connemara Sculpture*, 1971), and Robert Morris has also made a labyrinth (*Labyrinth*, 1974). The shape of Long's and Morris's labyrinths directly recall the Cretan labyrinth of initiation and ritual, and the spirals at the entrance to Newgrange in Co. Meath, a huge passage grave some 4,500 years old.

Herman de Vries created a circular walled *Sanctuarium* (1997) in Westfalen, Germany. Alan Sonfist planted a maze from oak trees at TICKON in 1993. In Dennis Oppenheim's *Maze* (1970), cattle are lab rats running after corn in a field. Dan Graham combined hedges and mirrors in his *Two-Way Mirror Hedge Labyrinth* (1989). Chris Drury has made circular mazes (some of which are reworked dew ponds). Drury also carved a maze from snow on a Sussex hill (1999). Bill Vazan has fashioned a number of earthworks on the ground, including a *Stone Maze* (1975-76,) and Richard Fleischner, Michelangelo Pistoletto, Hiroshi Teshigahara, and Vong Phaephanit have also created maze structures (Fleischner built a maze from turf in 1974 and one from a chain link fence in 1978). A number of (land) artists have made miniature labyrinths – maze models: Charles Simonds, Terry Fox and Patrick Ireland. Andy Goldsworthy has drawn lines on sand, or stitched grass stalks pinned together, in swirling, spiralling shapes which echo the primæval forms of the snake, the spiral and the labyrinth.

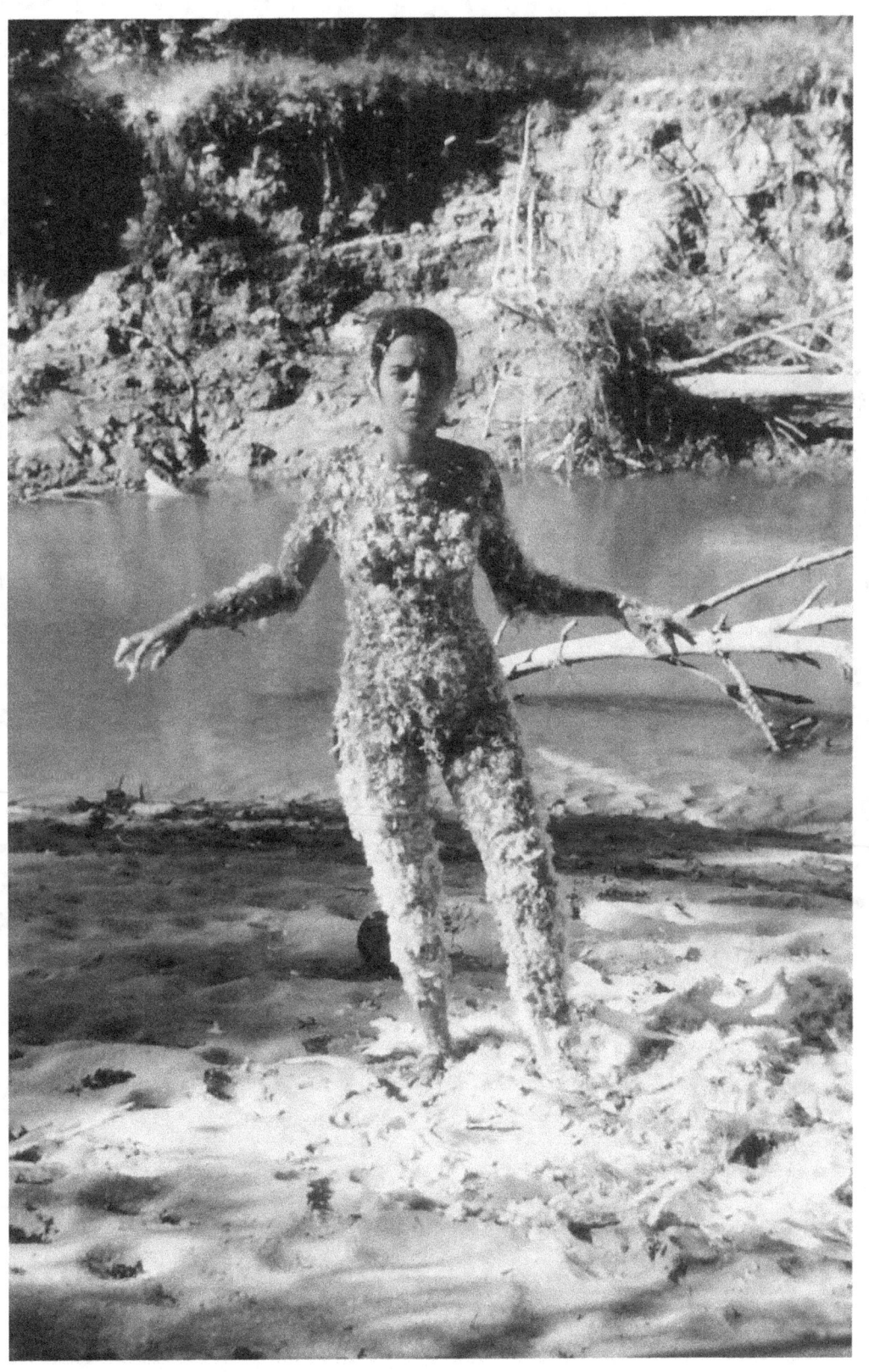

Ana Mendieta, Blood and Feathers, 1974

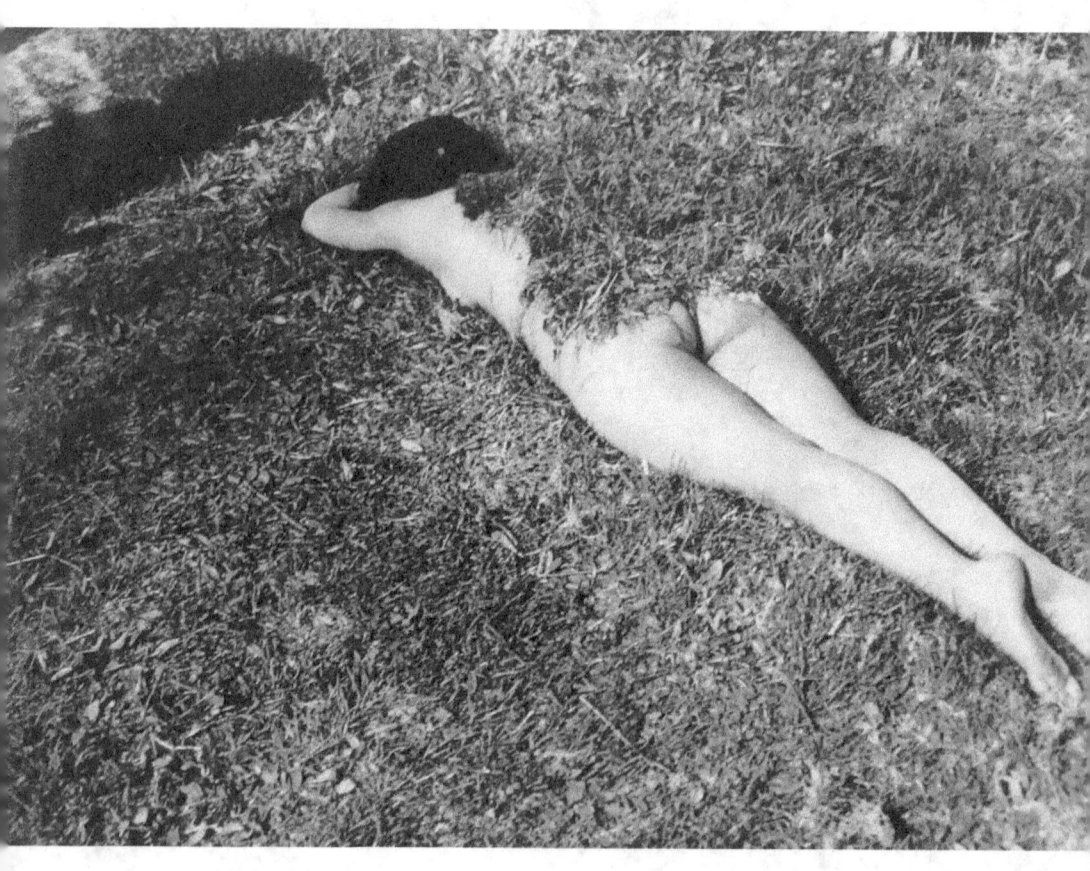

Ana Mendieta, Untitled (Grass On Woman), 1972

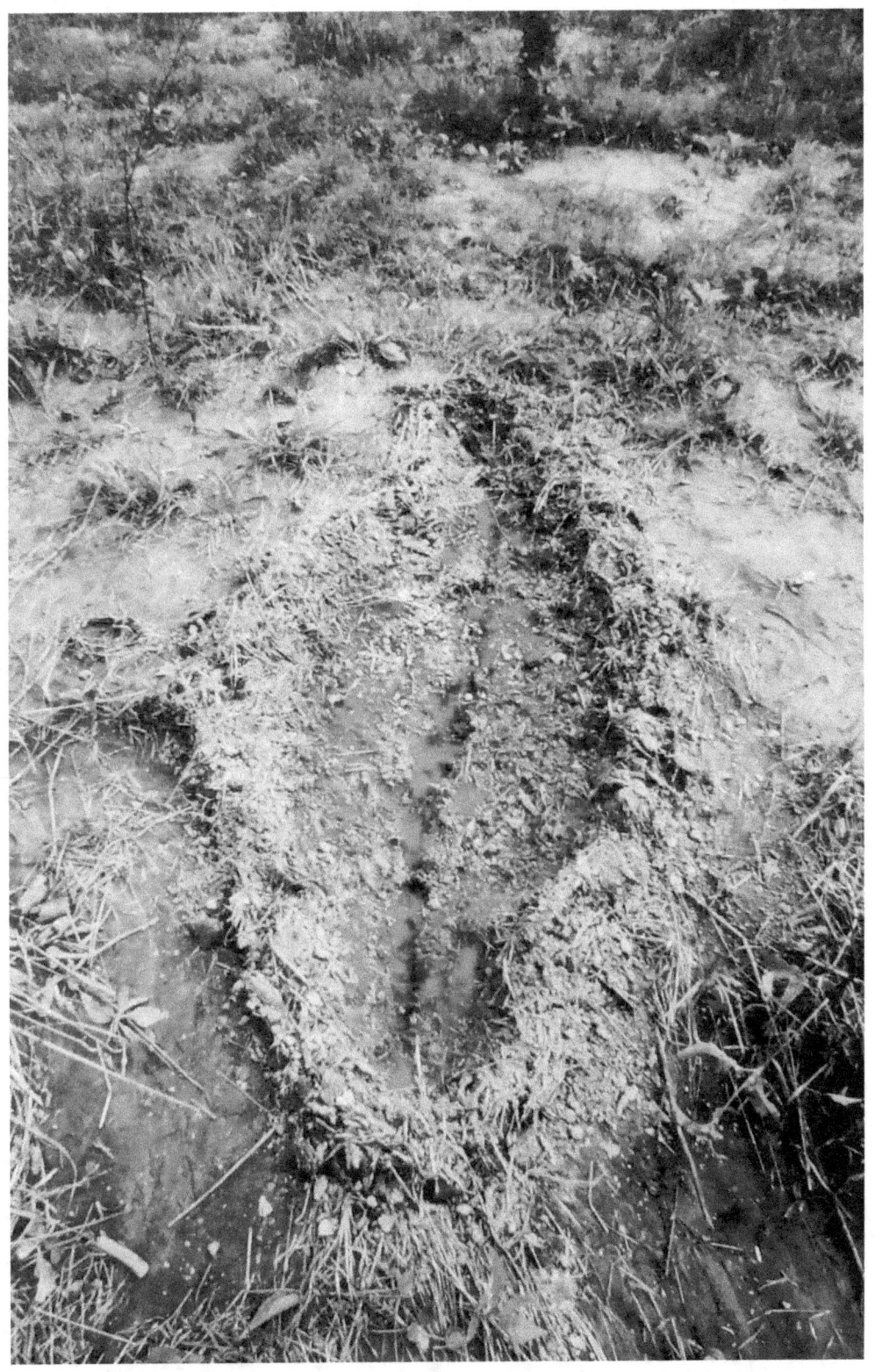

Ana Mendieta, Silueta Series, 1978

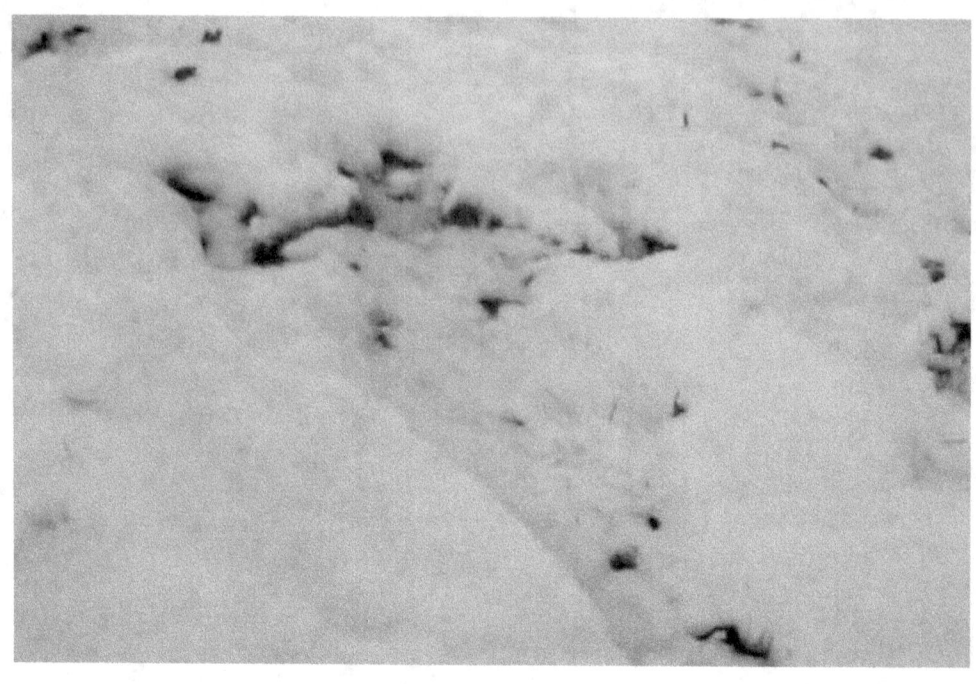

Anna Mendieta, Silueta series, 1979

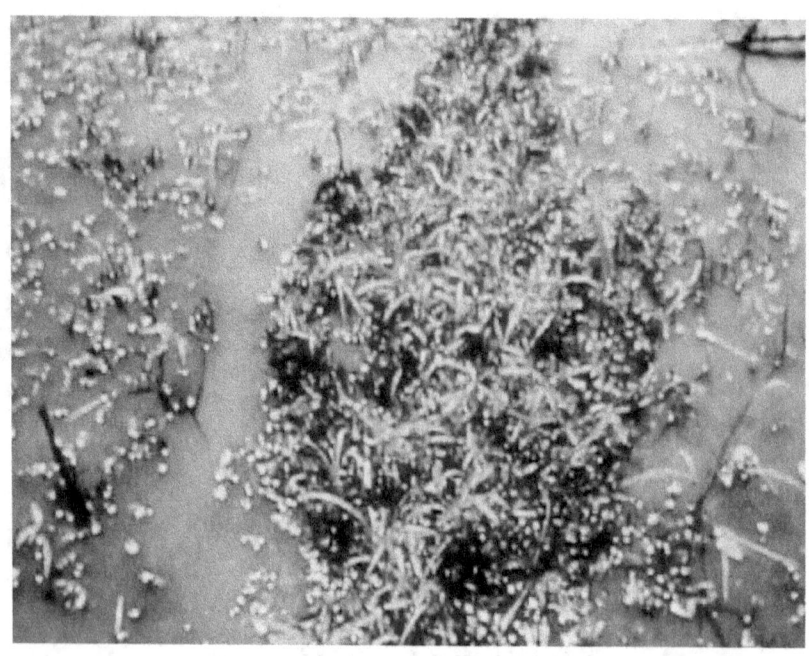

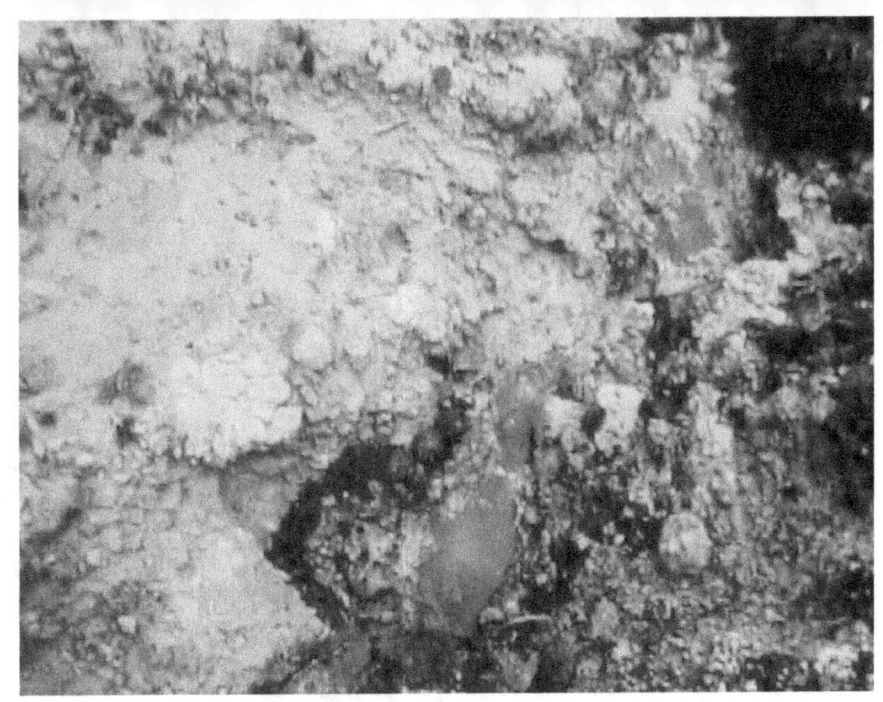

Anna Mendieta

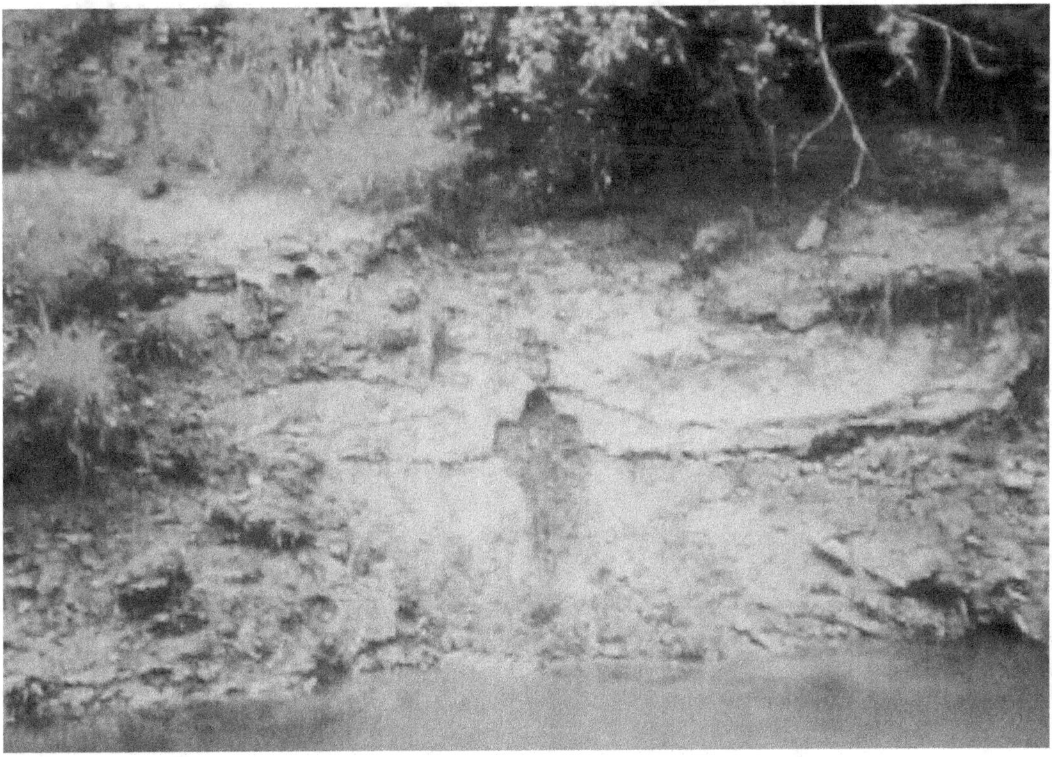

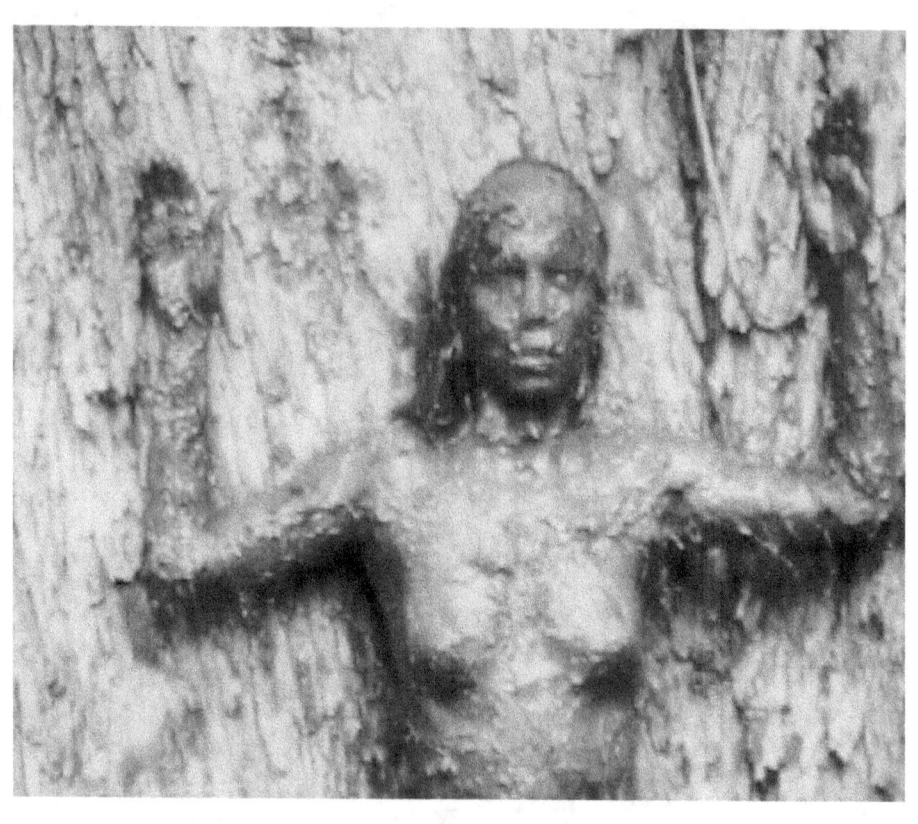

Anna Mendieta, Tree of Life series, 1977

5

Land Art and Religion

It's no surprise that the American form of land art should be sympathetic to Oriental mysticism, because Zen Buddhist and Taoism were particularly prevalent in Sixties culture (in Jack Kerouac, Allen Ginsberg, the 'Beats' and the 'dharma bums', for example). It was a natural development, it seems, from Parisian Existentialism of the 1940s and 1950s to Californian Zen Buddhism of the 1960s. Many of the chief precepts of Taoism and Zen Buddhism chime with those of land art, not only the American earthworks, but also the land art of Europeans such as Long, Laib, Nash, Drury and others. Matsuo Basho, an important Oriental poet, wrote:

> Go to the pine if you want to learn about the pine, or to the bamboo if you want to learn about the bamboo. And in doing so, you must leave your subjective preoccupation with yourself.[1]

Makoto Ueda glossed Basho thus: '[f]or learn means to enter into the object, perceive its delicate life and feel its feelings.'[2]

These notions of searching for the 'essence' are absolutely in tune with the æsthetics of sculptors such as Brancusi, Andre, Long and Judd. Goldsworthy spoke in exactly the same terms of trying to find the 'essence' of nature, of going out into the natural world in order to learn about it. Minimal art pursued the oft-used tenet that 'less is more', a radical reductionism and simplification. Or as Carl Andre put it, ''minimal' means to me only the greatest economy in attaining the greatest ends'.[3] Michael Heizer confessed he preferred to see art more as a religion than a recreational activity: 'if you consider art as activity then it becomes like recreation. I guess I'd like to see art become more of a religion'.[4]

The relation between land art and Oriental mysticism, in particular, Taoism and Zen Buddhism, has been noted by many commentators. Zen and Taoism, for instance, speak of (1) the 'here and now', (2) spontaneity, (3) satori or enlightenment, (4) intuition, (5) nature, (6) emptiness/ void, (7) change, (8) meditation, (9) cosmic unity – all these qualities can be applied to land art, and are sometimes elucidated by land artists.

(1) For example, the Zen notion of the 'eternal now' or 'now-streaming' (nunc fluens) as Alan Watts called it. Zen philosophy makes the present moment primary, the only true reality, and land artists too work in the present. Sculptors continually evoke the transient nature of sculpture: Hans Haacke's fog pieces; Chris Drury's fires; Ana Mendieta's snow and mud body prints; Wolfgang Laib's pollen. Goldsworthy's poppy lines are only there for an instant, then they are blown away by the wind.

(2) Spontaneity: this is as crucial in land art as it is in Zen and Taoism. The land artist works with whatever materials are to hand; s/he does not (often) use tools or machines; changes in weather must be accommodated into the artwork.

(3) The experience of viewing land art is not quite Zen *satori*, in the strict definition of *satori* or enlightenment, but certainly land artists aim for an 'epiphany', as James Joyce called the æsthetic shock, however brief it may be. In land art as object, there are 'no strings attached', i.e., 'what you see is what you get', as Frank Stella put it. One sees the whole thing there, and that is everything one gets. This instantaneous aspect of land art, as also in postwar painting, is a Zen-like notion. *Satori*, too, has affinities with the descriptions of land art/ sculpture that some land artists have given (Robert Morris's objecthood, for example).

(4) Most land artists value intuition highly, as do most poets and artists. The land artist trusts her/ his instincts, and works grow organically. Systems are adhered to, but land artists often veer off into intuitive areas.

(5) Nature dominates Zen and Taoism, as it does in land art. One is always encouraged in Taoism and Zen to 'follow one's nature', and to co-operate with the universe. Nature is the teacher in Zen and Taoism, as it is in land art.

(6) Easy to see the lure of the void of religions in land art, in those wildernesses beloved of American land artists such as Heizer, de Maria and Oppenheim. In the paradoxical bliss of Oriental mysticism, emptiness is also fullness, and to 'have' nothing is to 'have' everything. Zen and Taoism thrive on paradox, on the 'not-this-not-that' dialectic of philosophy, as a way of getting at the unsayableness of the essence. Similarly, Goldsworthy, in a paradoxical manner, speaks of the monumental aspect of sculptures made from leaves: the very small can also be very big, he says.

The imagery of Zen and Taoism is also that of land art: stones, mountains, rivers, water, flowers. China has a long tradition of landscape painting, and it is easy to see the many connections between the contemplative aspects of Chinese landscape painting and contemporary land art.

(7) Change is central to land art: all land art occurs within a changing landscape, whether it be the artificial (humanmade) changes in the gallery, or the natural changes of erosion, elements, water, light, season, and so on. Land art thrives on change, and many land artists have deliberately exploited time and change in their works, such as Nancy Holt with her *Sun Tunnels*, which change as the sunlight pours through the holes in the concrete tubes.

(8) Meditation is clearly not a goal of land artists – they make no pompous

claims concerning mysticism and meditation. Yet, clearly, meditation is a part of their work, as it is a part of all artists' work. Making land art often involves a mild form of meditation. Richard Long's walks, for instance, are meditations of a kind. 'A journey in the wilderness becomes a fantastic focus of concentration. I can get totally absorbed in the place and totally absorbed in my work', Long said.[5] Goldsworthy too speaks of an intense relationship with his subject as he works. The Cornish poet Peter Redgrove said that 'the ideal state for ordinary going about is the first stage of orgasmic arousal'. [6] This is 'walking' in the Taoist sense; that is, walking as another name for feeling ecstatic.

The very activity of walking releases chemicals in the brain that promote pleasure. Joggers get hooked on them sometimes. 'I think the sexual energy or the energy of creativity or the adrenalin energy you get from being on a mountain, sometimes they are all very close', Richard Long remarked.[7] The physical action of walking is soothing.

(9) Land art is close to Taoism in its worldview: like Taoists, land artists believe in a holistic view of things, where each part affects the rest. This interconnected worldview (sometimes called 'Gaia-consciousness') is also the philosophy of ecology and the offshoots of the ecological/ green movement: eco-feminism, Goddess religion, animal rights, eco-paganism, direct action, road activism, anti-hunting lobbies, and so on. Art now has a world consciousness, said Isamu Noguchi (1968).

In the Taoist view, inner and outer commingle, the individual and the mass interconnect. Land artists are (usually) very much concerned with ecological issues, and are careful to make sure their artworks do not scar the landscape. There is no litter in their photographs of their artworks. They are ecologically and societally conscientious artists, and thus Goldsworthy has been hailed as the UK's primary ecological artist. Long says, and Goldsworthy would agree with him, that his art is about finding a harmony between the human and the natural world, between the abstractions of humanity and the reality of nature. As Long puts it, his work is 'a balance between the patterns of nature and the formalism of human abstract ideas like lines and circles.'[8]

In *Being and Circumstance,* US artist Robert Irwin proposed four types of land art: 'site dominant', such as monuments and murals; 'site adjusted', in which some considerations are made towards the site, but it's still studio-made; 'site specific', in which steps are made towards integrating the work into the site; and 'site conditioned', work which responds to its surroundings. The 'site determined' category is the one Irwin preferred: it is also the type of sculpture favoured by many land artists. Irwin defines 'site conditioned' work as an 'intimate, hands-on reading of the site', which results from 'sitting, watching, and walking through the site'; it means being aware of water, weather, sound, surface, movement, history, and so on; such considerations determine whether the response 'should be monumental or ephemeral, aggressive or gentle, useful or useless, sculptural, architectural, or simply the planting of a tree, or maybe even doing nothing at all' (1985).

The land artist orients her/ himself to the four horizons, and to post-Renaissance time. The human level becomes the spiritual centre. The land art of whoever one cares to think of – in Erskine, Lipkis, Holt – puts people, not God or deities, at the centre of the cosmos. Land art, then, can be seen on one level as the reaffirmation of 'home', a re-instatement of the notion of 'homeland'. The 'homeland', though, is not primarily a physical place, but a cultural and spiritual space. Homeland is a state of mind as much as a landscape. Land art may be the manifestation of a spiritual re-orientation. In land art, the 'mythic centre' of one's life is reaffirmed.

Land artists always affirm the 'livingness' of their art, that they *live* their art. Their art, they claim, is not intellectually discussed or made at a critical distance. Rather, the artist is right in the middle of her/ his art, living it. There is no separation of art and life. Land art is a way of mythicizing one's sense of being-in-the-world, a way of making presence visible, tactile, *there*.

Some land artists include autobiographical material in their work. For some land artists, art and life cannot be easily separated (a common philosophy in modern art). One feeds the other, in a symbiotic relationship. One cannot say for certain where some land art ends and the artist's life begins. Land artists like Andy Goldsworthy and Richard Long see art as a continuation of life, where the feelings artists of the past had about nature (for example, the Hudson River school) feed on the same source as artists working today (that is, nature itself). Some people made their life their art (or was it the other way around?): Yves Klein, Salvador Dali, Joseph Beuys and Carolee Schneemann, among artists, and writers such as Quentin Crisp and Anaïs Nin. Most land artists are not quite larger than life personalities like Anaïs Nin or Quentin Crisp (yet). They often, however, keep a diary, and carefully record the daily progress of their art, and the manufacture of each work. Around each work, then, is an autobiographical residue.

Making land art is a religious activity because simply being in the world is religious. Land art, like all art, replays the primordial myth of Creation: each earthwork or land sculpture re-affirms the Creation. The land artwork, then, remakes the sacred in a profane world: 'the manifestation of the Sacred in any space whatsoever implies for one who believes in the authenticity of this hierophany the presence of transcendent reality', remarked Mircea Eliade.[9] Not only, then, do land artists make sacred spaces, as all artists do, they also create a sense of the 'real', a sense of beingness, a reaffirmation of the transcendent.

For the land artist, most, if not all, of the world is not just potential art material, but beautiful. Land artists, declining to admit to being romantic or emotional, nevertheless create art that is Earth-loving, nature-loving, ecologically-friendly, that is, in short, full of emotion.

Many land artists have their favourite haunts. Andy Goldsworthy, for instance, revisits certain stones 'many times over',[10] and gets very attached to places, which become like homes.[11] He also admits: 'I like touching stones touched many years ago.'[12] Like the Romantic poets, like the archaic shaman, Australian aborigines and 'primitive' people, Goldsworthy goes out into the landscape and communes with it,[13] knows every inch of it, knows this stone and that pool, this place for gathering strong grass stalks and that dramatic hilltop viewpoint. American land artists such as Michael Heizer and Robert Smithson were drawn to the deserts of the South-West.

Uncomfortable as they are with notions of 'spirituality' or 'mysticism', land artists such as Richard Long, Waleter de Maria, Chris Drury and Robert Smithson are religious artists, sensitive to the emanations of particular places. Richard Long, for instance, concedes that 'art is magical', as of course it is.[14] Art has been deeply associated with magic and religion for at least 40,000 years, and probably millennia more. Land art, like all art, is full of deep emotions. These emotions collect in clusters around certain places. It is understandable, then, that critics and the public see these emotions as potentially religious.

PART TWO

LAND ARTISTS IN AMERICA

6

Robert Smithson

Instead of putting a work of art on some land, some land is put into a work of art.

Robert Smithson[1]

Robert Smithson is the key land artist, the premier artist in the world of land art. And he's been a big favourite with art critics since the early Seventies. Smithson was the chief mouthpiece of American earth/ site æsthetics, and is probably the most important theoretician among all land artists.

Robert Smithson's theoretical statements were published in three essays. In "The Crystal Land" Smithson recounted a trip he made to a quarry with Donald Judd, the key Minimal artist. Robert Smithson evoked the decayed nature of the quarry, those aspects of entropy which would feature in his own work ('cracked broken shattered earth, of fragmentation, corrosion, decomposition, disintegration, rock crisis, debris slides, mud flow avalanche').2

In the second article, "Entropy and the New Monuments" (1966), Robert Smithson discussed the important Minimal show *Primary Structures* at the Jewish Museum. Smithson's themes were entropy in nature and art; he used the science of crystals and minerals as paradigms of the new art. Robert Smithson had collected crystals and rocks as a child. Crystallography, for Smithson, offered 'a way of dealing with nature without falling into the old trap of the biological metaphor'.3 No wonder, then, that when Smithson saw Donald Judd's pink plastic boxes he compared them to 'giant crystals from another planet' (RS, 19). The dissolution of crystals also provided Smithson with another analogy for his theory of natural entropy.

The third piece, "A Sedimentation of the Mind: Earth Projects" (1968), concerned notions of time and place. While sculptors such as Anthony Caro and his ilk still clung to the old-fashioned ideas of beauty, Smithson spoke warmly of artists such as Walter de Maria, Carl Andre, Michael Heizer, Dennis Oppenheim, Tony Smith and Douglas Huebler (RS, 85).

Robert Smithson was also interested in science fiction: the poetic elements of his art thus form a continuum: between the industrial wastelands he visited for his 'non-site' sculptures and the desolate planets of science fiction; between chaos theory in the New Physics and its exploration in postmodern science fiction; between the forms of crystals and Minimal sculptures, and so on. Robert Smithson's exaltation of lonely post-industrial sites was echoed in the speculative fictions of writers who evoked post- or near-holocaust worlds. J.G. Ballard, for example, wrote of post-industrial desert lands and run-down townscapes (in *The Drought, Vermilion Sands, High-Rise* and *Low-Flying Aircraft*). J.G. Ballard, as one would expect, took an eccentric view of Smithson's earthworks: Ballard mused on what kind of cargo might have been berthed at Smithson's *Spiral Jetty* and *Broken Circle*. Ballard wondered if the cargo was a 'very special kind' of clock... so many of Smithson's monuments seem to be a potent amalgam of clock, labyrinth and cargo terminal'.[4]

In the essay "Tour of the Monuments of Passaic", itself a sci-fi sort of title, Smithson wrote about 'great pipes, sand boxes, bridges with wooden sidewalks, all standing for the irreversibility of eternity. Under the dead light of the Passaic afternoon, the desert becomes a man of infinite disintegration and forgetfulness' (RS, 56). This sort of apocalyptic imagery is echoed in William Burroughs, J.G. Ballard, Tom Disch and other speculative fiction writers. It's the desolate wasteland imagery of Andrei Tarkovsky's film *Stalker* (1979) or *Mad Max* or *The Terminator* and other post-apocalyptic visions.[5]

For Robert Smithson, Andre, de Maria, Heizer, Oppenheim and Tony Smith were 'the more compelling artists today, concerned with 'Place' or 'Site''.[6] Smithson was impressed by Tony Smith's vision of the mysterious aspects of a dark unfinished road and called Smith 'the agent of endlessness'. Smith's æsthetic became part of Smithson's view of art as a complete 'site', not simply an æsthetic of sculptural objects. Smithson was not inspired by ancient religious sculpture, by burial mounds for example, so much as by decayed industrial sites. He visited some in the mid-1960s that were 'in some way disrupted or pulverized'. He said he was looking for a 'denaturalization rather than built up scenic beauty.'[7]

Robert Smithson said he was concerned, like many land (and contemporary) artists with the thing in itself, not its image, its effect, its critical significance: 'I am for an art that takes into account the direct effect of the elements as they exist from day to day apart from representation' (RS, 133). Smithson's theory of the 'non-site' was based on 'absence, a very ponderous, weighty absence'.[8] Smithson proposed a theory of a dialectic between absence and presence, in which the 'non-site' and 'site' are both interacting. In the 'non-site' work, presence and absence are there simultaneously. 'The land or ground from the Site is placed in the art (Non-Site) rather than the art is placed on the ground. The Non-Site is a container within another container – the room' (RS, 115).

> In a sense [Smithson wrote] my nonsites are rooms within rooms. Recovery from the outer fringes brings one back to the central point... The scale between indoors and outdoors, and how the two are impossible to bridge... What you are really confronted with in a non-site is the absence of the site. It is a contraction rather than an expansion of scale. One is confronted with a very ponderous, weighty absence... There is this dialectic between inner and outer, closed and open, center and peripheral.[9]

Smithson proposed a schema for 'non-site' art in his essay "Dialectic of Site and Non-Site" which ran thus:

Site	Non-Site
1. Open limits	Closed limits
2. A series of points	An array of Matter
3. Outer coordinates	Inner coordinates
4. Subtraction	Addition
5. Indeterminate certainty	Determinate uncertainty
6. Scattered information	Contained information
7. Reflection	Mirror
8. Edge	Center
9. Some place (physical)	No place (abstract)
10. Many	One (RS, 115)

The 'non-site' works were permanent, gallery works. Smithson's *Mirror Displacements* (1968) consisted of putting some mirrors in various settings and taking photographs of them before moving them somewhere else. *Mirror Displacements* was documented in Smithson's *Artforum* article "Incidents of Mirror Travel in the Yucatan". Sometimes Smithson put soil on top of the mirrors, to dirty them up, to sabotage 'the perfect reflections of the sky'. Smithson liked dirt, gravel, sand, sludge and sediment – indeterminate, malleable substances. Land artists often sabotaged the clinical nature of much of art – putting soil or horses in the clean, white gallery space, for example; of his Italian horse piece, which did just that, Jannis Kounellis said the aim was to increase awareness of the 'basic nature of a gallery, of its bourgeois origin', its economic and ideological aspects.[10]

Robert Smithson's other projects of the time included putting raw, natural materials into Minimal spaces, creating a tension of dialectic between 'site and non-site', as he called it. *Ziggurat Mirror* was completed by the use of mirrors. The sculpture needed the mirrors to work properly. Using the mirrors to create repetition, Smithson pointed to the delimited nature of the sculpture: with the right use of mirrors, a sculpture could be extended infinitely. Endless repetition was central to Minimal and Sixties art (Warhol, LeWitt, Andre, Morris, Judd, Stella and others took a simple unit and endlessly repeated it).

Before he made the famous *Spiral Jetty* Smithson had already been considering the scientific notions of rotation and equilibrium. His sculpture *Gyrostasis* (1968) was a 75 by 57 by 40 inch painted steel structure based on the spiral. Smithson explained that *Gyrostasis*, as the title implied, was about how rotating bodies maintain their equilibrium: '[t]he work is a standing triangulated spiral. When I made the sculpture I was thinking of mapping procedures that refer to the planet Earth' (RS, 37).

Robert Smithson's famous *Spiral Jetty* is a 'monumental' earthwork, though the use of the spiral motif has connotations with the ancient symbols of the Goddess.[11] Of his *Spiral Jetty*, Smithson wrote:

> As I looked at the site, it reverberated out to the horizons only to suggest an immobile cyclone while flickering light made the entire landscape appear to quake. A dormant earthquake spread into an immense roundness. From that gyrating space emerged the possibility of the Spiral Jetty. No idea, no concepts, no systems, no structures, no abstractions could hold themselves together in the actuality of that phenomenological evidence.[12]

Smithson was impressed by the characteristics of the Great Salt Lake site, the pinkish mud, the faintly violet water surrounded by limestone hills, and the 'crushing light' of the sun. He had been reading about salt lakes in Boliva, where bacteria turned the water red to match the colour of the flamingos. Smithson found out that the Utah salt lakes were also red and pink, but due to algæ and mineral waste. Smithson and his wife, Nancy Holt, surveyed the area and chose a lake at Rozel Point in Utah, which had a number of cracks in the mud under the shallow water. Smithson began building it in April, 1970, excavating 6,650 tons.

Spiral Jetty was made from rocks, water, mud and precipitated salt crystals. It was 1,500 ft long and 15 ft wide. Smithson was aided by Virginia Dwan and the Ace Gallery of Vancouver. As with many other projects of the time a film was made of the construction of *Spiral Jetty*. Smithson related the work to spiral nebulæ, to salt crystals and microscopic organisms. Smithson thought in terms of eons of time, and mused on how entropy would overtake the site.[13]

Robert Smithson used one of the primary forms of land art, the circle, in many works, combining it with ideas taken from science (such as *Gyrostasis*, which, said Smithson, 'refers to a branch of physics that deals with rotating bodies').[14] Smithson was not adverse to religious feelings about art: when he visited the site of his *Spiral Jetty*, in the Utah salt flats, he experienced a feeling of 'a rotary that enclosed itself in an immense roundness' (ib., 111).

The two elements – rational, mathematical, scientific precision and intuitive, emotional, religious feeling – are two of the chief characteristics of land art. On the one hand, land artists talk about measurements, practical details, materials, maps and spatial data. On the other hand, they hint at religious awe, spiritual feelings, prehistoric art and the influx of the numinous into modern art.

Smithson also identified his *Spiral Jetty* with a mythic whirlpool that sprang up from a tunnel connected to the Pacific Ocean. His *Spiral Jetty* was an 'immobile cyclone', it spiralled inwards from the outside: the track leaves the shore and twists round and round to the centre. *Spiral Jetty* was also linked with notions of decay in nature. In "A Sedimentation of the Mind: Earth Projects" Smithson had written '[e]very object, if it is art, is charged with the rush of time, even though it is static' (RS, 90). Ironically, Smithson's *Spiral Jetty* was itself subject to natural entropy: the water level rose and *Spiral Jetty* was submerged under water. It was ironic too that Smithson died in a plane crash while he was flying over and inspecting a site in Texas.

Smithson's 1971 *Broken Circle* was another large earthwork using circular motifs that was set adjacent to the land and extended out into a lake. Smithson chose a quarry site near Emmen, Holland. Again, the site had an interesting geological aspect, which was in keeping with Smithson's love of rocks and minerals. Glacial action had formed unusual layers of soil.

Unlike *Spiral Jetty*, which was subsequently submerged, *Broken Circle* remains on display, and is maintained by local funds. It is a 140 foot circle comprising one half of soil and one half of water, with a twelve foot wide canal cutting round the earth section of the circle, forming a semicircle. At the centre of *Broken Circle* is a very large glacial boulder. It was supposedly one of the largest in the Netherlands. Significantly, Smithson allowed nothing at the centre of *Spiral Jetty*: the spectator walked round the inward-turning spiral to find nothing. Smithson was exasperated by the prehistoric stone at the centre of his *Broken Circle*, but he let this 'accidental center' stay there, commenting 'it became a dark spot of exasperation, a geological gangrene on the sandy expanse'.[15]

Robert Smithson's last major work, before his untimely death, was *Armarillo Ramp*, one of many land artworks conceived as an observation structure. Nancy Holt worked with one of the major American sculptors of the era, Richard Serra, to complete Smithson's plans. *Amarillo Ramp*, 15 miles North-West of Amarillo in the Texas Panhandle, is a huge inclined ramp or road, made from quarried rocks. The summit of *Amarillo Ramp* is a viewing point.[17]

Taken together, Smithson's three large-scale earthworks, *Spiral Jetty, Broken Circle* and *Amarillo Ramp,* all revolve around circular or spiral motifs, a sense of temporality, of decay and transience, and each uses primitive, mythic forms and gestures in a monumental manner. Two of them are set in wilderness spaces, where the marks of humanity are at their weakest. Yet each earthwork of course speaks acutely of the mark of humanity upon the Earth, and a very particular kind of mark: that of late 20th century American art-making.

Robert Smithson's influence on land art has been immense, probably more than any other single artist. One example would be Andy Goldsworthy's Durham earthwork *Maze* (1989, at Leadgate), which draws as much on the legacy of Smithson's art as also on ancient mythology and symbolism. It uses the labyrinth motif. Goldsworthy's *Maze* can seen a part of the resurgence of interest in mazes which occurred in the 1980s (aligned, as ever, with green/ ecological/ occult/ New Age trends). New mazes were commissioned, and 1991 was designated the 'Year of the Maze' in the U.K. Like *Lambton Earthwork* (but unlike most of Goldsworthy's works), *Maze* was intended to be used by the general public. As with Smithson's *Broken Circle* or the *Armarillo Ramp* the public was invited to walk around Goldsworthy's earthworks. Both *Maze* and *Lambton Earthwork* were about responses to the energies in nature – thus the public was invited to explore similar things as they physically walked around the earthworks. Goldsworthy also designed an earthwork which was a curving ramp, exactly like *Armarillo Ramp*, though on a much smaller scale.

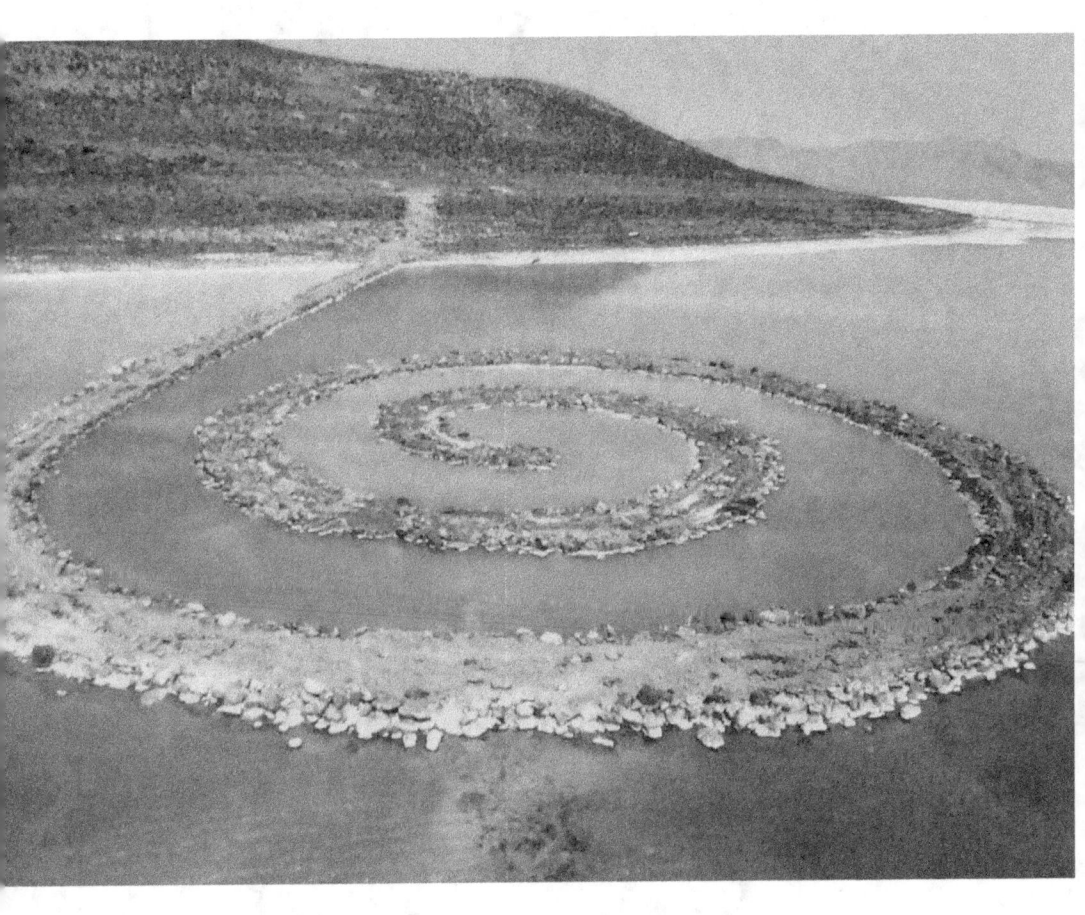

Robert Smithson, Spiral Jetty, 1970

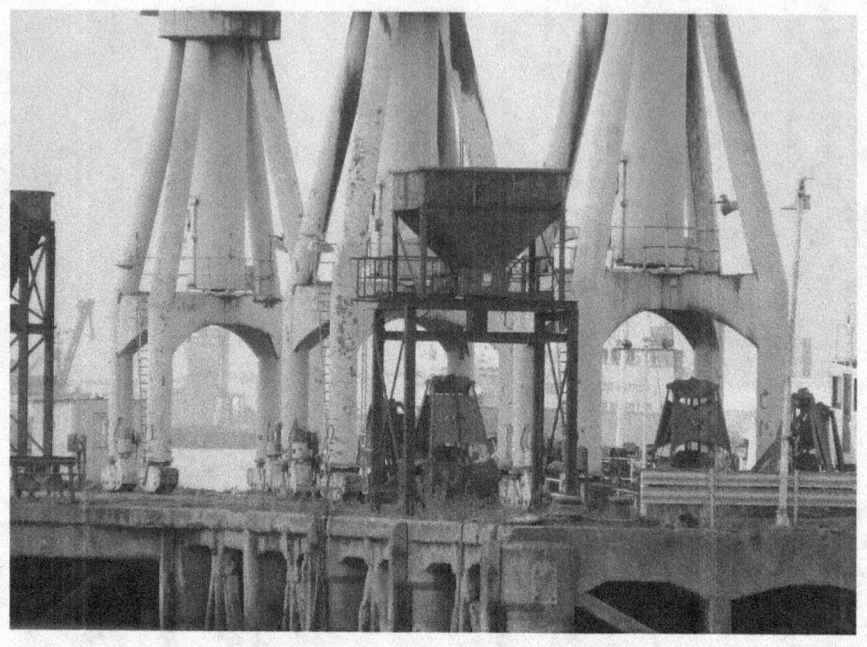

The kind of heavy industry which inspired land artists such as Robert Smithson and Dennis Oppenheim (Photos: Cassidy Hughes, London)

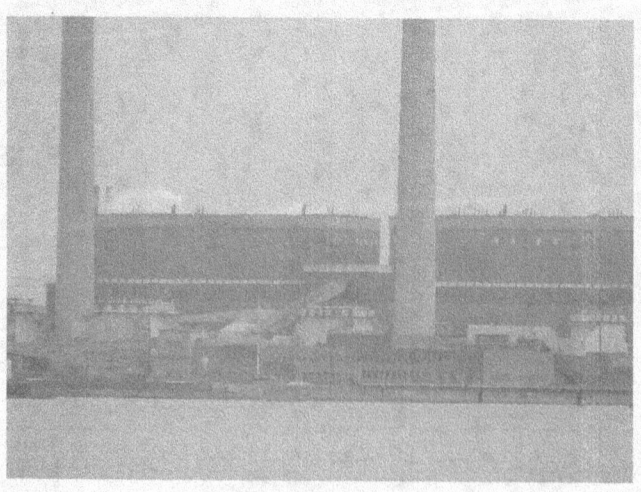

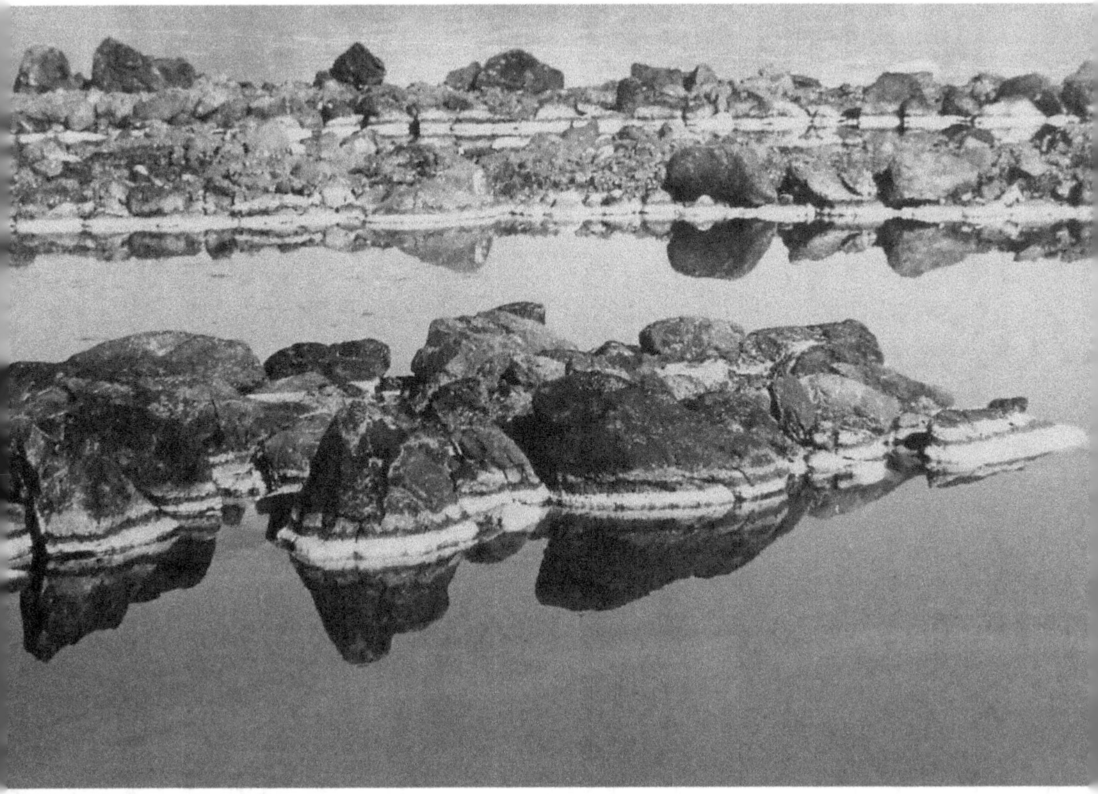

Two closer views of Robert Smithson's Spiral Jetty (photos: Gianfranco Gorgoni)

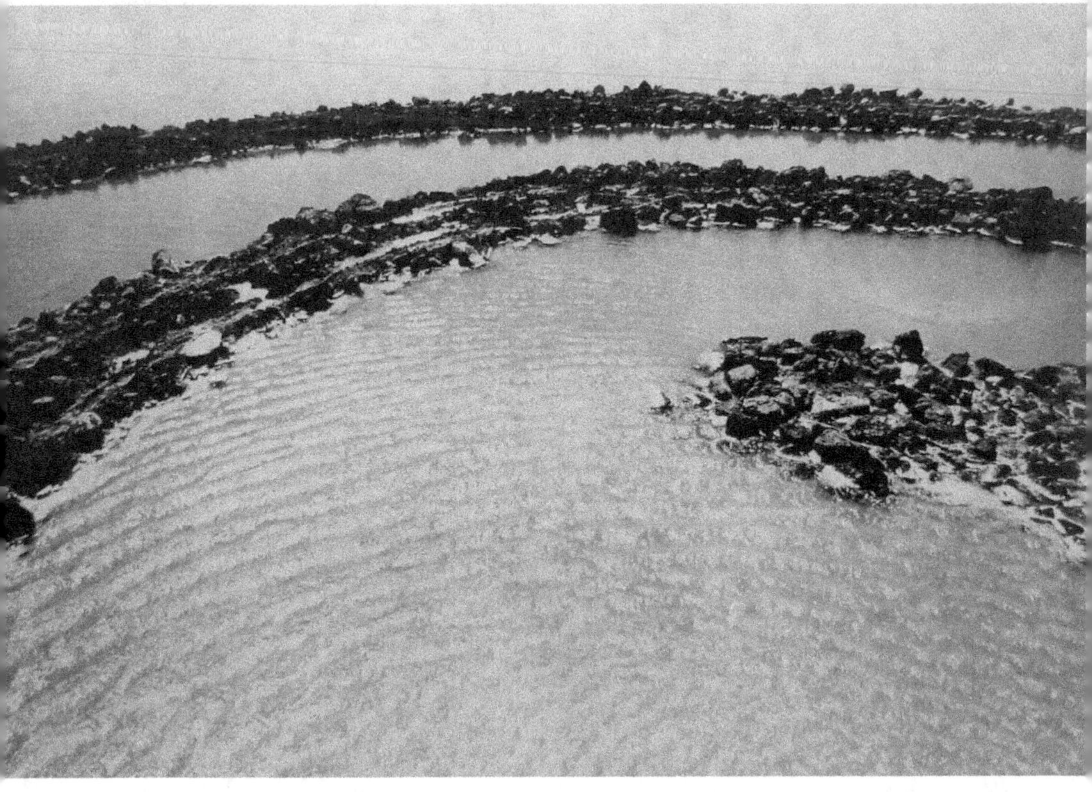

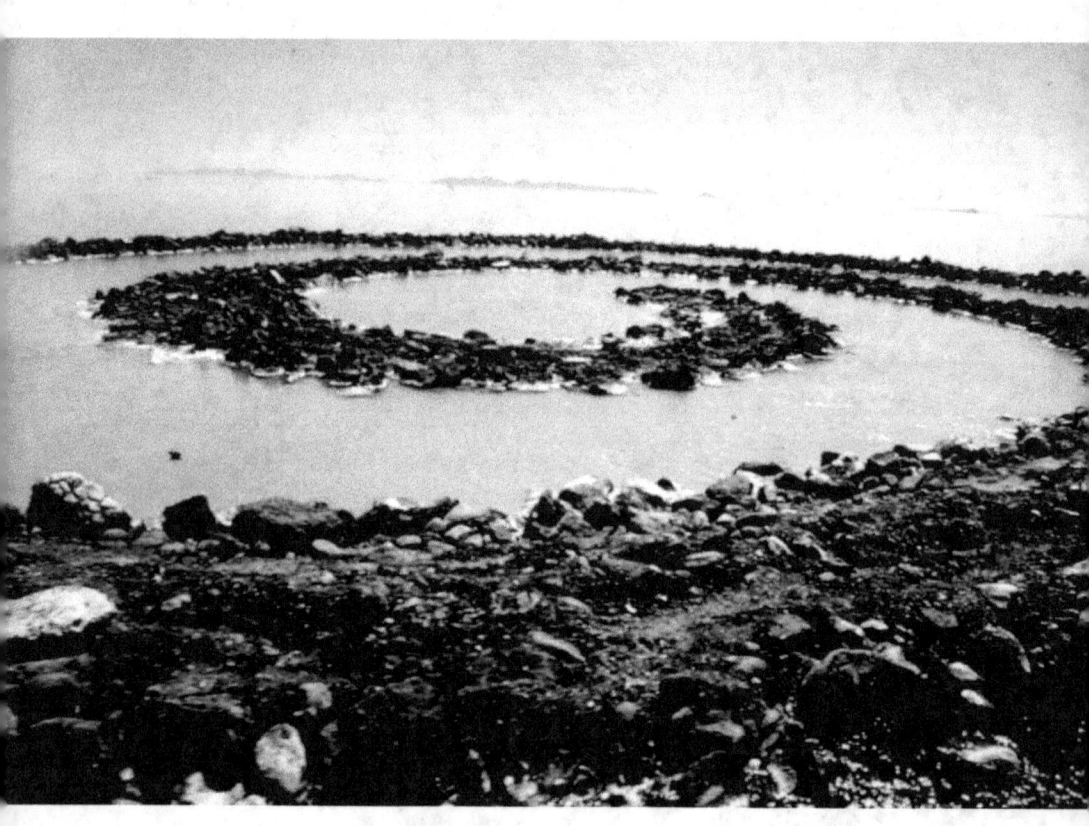

Robert Smithson, Spiral Jetty

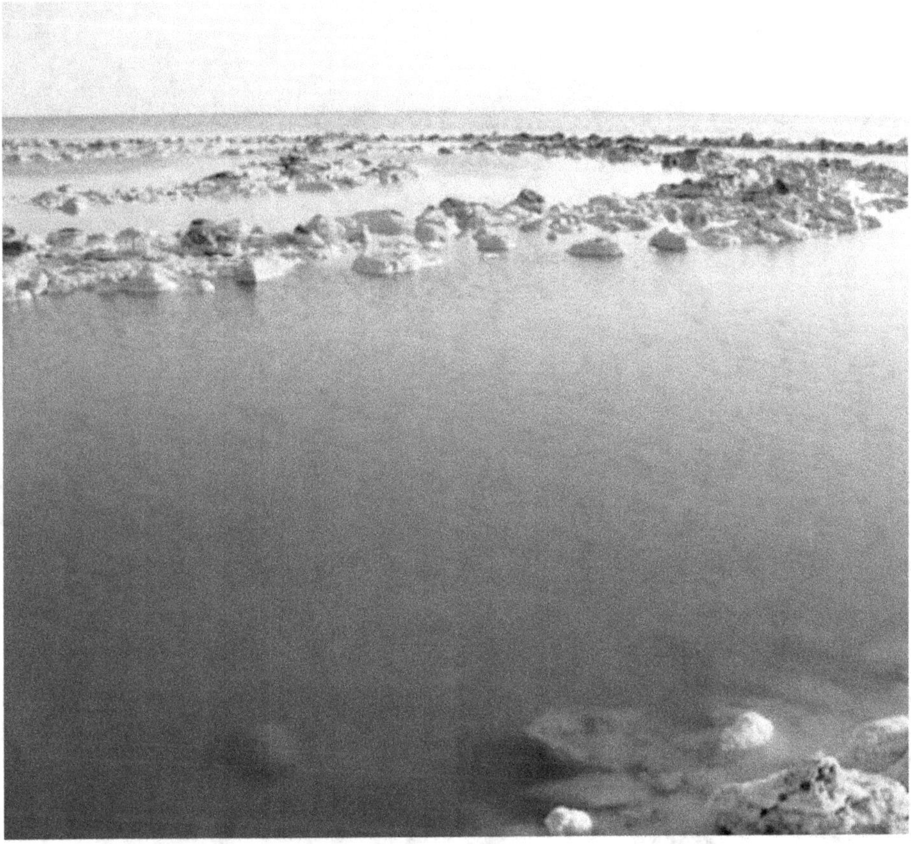

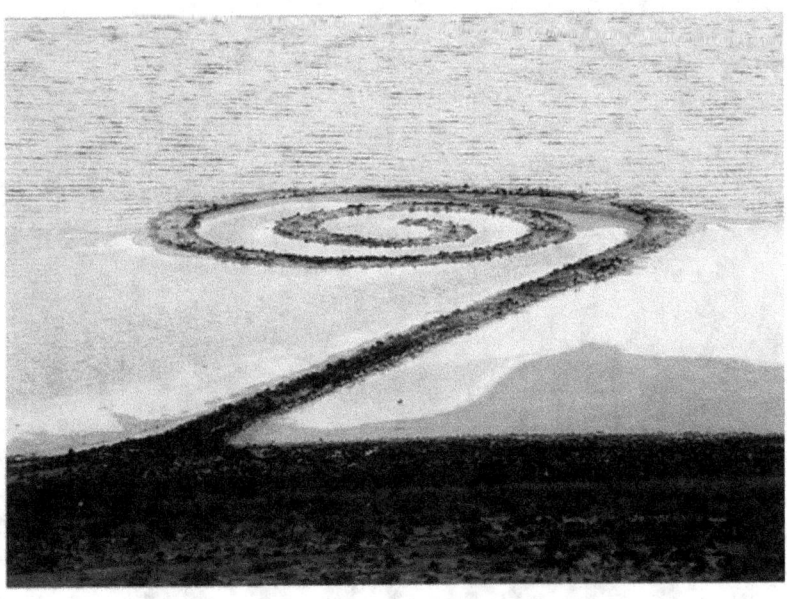

Watery views of Robert Smithson's Spiral Jetty

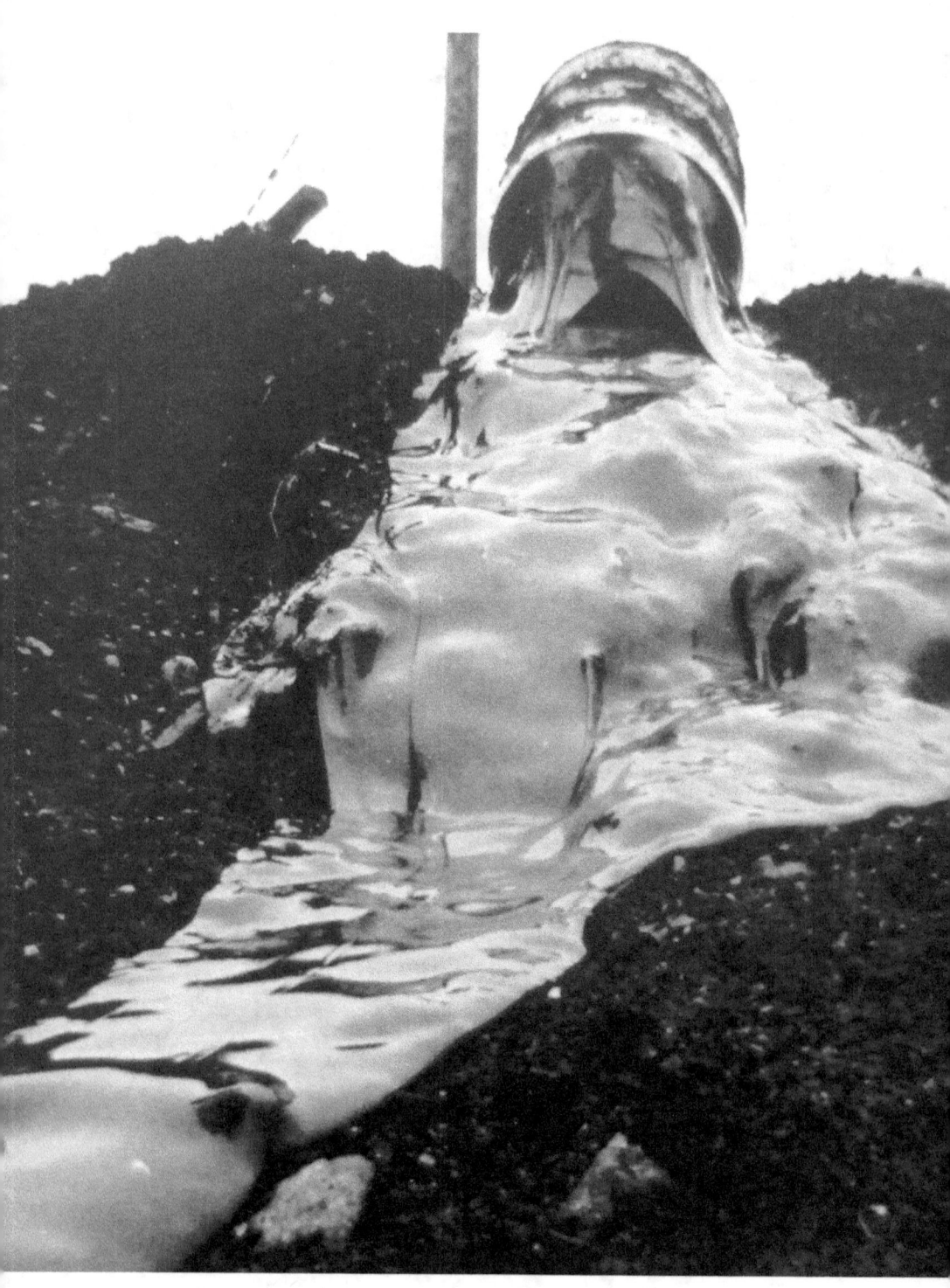

Robert Smithson, Glue Pour, 1970

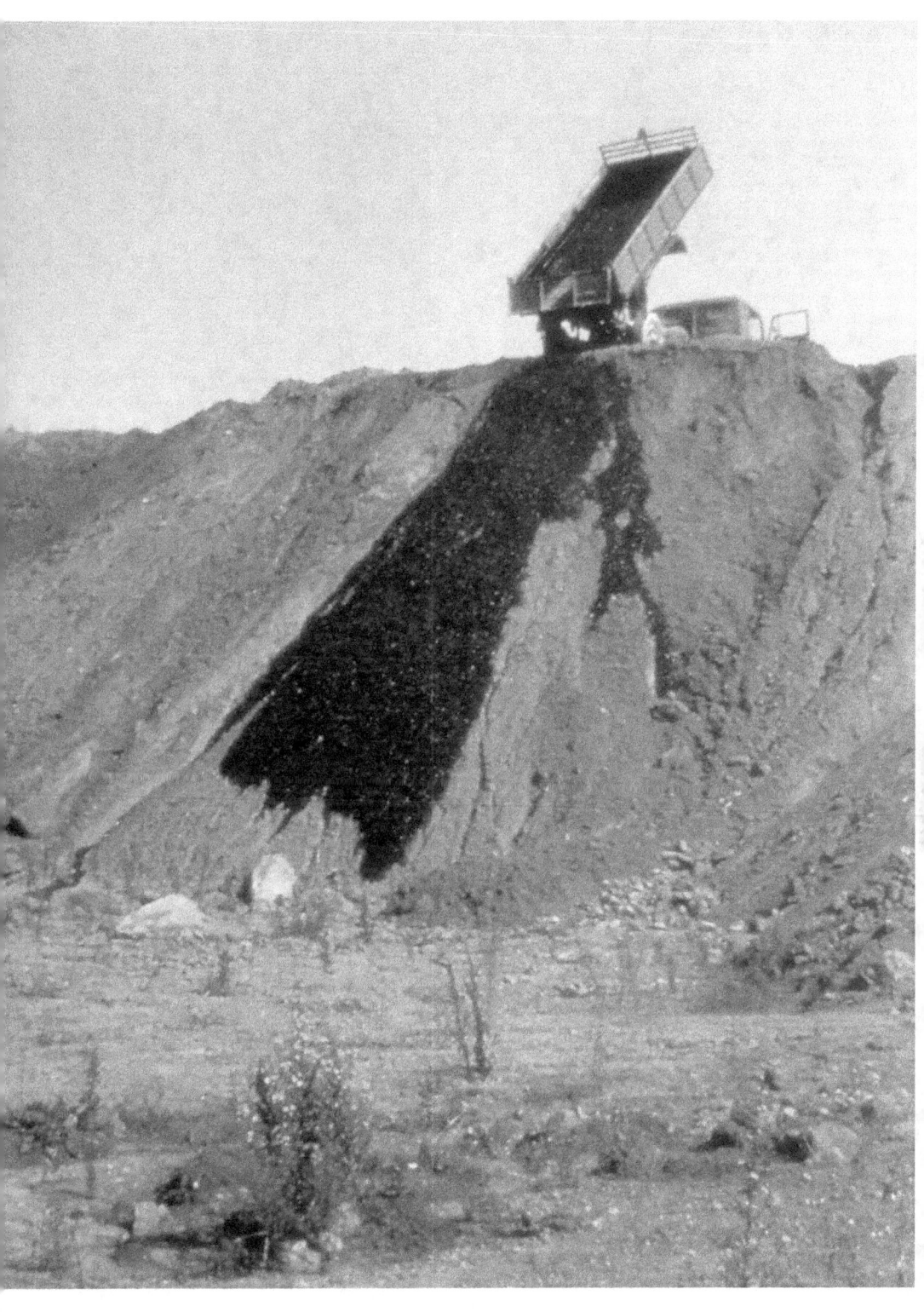

Robert Smithson, Ashphalt Rundown, 1969

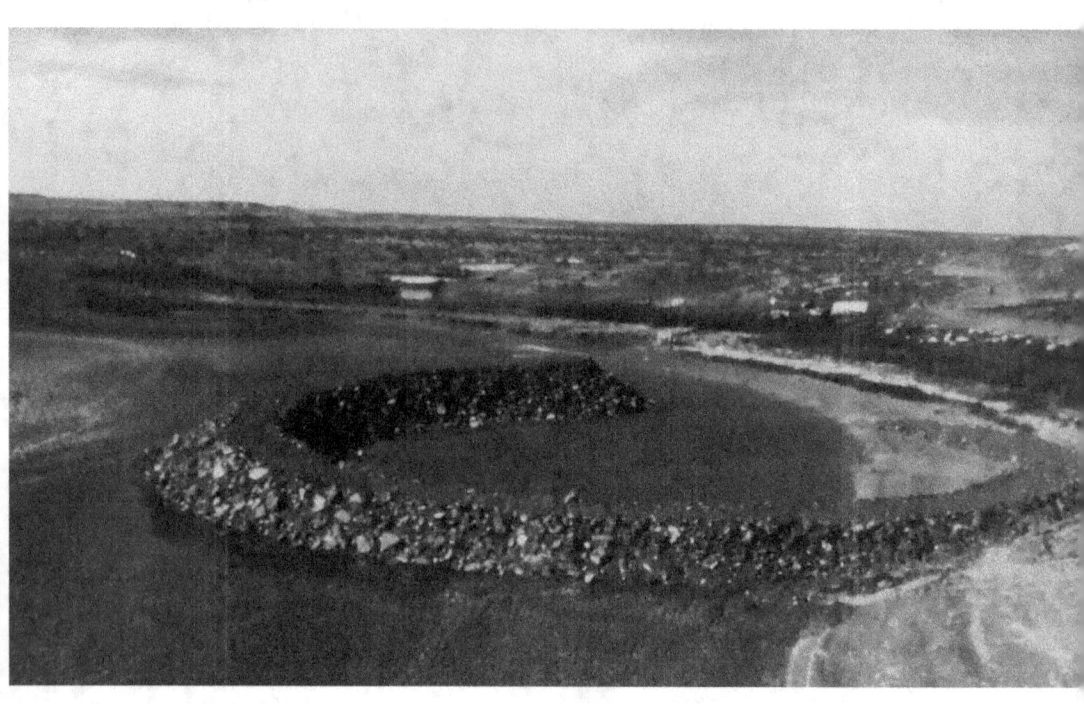

Robert Smithson, Amarillo Ramp, 1973

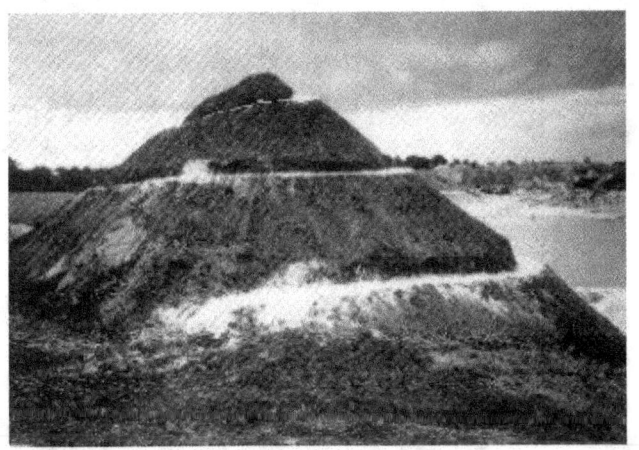

Robert Smithson, The Spiral Hill, 1971

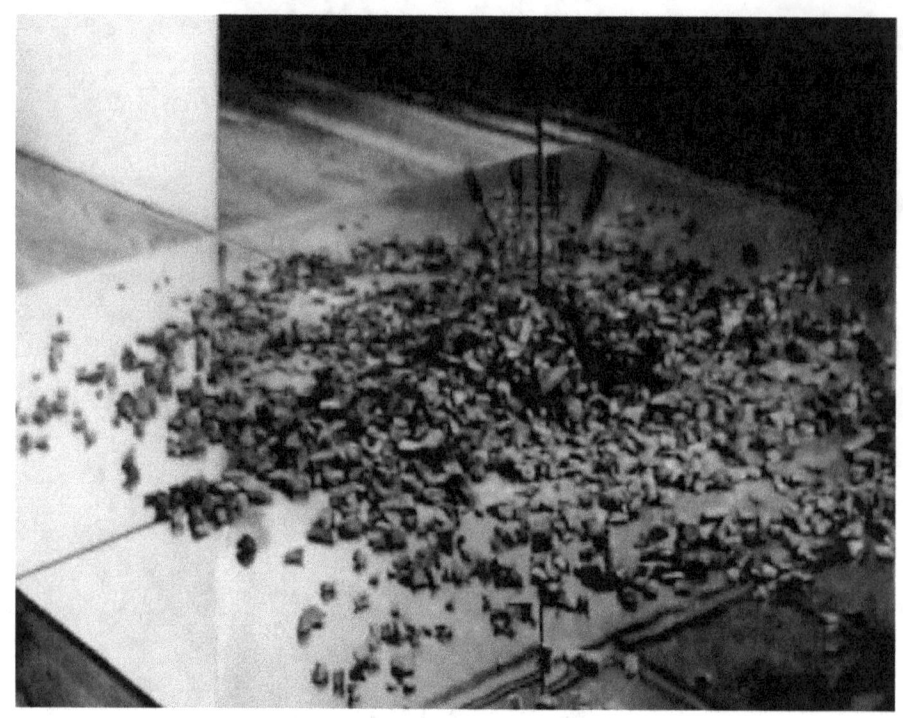

Robert Smithson, non-site works

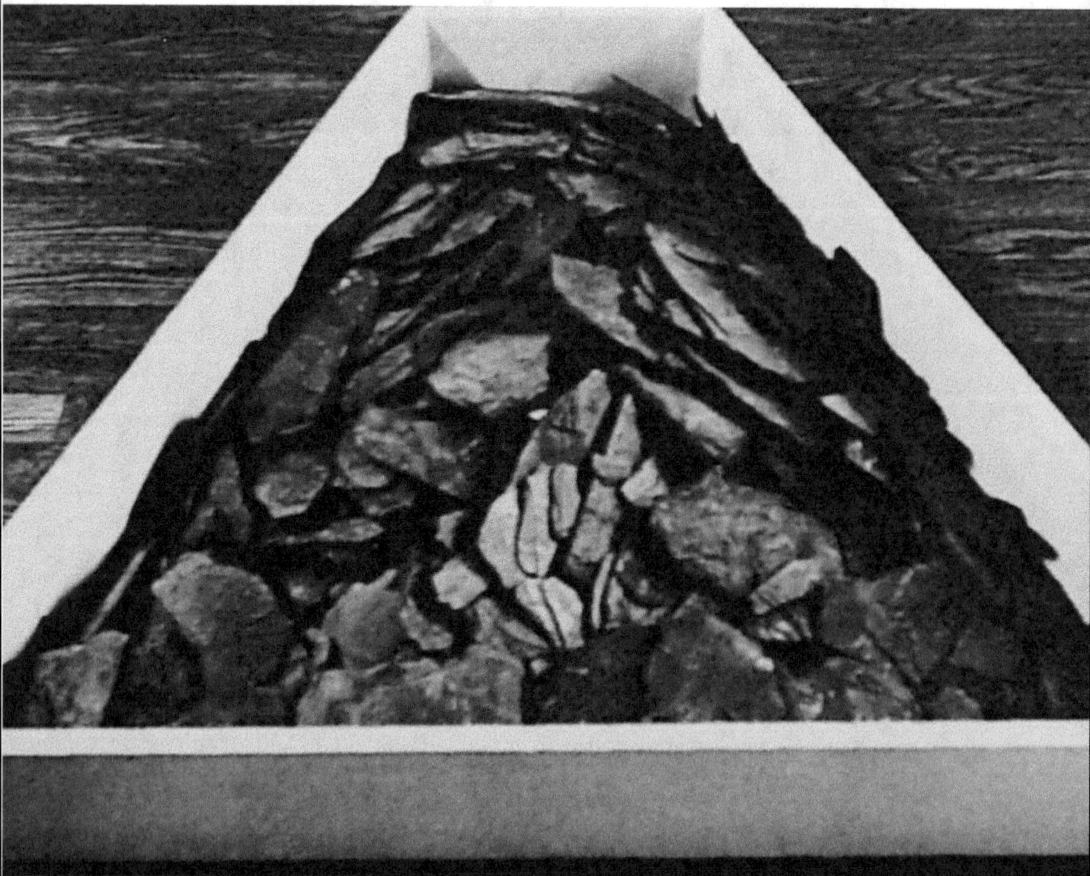

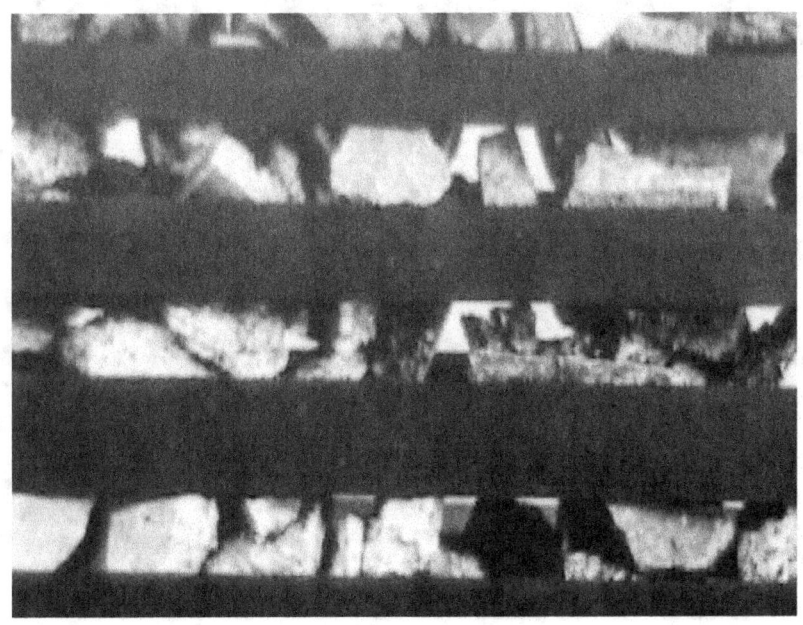

Robert Smithson

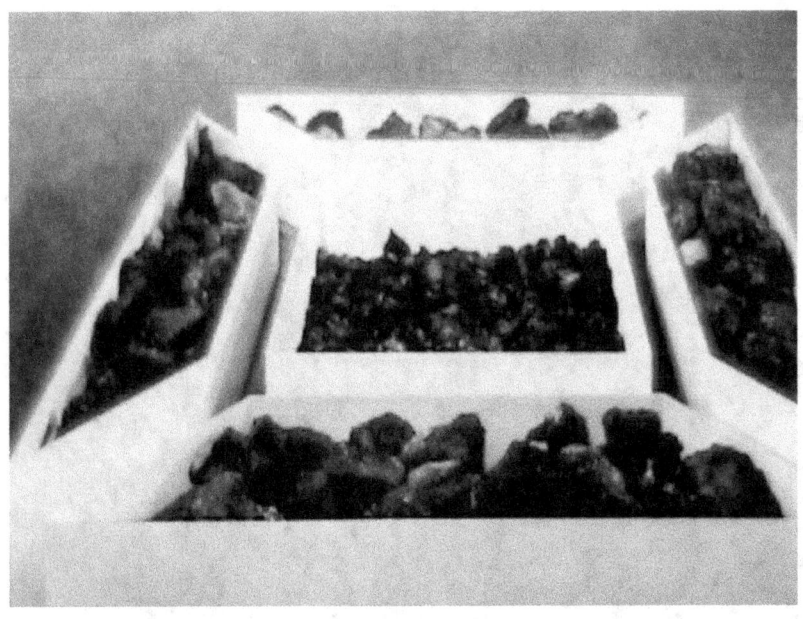

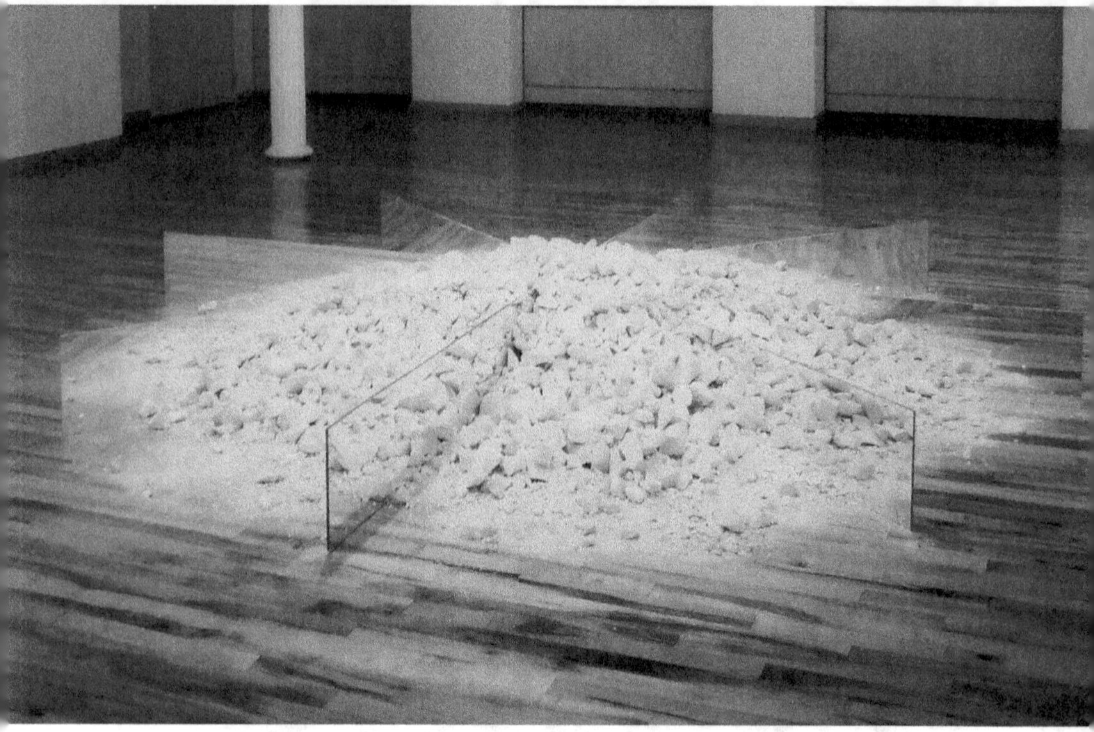

Robert Smithson: Chalk-Mirror Displacement, 1969/ 1987 (above),
Mirrored Zigurat, 1966 (below)

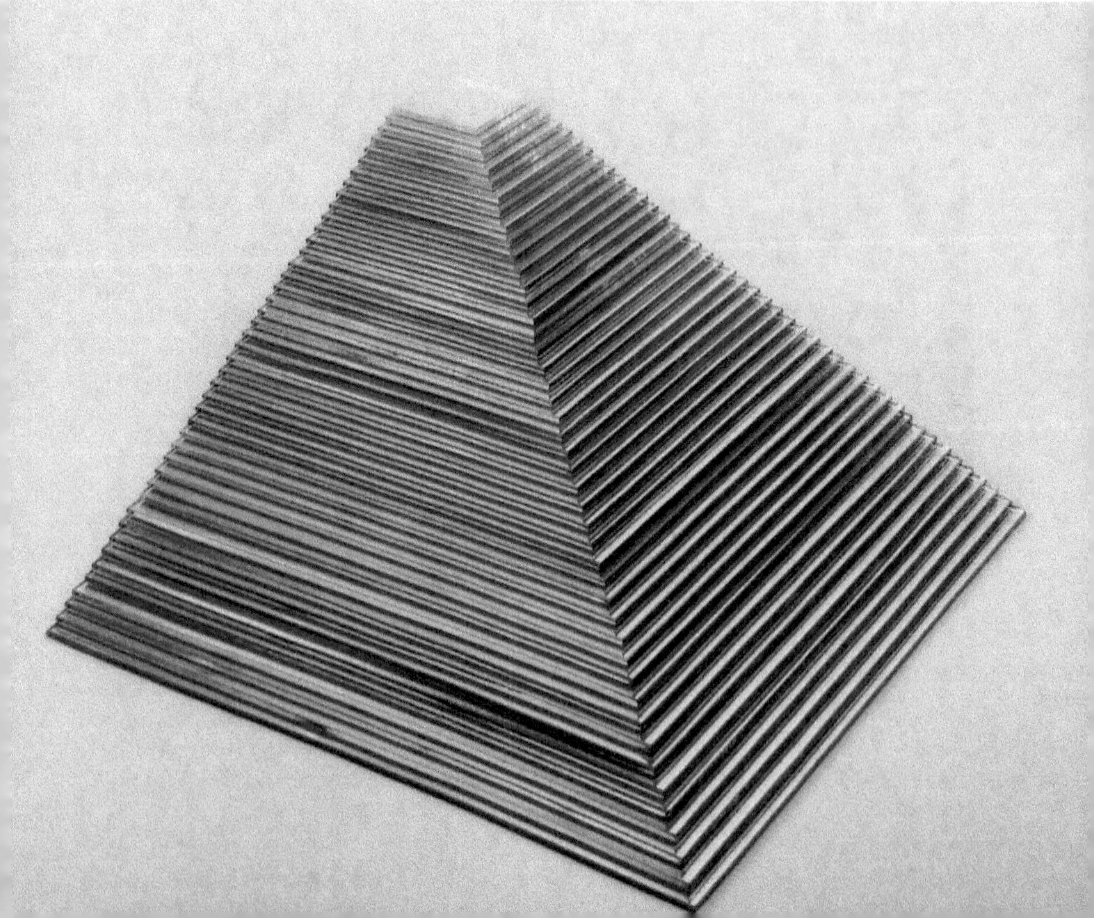

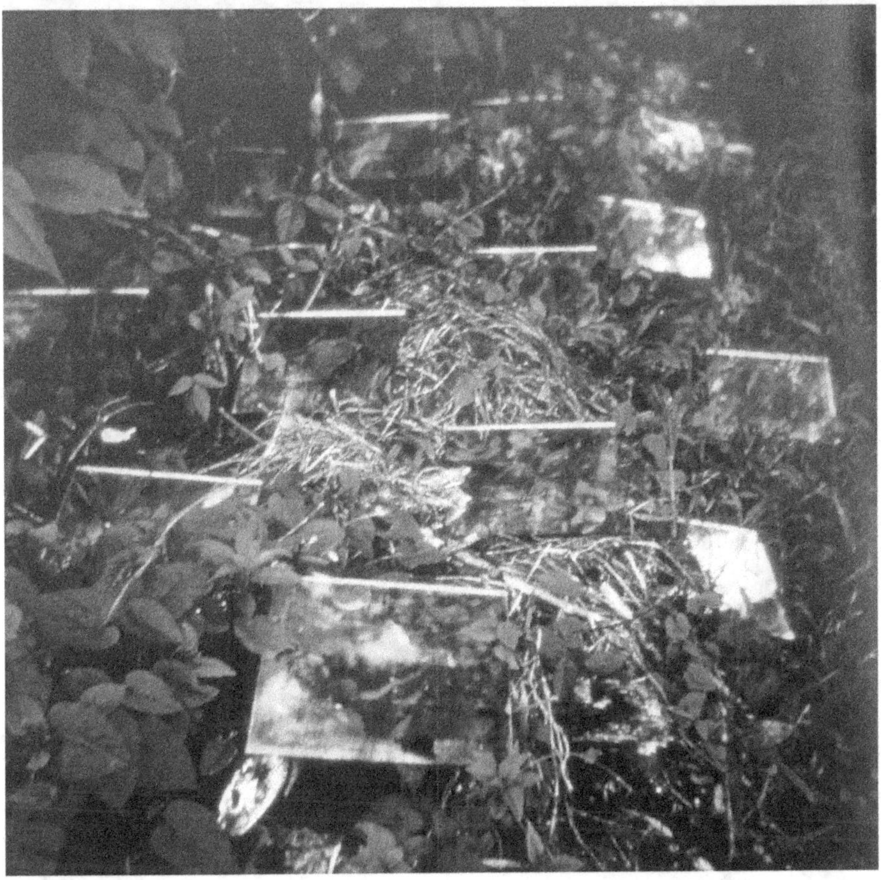

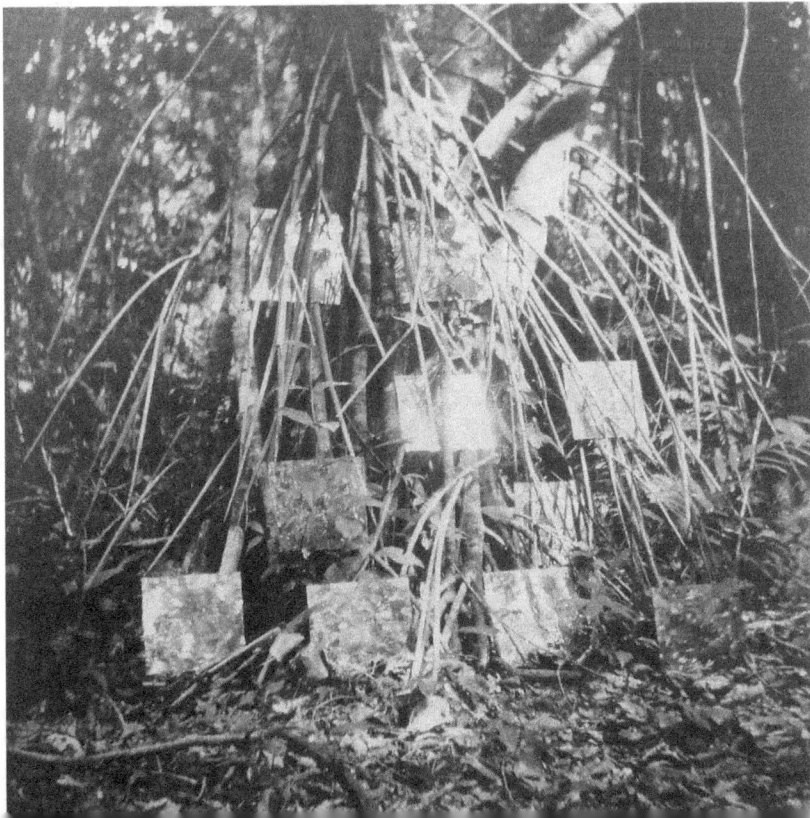

Robert Smithson, Yucatan Mirror Displacements, 1969

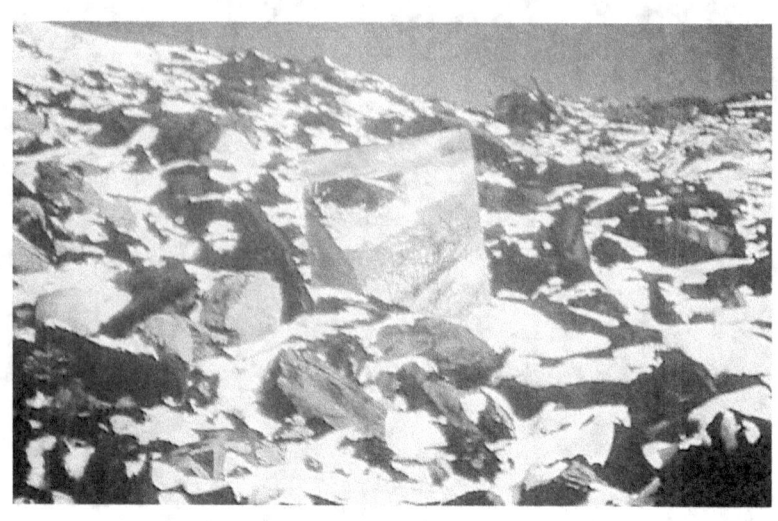

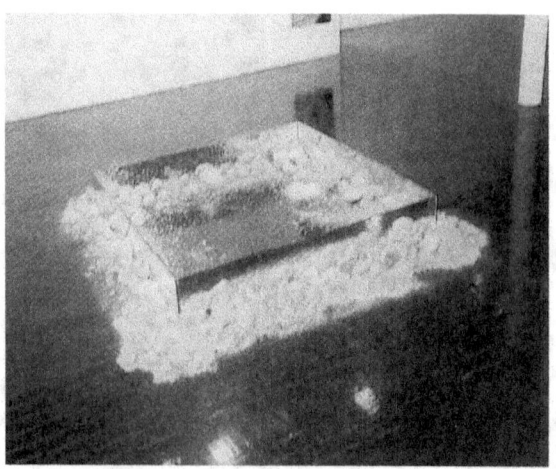

Robert Smithson, more mirror works

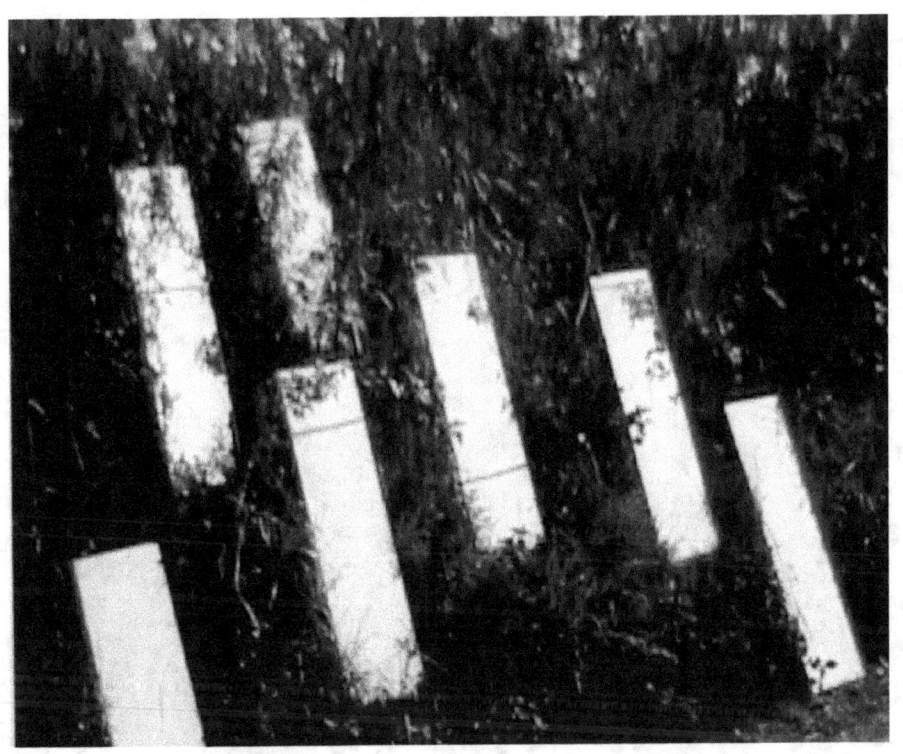

Robert Smithson, Mirror Displacements

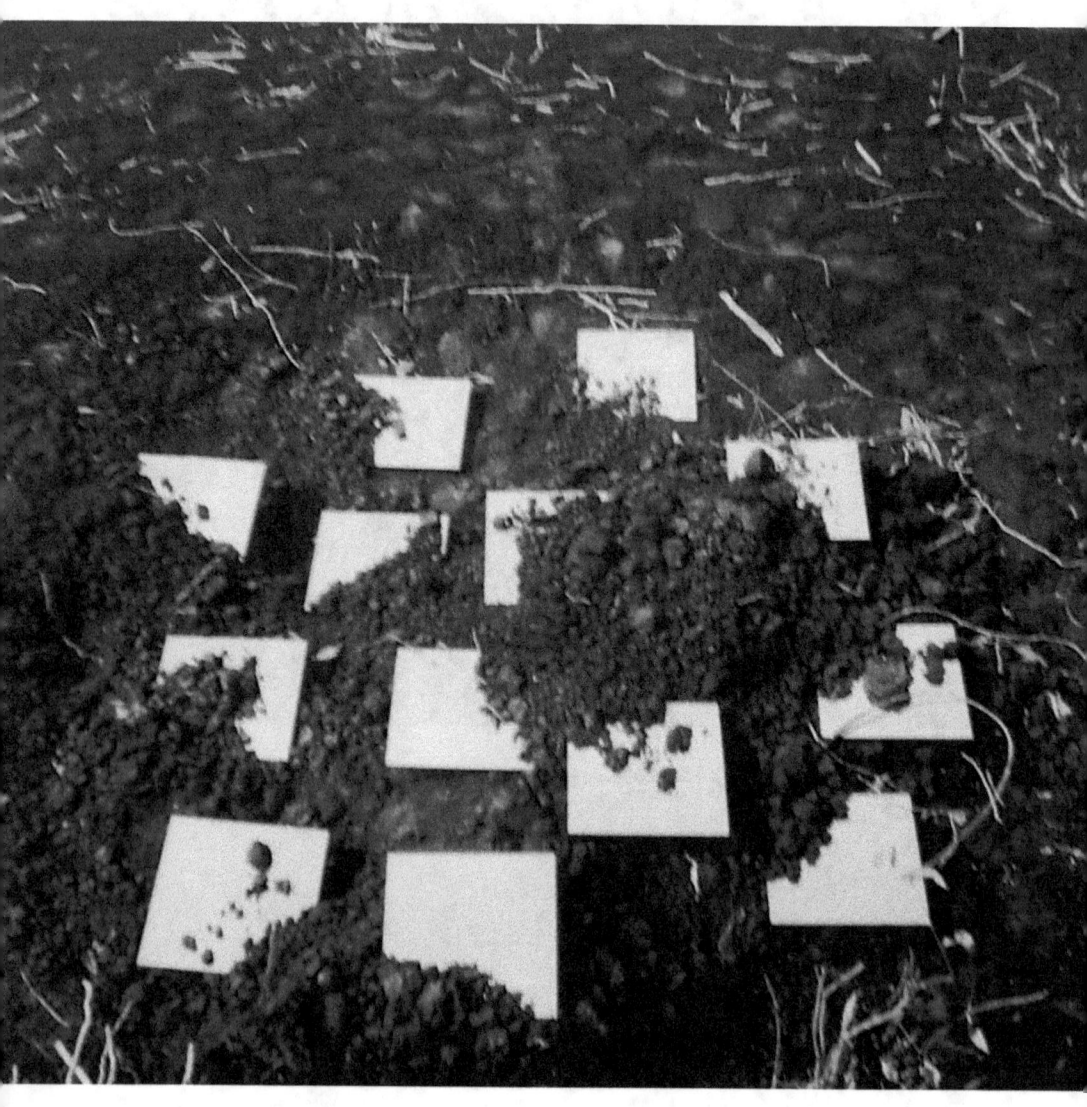

Robert Smithson, Mirror Displacements

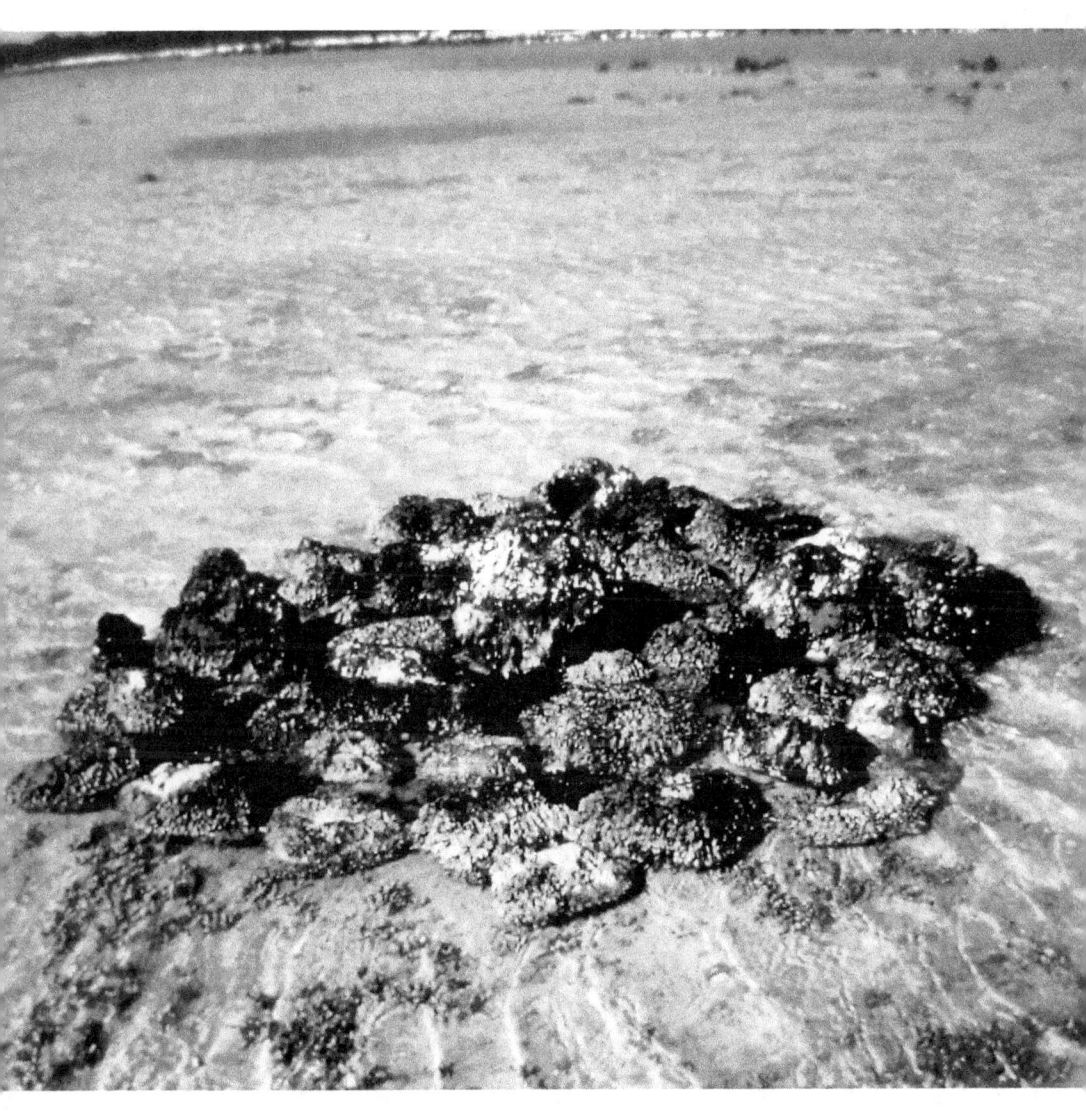

Robert Smithson, Sunken Island, 1971, Florida

7

Carl Andre

Since the 1960s, the statements of a handful of artists have proved to be the most illuminating about 1960s art, and land art in particular. Smithson, Judd, Morris and Andre have been among the most lucid of theorists among artists (and Clement Greenberg, Michael Fried, Lawrence Alloway, Bruce Glaser, Mel Bochner, David Bourdon, Lucy Lippard and Harold Rosenberg among art critics). Carl Andre (b. 1935) has many pertinent things to say about sculpture. His mid-1960s summary of the history of sculpture applies directly to land art:

> The course of development
>   Sculpture as form
>   Sculpture as structure
>   Sculpture as place.[1]

Andre's biography is often cited in accounts of his art. He worked on the railways, as a freight conductor and brakeman (in Newark, at the Pennsylvania Railroad) from 1960-64, and this is used to explain Andre's use of modules and units which join together to form a work. Like Sol LeWitt and Donald Judd, Andre took one unit and multiplied them until he had a line or a square. Before working on the railroad, Andre was 'a wood-carving disciple of Brancusi', carving chunks out of wood beams. For a long time the shadow of Brancusi lay over Andre's art. When he came to explain his floor-standing works, such as *Lever*, a line of firebricks, he said he was

> putting Brancusi's *Endless Column* on the ground instead of in the sky... Most sculpture is priapic with the male organ in the air. In my work, Priapus is down on the floor. The engaged position is to run along the earth.[2]

The sexualization of sculpture in Andre's remark is no accident: Andre has spoken in interviews that the best creative work is erotic. In a 1970 radio discussion (with Lucy Lippard, Douglas Huebler, Dan Graham and Jan Dibbets on WBAI FM), Andre said desires, not ideas, were important.

> I have very few ideas, but I have strong desires.... I agree with Dr Guillotine that all ideas are the same except in execution... You can't cut off desires except painfully.[3]

Nature was also crucial: Andre said he disliked Conceptual art because it was cut off from nature (ibid.). Andre said his art 'has never been conceptual in any way'.[4]

While he was in New Hampshire in 1965, canoeing on a lake, Andre (apparently) realized that sculpture ought to be level, like water. After this, most of his sculpture was floor-standing and flat. Andre did not make boxes in the usual Minimal manner. Andre's sculptures were modular in the sense that one piece could be removed and put somewhere else without altering the whole (Andre's 'anaxial symmetry').

Lines of bricks or squares made from plates of metal were typical Andre works. Andre's use of materials was not 'poetic' or 'spiritual' in the usual sense of the word. In works such as *Cedar Piece* (1959/ 64), *Pyre* (1971, S. & C. Gilman), *Herm* (1976, Guggenheim), *Stile* (1975) and *Well* (1964), which were made out of wood, Carl Andre was using materials as themselves, but 'not to evoke nature'.5 Andre did not intend his materials to refer to other things, to be allusive in the art historical or lyrical sense. His Styrofoam planks were not alluding to marble, as some viewers mistakenly thought.6

Carl Andre's notion of the 'dematerialization' of sculpture was central to his art, and also to land art. When they were not being exhibited, Andre's sculptures simply disappeared. They were not objects on permanent display, but were made specially for each occasion and space. Most land art is like this. Andre's works outside of shows exist as ideas, photographs, descriptions, memories, and so on, but not as actual works. Much of land art is also this ephemeral, made for a particular occasion then dismantled (Christo, Drury, Morris). This emphasis on the materiality and dematerialization of his works lead Andre to regard his art as non-spiritual. He said:

> My work is atheistic, materialistic, and communistic. It's atheistic because it's without transcendent form, without spiritual or intellectual quality. Materialistic because it's made out of its own materials without pretension to other materials. And communistic because the form is equally accessible to all men.7

This is a humble, self-effacing view of his own art. His art was materialistic, Andre said, because it does not pretend to be anything else other than itself. However, at other times (in interviews, for example), Andre comes across as a warmly Romantic artist. It is this aspect of his art that annoyed people when the Tate Gallery in the UK bought, with public money, one of his piles of bricks. The form (a low oblong shape) and the material of the work (brick) seemed available to anyone who visited a household supply store and bought a few bricks and arranged them in a certain way. Yet Carl Andre's art is of course not as simple as that, and not as easy to produce as that.

Carl Andre's *37 Pieces of Work* is a good example of Minimal æsthetic permutations taken to extremes. It is a sculpture that is typical of Andre's art:

> Taken as a whole *37 Pieces of Work* consists of 1,296 plates, 216 each of aluminium, copper, steel, magnesium, lead and zinc. Each metal appears alone in individual six-foot square plains. Then alternates with another, checker-board fashion, in every possible permutation. Since each of the six metals in the large piece was laid out in the alphabetical order of its chemical symbol, alternating successively with the others, there are two versions of each combination.[8]

Andre's *Element* series consisted of wood-carved beams that recalled Brancusi; Andre's *Equivalents* were 'floor-hugging' sculptures shown in 1966. The magnet pieces, which preceded the metal squares, also hugged the floor, so much so that the third dimension was nearly expunged. The floor-pieces neatly rid the sculptor of dealing with pedestals. They became 'place-markers'.[9] They have no space, according to one critic, they have 'no appearance of inside or center. Rather they seem to be coextensive with the very floor on which the viewer stands'.[10] Place, not space or sky, became what matters for Andre. Andre's floor-pieces are viewer-friendly, too: the viewer is invited to (or allowed to) walk over them. Like Judd, Andre wanted his sculptures to be seen from a variety of viewpoints. Instead of a single viewpoint, one could have a number of angles; he compared viewing his sculptures to walking on roads: '[t]hey cause you to make your way along them or around them or to move... over them' (1970, 57).

Andre's works seem to be slight, almost insubstantial, but, simultaneously, 'their matter-of-factness that makes them in a multiple sense *present*'.[11] Stella influenced Andre's way of making sculpture: Andre often stayed with Stella in the early years, and worked in Stella's studio: when Andre was working on a large log, Stella told him that unworked wood could be sculpture too. Andre considered what Stella had said, and thereafter used materials in an untouched state, 'using them as 'cuts' in the space that surrounds them, shaping the space itself'.[12]

Carl Andre's works are extremely sensuous, with their shiny or dull surfaces of copper, zinc, steel or aluminium. Andre's *Sixteenth Copper Cardinal*, sixteen square copper slabs, is a work that could be described as luscious. People are used to marble and stone being beautiful, and also certain metals – bronze, silver and gold in particular have been central to sculpture for millennia. Why not zinc and copper, too? After all, much jewellery is made from copper. Carl Andre, like other Minimal sculptors, introduces the viewer to the sensuality of copper, bronze and zinc shaped into nothing more than... a simple shape, like a slab, put on the floor. Andre's slabs are not 'narrative' or anthropomorphic or literal or allusive; they do not 'depict' animals or gods or people; but they are no less beautiful, as objects in their own right. Spectators are invited to walk on his sculptures, offering a new relation with the work.

If land art is in a gallery, one sees it as art (and a particular kind of Western, bourgeois art, the sort of art that is exhibited in Western, bourgeois galleries). Carl Andre explored the relation between real and represented objects with his controversial pile of bricks. The sculpture was 'controversial' because the general public (whoever they are) perceived, via the media, that Andre had simply stuck some bricks into a gallery. Or rather, that taxpayer's money had been used to purchase Andre's bricks. A pile of bricks on a building site is... a pile of bricks. A pile of bricks in an art gallery is... sculpture. Context is everything here. This is what Carl Andre explored, whether consciously or not: the *response*, affected by so much of culture, socialization, physical context, education, and so on, makes objects sculptures. People make art. A leaf simply exists, but if someone puts it in a gallery or an art book, it becomes art (as well as remaining a leaf). If people think something is art, then it's art, as Donald Judd said.

Andre commented:

> The materiality, the presence of the work of sculpture in the world, essentially independent of any single individual, but rather the residue of many individuals and the dream, the experience of the sea, the trees and the stones – I'm interested in that kind of essential thing.13

('I will try to have in my work only what is necessary to it' Andre said [1984]).

Carl Andre's *Stone Field* (1977) was one of his site-specific works of the 1970s, consisting of 26 very large glacial boulders (one of his more obviously land artworks). It was an imposing piece, introducing the idiosyncratic, organic shapes of nature into the 'geometric wilderness' (D.M. Thomas's term) of the city (Hartford, Connecticut). Andre made a line of hay bales, placed end to end, in a field in Vermont (*Joint*, 1968). 14 It was a line like Richard Long's stone rows, or Tony Cragg's floor spreads. 'Many of the activities in farm work are sculptural: stacking the hay bales, ploughing fields, feeding animals; also the marks left behind by the animals or made by farmworkers, tractors... the texture of the land' Goldsworthy remarked.15

Andre made one of his floor pieces of slabs of metal deliberately so it would be altered by being outside. It was called *Small Weathering Piece* (1971), and contained a large number of metals (large for an Andre sculpture): lead, zinc, aluminium, copper, steel and magnesium.

One of Carl Andre's most intriguing theoretical statements is this: 'my ideal piece of sculpture is a road'.[16] This applies not only to Andre's lines of bricks or hay bales, but to Long's lines of stones and walks along roads, to Christo's *Running Fence*, to Goldsworthy's stone walls, and to other land artworks.

Andre's notion of the ultimate earthwork as a road has a parallel with the famous anecdote of US artist Tony Smith who, when driving along the New Jersey turnpike, was impressed by the 'dark pavements moving through the landscape of the flats, rimmed in the distance, but punctuated by stacks, towers, fumes, and colored lights'.[17] Something in such a long stretch of empty roads, as with airstrips (and, more dubiously, a drill ground at Nuremberg) impressed Tony Smith, who wrote '[i]t seemed that there had been a reality there that had not had any expression in art'.[18] Roads are not 'art', not wholly functional either – they have an aura or mystery which Smith tried to explain. Richard Long emphasizes the functional or workaday aspect of his walks. He sees his walks as hard work; roads, in the Tony Smith view, are also for and about labour and functionality. The road, for the Minimal or Process artist, in the Carl Andre manner, embody materially the sense of a sequence or process. One unit (the foot or brick or slab of tarmac or concrete) is placed next to another, forming a road. Artists such as Carl Andre (and LeWitt, Bladen and Judd) did exactly the same, putting one unit next to another, creating a line or sequence of units.

The road also may have no obvious end: endlessness was crucial to Minimal, Process and Conceptual art, as it is to land art. Many land artists emphasize art that goes on and on. Christo's fence, for example, goes on and on for 26 miles. One imagines that Christo would love a fence that could run across a whole country, or, even better, a whole continent. Similarly, Long's walks could extend far beyond their limits, and the modular art of Judd, Bladen, Morris and LeWitt could expand indefinitely, once the basic pattern had been established. The seriality or endless process of art was identified by Judd as the idea of 'one thing after another'.[19]

Carl Andre's concept of the road as the ideal artwork fits in with this urge towards endless process and seriality. The road motif also fits in well with stereotypical American culture, with its love of the 'open road', Robert Frank's famous photograph, road movies (*Easy Rider, Duel, Thelma and Louise, Natural Born Killers*), the frontier spirit (in Westerns), and in hippy and beatnik culture (Jack Kerouac's *On the Road*, Allen Ginsberg and the 'dharma bums' who drifted around from state to state).

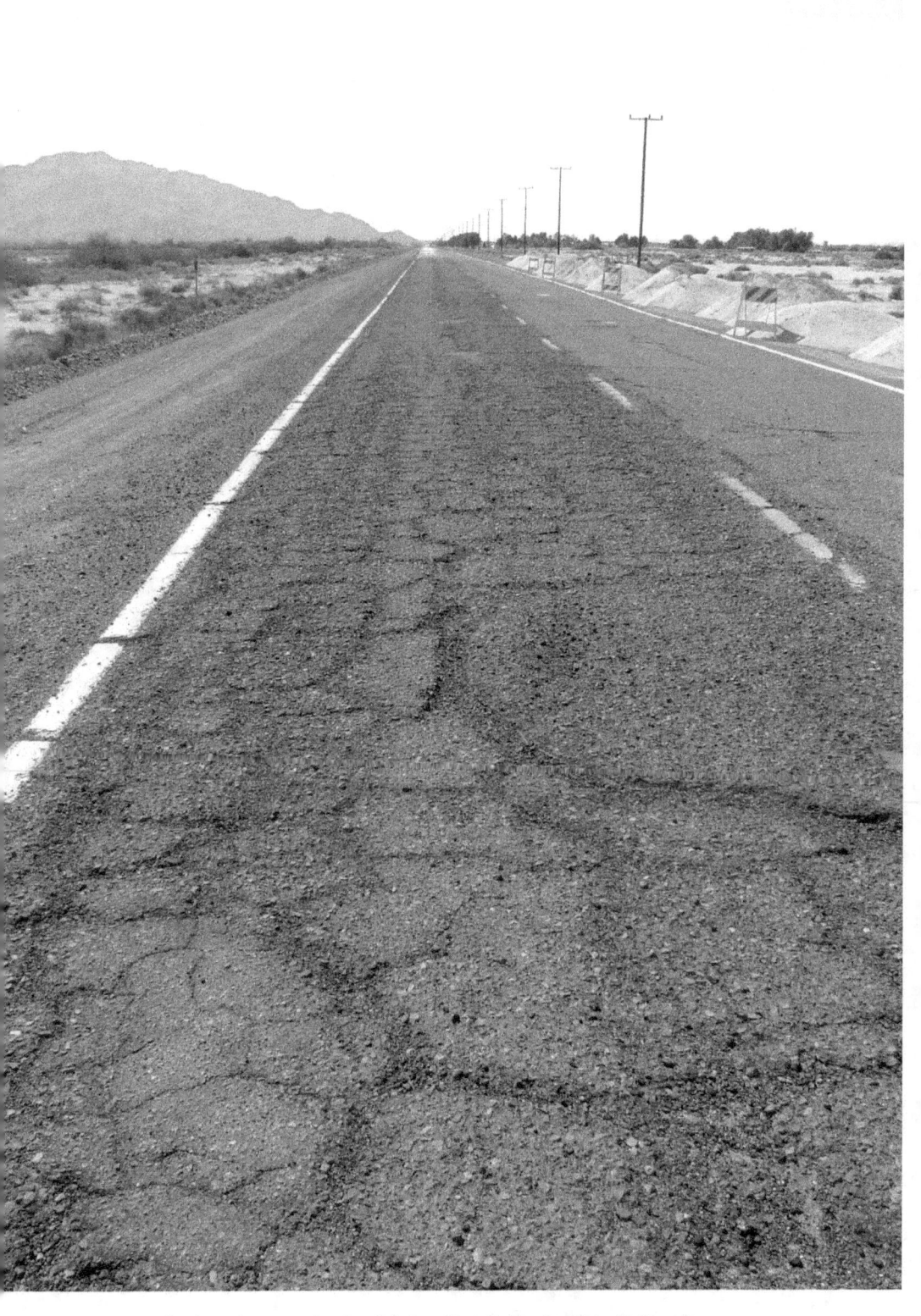
An American road – the 'Mother Road', Route 66 in California
(Photo: Cassidy Hughes, 2008)

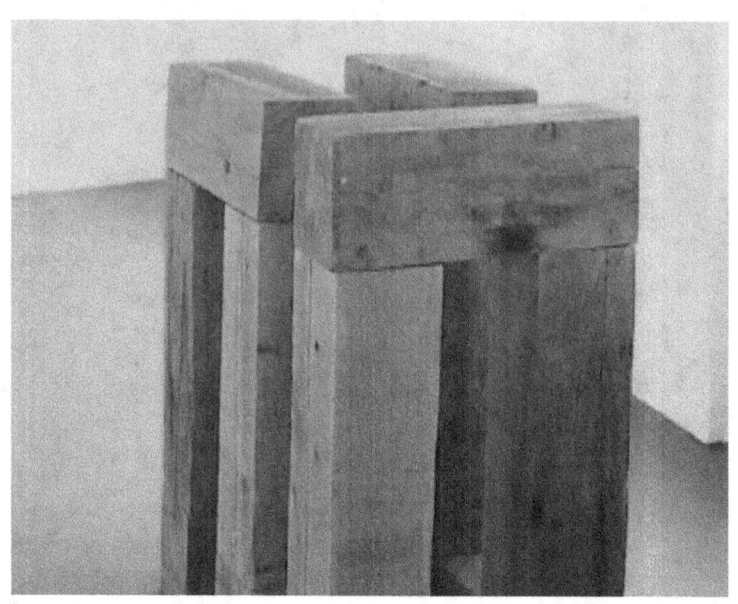

Carl Andre, Furrow, 1981

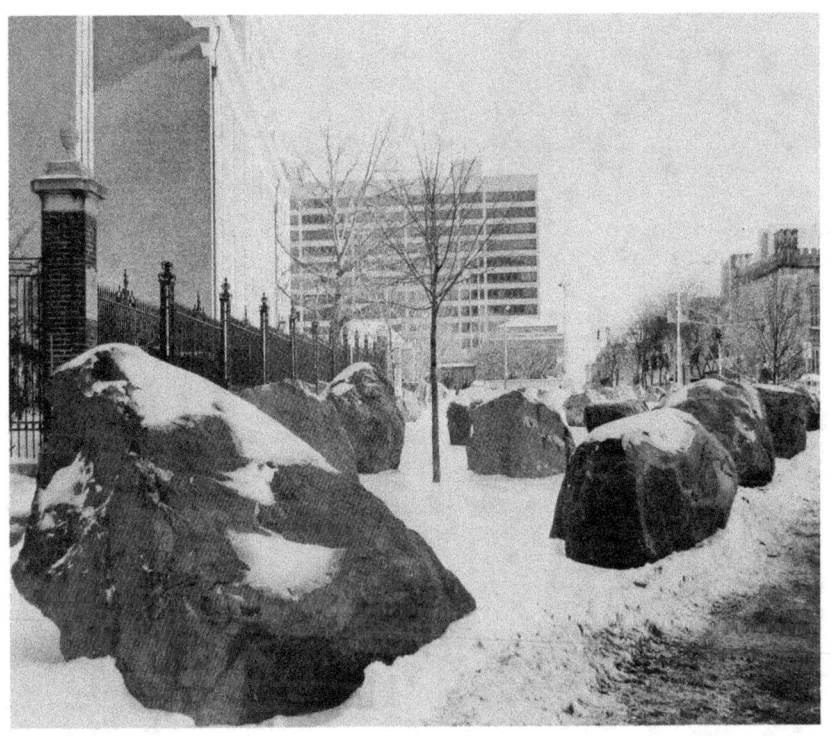

Carl Andre, Stone Field, 1977

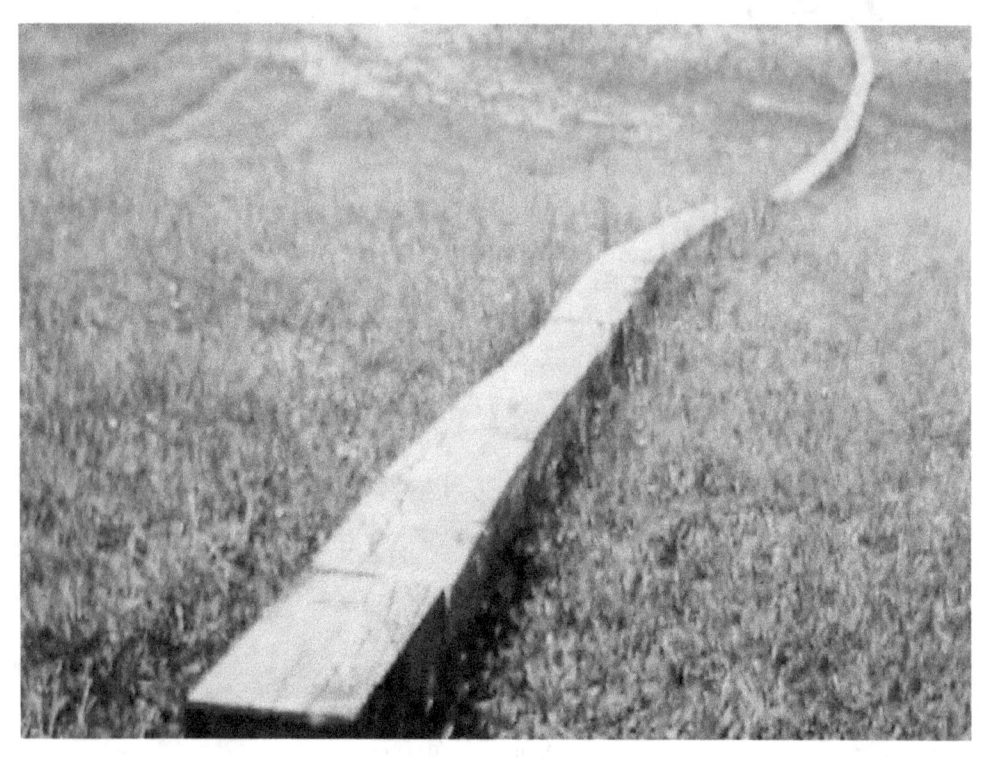

Carl Andre, Secant, 1977

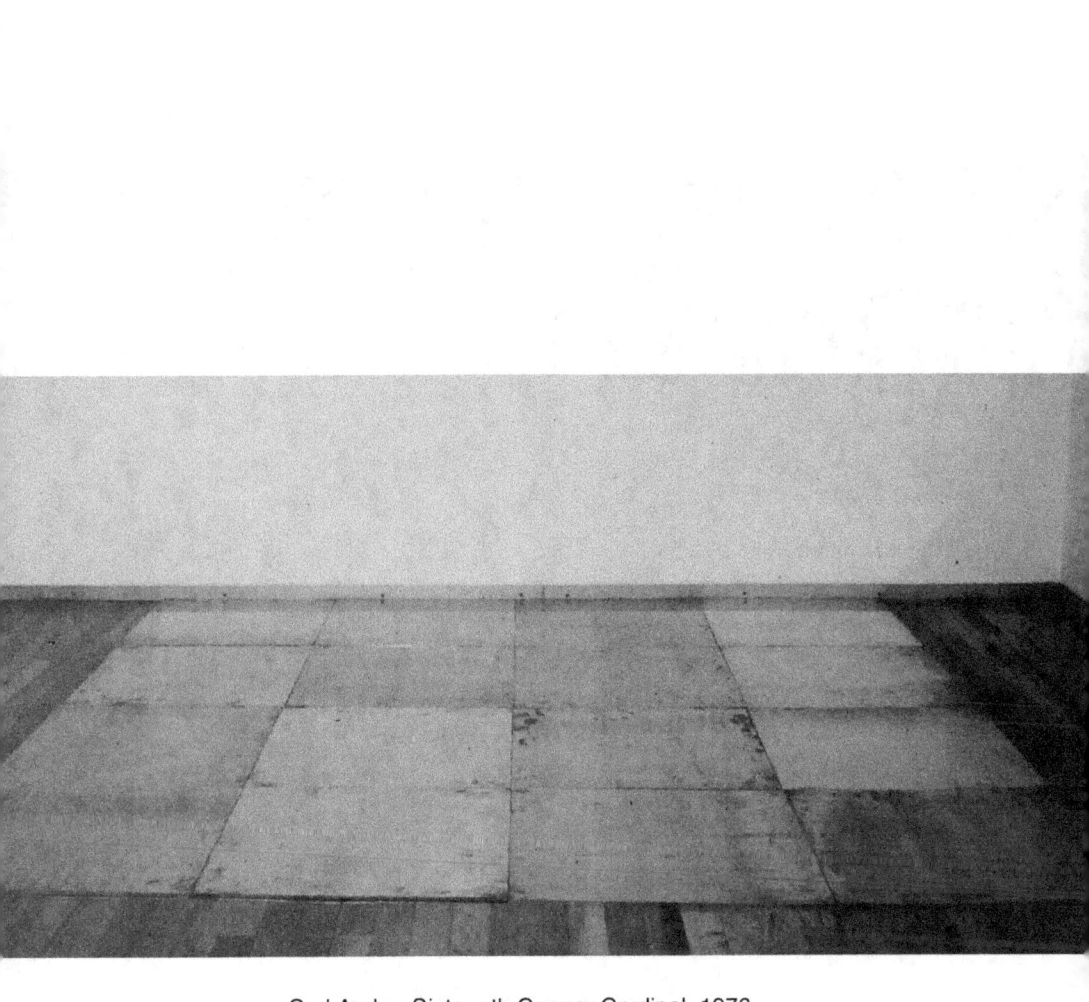

Carl Andre, Sixteenth Copper Cardinal, 1976

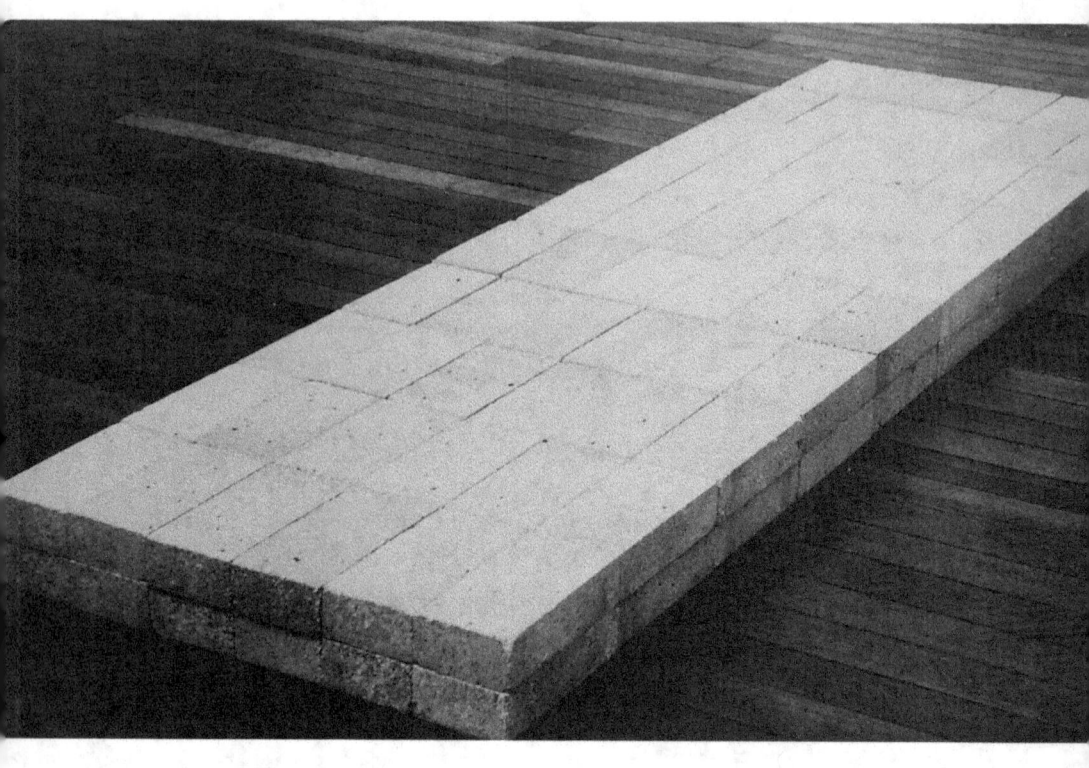

Carl, Andre, Equivalent VII

8

James Turrell

James Turrell (b. 1943) was a land artist who worked with light, earth and the sky. He was famous for his 'skyspaces', the most celebrated being his *Roden Crater Project* – 'skyspaces', tunnels, observatories and chambers in an extinct volcano near Flagstaff, Arizona. It's one of the biggest works of land and environmental art. Begun in 1974, it was funded by many different sources and administered by the Skystone Foundation.[1]

The first stage of Turrell's on-going *Roden Crater* project involved bull-dozing 200,000 cubic yards of earth from the volcano's rim, 'so as to shape the sky'. Turrell planned tunnels, pools and viewing chambers at *Roden Crater*. There were spaces at *Roden Crater* where clouds were projected onto the floor during the day, which at night were related to the procession of equinoxes. Many of the spaces planned at *Roden Crater* were built around celestial events, such as full moons, solstices, equinoxes, the movement of the sun, or just being able to view stars and some planets. The connection with the heavens was important for Turrell: most of his works have openings to the sky, and the relationship with the sky is the centrepiece of the works. It's important for Turrell, in short, to see the stars.

The *Roden Crater* work was about the relationship between the viewer and the elements, in particular the sky, celestial events, and light. Turrell said:

> My art is made for one person. I like the solitary experience. Standing alone at night, perceiving the Roden Crater and the moon and stars, you really feel the vastness of the universe and yourself entering into it'.[2]

The environment was a volcano, relating to geological time. 'The work I do intensifies the experience of light by isolating it and occluding all other light. Each space essentially looks to a different portion of sky and accepts a limited number of events' Turrell explained (1995, 67). Thus, each space at *Roden Crater* was designed to highlight some celestial event. The subject of some spaces was the vaulting of the sky, and the curvature of the Earth. Some were about daily events, such as sunrises and sunsets, or the movement of the stars.

The North section of *Roden Crater* is about looking North, the North Star, the rotation of the Earth, changing light, and includes a *camera obscura* (which projects whatever is overhead onto a white sand floor), and a seat for viewing Polaris. The Eastern space is for witnessing sunrise, and a 'skyspace' overhead. *Bath Space* projects a magnified image of the sky above onto a white sand floor, using a water bath above a large sphere as a lens.

The *Sun and Moon Room* was constructed around the furthest south moonset (every 18.61 years), the furthest North sunrise and the Summer solstice. *Tso Kiva* is a hemispherical space in the centre of the volcano, for observing light, shadows, shapes and the horizon. The *South Space* is an astronomical observatory and star chart. The *West Space*, as one would expect, is for the sunset, and the 'twilight arch', the projection of the Earth's shadow into the atmosphere at nightfall. Turrell said he didn't want Roden Crater to be 'a mark upon Nature, but to be enfolded in Nature in such a way that light from the Sun, Moon, and stars empowered the spaces' (1995, 66).

James Turrell's creative task as he saw it was not to impose his own vision or aesthetics on the viewer, but to encourage them to see things for themselves, to create the situation in which they could have their own experience. These were aesthetics common in much of land art. As he said in 1987, the goal was not to turn an experience into art, but

> to set up a situation to which I take you and let you see. It becomes your experience... not taking from nature as much as placing you in contact with it.[3]

Turrell regarded his art as a 'seeing aid', as showing the observer something that was already there but that they might not have noticed.

On the indoor-outdoor debate, which exercised so many land artists, James Turrell said that, instead of bringing nature into the museum, he wanted to 'bring culture to the natural surround as if designing a garden or tending a landscape' (1995, 66). The artwork became something to visit in itself, rather than one of many artworks in a museum to see. The viewer travelled specially to see the artwork, as they visited *Double Negative,* or Marfa in Texas, or Robert Smithson's earthworks.

James Turrell's primary material was not earth or stone or the usual materials of land art, but light itself, what he called 'light in the space itself'. Turrell wanted to use light as a thing-in-itself, which had presence, just as the sculptor used a physical object which had presence. He achieved this, he said, by setting limits on the space in which light manifested itself: 'I give light thingness by putting limits on it in a formal manner. I do not create an object, only objectified perception' (1995, 65).

Turrell was attempting to create spaces in which viewers could perceive the subject of his works, light itself, and celestial events. It was important also for Turrell that the viewer was able to enter those spaces physically, not virtually. Turrell's art was not about creating illusions or artificial scenarios or a record of the artwork.

Turrell called it 'non-vicarious seeing': '[t]he subject of my work is your nonvicarious seeing. You are not looking at a record of my seeing' (1995, 64). Thus, Turrell's art was not about recording some event that took place elsewhere, or taking photographs of his art, or writing down what happened, as in some land art. Rather, Turrell wanted to place the viewer right into the artwork, to have them able to walk into and around the artwork, and to experience of the artwork for themselves.

Many of Turrell's artworks were about working with not just light, but with the sky. The archetypal Turrell space was an enclosed area (a 'skyspace') which had an opening above onto the sky. Turrell spoke of the vaulting of the sky, how the sky looked when the viewer was standing up, or sitting down, or lying down.

Some of Turrell's 'skyspaces' – indoor rooms or spaces which are open to the sky above – include *Spaces That Sees* (1992) in Jerusalem, *Heavy Water* (1992, Poitier) and *Razor* (1991, London). *Kielder Skyspace* is open to the public, situated outside the village of Kielder near the Scottish border. Turrell has also constructed pools of water which combine water and light: in these works (at *Roden Crater*, and Poitier, France), the viewer is invited to dive under the water to reach a space beyond which's open to the sky.

James Turrell emphasized the spiritual aspects of light in his land art. 'I am interested in light because of my interest in our spiritual nature and the things that empower us. My art deals with light itself, the bearer of revelation, but as revelation itself' (1995, 64). The kind of effect Turrell was after in his light works he compared to staring into a fire, a kind of meditation or daydreaming. Turrell encouraged the viewer to sit or lie down and contemplate light itself, and the effects of light in a particular space. Thus, the spaces that Turrell constructed were furnished with viewing platforms, or benches, or places to lie down and look up at the sky. Situating the spectator in relation to the subject of the artwork (light itself) was Turrell's goal.

As well as drifting off by looking at a fire, Turrell also often spoke of the experience of flight, of being in a plane and rising into new zones of light, different kinds of light. Turrell also spoke of the curvature of the Earth when seen from a plane (and how, between 600 and 3,000 feet, the Earth seems to curve the wrong way). The Roden volcano was chosen partly because of its relation at that particular place in the Painted Desert to the curvature of the Earth. The low mound of the volcano and its relation to the curvature of the Earth and the sky above had the right mixture of components Turrell was seeking.

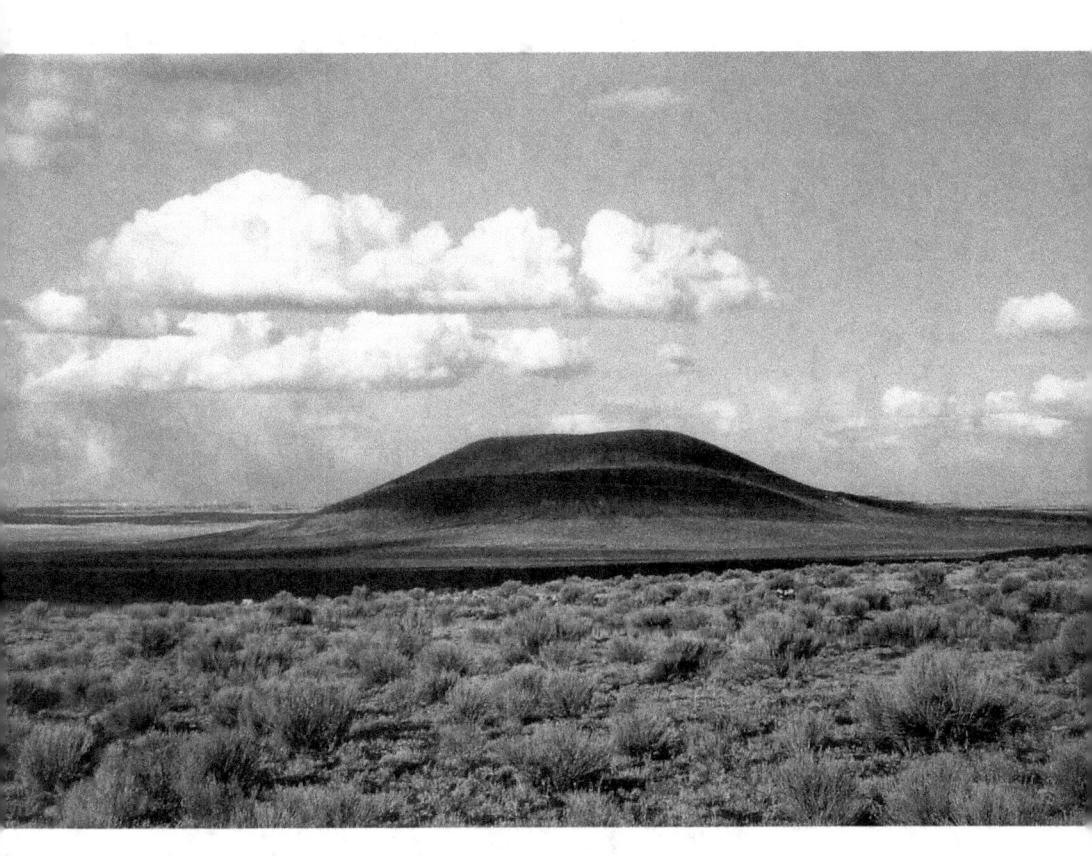

James Turrell, Roden Crater

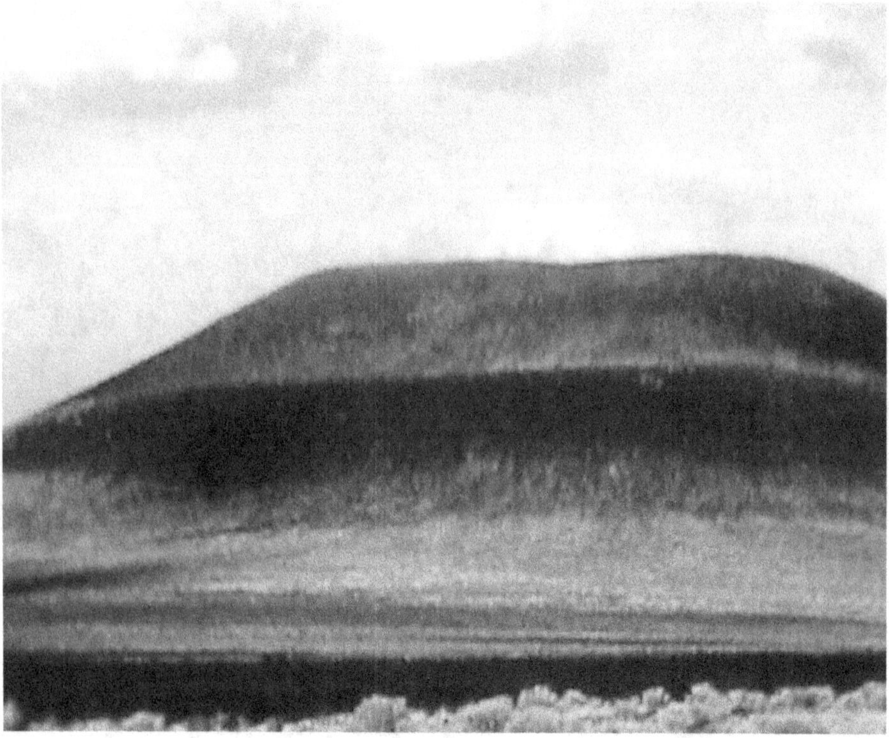

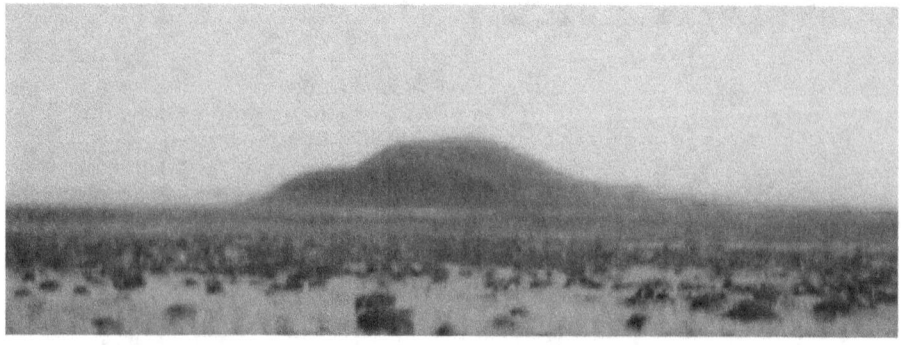

James Turrell, Roden Crater

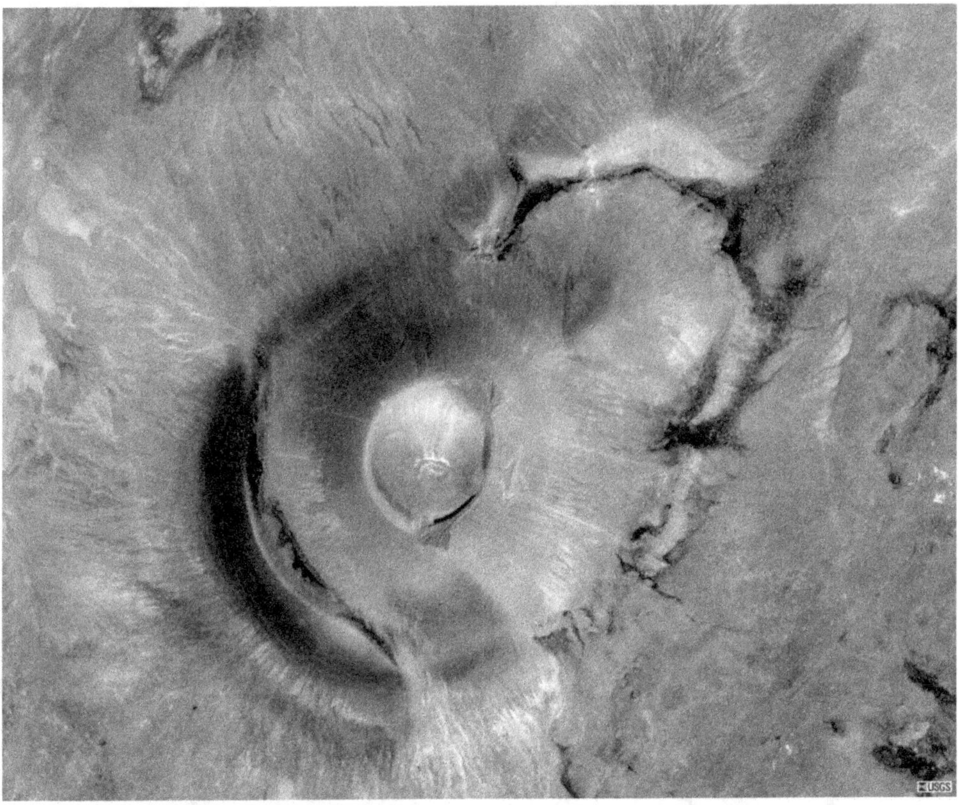

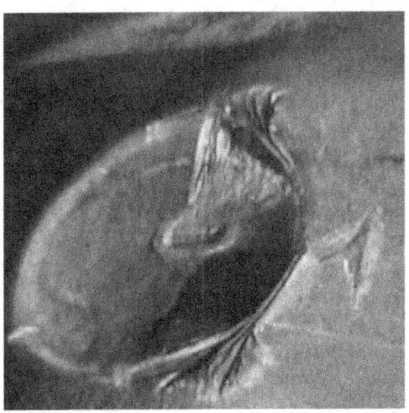

James Turrell's Roden Crater seen from above

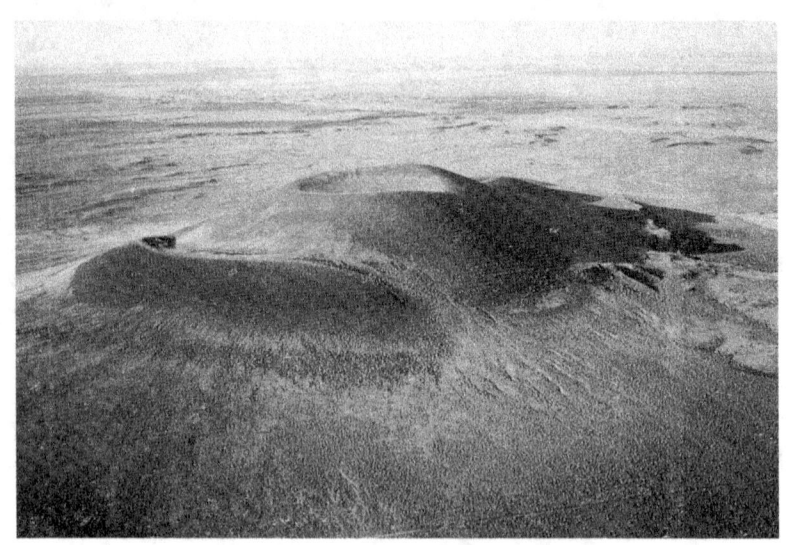

James Turrell, Roden Crater, 1974-

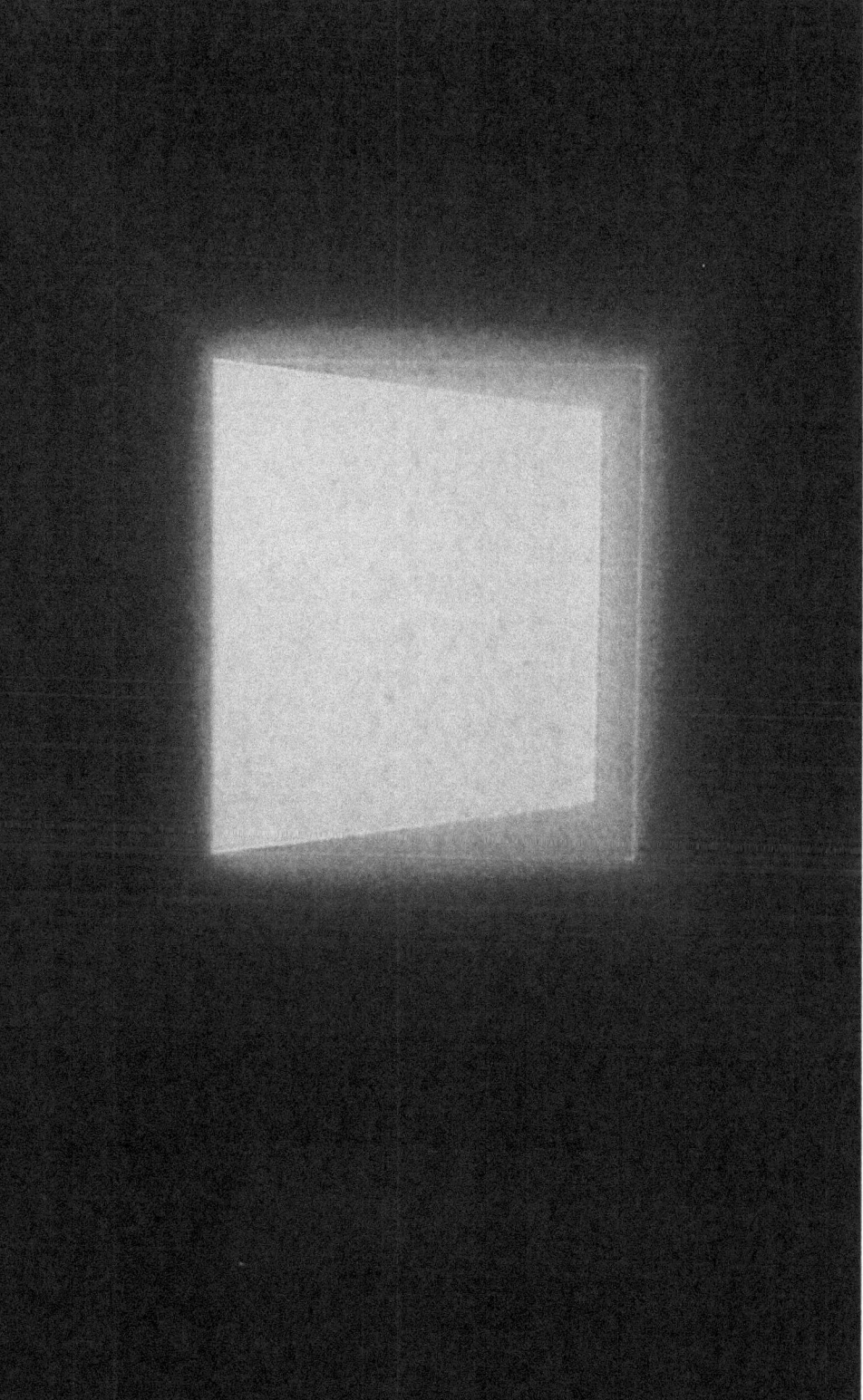

James Turrell, Milk Run III, 2002

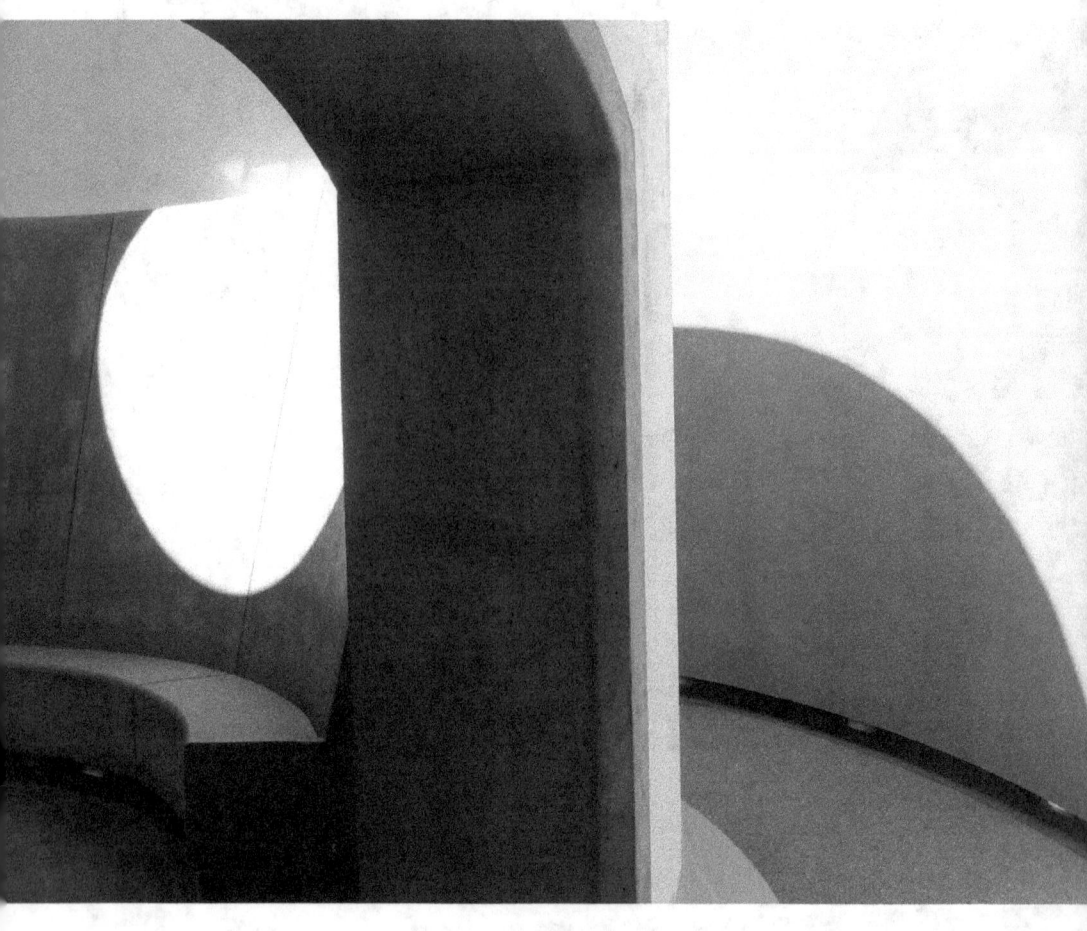

James Turrell's skyspace at the de Young Museum in San Francisco
(Photo: Cassidy Hughes)

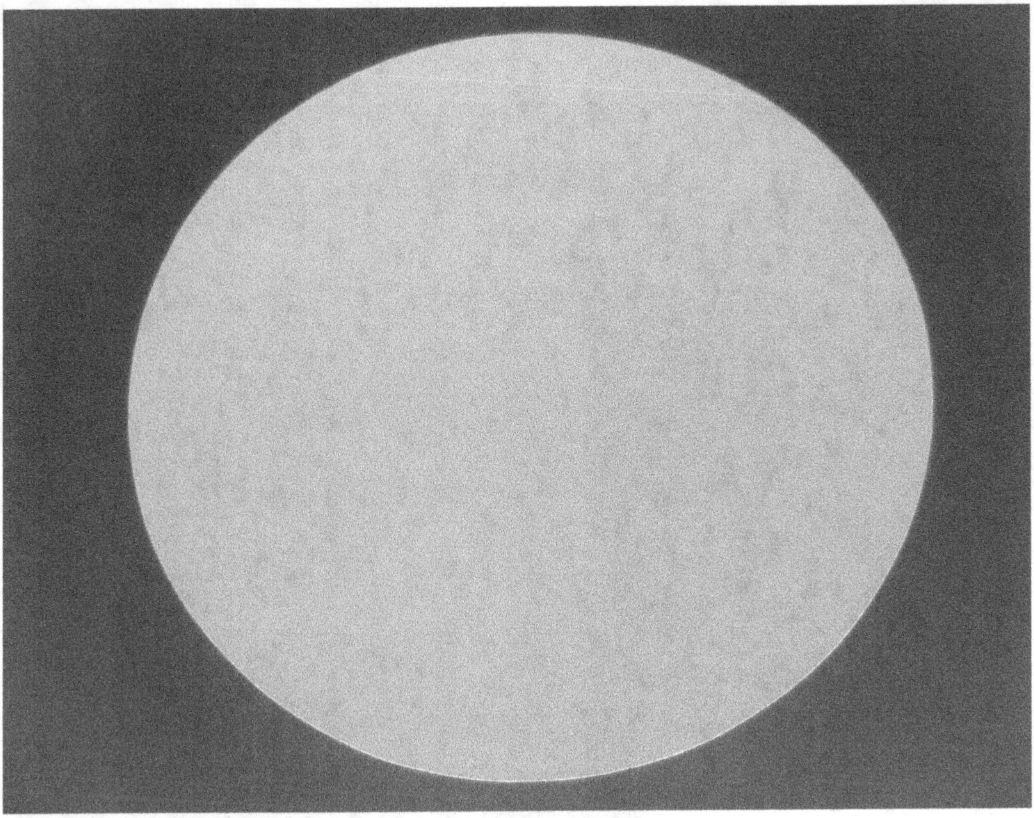

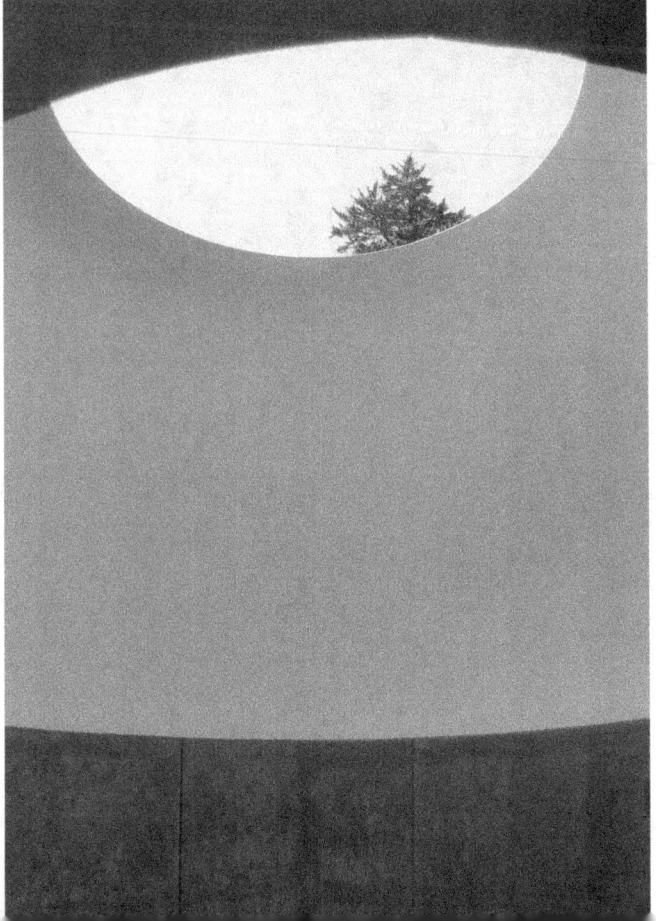

James Turrell's skyspace
at the de Young Museum
in San Francisco
(Photo: Cassidy Hughes)

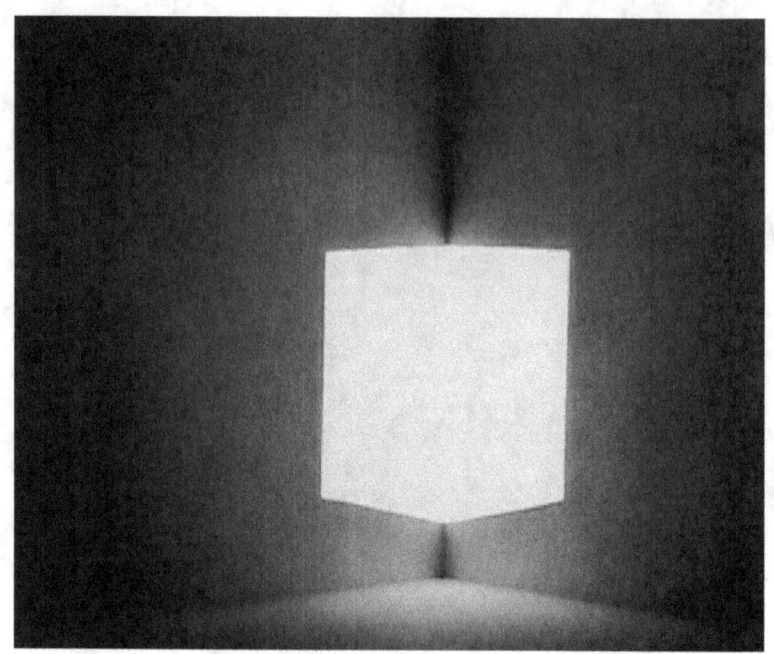

James Turrell

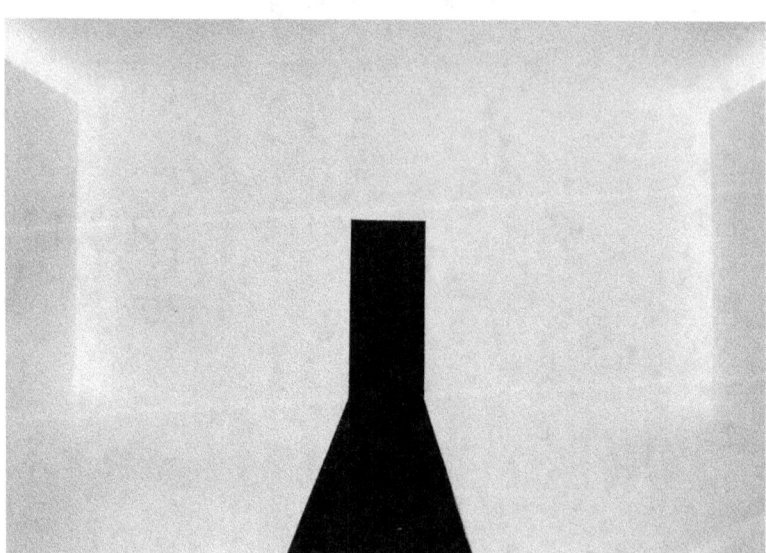

9

Dennis Oppenheim

Like Robert Smithson and James Turrell, Dennis Oppenheim (b. 1938) was one of the most interesting of US land artists, an artist who produced an amazing body of work. It's significant, for instance, that Dennis Oppenheim was the first US land artist to work with snow on a grand scale. Oppenheim began making snow works in the late Sixties. The only other important environmental artist who regularly used snow and ice, really, was Hans Haacke. But, more than any of the other first generation land artists, Oppenheim made snow one of his primary media.

Oppenheim's *Annual Rings* (1968), a series of concentric circles that straddled the Canadian/ American border, was made with snow (one of Oppenheim's recurring motifs was the border zone, margins and thresholds in time and space and concept). Oppenheim has drawn a number of snow works with a snowmobile: *One Hour Run* (1968) was a continuous track created in the snow in Maine. Two tracks, side by side, were carved in the snow between Fort Kent, Maine and Clair, New Brunswick, Canada, in 1968, for *Time Line*, a work which explored the different time zones. Oppenheim's *Negative Board* (1968) was a dark cut in the snow and ice in Maine.

Oppenheim burnt circles onto grass in *Branded Mountain. Accumulation Cut* (1969) was made at Cornell University: a hundred foot long cut made in the ice, running away from a waterfall. Also at Cornell, Oppenheim took the floor outline of gallery 4 of the Andrew Dickson White Museum of Art and drew it into the snow and ice outside (1969). Another *Gallery Transplant* was made in 1969, transplanting the floor plan of a gallery in the Stedelijk Museum in Amsterdam to a snowy hillside in New Jersey.

Oppenheim's *Whirlpool Eye of Storm* (1973) was an ephemeral piece of land art in the Hans Haacke vein: a jet trail created in the sky by a plane flying above the desert at El Mirage Dry Lake in California. *Directed Seeding* (1969) parodied Action Painting by harvesting a wheat field.

In *Cancelled Crop* (1969) Oppenheim cut a giant 'X' in a field in the Netherlands, and kept the grain, as if he were preventing the material he'd cultivated for his art from becoming the raw material for other (illusionistic) art: 'isolating this grain from further processing becomes like stopping raw pigment from becoming an illusionistic force on canvas'.[1] Another 'X' was laid onto the landscape at El Mirage Dry Lake out of asphalt primer (covering an area 610 metres square), entitled *Relocated Burial Ground* (1978) (The 'X' shape, as Lucy Lippard noted, was a favourite motif with male land artists: Chris Burden, Richard Long and Robert Smithson also created 'Xs').[2]

Many of Oppenheim's artworks are conceptual pieces in the great tradition of

Sixties Conceptualism. That is, many are works made to be exhibited in galleries, on walls. They comprise photographs, drawings and maps, with Oppenheim's type-written captions and explanations: *Three Downward Blows* (1977), *Salt Flat* (1969), *Boundary Split* (1968), and *Negative Board* (1968) (maps were central to Oppenheim's art).

Many of Oppenheim's land artworks also existed as these framed photo-text-sketch-map works. One of Oppenheim's specialities was to impose humanmade geometries, symbols and ideas onto the landscape: to transpose map contours, for instance, or the rings of a tree trunk onto snow (in *Annual Rings*), or the International Date Line in snow (*Time Pocket*). Robert Smithson remarked that Oppenheim was 'transforming a terrestrial site into a map'.3 Generally, Oppenheim tended to enlarge symbols or ideas or images, and recreate them on a colossal scale in the landscape.

In *Time Pocket* (1968) Oppenheim 'drew' the International Date Line with a diesel-powered skidder in snow in Maine. In *Boundary Split* (1968) Oppenheim carved lines perpendicular to the Time Boundary between Canada and the US. *Star Skid* (1977) was Oppenheim's proposal for a series of concrete and glass stars that would look from the air as if they had landed on Earth and skidded to a halt.

In *Salt Flat* (1969) Oppenheim created a 'salt flat' (a favourite place for land artists to make work in the US) in New York City, with a thousand pounds of salt. The rectangle of salt was recreated in the sea in the Bahamas, and in the Salt Lake Desert. In *Directed Harvest* (1969) Oppenheim carved up fields of crops. Oppenheim set off underground explosions in *Three Downward Blows (Knuckle Marks)* in Montana in 1977.

In *Ground Mutations – Shoe Prints* (1969) Oppenheim created shoe print works over the course of three Winter months (by wearing shoes with a 1/4 inch groove cut in the sole and heel): 'I was connecting the patterns of thousands of individuals... My thoughts were filled with marching diagrams'. The use of shoes and prints links with Andy Goldsworthy's direct use of the body and Richard Long's walks.

Speaking in 1970, Oppenheim opined that art now 'more concerned with the location of material and with speculation' (i.e., locations or ideas). Now, art was meant to be visited (location) or 'abstracted from a photograph' (conceptualized).4 Oppenheim moved towards a kind of art that would be discovered or visited by the spectator, rather than 'made' in the old, traditional manner (this was part of the 'dematerialization' of the art object in Sixties art). Oppenheim moved away from the idea of the special, unique art object, towards found objects, and utilizing existing sites. Oppenheim was replacing objects with locations.

The *Site Markers* series (1967) comprised posts in locations which were documented with texts, maps and photos. The maps and photos explained where the posts were situated, so that the location, rather than the object, became the centre of the piece. As Oppenheim pointed out, the *Site Markers* works were intended to be about the sites themselves, rather than the manipulation of replication of an object: 'beginning with the site-markers started in a sense a journey: art is travel'.5

One of Oppenheim's more Conceptual pieces (*Sound Enclosed Land Area*, 1969) comprised four tape recorders buried in cages in Paris enclosing an area 500 by 800 metres. Each machine played a tape loop which had a voice repeating its position (North, South, East or West). *Contour Lines Scribed in Swamp Grass* (1968) transposed contour lines on a map in two different locations (a swamp and a mountain). The use of aluminium filings poured onto grass in concentric circles recalled Long's stone circles.

The contours of Oppenheim's own thumbprints were the basis for *Identity Stretch* (1970-75), where a truck sprayed white paint on the ground, using the thumbprint (which Oppenheim had elongated) as a guide, within a grid. In 1970 Oppenheim created a performance piece, entitled *Parallel Stress*, made between a collapsed concrete pier and a wall at Manhattan and Brooklyn bridges. Oppenheim stretched his body between the wall and the pier, echoing the New York bridges nearby. The same body position was recreated at an abandoned sump in Long Island.

Like many land artists, Oppenheim produced a maze (in 1970). But Oppenheim's *Maze* was just a little different: it was the design of a maze used in a scientific laboratory for rats transposed onto a large field, with cows as the rats, lured around the maze by the promise of food.

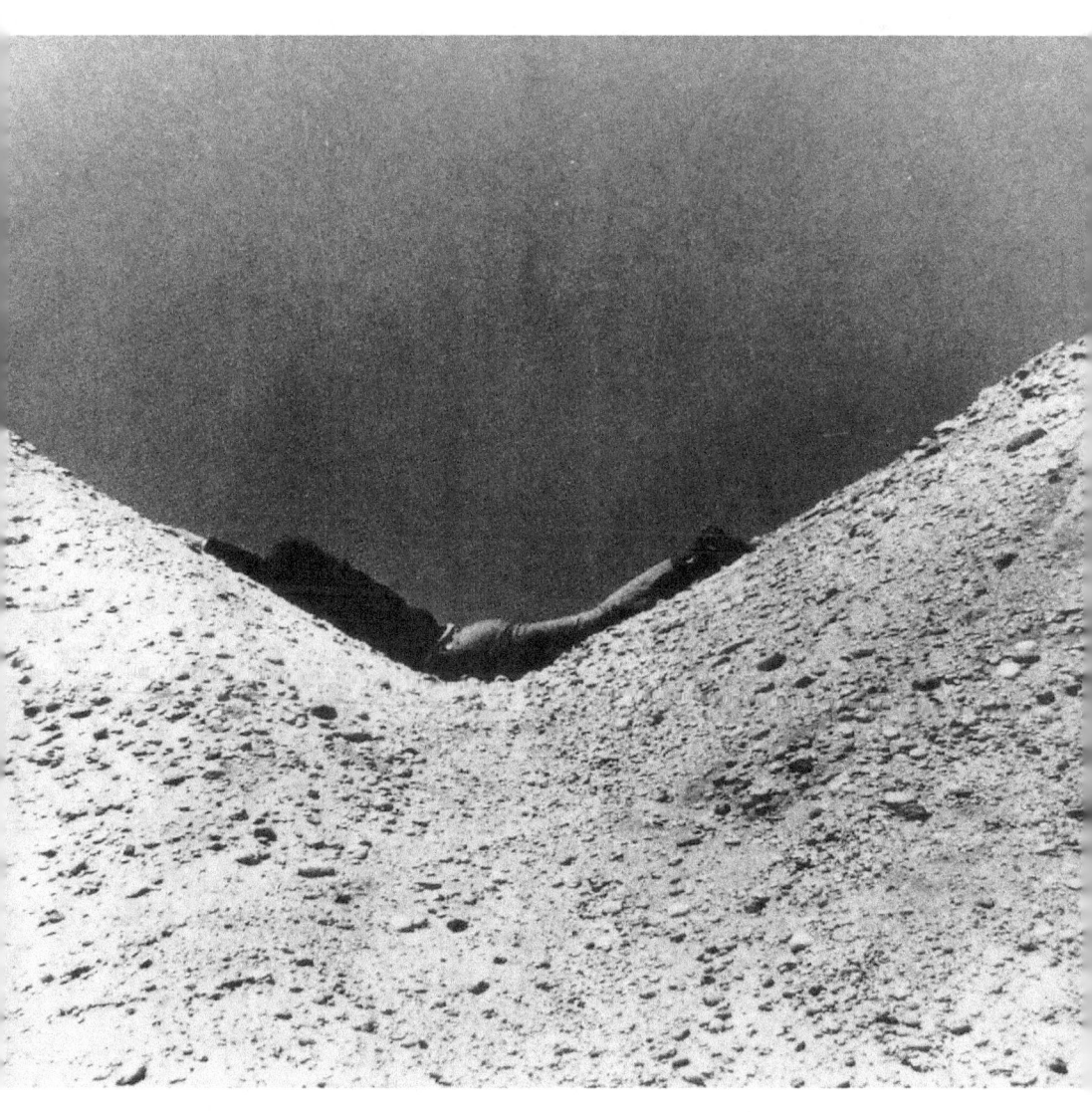

Dennis Oppenheim, Parallel Stress, 1970

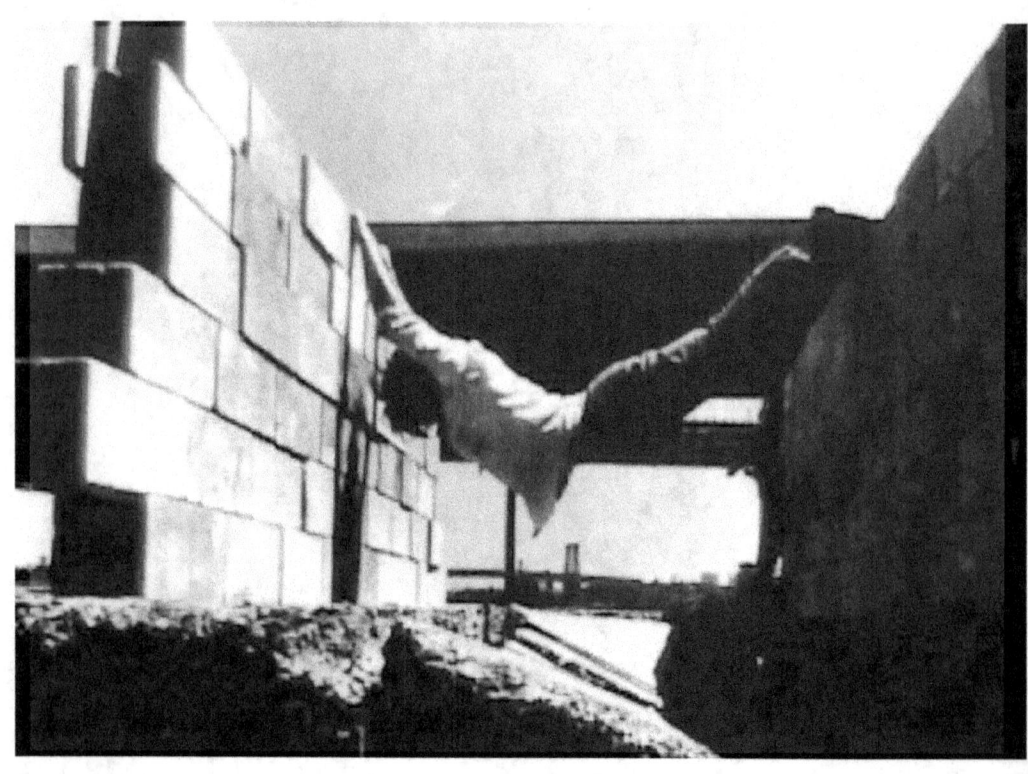

Dennis Oppenheim, Parallel Stress, 1970

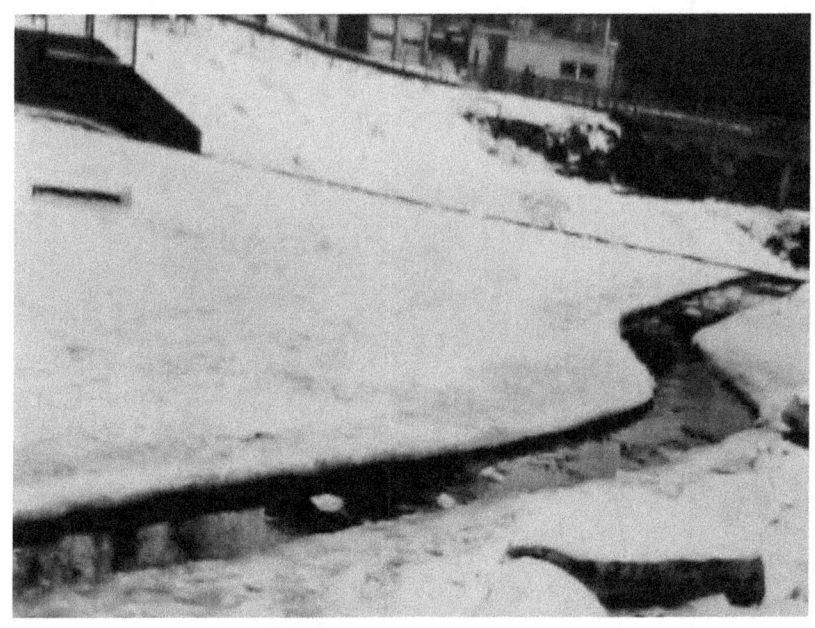

Dennis Oppenheim, Branded Mountain, Accumulation Cut,
1969, Cornell University

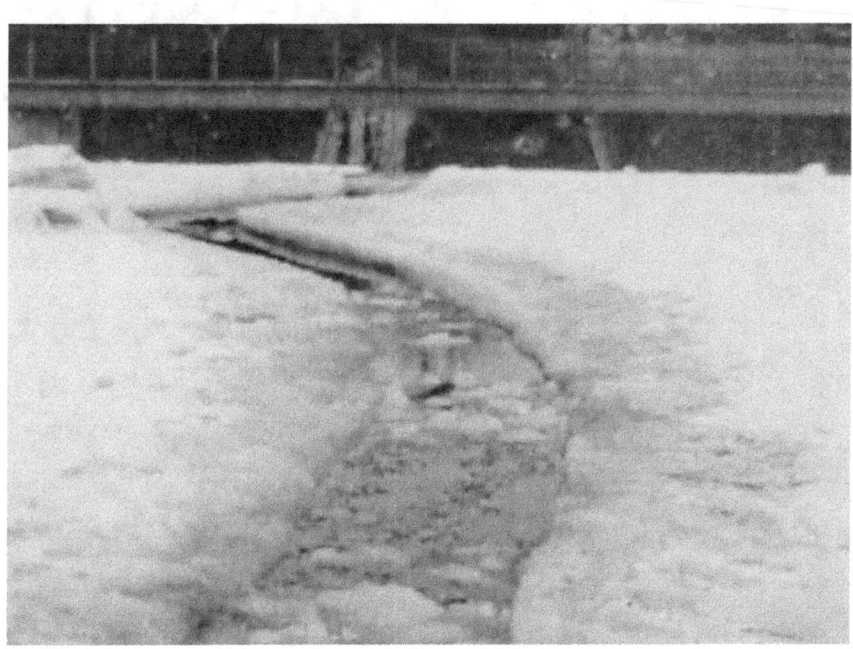

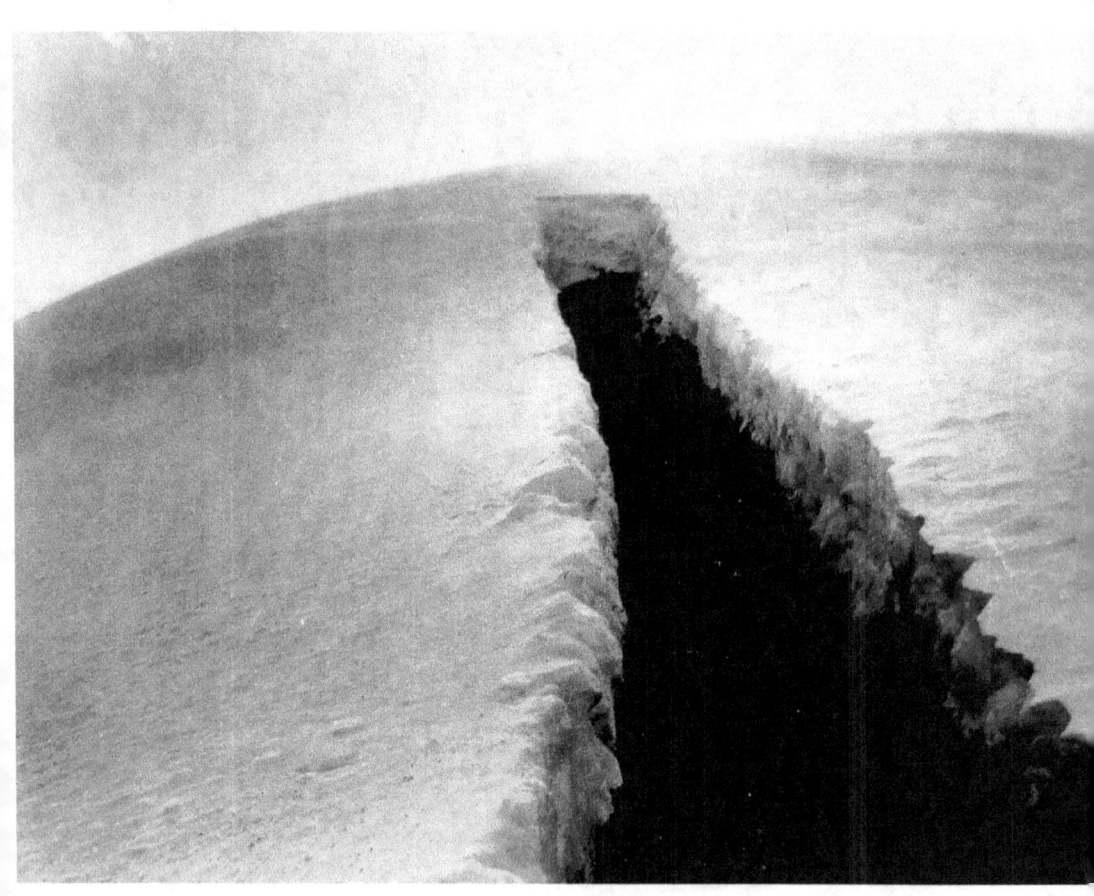

Dennis Oppenheim, Negative Board, 1968

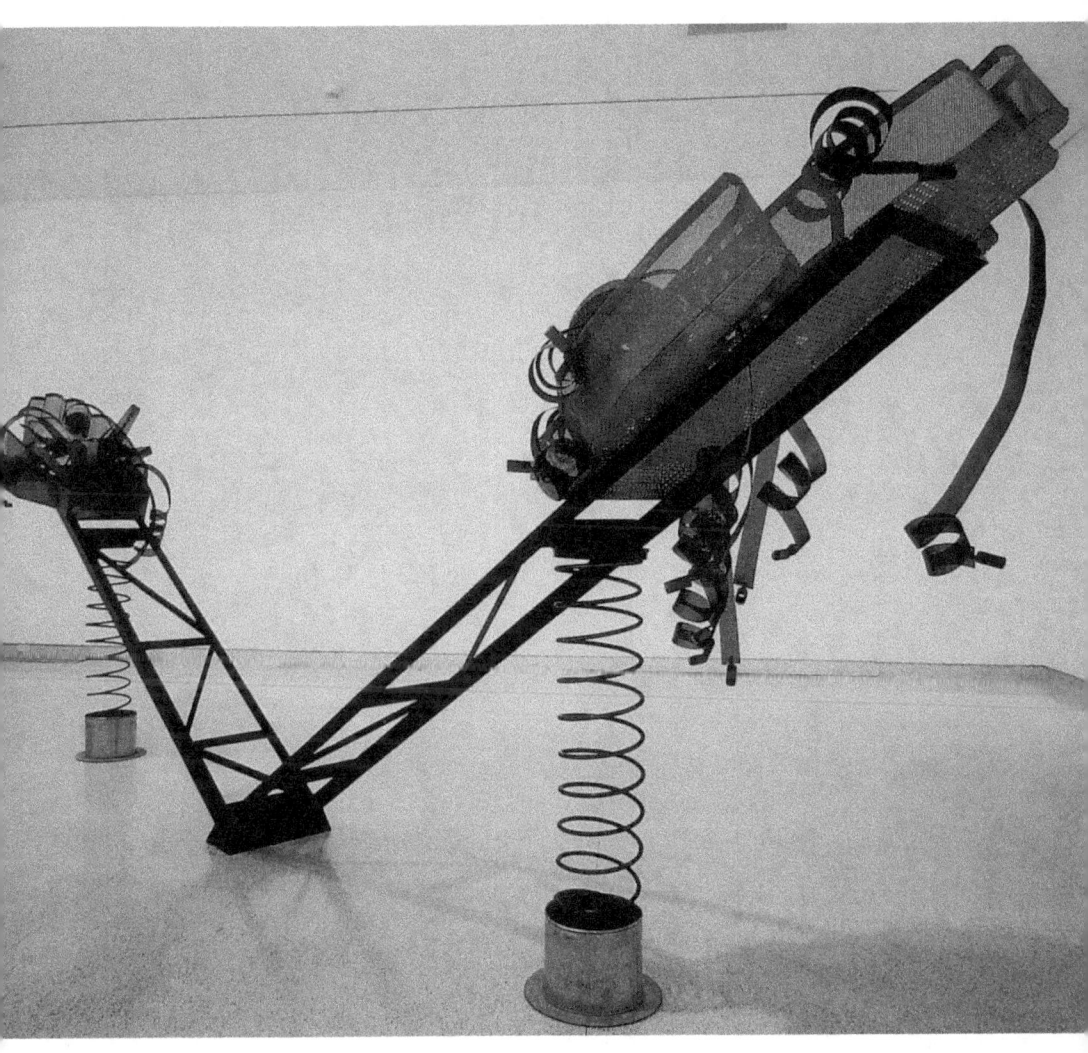

Dennis Oppeneheim, Power Fingers, 1983

10

Robert Morris

Robert Morris (b. 1931) was one of the most eloquent theorists of Sixties, Minimal and Postminimal sculpture (along with Donald Judd and Carl Andre). Robert Morris had, like Donald Judd, begun by working in painting, but moved on to sculpture. Morris studied at Kansas City Art Institute, California School of Fine Arts and Hunter College, New York. In San Francisco in 1961 he worked with the dancer Anna Halprin. He was part of the Fluxus school, alongside Yoko Ono, Simone Forte, Walter de Maria and Henry Flynt.

Morris wrote many artistic statements, the most famous probably being the articles published in *Artforum* entitled "Notes on Sculpture". For Morris, one of the things that was new about 1960s sculpture was the object's relationship with the viewer. Before then, Morris argued, the viewer related to the object as something separate; the new æsthetic put the viewer into the same space as the object. 'One is more aware than before that he himself is establishing relationships as he apprehends the object from various positions and under varying conditions of light and spatial context.'[1] This is a crucial concept in Minimal art, which is nearly always viewed in an object-viewer continuous space.

Robert Morris's concept of 'objecthood' was central to his notion of sculpture. 'Morris wants to achieve presence through objecthood, which requires a certain largeness of scale, rather than through size alone' wrote Michael Fried (1967). Just as important as the object itself was the sense of space around it, the spatial context in which it was displayed. Robert Morris wanted to emphasize that 'things are in a space with oneself', rather than the notion that 'one is in a space surrounded by things' (ib., 127). The whole context of the object in its space ('the entire situation') was important to Morris's notion of the new sculpture. One might say the new, 1960s sculpture, like land art, was about the 'thing in itself', a notion borrowed from Existentialism, but also about the 'thing in its space'. Although Robert Morris denied being an 'environmental' artist, the context was important to his art.[2] For one critic, Morris's sculpture 'redirect[s] the entire environmental experience'.[3] Referring to Donald Judd's "Specific Objects" article, Morris said he did not separate the two, he did not think that something must be either an object or an environment.[4] As he moved towards Postminimalism, Morris advocated doing away with a figure-ground relationship; instead, heterogeneous 'stuff' should be used, an 'accumulation of things or stuff'.[5]

In 1975 Robert Morris wrote "Aligned with Nazca", an article in one of the key magazines of the period (*Artforum*), which related earthwork art with ancient art such as the Nazca lines. However, such connections with ancient art had already been made by artists and critics of land art.

Among Robert Morris's stranger concepts was his 'mobile' mausoleum: in an aluminium tunnel 3 miles long a coffin made from iron and suspended from pulleys would be moved intermittently. An attendant with a magnet would shift the coffin from above. By the entrance to the tube would be swooning maidens in marble, carved in the style of Canova.6 'If something is still capable of moving, is it dead?' Morris wondered.7

Morris produced some works of a highly 'ephemeral' nature, such as his 'steam piece' (*Untitled*, 1968-69), which was made out of doors on a patch of grass. How the work turned out was dependent upon physicalities such as humidity, air pressure, wind speed and direction, and temperature. Clouds of steam drifted over the grass.

British artist Rose Finn-Kelcey has produced a steam work: her *Untitled* (1992, London) comprised of water placed on a sheet metal base, with an extractor hood hung above it. In between the two was a cloud of steam, made dramatic by the lighting. Some of Hans Haacke's most intriguing works were with ephemeral natural events such as steam, ice, condensation, fog and flooding. Peter Hutchinson made a cloud piece (*Dissolving Clouds*, 1970) using Hatha yoga meditation techniques, trying to dissolve clouds through thought. The work consisted of a sequence of 6 photographs of clouds. Alice Aycock also made a *Cloud Piece* (1971), photographs of cumulus clouds which melted after a few minutes.

In *Pace and Progress*, Robert Morris produced a work by walking a horse back and forth over a piece of grass until a path had been worn. The action of walking the horse rubbed down the grass. One of Morris's largest commissions was the *Grand Rapids Project*, in Michigan (1973-74), consisting of huge ramps leading up to a plateau. Another large Morris sitework was created in King County, Washington (1979), a series of oval terraces recalling Iron Age hillforts.

Morris's later works included the felt sculptures, where an element of randomness and chance dictated how the felt strips would hang. Each installation would be different. Some of the later felt pieces used thick felt (such as in *Untitled 1996* [collection: the artist]). Another work entitled *Untitled 1996* (collection: the artist) was modelled, the felt being draped symmetrically over a pole. *Untitled 1996* recalled a human figure.8

Morris's wall drawings were made by the artist covering his hands with graphite and dabbing them on the wall blindfolded. The large areas of smeared graphite (in *Blind Time IV*, 1991, for example) recall Richard Long's mud wall drawings. The links between Morris and other land artists would include an emphasis on spontaneity, materiality, chance, randomness, change and ephemerality.

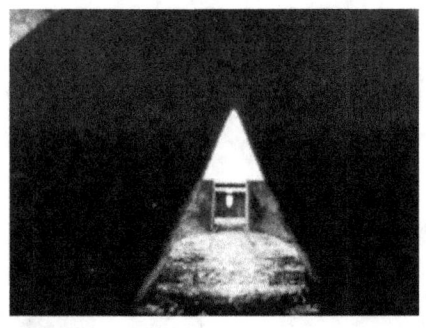

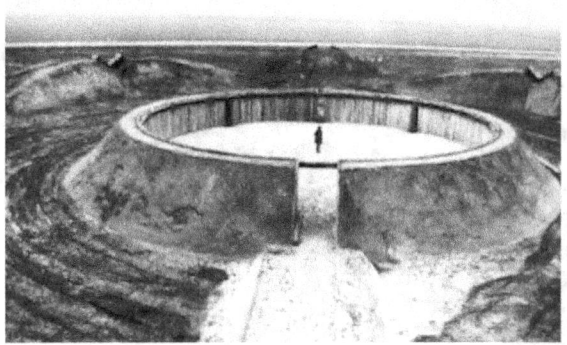

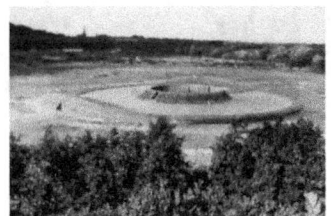

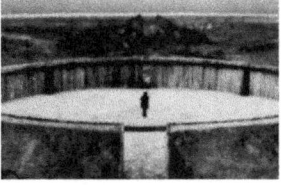

Robert Morris, Observatory

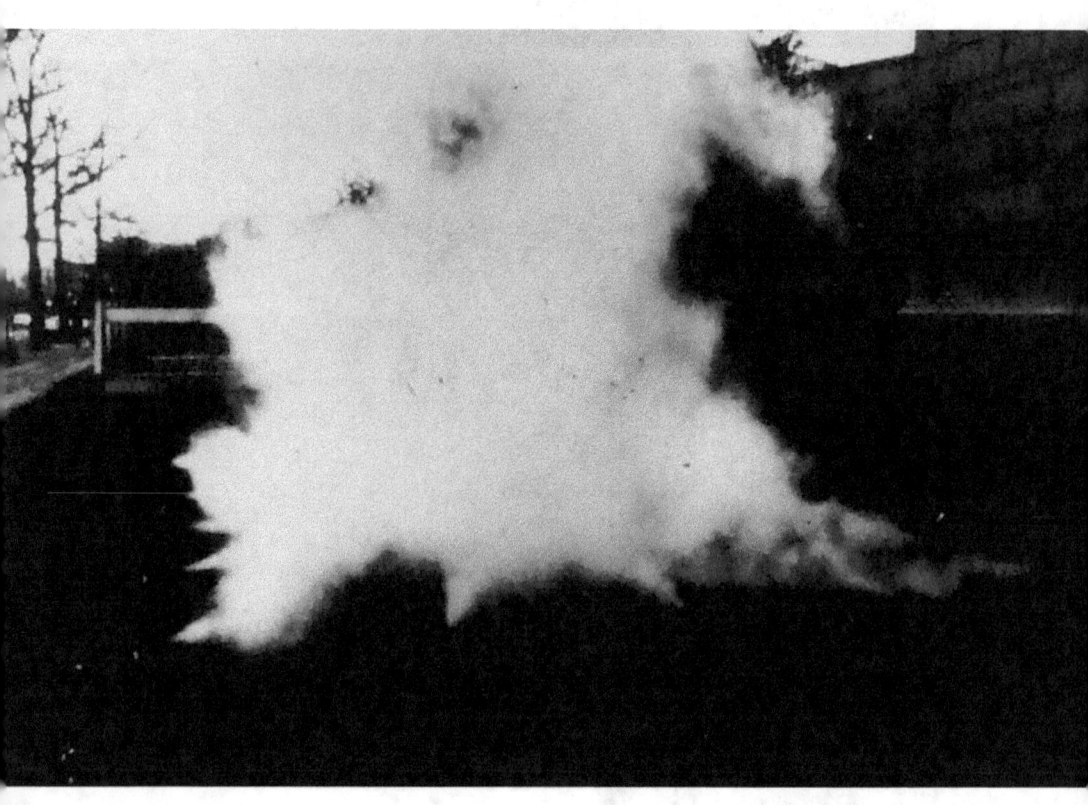

Robert Morris, Steam Piece, 1969

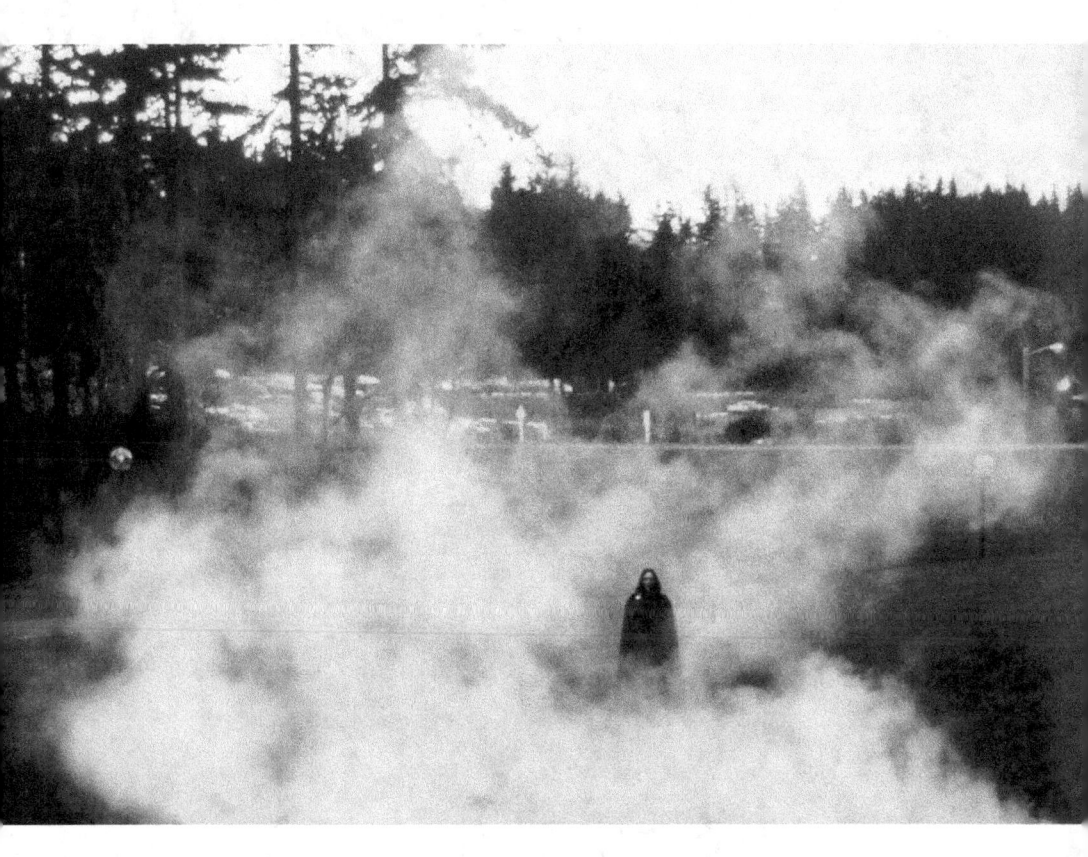

Robert Morris, Untitled (Steam Piece), 1968-69

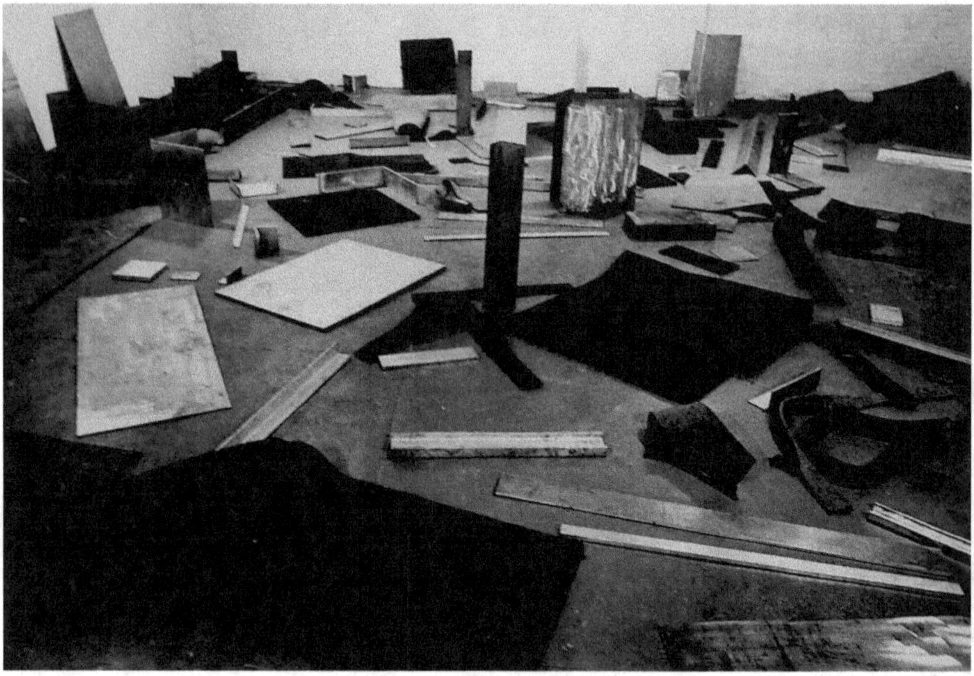

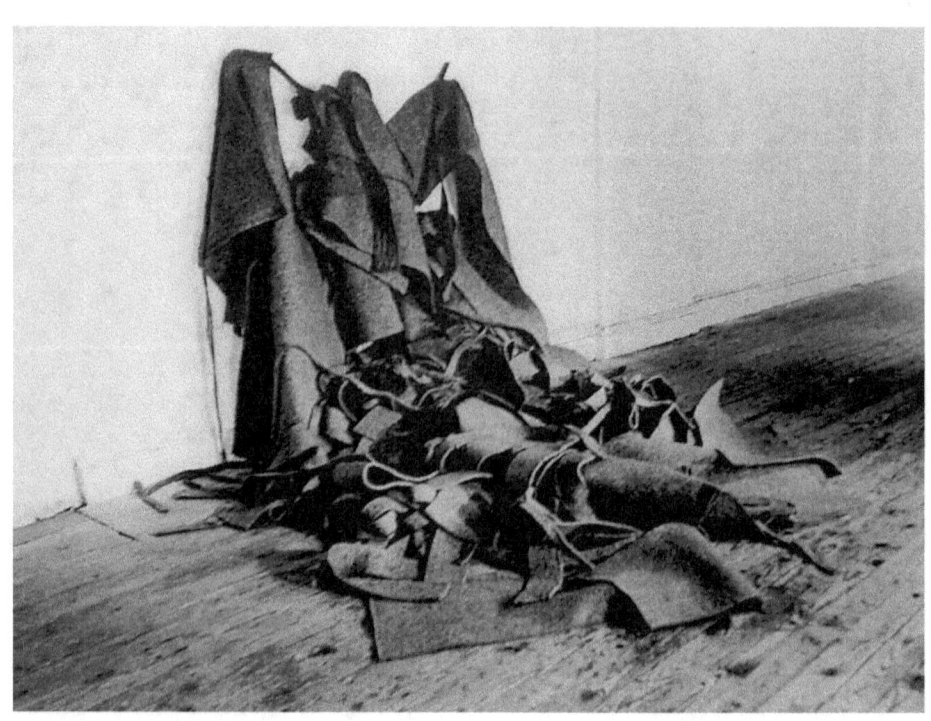

Robert Morris, felt works

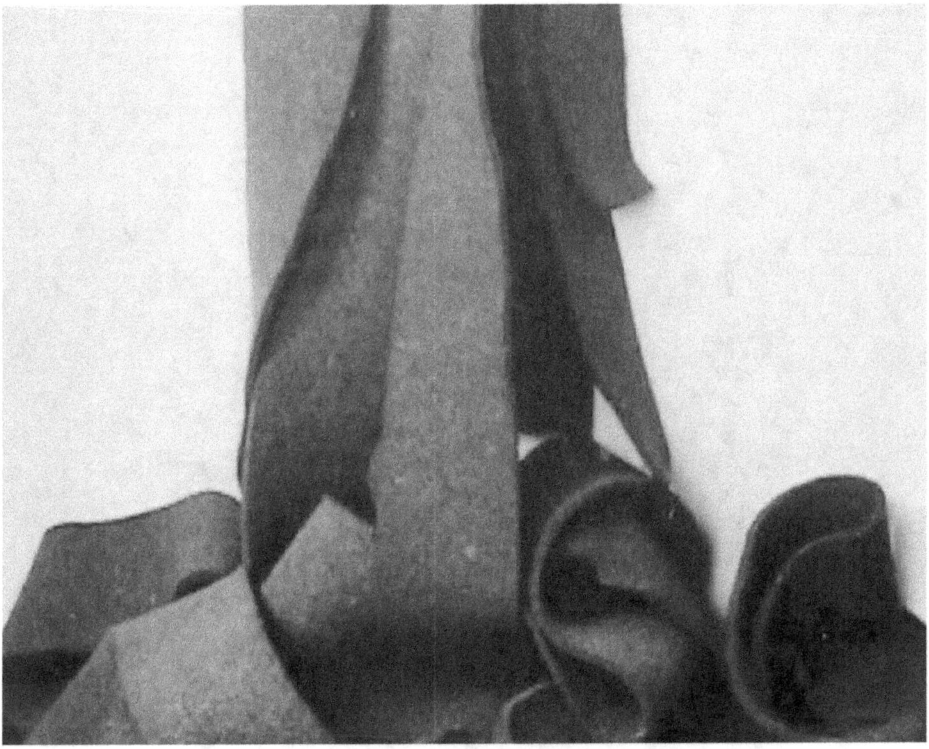

Robert Morris, felt works

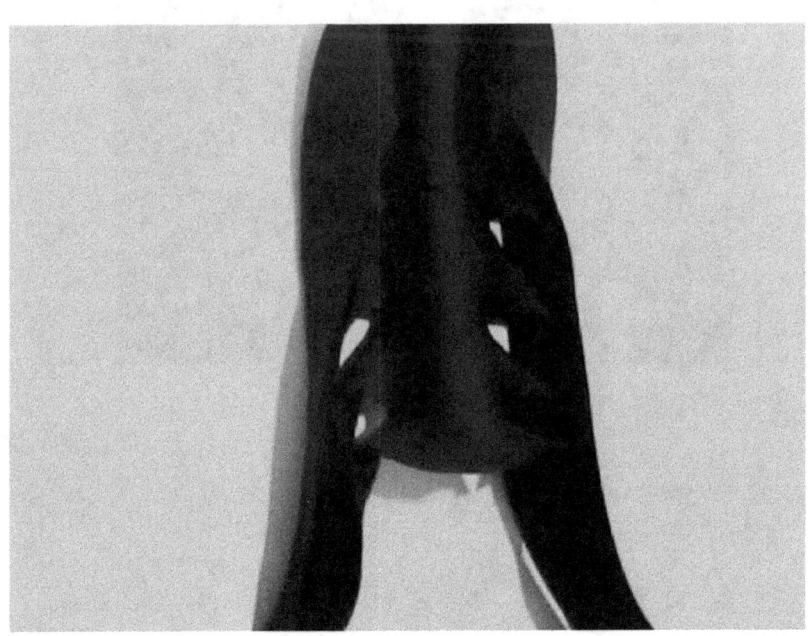

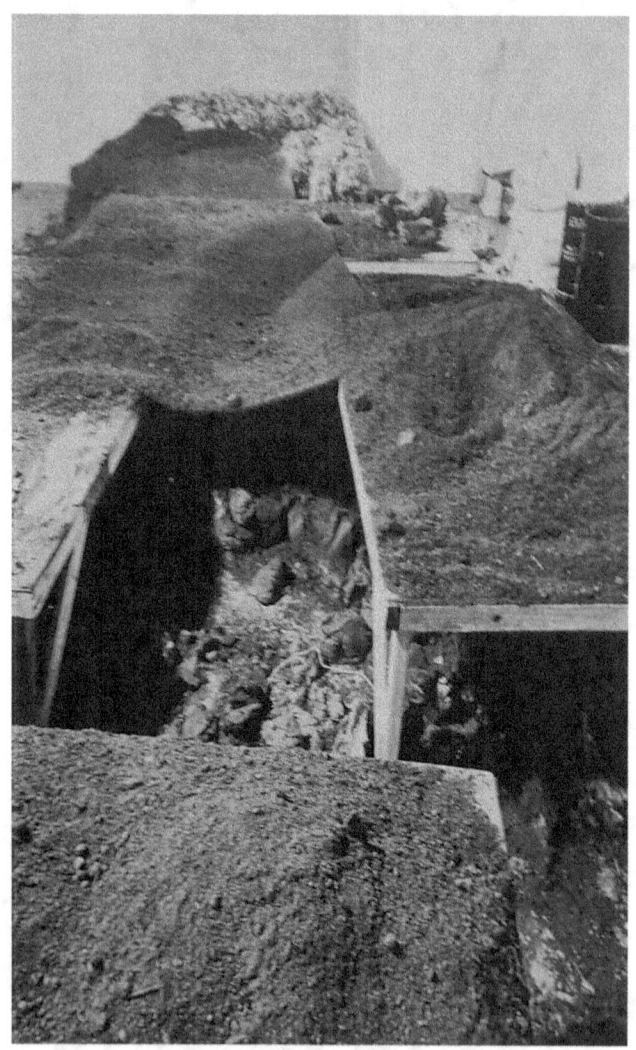

Robert Morris, installation

11

Nancy Holt

Nancy Holt (b. 1938) married the key land artist, Robert Smithson, in 1963. She worked with him on his non-site projects, including the famous *Spiral Jetty* and *Amarillo Ramp.* Nancy Holt's art, with its large, heavy landscaping gestures (such as her *Dark Star Park*), is comparable with the male land artists. The globes and pools of water, though, are traditionally seen as 'feminine' volumes, but here given a new, monumental turn. Holt's art concerns the movements of the heavens. Her sculptures focus the viewer on the motions of the earth, moon, sun and stars. Holt's art is concerned with the notion of time, in particular with geological time, the relation between time and the Earth. Holt was impressed by the desert when she visited it in the late 1960s with Smithson and Michael Heizer.

> Time is not just a mental concept or a mathematical abstraction in the desert [Holt wrote]. The rocks in the distance are ageless; they have been deposited in layers over hundreds of thousands of years. Time takes on a physical presence.[1]

Nancy Holt has said she is interested in 'conjuring up a sense of time that is longer than the built-in obsolescence we have all around us.' Hence she uses long-lasting materials, such as steel and rocks. Using enduring materials does not stem from a sense of vanity, of wanting one's works to last forever, but rather because Holt wants to create a sense of time that extends beyond the human lifespan.[2]

While working on Smithson's enormous *Amarillo Ramp* after his death in a plane crash, Holt developed the idea for the gigantic *Sun Tunnels*, 18 foot long pipes that were 9 feet high with many holes punched in the side, to let light in.[3] She searched for a suitable site – a desert floor surrounded by low hills. The site she chose (and bought) was in the Great Basin Desert of Utah.

Sun Tunnels was finished in 1976, with holes in the side of each concrete tube 7, 8, 9 and 10 inches diameter. The holes corresponded with star constellations (Capricorn, Draco, Columba and Perseus), as with *Hydra's Head*. During the day the sun creates points of light on the bottom of the tunnels that move. The moon also shines through the holes by night. *Sun Tunnels* links together the movements of celestial objects and the viewer on the planet. Holt said she had the idea for *Sun Tunnels* while being out in the desert and watching the sun rising and setting. The flat desert area evoked 'a sense of being on this planet, rotating in space, in universal time' (1977). It is a cosmological piece of land art, something of an observatory, like the Bronze Age stone circles of Europe. 'I wanted to bring the vast space of desert back to human scale' (1977). The astronomical observatory has been an enduring theme in land art. Robert Morris, Michael Dan Archer, Julia Barton and Andy Goldsworthy have also made viewing sites.

Nancy Holt's *Hydra's Head* (1975) also concerned the relation between the heavens and earth. Next to the Niagara River at Art Park, Lewiston, New York, Holt sank 6 concrete tubes into the soil. Each three foot pipe was filled with water, so they formed circular mirrors flush with the ground. Again, Holt based the position of the concrete pits on a constellation (Hydra). *Hydra's Head* combined the presence and noise of the rushing Niagara River with the reflections of the sky, stars and moon. Holt's concrete pipe sculptures use the prime symbol of change and all things cosmic, the circle. The *Sun Tunnels* are like enormous telescopes or astrolabes, while *Hydra's Head* evokes six fallen stars, the circles of water reflecting the sky and stars.

Holt's romantic evocations of stellar, cosmological themes in concrete and soil flourished again with *Stone Enclosure: Rock Rings* (1977-78), constructed at Western Washington University Bellingham. Holt's *Stone Enclosure* directly recalled, even emulated, prehistoric stone circles, in particular Stonehenge. Holt used ancient schist rocks, between 200 and 230 million years old (known as brown mountain stone) to construct two concentric rings 10 feet high. In each wall of stone Holt made 4 arches, each 8 feet high, and 12 'portholes'. It was not a large stone ring, in terms of diameter (outer diameter was 40 feet), but being ten feet high it was much taller than most Bronze Age stone circles. The arches and holes provided views to the cardinal points, and to NE, SW, EW, NW-SE.

Holt's *Stone Enclosure* makes the connections with ancient astronomy and stone circle building explicit, not slyly implied, as in much of land art. Holt is clear that she is dealing with the ancient astronomical realities of weather, seasons, cycles, stars and time.

Another work, *30 Below* (1980), a tower with arches facing the points of the compass, was positioned around the North Star. The still point in the heavens, the Pole Star, was also one of the keys to *Stone Enclosure*, which, Holt said, related to a true North, a dead centre.[4] *Annual Ring* (1981) was an 'open hemi-dome' of steel bars, 30 feet in diameter and 15 feet high, constructed in Saginaw, Michigan. Again, Holt built the dome to highlight celestial events: the sun at the Summer solstice, the equinoxes, and the North Star.

One of Holt's biggest projects was the *Sky Mound*, begun in the late 1980s (the first phase cost $11 million). Situated in amongst Amtrack and NJ Transit train tracks, highways, bridges, the Pulaski Skyway, the New Jersey turnpike, and metropolitan

New Jersey and New York, with views over Newark and Manhattan, *Sky Mound* was a converted landfill which Holt turned into an observatory to mark solstices, equinoxes, and the stars Vega and Sirius.

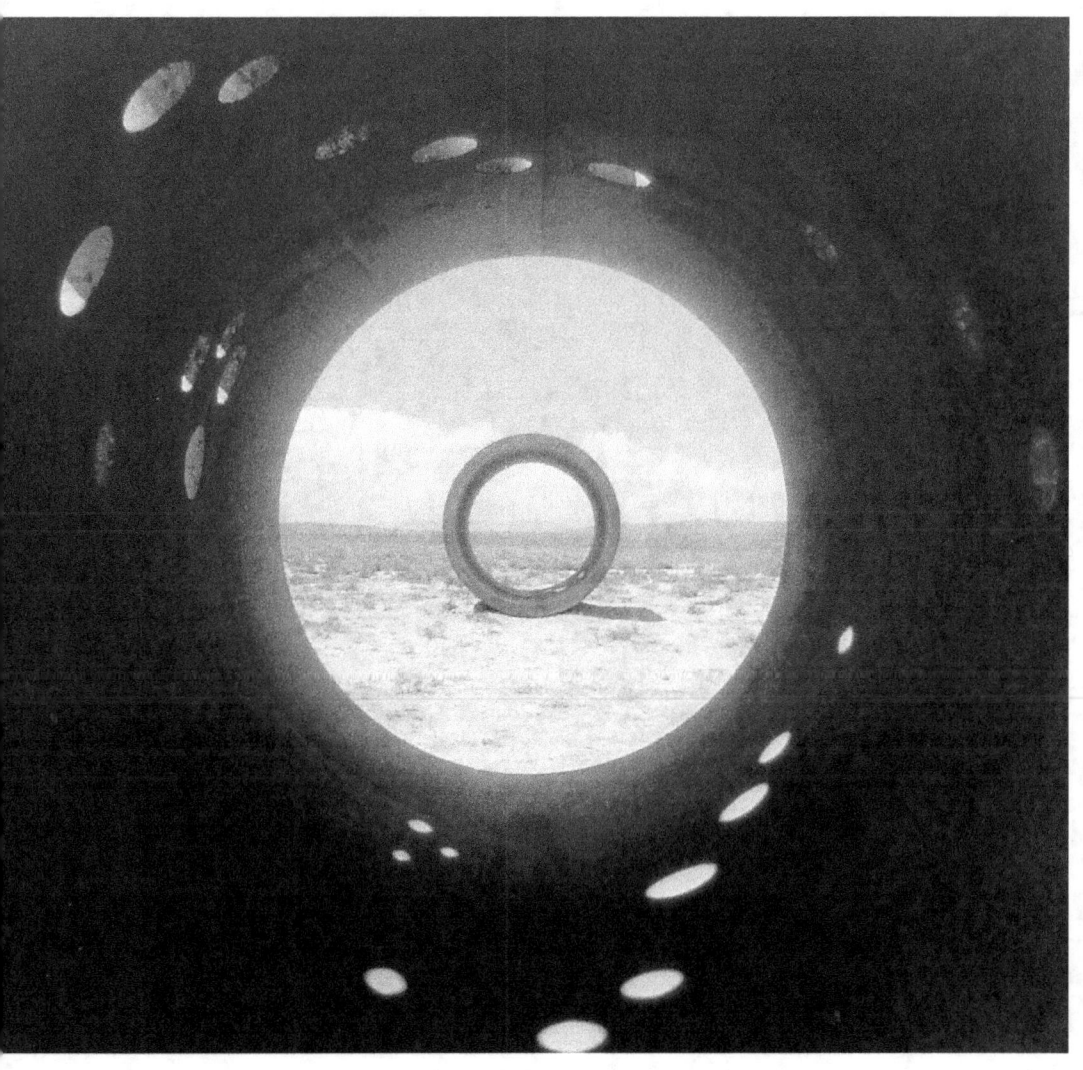

Nancy Holt, Sun Tunnels, 1973-76

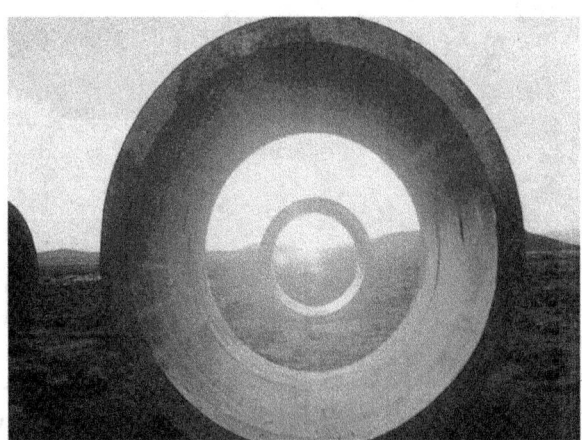

Nancy Holt, Sun Tunnels, 1976

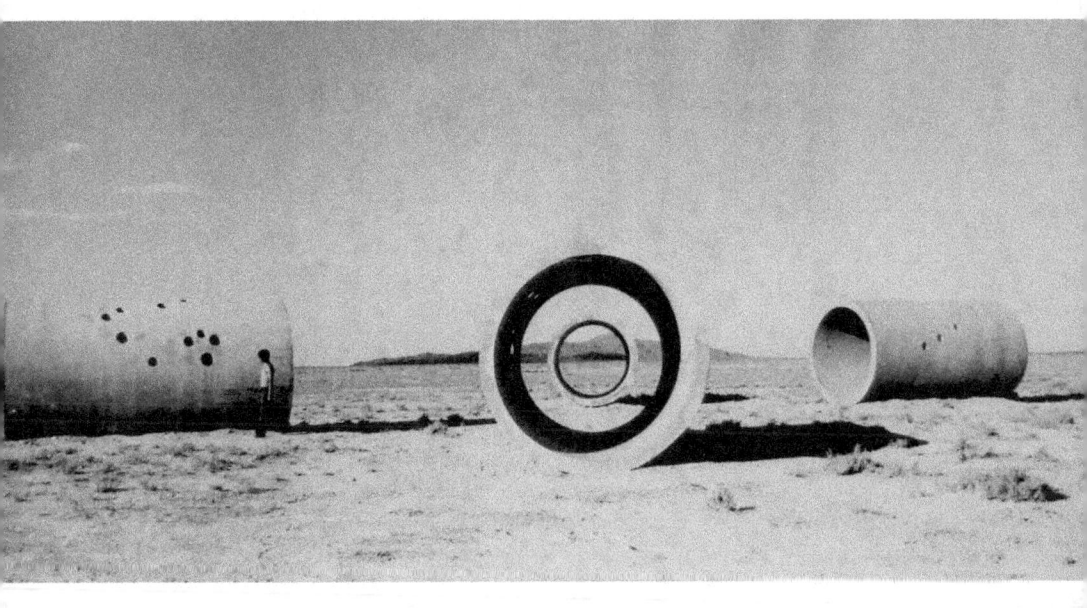

Nancy Holt, Sun Tunnels, 1976

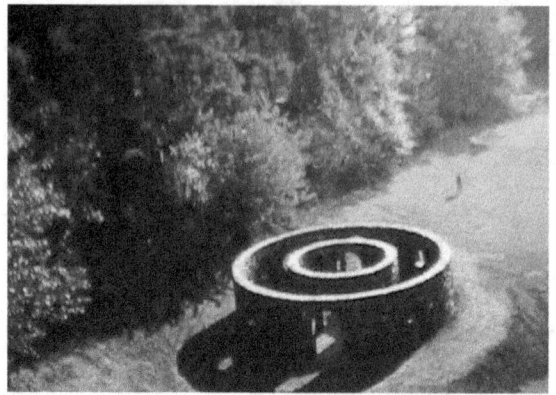

Nancy Holt, Stone Enclosure - Rock Rings, 1977-78

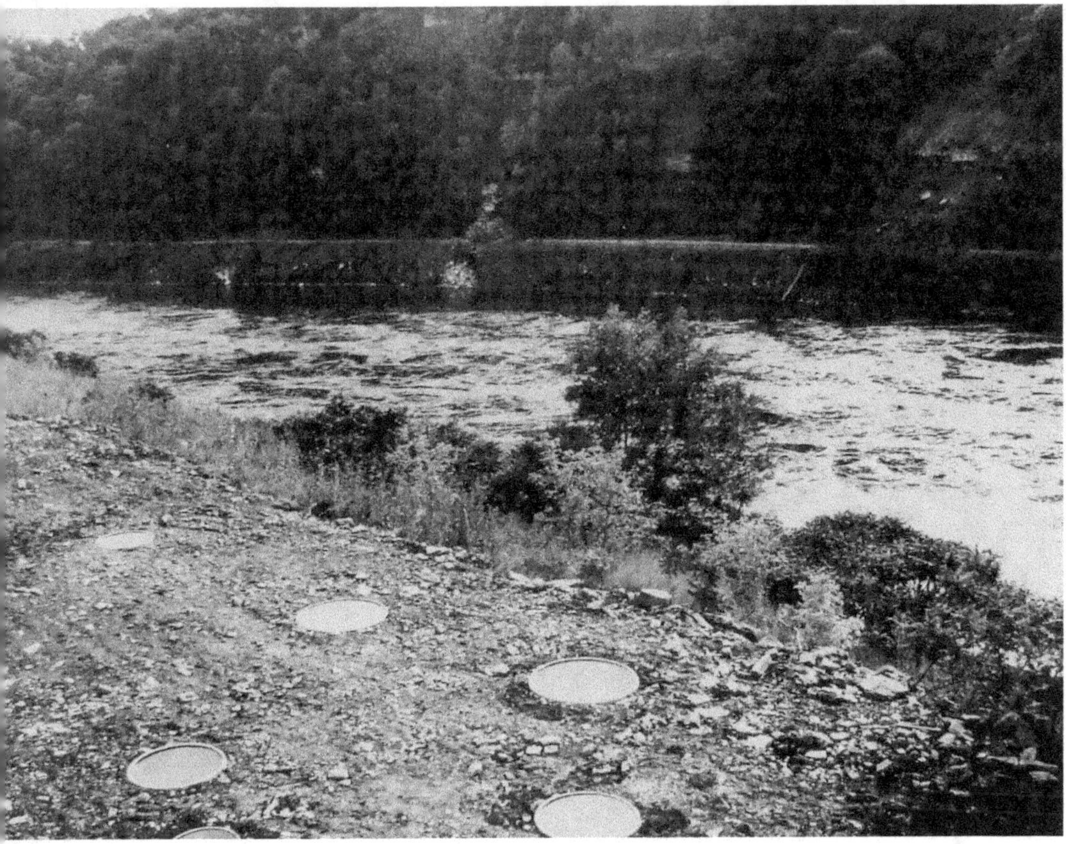

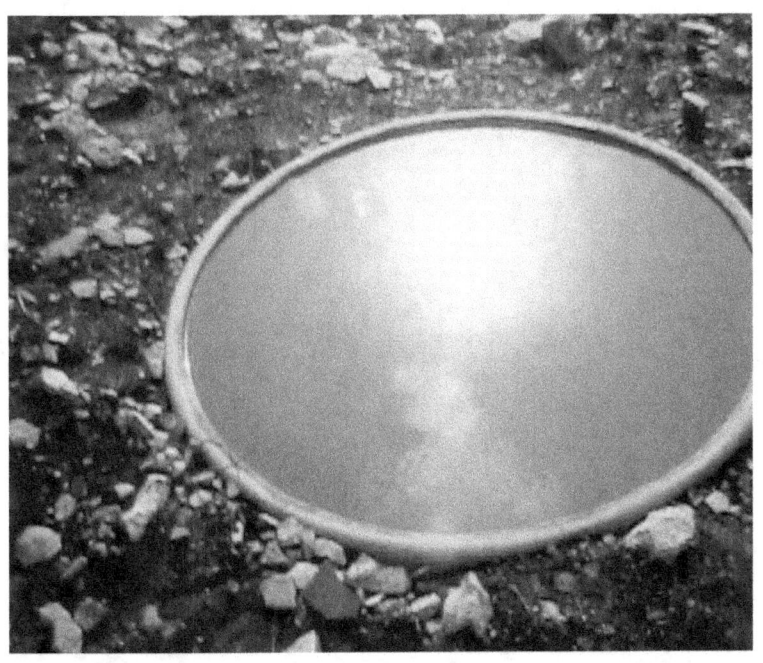

Nancy Holt, Hydra's Head, 1975

12

Alice Aycock

Alice Aycock's (b. 1946) environmental artworks are much more ambiguous and deliberately problematic than Nancy Holt's or Carl Andre's works. Many of Alice Aycock's land sculptures involve underground passages and spaces. In 1972 she constructed a series of underground spaces in *Low Building Made with Dirt Roof (For Mary)* in Pennsylvania. The spectator entered the 20 by 12 feet work through a doorway thirty inches high. The work was experienced by crawling through it. Aycock's intention was to evoke an experience of claustrophia, of being in a cellar. Aycock's works had titles such as *The Machine That Makes the World* (1979), *A Theory of Universal Causality* (1983) and *How to Catch and Manufacture Ghosts* (1979) – Aycock is brilliant with titles.

Alice Aycock's sculpture and land art explored the rationality of machines and technology and irrationality of ghosts and magic.[1] Aycock's 1972 *Maze* had direct parallels with the observatories and labyrinths of Robert Morris, Nancy Holt, Julia Barton and Michael Dan Archer. *Maze* consists of 5 concentric wooden rings, each six feet high, forming a 12-sided labyrinth. Essentially it is a fence maze, the kind that can be seen at theme parks and country houses. However, Aycock's New Kingston, Pennsylvania *Maze* is intended to be a labyrinth of the ancient type, a structure in which one is meant to get lost. Aycock stated that she wanted 'to create a moment of absolute panic – when the only thing that mattered was to get out.'[2]

Aycock's intentions, then, are quite different from, say, Nancy Holt's, who wishes to infuse a sense of celestial contemplation, or James Turrell's, who was after light and revelation. Aycock wants viewers to be confused, even frightened, by her underground passages and mazes. Aycock did not wish the viewer to be able to get out of her labyrinth easily (it was partially based on a circular Egyptian labyrinth (designed as a prison), the Zulu kraal and the Amerindian stockade. Aycock also cited a circular Greek temple at Epidarus, a 'Place of Sacrifice').

Aycock has spoken of the relations between her art and her own childhood dreams and fears. Her works recreate disturbing moments from her childhood, such as when she was trapped in a revolving barrel at an amusement park. Aycock's works deal with such moments of fear, confusion, strangeness and risk. Aycock also remarked that her structures were inspired by visits to the Pyramids in 1970 and the Greek tombs at Mycenae, and fantasies of being buried alive.

Alice Aycock's *A Simple Network of Underground Walls and Tunnels* (1975) was made in a corn field at Far Hills, New Jersey. It consisted of 6 square wells in two rows of three excavated out of a 20 by 50 foot area. Two of the wells had 7 foot ladders that enabled the spectator to climb down and explore the dark connecting tunnels. Some of the wells were capped, others were open. The effect was a series of spaces that recalled 'ominous historical precedents, caves, catacombs, dungeons and beehive tombs', wrote Roberta Smith.3

Aycock's 1974's *Walled-Trench/ Earth Platform/ Center Pit* was a series of three concentric walls made from concrete blocks. A platform of earth was made between the inner two walls: it was possible to jump onto this platform over the outer pit. Only when the spectator is standing on the inner platform does another aspect of *Walled-Trench/ Earth Platform/ Center Pit* become visible: a tunnel which leads into a dark inner chamber.

The fear and fantasy element in Alice Aycock's land and site work found a new level of ambiguity in her 1976 *Circular Building with Narrow Ledge for Walking*. Again, the spectator was invited to explore this artwork physically (and psychologically). *Circular Building with Narrow Ledge for Walking* was a round structure thirteen feet high. Inside the well were three concentric ledges, only 8 inches wide. The wall went 7 feet into the ground, and was 'no more perilous or threatening than a treacherous cliff', the artist said, reassuringly.4 Again, the spectator was invited to investigate the work by climbing a ladder outside the building, then edging her/ his way along the ledges. Indeed, the only way to fully appreciate *Circular Building with Narrow Ledge for Walking,* as with Aycock's other works, was to experience it directly.

Aycock experimented with installing guillotines and motorized blade machines in works such as *The Machine That Makes the World* (1979) and later pieces, such as *A Salutation To the Wonderful Pig of Knowledge (Jelly Fish, Water, Spouter...), There's a Hole In My Bucket, There's a Hole In My Head, There's a Hole In My Dream* (1984).

The structure *From the Series Entitled How To Catch and Manufacture Ghosts* (1980) was a much larger development of the earlier *How to Catch and Manufacture Ghosts.* It was a combination of steel, pipes, spheres and galvanized drums that drew inspiration from early experiments with electricity and magnetism, Marcel Duchamp's *Bachelor Apparatus,* Montgolfier's balloon launch pad, and an oil refinery on the New Jersey turnpike.

A later work, *Tree of Life Fantasy: Synopsis of the Book of Questions Concerning the World Order and/ or the Order of Worlds* (1990-92), drew on influences from Renaissance illustrations of people walking into the sky to Heaven, DNA helices, ancient Indian observatories, and Walter Gropius's designs for theatres.

With Aycock's bewildering and unsettling catacombs and mazes one had to move 'one's body through them', a process which also involved descending back through time and memory.5 Confronted with the subterranean passage or the *Circular Building with Narrow Ledge for Walking* it is soon apparent to the spectator that one is not dealing simply with an art object to be admired for its formal characteristics alone. Aycock wants the spectator to become physically involved in the sculpture: the physical actions of climbing and scrabbling over and through the sculpture trigger an exploration of one's own psychology and memory.6 The physicality of the body as a tool for exploration in Aycock's works soon becomes a pretext or an inspiration for an exploration of personal psychology. Spectators are invited to risk themselves in exploring her works. Her land/ site art offers seductive as well as potentially dangerous spaces. Aycock wants the spectator to enter, but then confronts her/ him with a door that opens onto a wall, or a tiny passage to crawl through, or a ledge over a precipice, or a pit to vault over. Such devices go straight back to childhood, to acts of dare and bravado (such as walking along a high brick wall, egged on by other children).

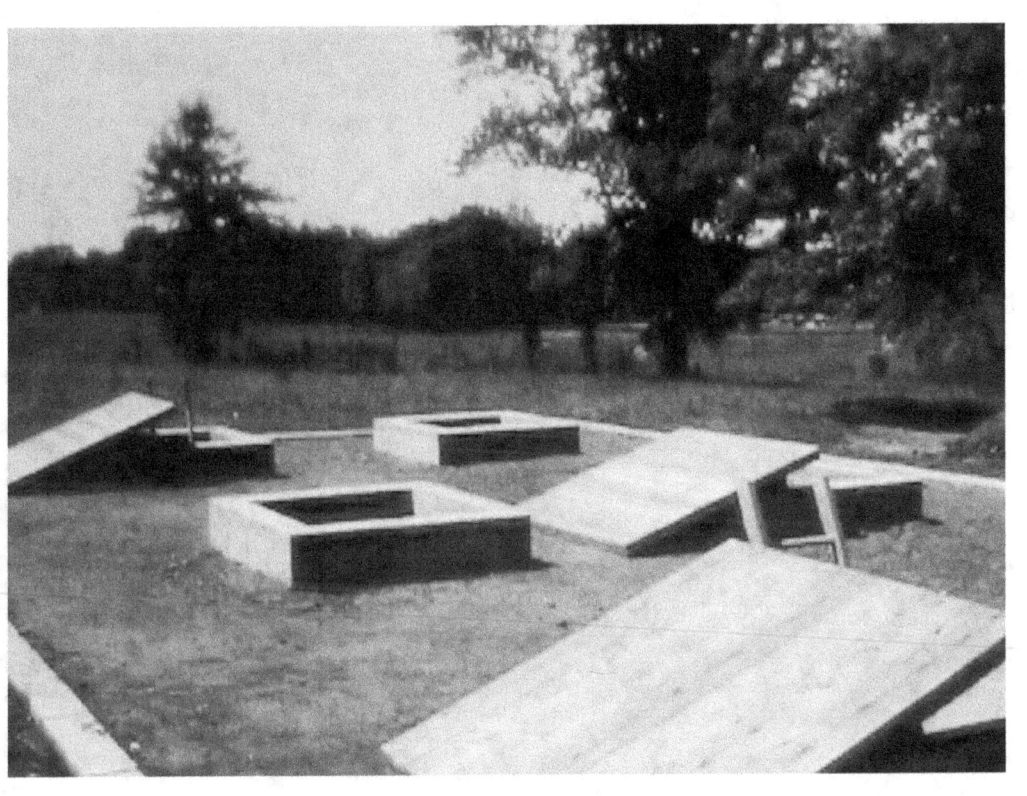

Alice Aycock, A Simple Network of Underground
Walls and Tunnels, 1975

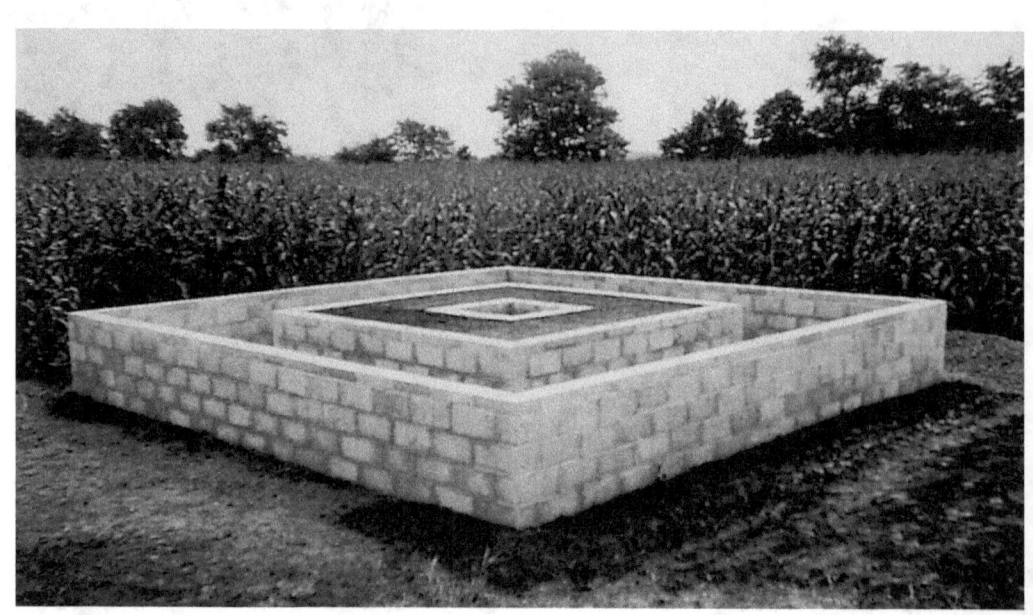

Alice Aycock, Walled Trench

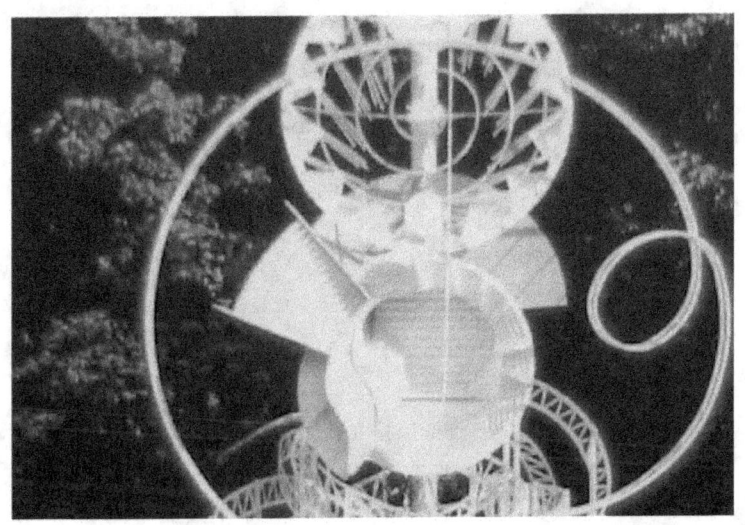

Alice Aycock

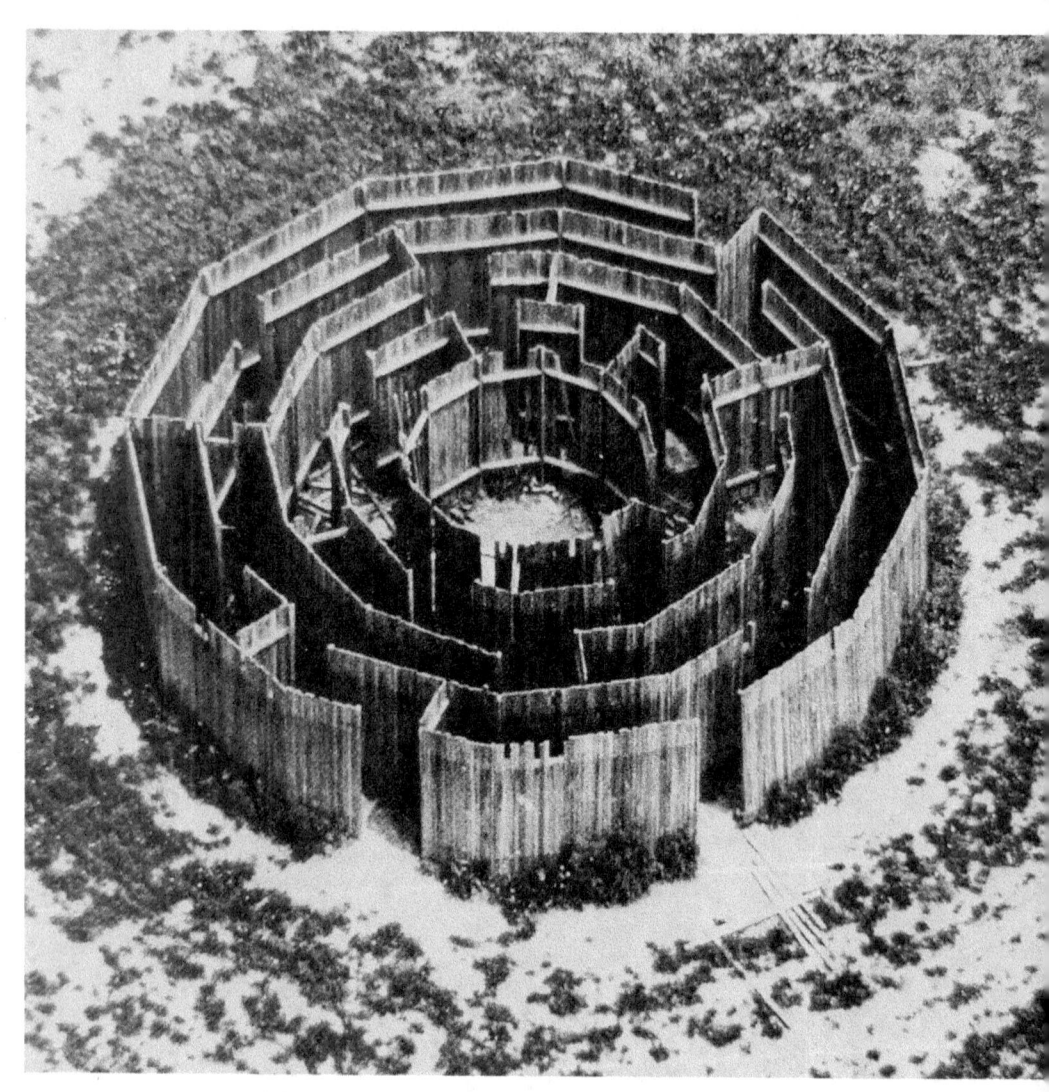

Alive Aycock, Maze, 1972

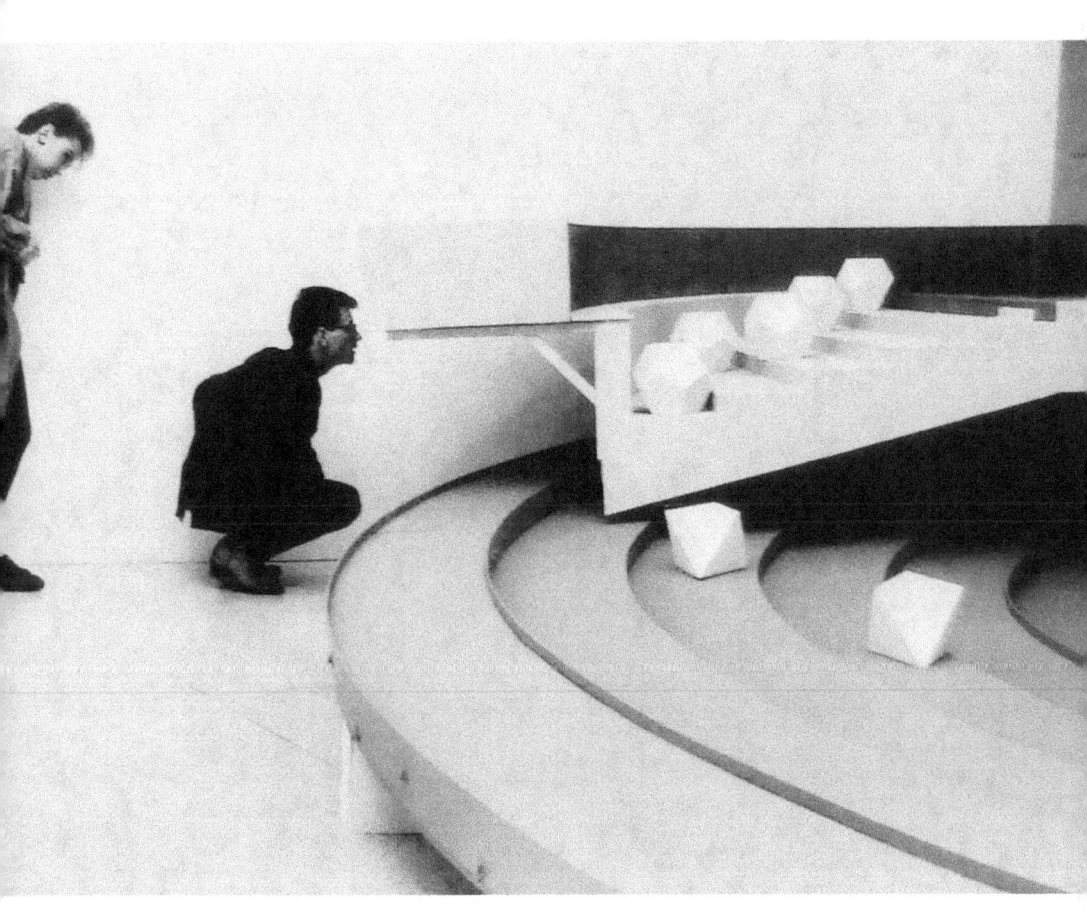

Alice Aycock, The Glass Bead Game, 1986

13

Mary Miss

Mary Miss (b. 1944) attended the University of California at Santa Barbara. In Summer, 1963 she studied sculpture at Colorado College. After graduating in 1966 from the University of California Miss studied at the Rinehard School of Sculpture at the Maryland Art Institute until 1968. Early works included a 'water-line': at Fountain Creek in Colorado Miss suspended a double knot of hemp rope 100 feet over a dry riverbed; every twenty feet were lines of rope. At War's Island in New York Miss threw 15 foot long wooden stakes into the water which were weighted with rocks.

In the middle of a wood in Connecticut in 1974 Miss made *Sunken Pool*: it was a circular wooden structure, 10 feet tall, filled with one foot of water in a galvanized steel interior. *Sunken Pool* was sunken because Miss set it in a hole three feet deep and 20 feet across. As with the large site work of Alice Aycock and Robert Smithson, the spectator was invited to explore Miss's *Sunken Pool* physically, either by stepping into the water, or by climbing up the outer part of the wooden structure and looking over the top. Like Aycock's underground caverns, Miss's *Sunken Pool* was secretive, hiding away in a dense wood, with tall wooden sides. It seemed to speak, like Aycock's works, of childhood memories and half-remembered spaces.

Mary Miss's 1978 work *Perimeters/ Pavilion/ Decoys* was constructed in Roslyn, New York, in a field that was part of the Nassau County Museum's ground. *Perimeters/ Pavillion/ Decoys* consists of three wooden towers, which look like tree houses with four platforms on stilts, two mounds of earth, and an underground space which's accessed by a ladder. The wooden towers are not for climbing on, but for viewing. The tallest is 18 by 10 by 10 feet. The subterranean atrium was for exploring. It was a 16 ft² pit with a seven foot hole acting as an entrance; visitors climbed down a ladder to explore the various underground spaces, some with wooden, others with soil walls.

Perimeters/ Pavillion/ Decoys was related to Pueblo Indian structures, Pompeiian and Mexican courtyards, and Mesopotamian brick complexes. The site explored the physical and psychological aspects of 'inside/ outside, above/ below, light/ dark, open/ closed, nature/ artifice'.[1] Miss's works are often large, spreading over a wide area of ground. In Illinois she created a 5-acre scale work.[2]

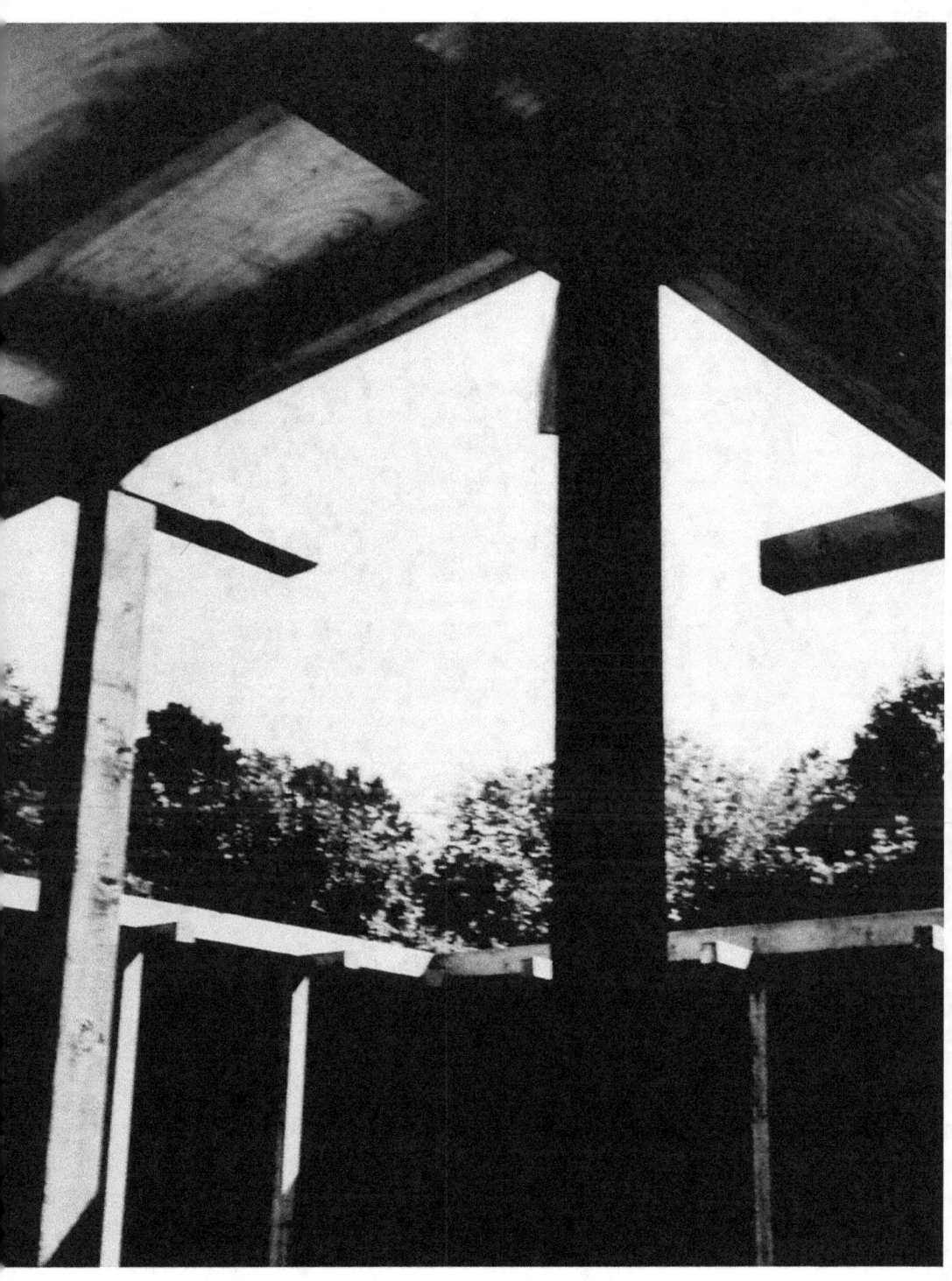

Mary Miss, Perimeters/ Pavilion/ Decoys, 1978

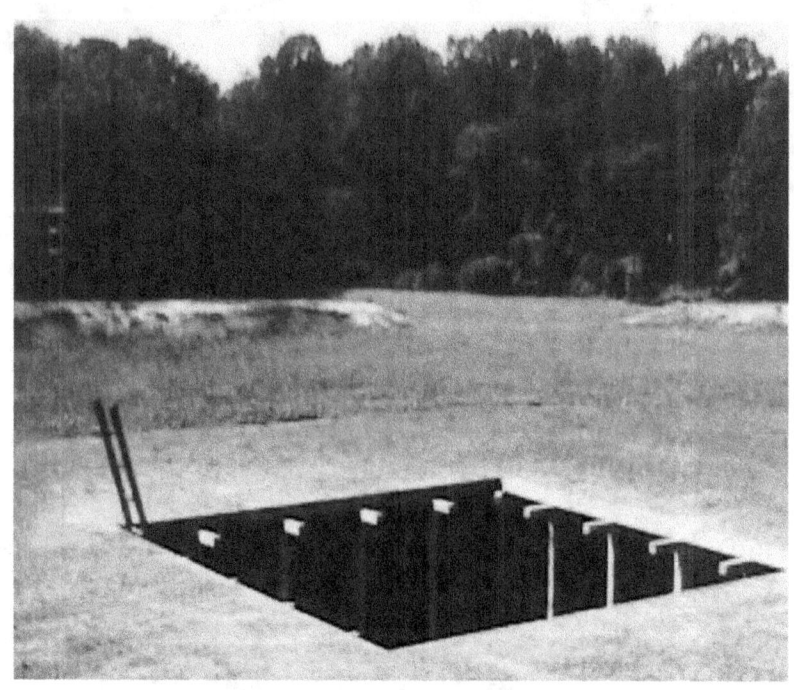

Mary Miss, Perimeters/ Pavilion/ Decoys. 1978

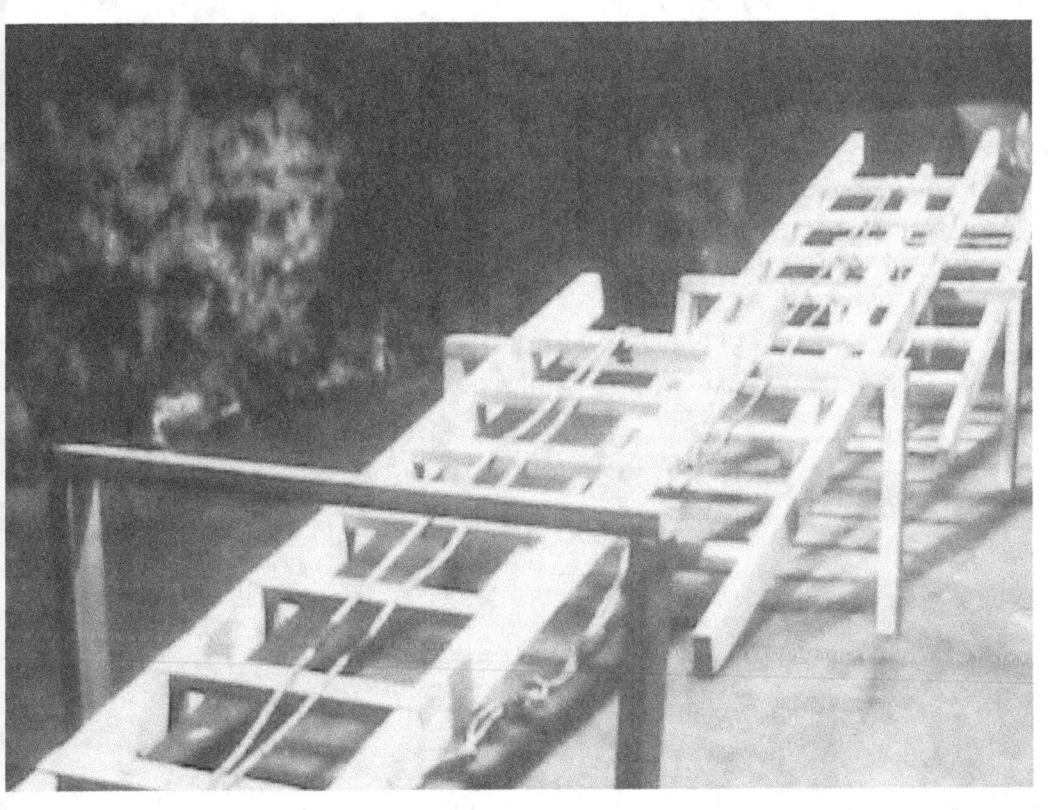

Mary Miss, Ladders and Hurdles, 1970

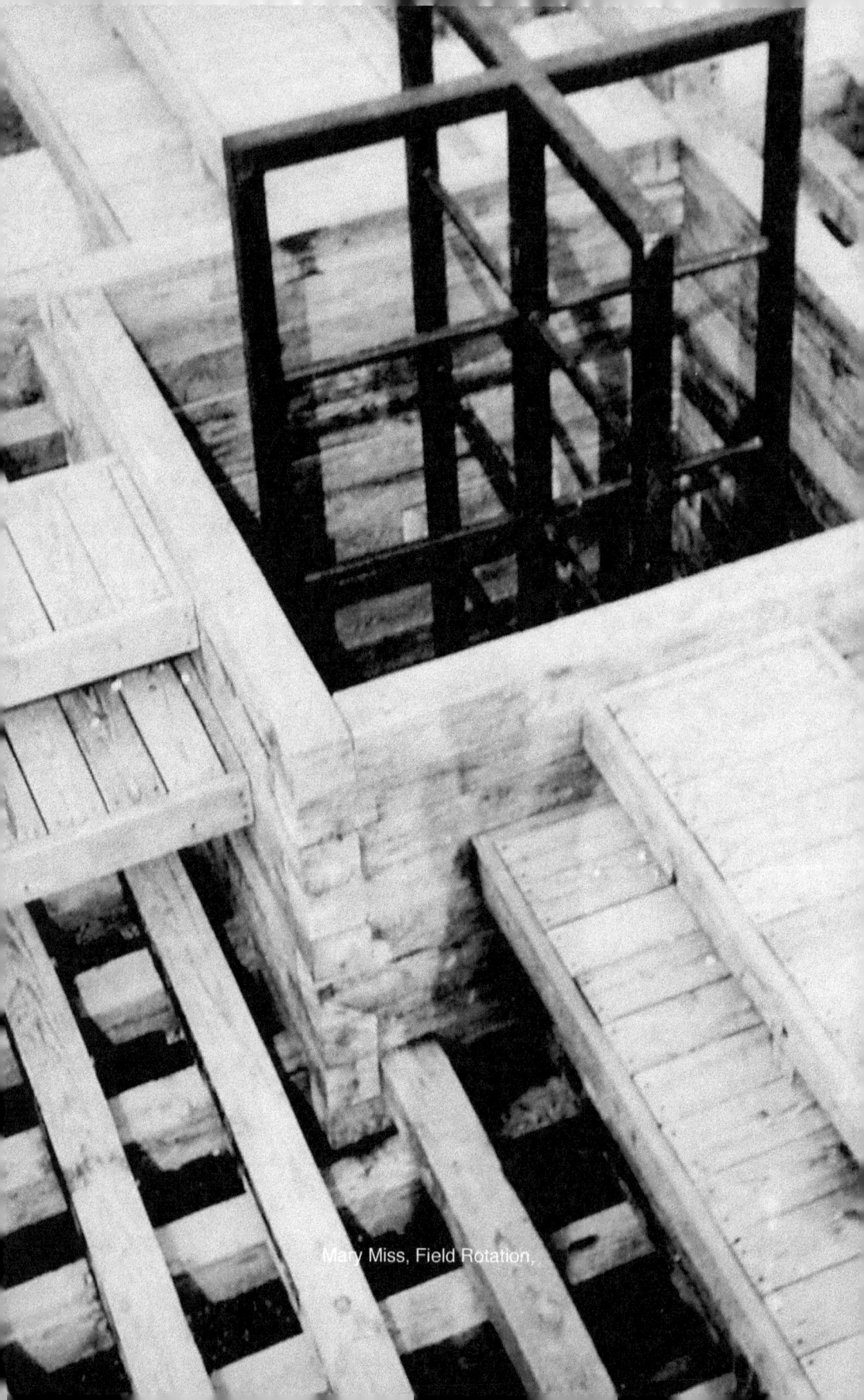
Mary Miss, Field Rotation,

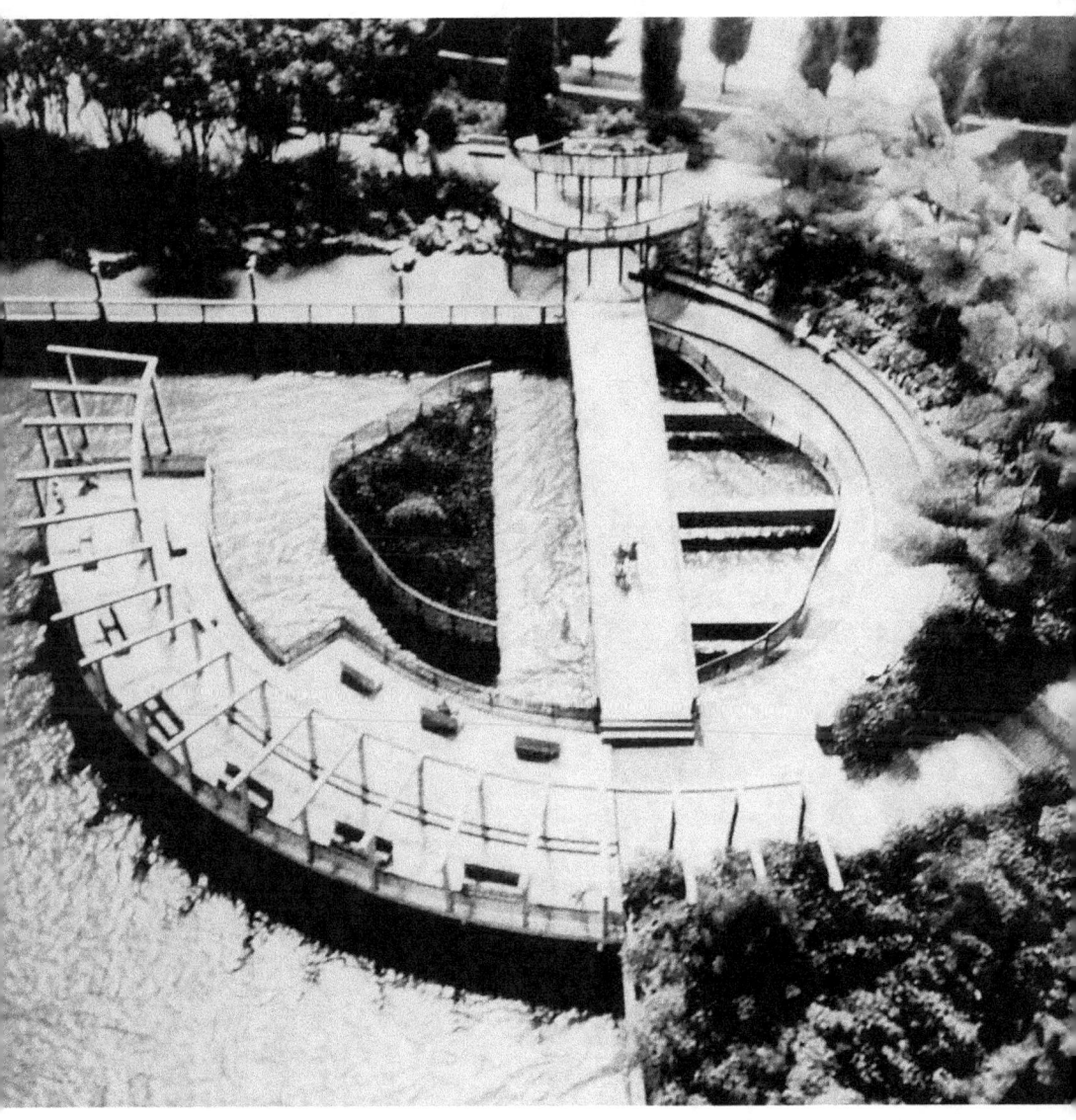

Mary Miss

14

Michael Heizer

My work is closely tied up with my own experiences; for instance, my personal associations with dirt are very real. I really like it, I really like to lie in the dirt.

Michael Heizer[1]

Land artworks are some of the biggest, most prominent and even phallic of contemporary artworks.2 Christo works on a gigantic scale, for instance, wrapping buildings or stretching curtains across valleys or surrounding islands. Some of the most phallic, domineering works of land art are by Michael Heizer (b. 1944).3 In his *Double Negative* (1969-70), his most well-known piece, and one of the most famous examples of land art, he took two chunks out of the earth, a gigantic 'violation' of the planet, in ecological/ green terms.4 Heizer claimed *Double Negative* is 'the smallest piece I've done in relation to the size of the site'.5 Heizer directed the gouging out 240,000 tons of earth from the site at Mormon Mesa in Nevada with bulldozers. The cuts are ramps, going down 50 feet through the cliff of the canyon. The spectator can walk down them. The overall dimensions of *Double Negative* are 1,500 x 42 feet.

Michael Heizer is very much concerned with *scale*, as well as other formal characteristics of a work. Heizer said he liked working outside because of the scale; he could work large. He also said that '[m]an will never really create anything large in relation to the world.'6

Michael Heizer's *Double Negative* is a widely celebrated example of land art. The photographs of it have been reproduced in many art history books. *Double Negative* appeals to trendy 1960s notions of Zen, existentialism, negativity and emptiness. The point about *Double Negative* was its sense of symmetry and relationship, the one cut reflecting the other across the Nevada canyon.

Some viewers saw Heizer's enterprise as combining the subliminity and grandeur of Abstract Expressionism with the emblematic forms of Minimalism. American earthworks art rejuvenated the myth of the sublime West.7 Mary Miss was not convinced. When she looks at the work of Heizer or Smithson 'there's always been an aspect which impedes my relating to it... It's like a mark on the earth'.8

Heizer went on archaeological digs as a child with his father. He started out with the ambition to be a painter, which he studied in San Francisco. He made his first earthwork in 1967, and accompanied Smithson on geological expeditions. In 1968, Heizer collaborated with Smithson and Nancy Holt on a Super-8 film, *Mono-Lake*. (Heizer had invited Holt and Smithson to his parents' house at Lake Tahoe). Heizer's motorbike earthwork was entitled *Circular Surface Displacement*, it was made at Mono Lake.

Heizer's other works include gouging huge holes in the ground and putting great chunks of rock in them. *Nine Nevada Depressions* (1968) comprised five cuts in the Blackrock desert, each one twelve feet long in an area 50 by 50 feet. *Munich*

Depression (1969) was another cut, a line 15 feet deep. Heizer's *Complex One* (1972) was a huge bunker-like mass of earth built with the aid of two assistants in Nevada. It was 23.5 feet high and 140 feet long. Each end of the hill had a cut-off triangle of reinforced concrete like giant book-ends. Over the work were cantilevered concrete beams. '*Complex One* is a magnificent spectacle. Even its minatory look, suggesting a bunker, seems proper to the site – the edge of the Nevada nuclear proving-ground', remarked Robert Hughes.[9]

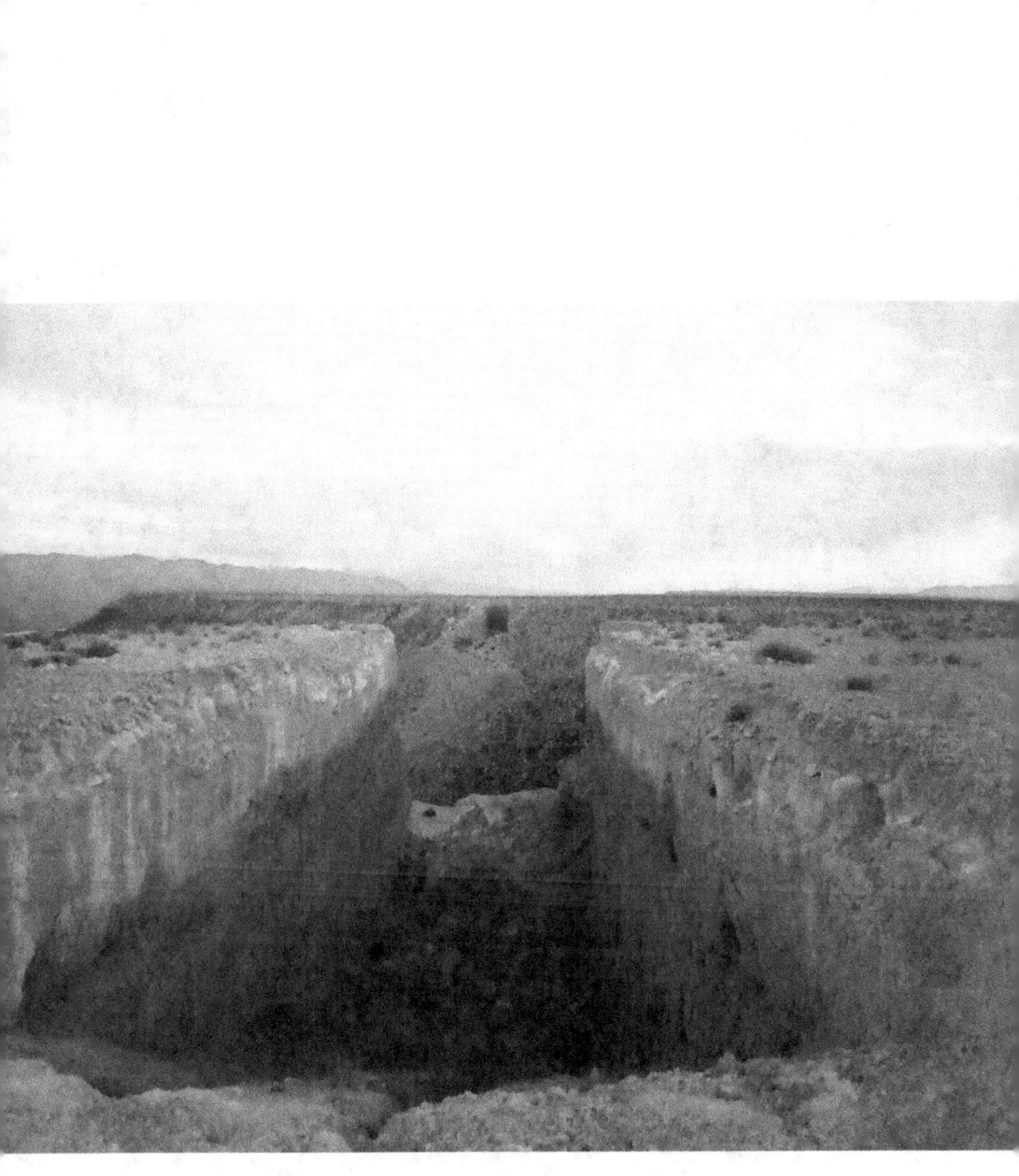

Michael Heizer, Double Negative, 1970

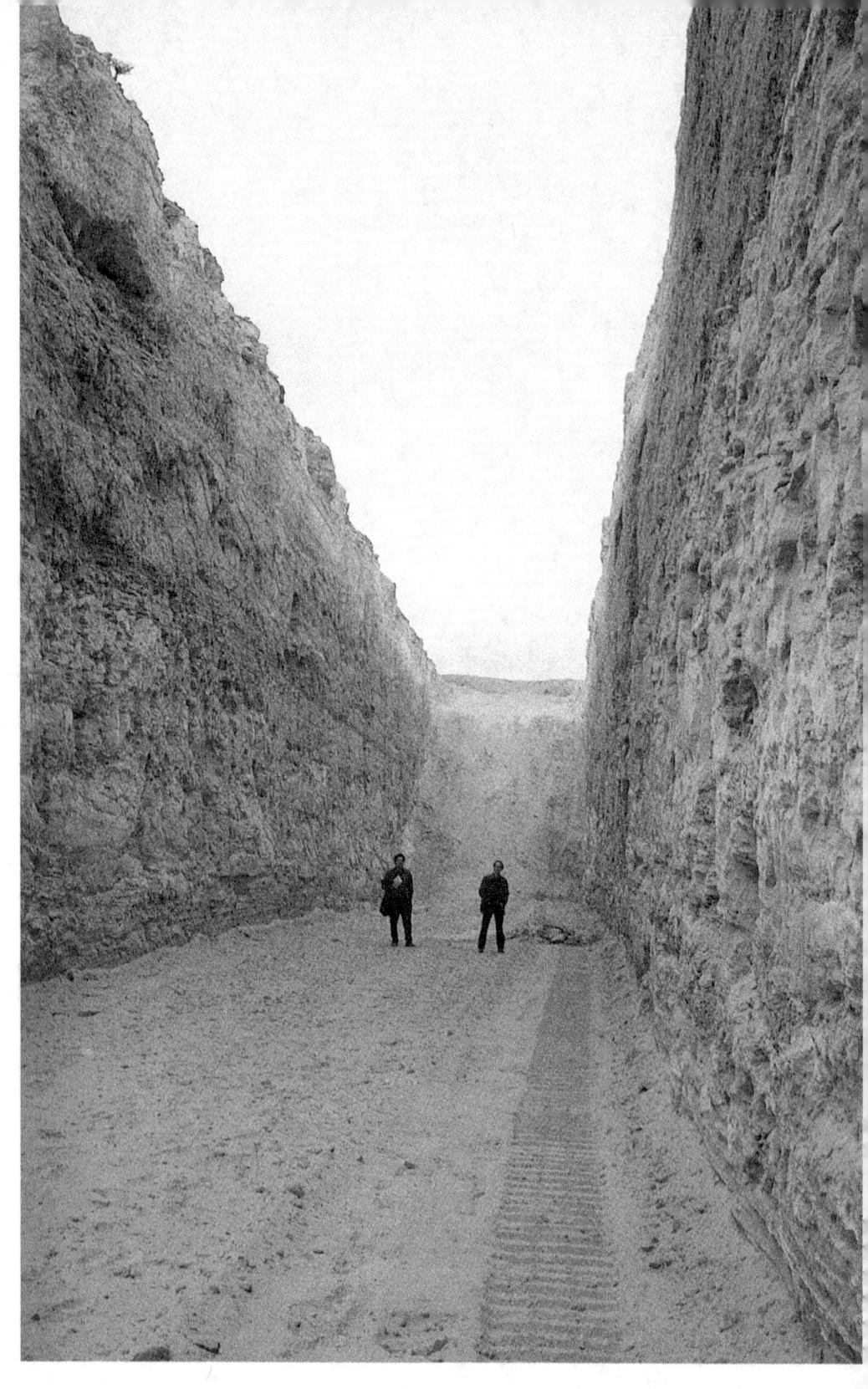

Michael heizer, Double Negative, 1970

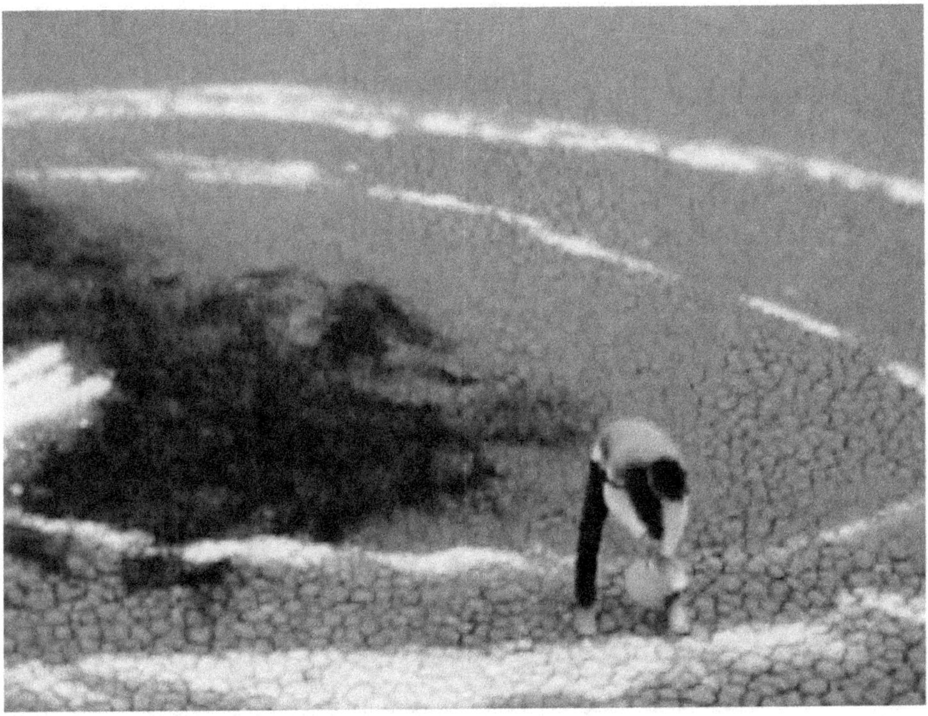

Michael Heizer at work in the American desert

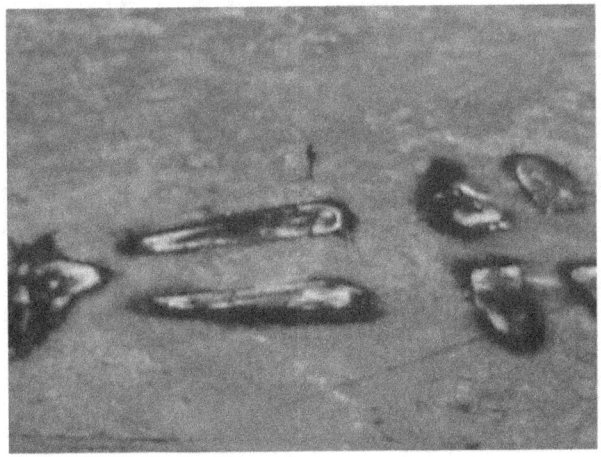

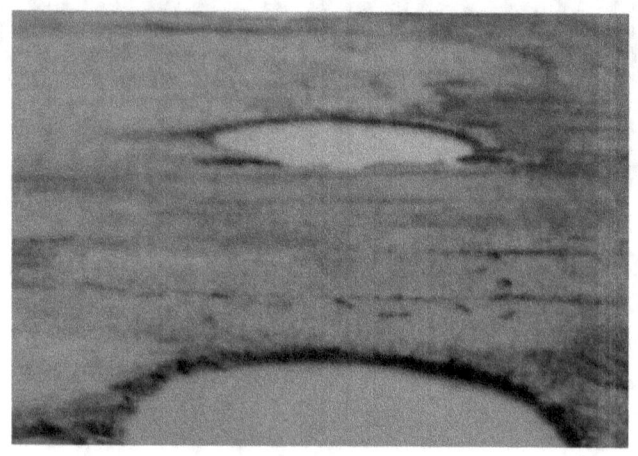

Michael Heizer, Nine Nevada Depressions,
1968

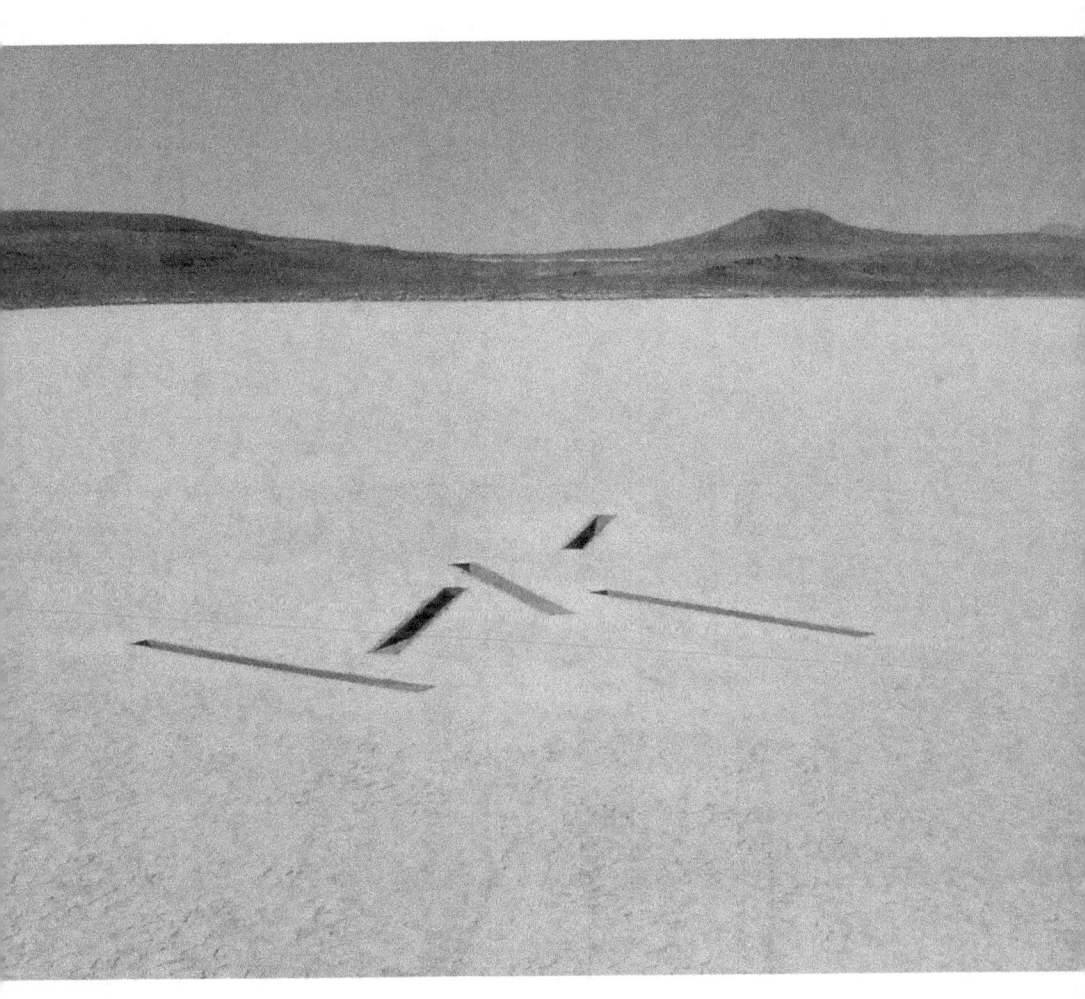

Michael Heizer, Nine Nevada Depressions, #8, 1968

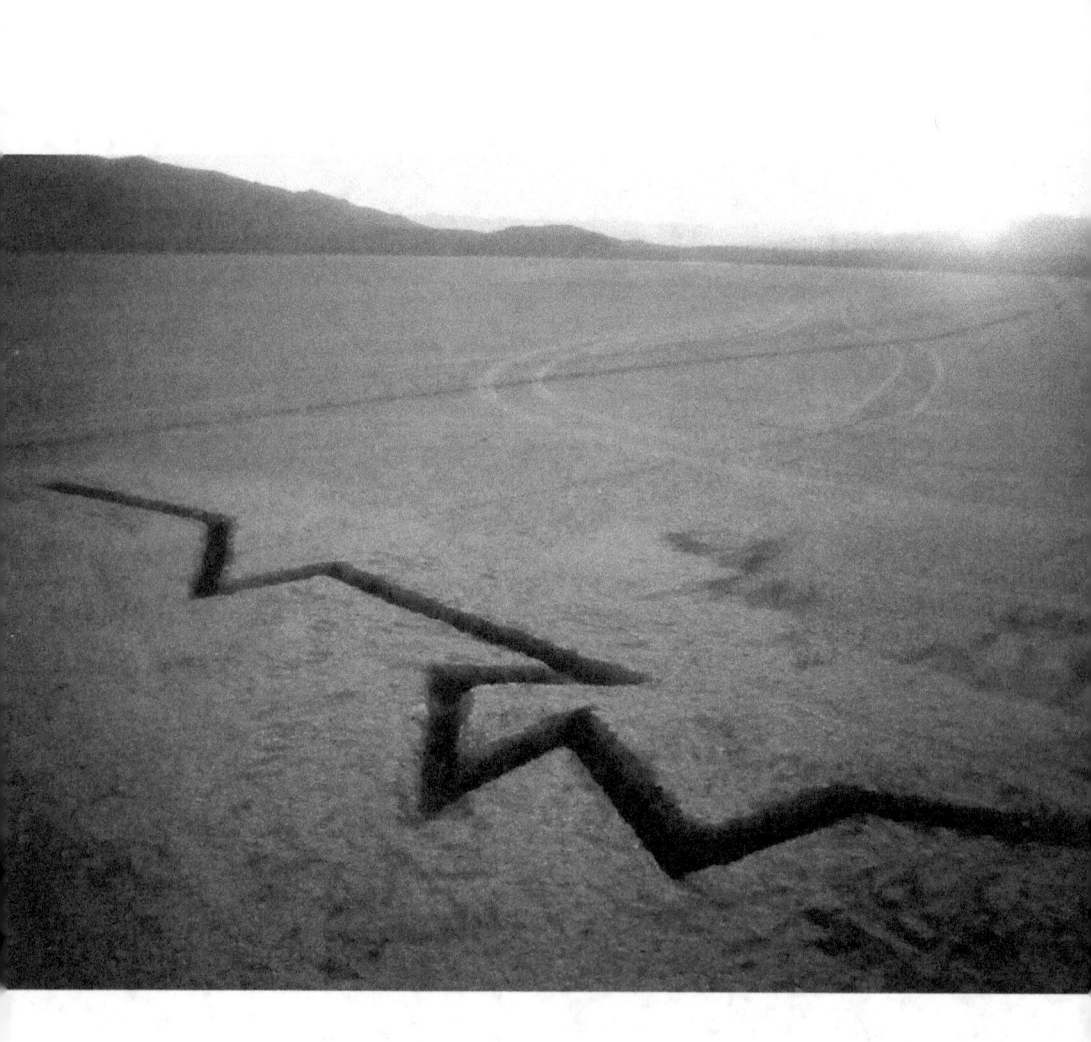

Michael Heizer, Nine Nevada Depressions, #1, 1968

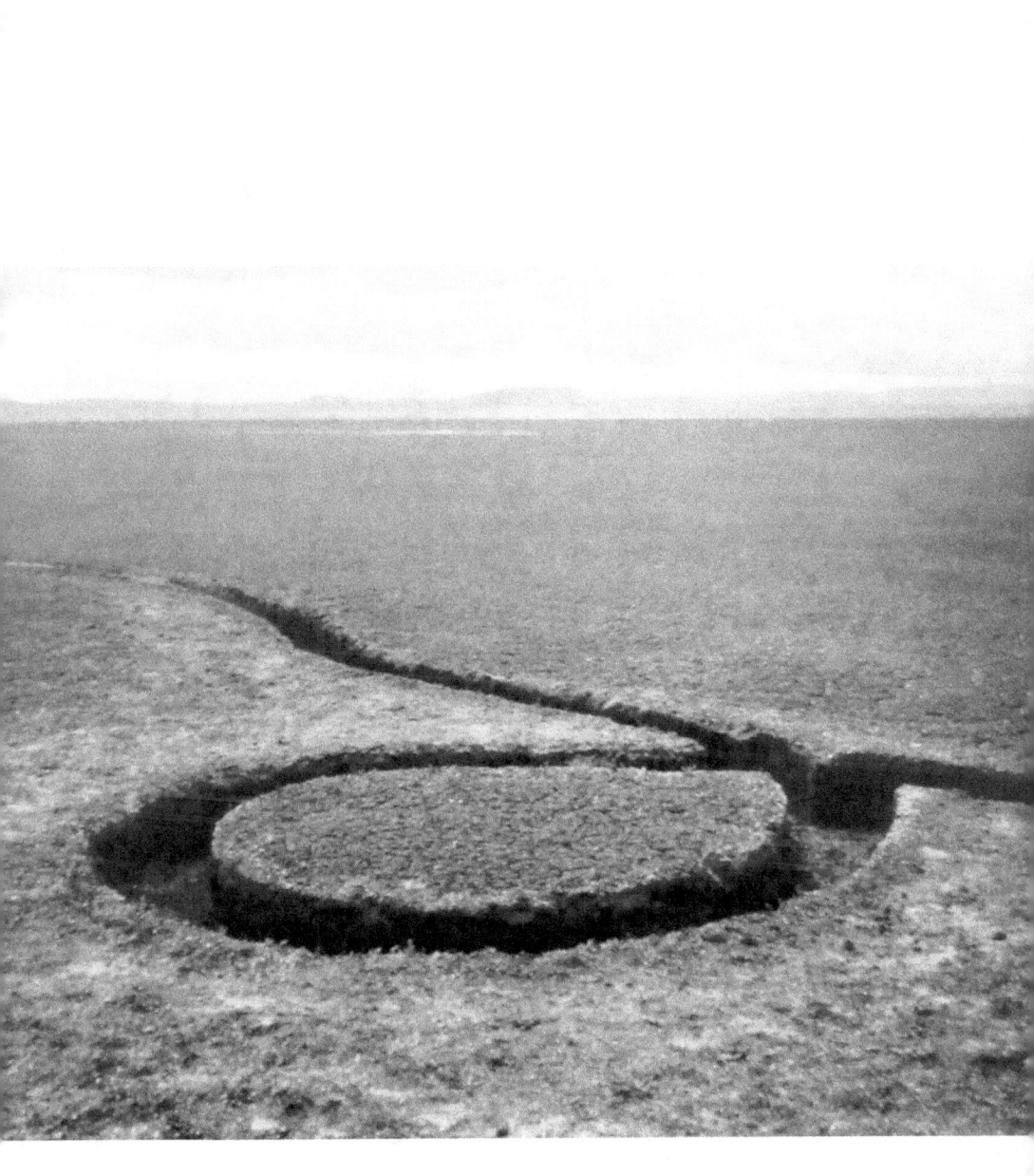

Michael Heizer, Nine Nevada Depressions, #9, 1968

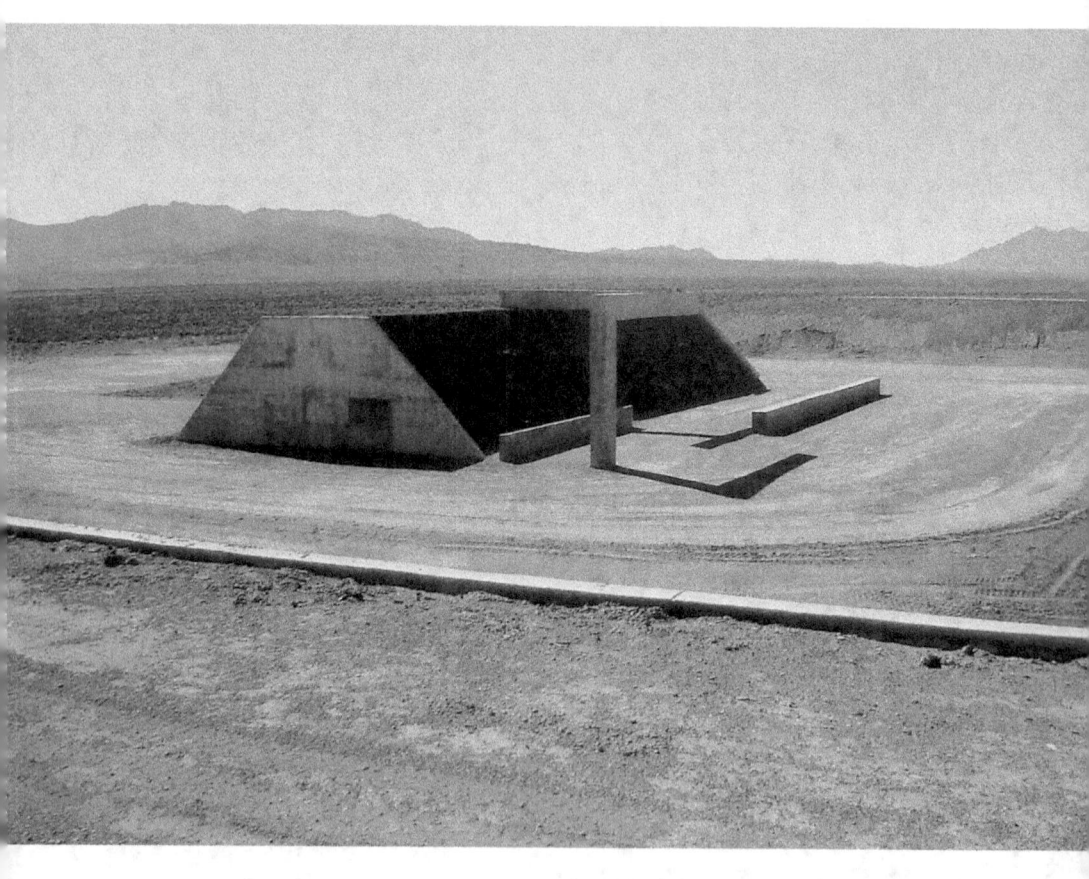

Michael Heizer, Complex One, 1972-76

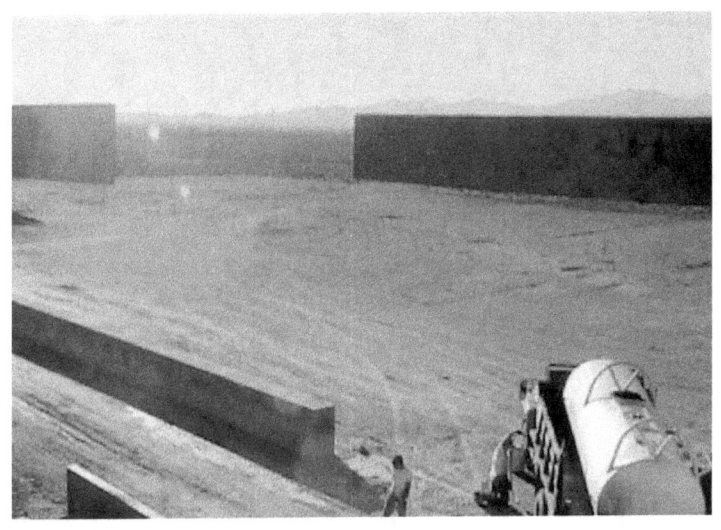

Michael Heizer, Complex One, 1972

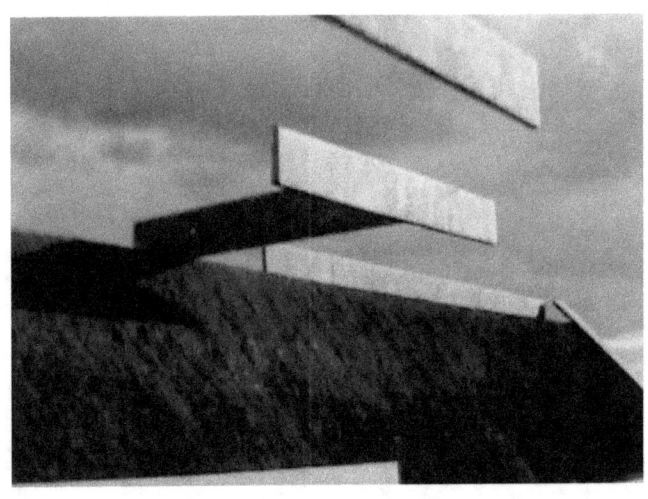

15

Walter de Maria

Walter de Maria (b. 1935), one of the most famous of the first group of US land artists, made a dramatic land art gesture when he cut a 4.5 mile-long 6 foot-wide scar in the desert in Nevada with a bulldozer (*Las Vegas Piece*, 1969). Commentators have spoken of this cut as a 'wound' or 'scar' on the Earth (a wound in the body of the Earth in its Great Mother persona). The ultimate in ithyphallic, male land art must be de Maria's *Vertical Earth Kilometer*. At a cost of $500,000, de Maria sunk a one kilometre brass rod into the planet. Nothing can be seen of it except a 2 inch brass disc on the ground.

The making of de Maria's work is perhaps far more interesting than the artwork itself. It must be the ultimate art statement/ non-statement. De Maria's *Vertical Earth Kilometer* remains practically invisible. It neatly melds two 1960s æsthetic movements: Conceptualism (wow, what an idea, sticking a kilometer of solid brass into the Earth!) and Minimal art (there's nothing to see of it except... a two-inch brass disc!). Yeah, that's *real art*, a kilometer-long piece of metal stuck into the ground with nothing of it showing except a tiny disc. This is, in Richard Long's words, '[t]rue capitalist art', an art of excessive cost, and maybe excessive waste (it took 79 days to bore the shaft).[1]

Shown at Kassel Dokumenta 6 in 1977, de Maria's *Vertical Earth Kilometer* upset British artist Stuart Brisley so much he made *Survival in Alien Circumstances*. This was a hole in the earth dug with his bare hands, which Brisley lived in for 2 weeks, intending to mock de Maria's overblown American earthwork. But then, art has been full of idiotic amounts of money and out-size projects for ages. In 1979 de Maria exhibited *The Broken Kilometer*. 500 brass rods each two metres long arranged in rows on the floor of a New York gallery.

Walter de Maria started out as a musician rather than, like many land artists, as a painter or sculptor. He played drums with the art rockers Velvet Underground. One of his early ideas (in 1962) for an earthwork was a mile-long pair of walls that would be 12 feet high and 12 feet apart. De Maria said that 'when you walk between, you can look up and see the sky'.[2] After carving a four and a half mile bulldozer square cut in the Earth, de Maria made a chalk drawing in the desert.

De Maria's *Earth Room* was a gallery full of dark earth made in 1968 in Munich and later in New York (*The New York Earth Room*, SoHo Gallery, 1977). It consisted of 125 tons of soil, taking up 3,600 square feet, 22 inches deep. This was a vivid (and aromatic) example of bringing the Outside inside, one of land art's key projects. The contrasts were immediate, between the flat, clean, white, controlled gallery space and the 1,600 cubic feet of uneven, 'dirty', dark, organic soil. Roberta Smith said it was a 'shock' to see the soil taking up the interior space usually reserved for things such as furniture and people. 'The dirt carried its own absence, was somehow a living substance'.3 A related work, *5 Continents Sculpture* (1987-88), comprised white rocks filling an area 42 by 77 feet in a Stuttgart gallery.

De Maria's *Bed of Spikes* (1969) was called 'a piece of Dadaist Sadism' by Harold Rosenberg.4 *Bed of Spikes*, an installation at the Dwan Gallery, was 153 metal spikes set in five planks on the floor. Interestingly, spectators were asked to sign a release that exempted the gallery for being responsible for any accidents on viewing the installation. *Bed of Spikes* looked forward to *Lightning Field*.

Critic Kenneth Baker called Walter de Maria's most famous work, the *Lightning Field,* the 'grandest Minimalist work of the 1970s' and 'the closest thing to a masterpiece to come out of Minimalism'.5 De Maria's first *Lightning Field* was sited 40 miles from Flagstaff in Arizona, consisting of 2 inch diameter steel poles, 18 feet tall, 30 feet apart, in five rows of seven.

The second, larger *Lightning Field* is a grid of 400 stainless steel poles, 16 along the width, 25 along the length, each about 20 feet high, set in the New Mexico desert.6 The poles were set in concrete, one foot below land, able to withstand winds of 110 mph. The site was chosen for its flatness, isolation and lightning activity. The most lightning activity occurs during May-September; there are about 60 days when thunder and lightning can be seen from *Lightning Field*.7

Lightning Field is about a mile by a kilometre in size. The poles in *Lightning Field* stand alone, about 220 feet apart. Nothing remains on the ground of the work needed to set them there. The tips of the poles define a plane in space parallel to sea level: the length of each pole varies according to the contours of the landscape. The *Lightning Field* is an exact, mathematically-precise human site laid onto nature, where the poles are tiny mirrors which mark out and calibrate the landscape. The site looks like a scientific or industrial project – like a radio telescope site, say, or a military communications centre. *Lightning Field* is spectacular, with masculine and phallic connotations (lightning is related in symbolism to male creativity, sperm, fire, power and shamanism).

Lightning Field is ambiguously associated with the Dia Art Foundation, which financed its construction. The site recalls technological experiments, while the poles themselves recall Brancusi's *Birds in Space*, and his *Endless Column*.

De Maria's *Lightning Field* attracts lightning, and a storm, as anyone knows, is about the most erotic and spectacular phenomenon in nature.8 May to September is the season of the great storms in the area, sometimes 'two or three a week cross this field of poles'.9

Joseph Beuys produced a striking piece entitled *Lightning* (1982-85): a gigantic chunk of bronze, narrow at the top, splaying out towards the bottom, as if he was trying to make manifest the bolt of energy leaping down to the Earth. Justin Holland too used lightning in artworks; he collaborated with Westinghouse Electric, making humanmade lightning, and 'seeded' clouds to produce storms. Peter Hutchinson and Alice Aycock also made cloud works.

Walter de Maria, Las Vegas Piece, 1969

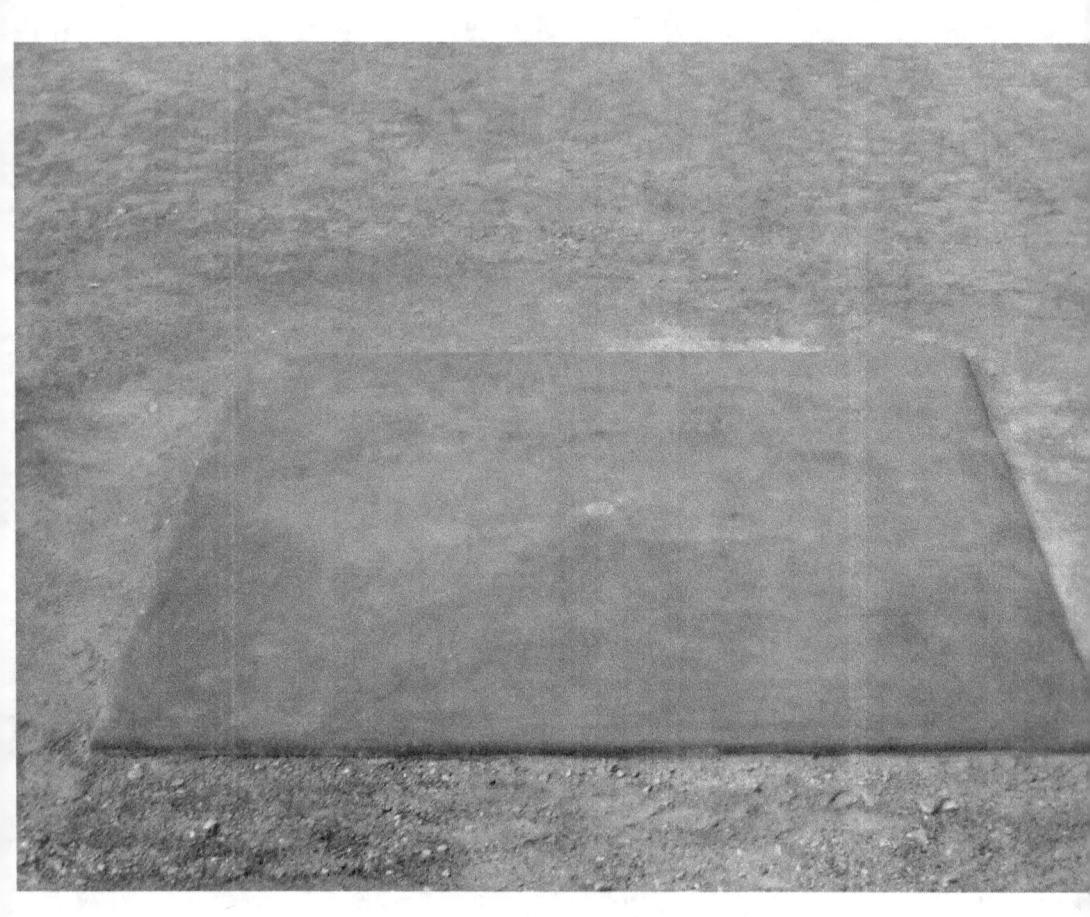

Walter de Maria, Vertical Earth Kilometer, 1977

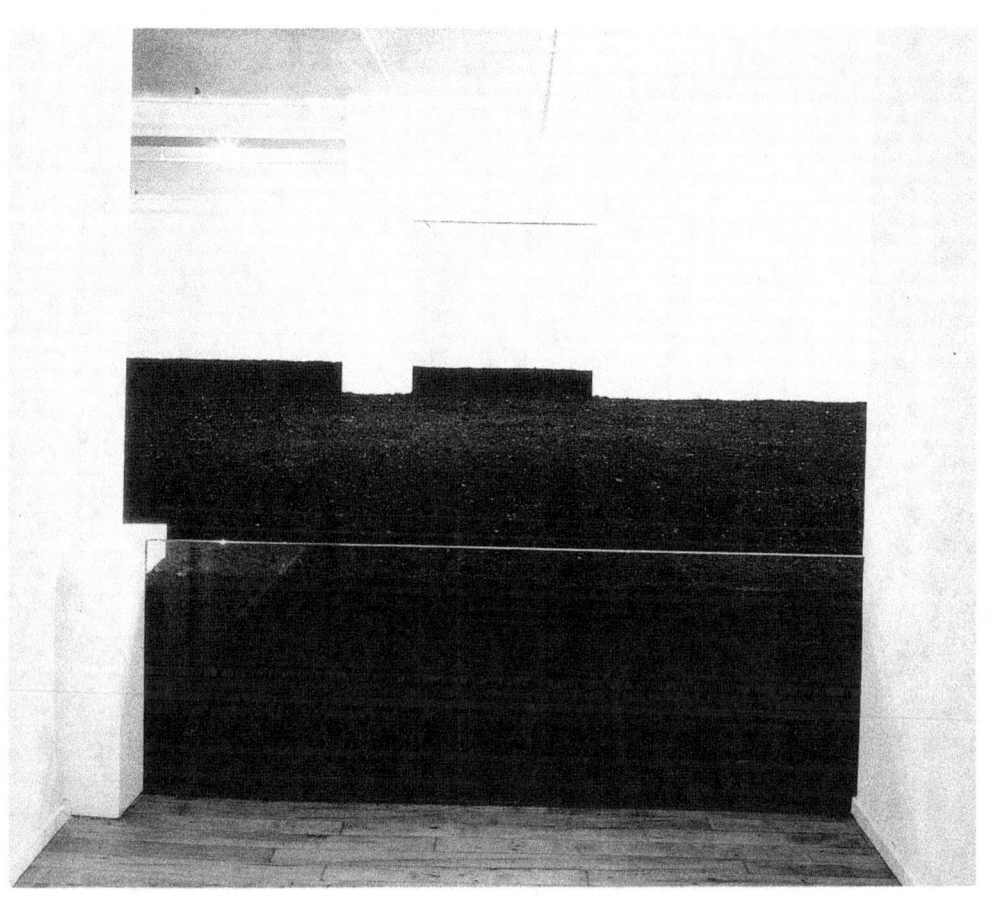

Walter de Maria, Earth Room, 1977

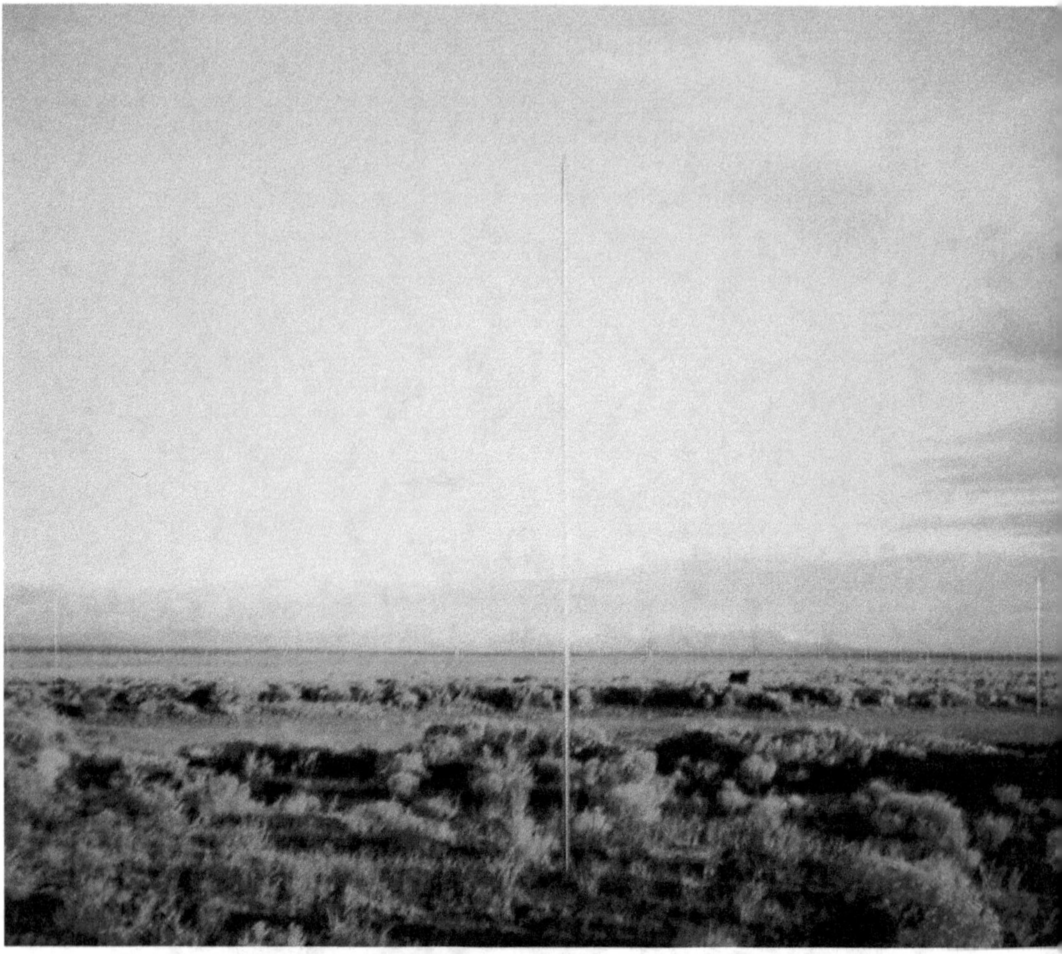

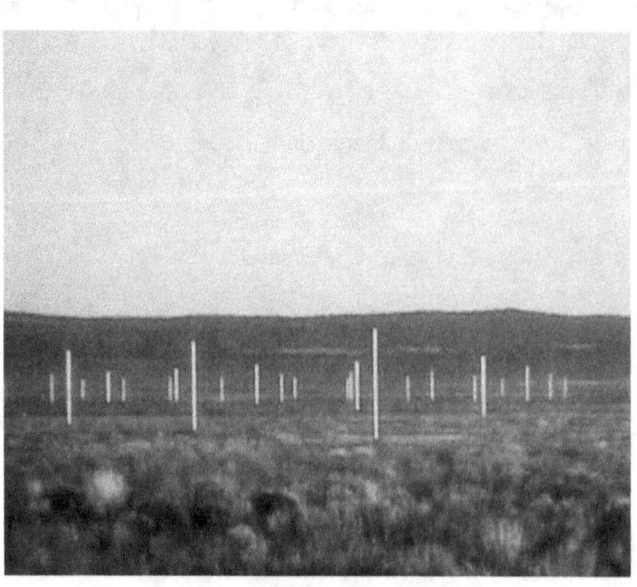

Walter de Maria, Lightning Field, 1977

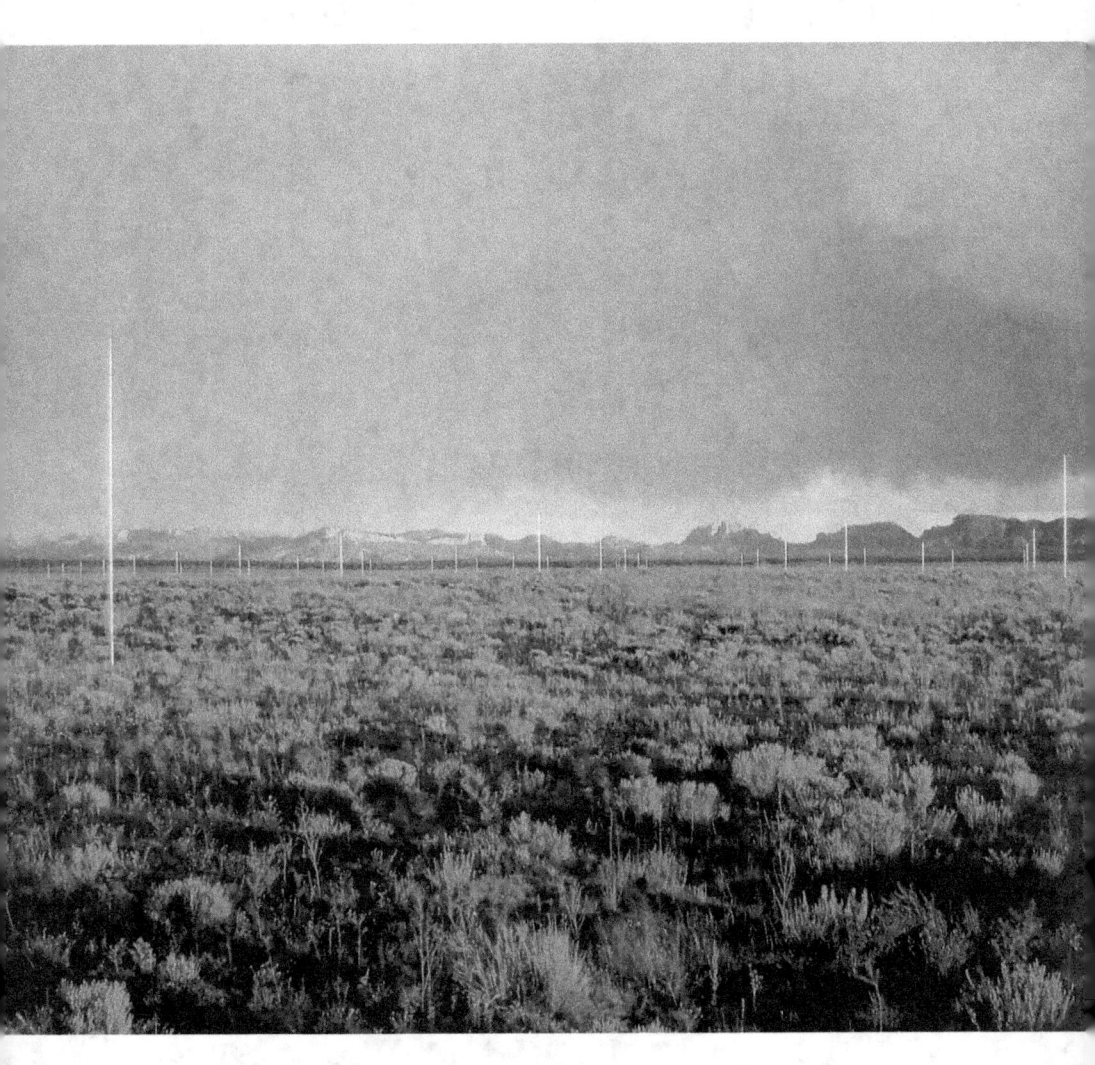

Walter de Maria, Lightning Field, 1977

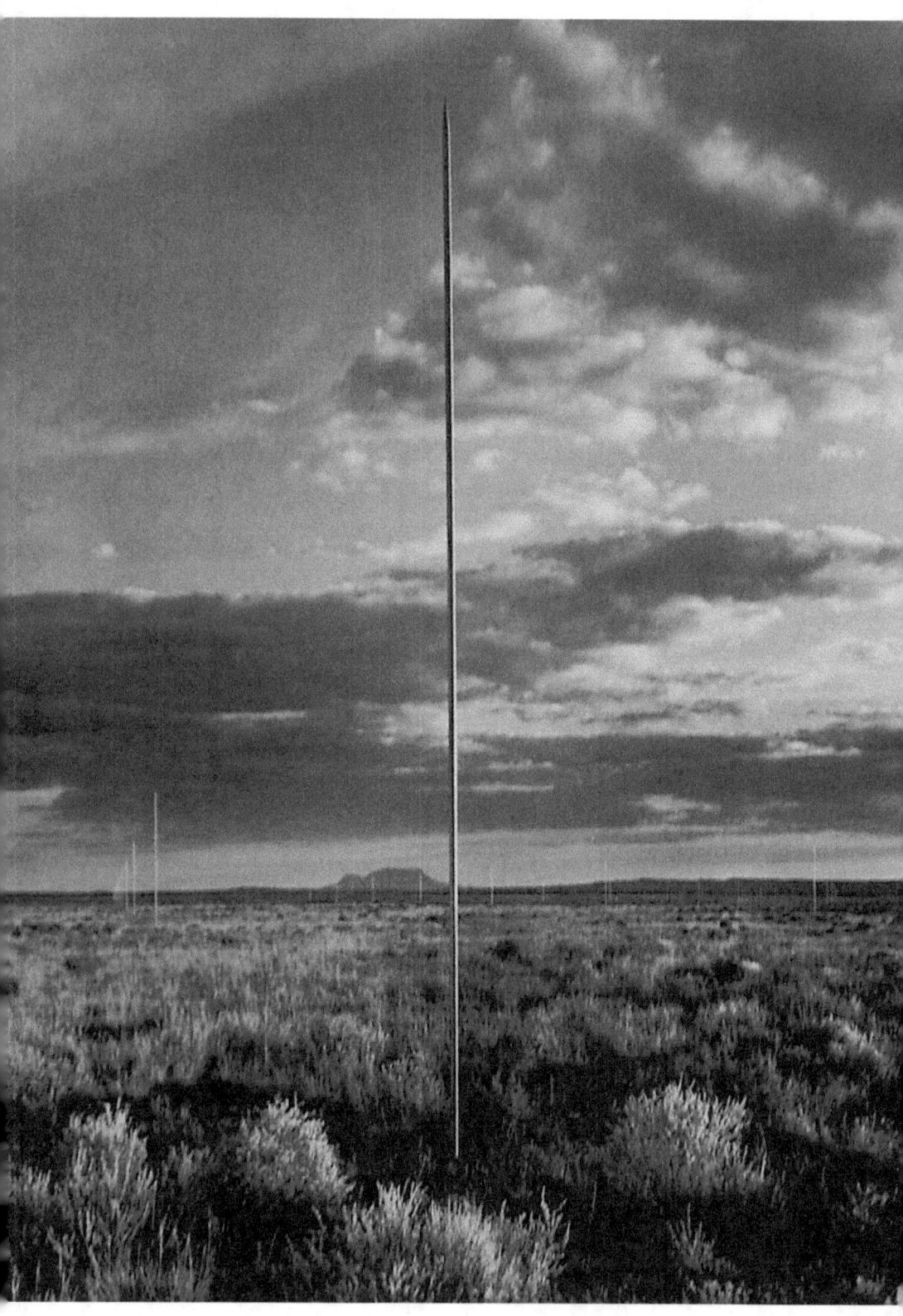

Walter de Maria, Lightning Field, 1977

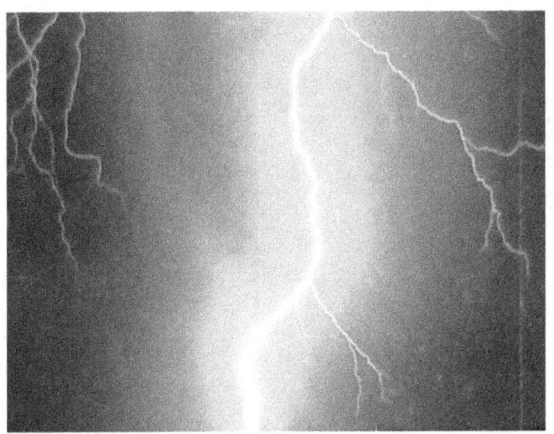

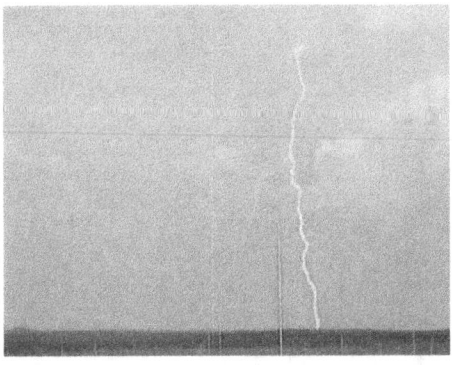

Walter de Maria, Lightning Field, 1977

16

Other American Land Artists

Some other artists living and working in North America include:

JAMES PIERCE

James Pierce created a series of earthworks at Pratt Farm in central Maine in the 1970s: there was a triangular turf maze; a small earth *Observatory*; a *Serpent* made from large rocks; a *Stone Ship*; a *Burial Mound*; a stone *Altar* (in the shape of male genitals); and various figures built out of grass and soil: *Earthwoman* and *Suntreeman*. Pierce's *Earthwoman* (1976-77) was a recumbent female shape, with prominent buttocks, evoking the erotic gardens of the 18th century, and the links between prehistoric earth mounds, fertility and femininity.

HERBERT BAYER

Herbert Bayer (1900-85) created earthworks which directly evoked prehistoric structures: Bayer's *Earth Mound* (1955) in Aspen, Colorado, contained the familiar motifs of ancient religions and cultures: a circular rampart enclosing a small mound; a standing stone and a hollow were placed beside the mound. In Kent, Washington, Bayer built a series of earthworks (*Mill Creek Canyon Earthworks*, 1979-82) which featured circular ramparts, circular moats, mounds surmounted by walkways, and circular ramparts split by a path.

PATRICIA JOHANSON

Patricia Johanson's (b. 1940) most well-known work is probably the large water park she fashioned in Dallas, Texas, between 1981 and 1986. *Fair Park Lagoon* comprised a series of interlacing walkways above the pool in an 'organic', Gaudiesque manner, and cost over $2 million.

GORDON MATTA-CLARK

Gordon Matta-Clark (1943-78) transformed buildings by knocking enormous holes in them (*Conical Intersect,* 1975), or cutting a house in New Jersey in half (*Splitting,* 1974). But these were not sculpted spaces or physical gestures so much as Conceptual reorganizations of a structure. It's easy to discern the influence of Matta-Clark's interventions in houses and buildings (which he called 'unbuilding') on Andy Goldsworthy's holes and Rachel Whiteread's works (such as her impressions of rooms and houses).

Matta-Clark bought up pieces of land in the borough of Queens (in 1973), in another Conceptual piece; none of them were big enough for housing of for much else (some were only 2 by 3 feet, tiny strips of land). *Reality Positions, Fake Estates* explored the notion of land ownership. Matta-Clark explained:

> One or two of the prize ones were a foot strip down somebody's driveway and a square foot of sidewalk. And the others were kerbstone and gutterspace. What I basically wanted to do was to designate spaces that wouldn't be seen and certainly not occupied. Buying them was my own take on the strangeness of existing property demarcation lines. Property is so all-pervasive.[1]

ANA MENDIETA

Ana Mendieta (1948-85) covered herself in mud (while nude, of course) and stood against a tree (for *The Tree of Life* series, 1977, made in Old Man's Creek, Iowa), a combination of Goddess art, performance art and environmental art. In *The Tree of Life* series, Mendieta left the outline of her body in leaves on a tree trunk. In the *Silueta* series (1979), Mendieta imprinted her body in the snow in Amana, Iowa, and in mud on a riverbank, or set the form on fire in the earth, or made a silhouette from flowers.

These pieces echo Andy Goldsworthy's rain and snow 'body prints' (however, Mendieta's art has an undisguised ideological, spiritual and ecological agenda; some of Mendieta's works are explicit performance explorations of rapes, and Mendieta was also exploring her Cuban and Latin American heritage).

In some pieces Mendieta remodelled the entrance of a cave and a ravine into her Goddess shape. She also buried herself under turf – a literal Earth-Goddess mound, and had herself photographed in an ancient Mexican stone grave.[2] Mendieta also lit fires in sculptures (such as *Volcano*, 1979), like Chris Drury and David Nash, and lit candles and fireworks in the shape of a woman.

Ana Mendieta was married to Carl Andre, and their relationship ended tragically when Mendieta fell to her death from a skyscraper in New York City. It was one of the more notorious incidents in contemporary art, and, like Robert Smithson's early death, a great loss to the art world.

DONNA DENNIS

Donna Dennis (b. 1942) took the vernacular architecture of New York City as her starting-point in her 1970s works: *Tunnel Tower* was based on the entrance building to the Holland Tunnel. Later, nostalgic works, such as *Deep Station* (1981-85), recreated the shadowy recesses of subway stations (in full-scale, something like a movie set or an installation).

CHARLES ROSS

Charles Ross constructed a large observatory, *Star Axis* (1989), which recalled the celestial viewing spaces of Turrell, Holt and Morris. It was designed for viewing the North Star (the North Star was undoubtedly the land artists' favourite star – apart from the sun – appearing in works by James Turrell and Charles Ross, among others). Charles Simonds made an *Abandoned Observatory* (1976), in model form. Juan Geuer has also worked with the sky: he mounted four pairs of large mirrors in the National Gallery of Canada in order to reflect the sky in the glass cupola above (*Karonhia*, 1989).

DOUGLAS HOLLIS

Douglas Hollis (b. 1948) constructed 'sound gardens' – a series of wind organ pipes mounted on towers beside the shore in Seattle, WA (1980). Hollis's *Field of Vision* (1980) comprised 900 wind vanes at Lake Placid, NY, to 'explore the choreography between windscape and landscape'.[4] In the Seventies Hollis experimented with sending up kites that emitted sound (*Sky Soundings*, 1975).

Other American land artists include: Elyn Zimmerman, who created large-scale ecological land art, such as her *Keystone Island* (1989), a 50-foot wide artificial island built on a lagoon in a mangrove swamp. Jackie Ferrara's works include *Garden Courtyard* (1989), a large piece of landscape art involving steps, grass, trees, seating, platforms and walkways at the Fulton County Government Center in Atlanta.

At a quarry in upstate New York William Bennett fashioned a *Wedge (Stone Boat)* (1976), an 80 foot long smooth-sided channel in the limestone. Christine Oatman lit a fire on a frozen lake in the centre of a circle of tall icicles in *Icicle Circle and Fire* (1973). Teresa Murak, in a Mendietan gesture, covered her naked body with cress seeds, while lying in a bath (in *Seed*, 1989). 'They sprout, swell and begin after a few hours to grow right on my body'.[3]

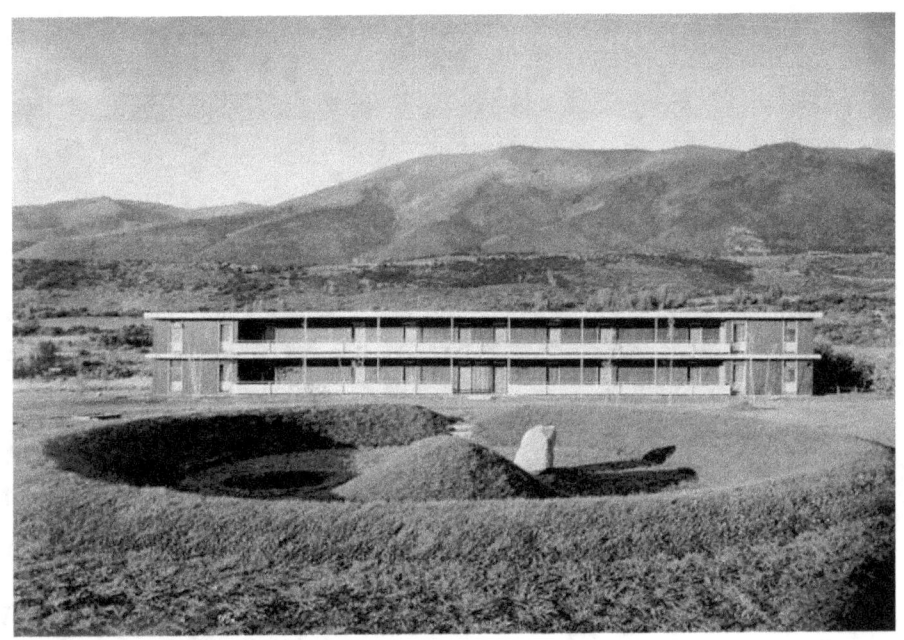

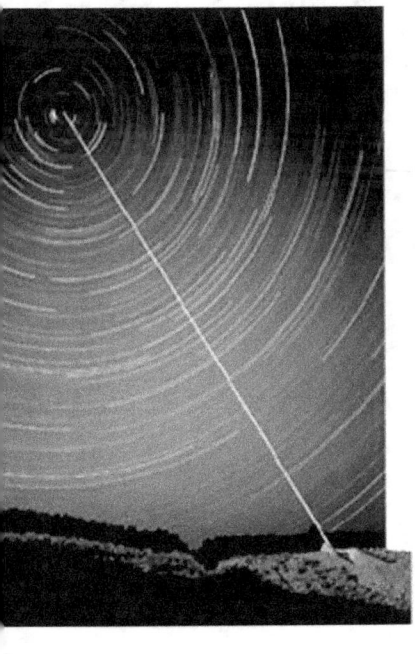

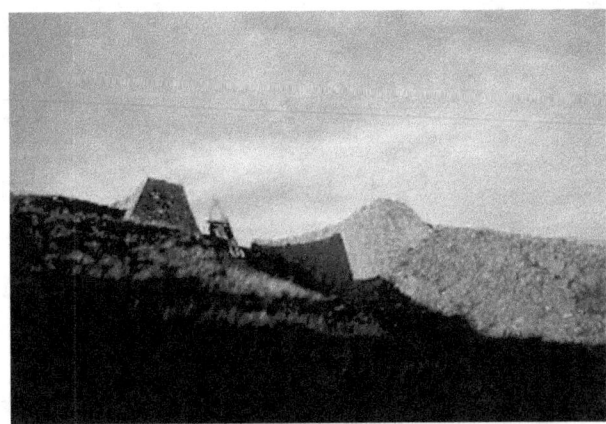

Herbert Bayer in Aspen, top.

Charles Ross, Star Axis, above.

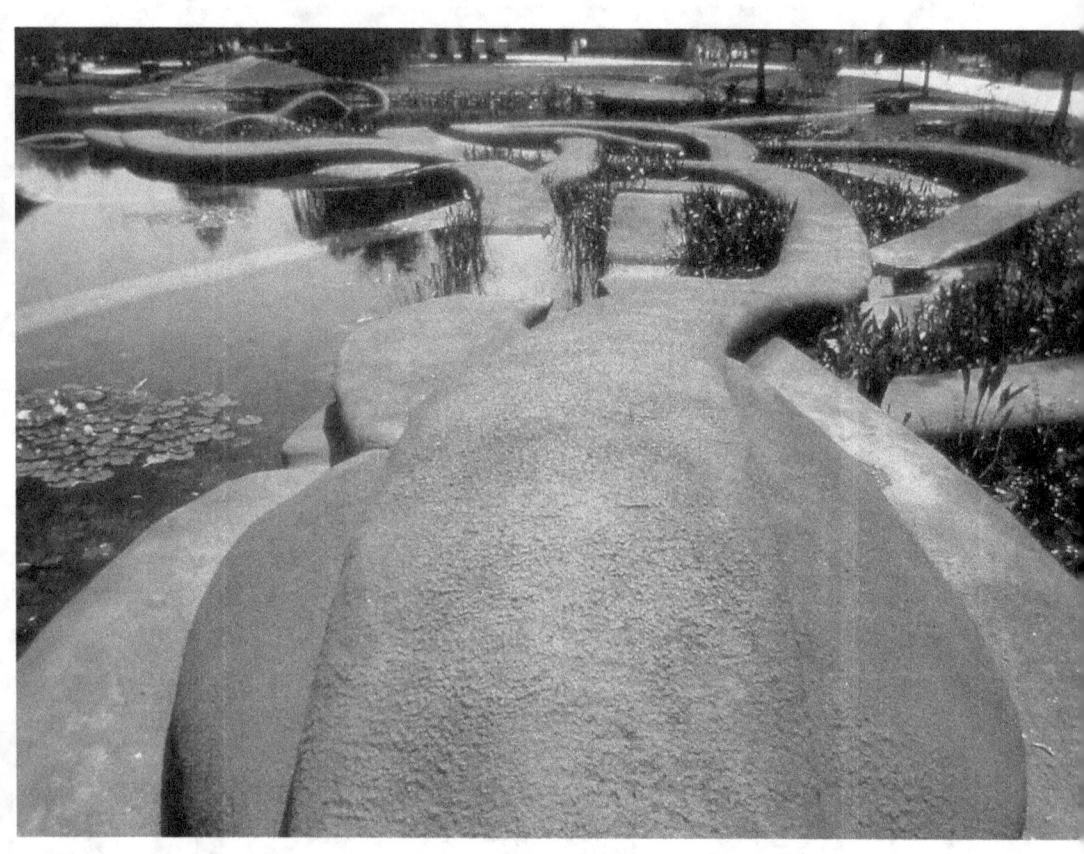

Patricia Johanson, Fair Park Lagoon, 1981-86

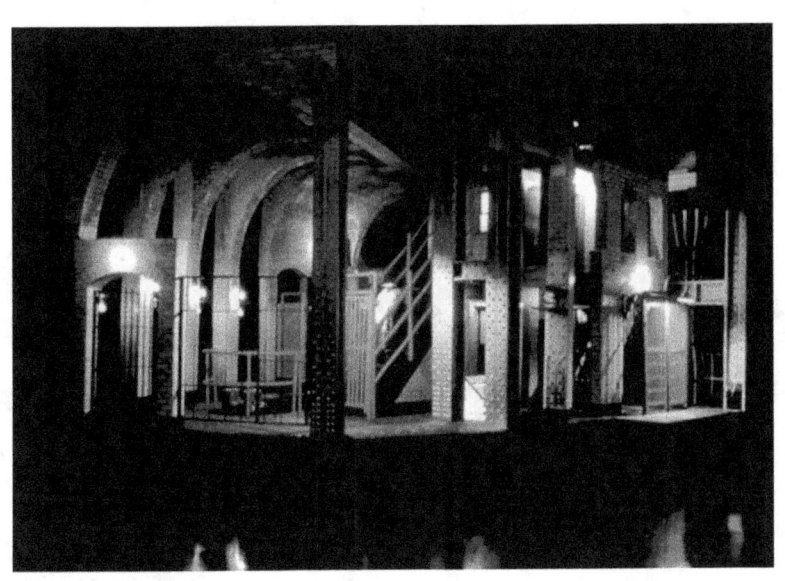

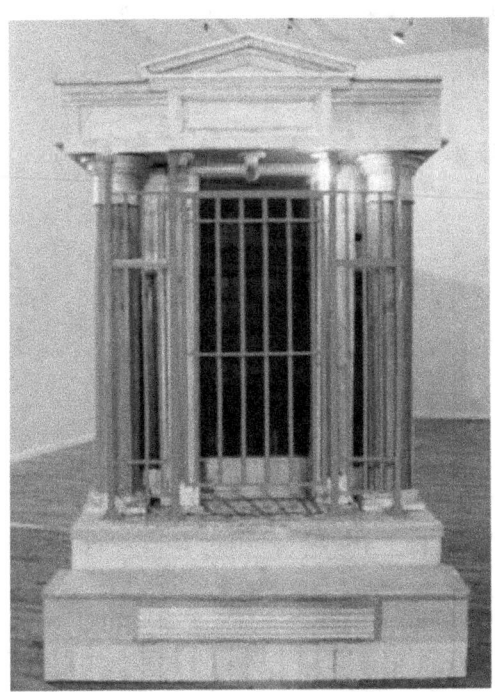

Donna Dennis, Deep Station, 1981-85, top.
Subway With Yellow and Blue, 1974-76, above.

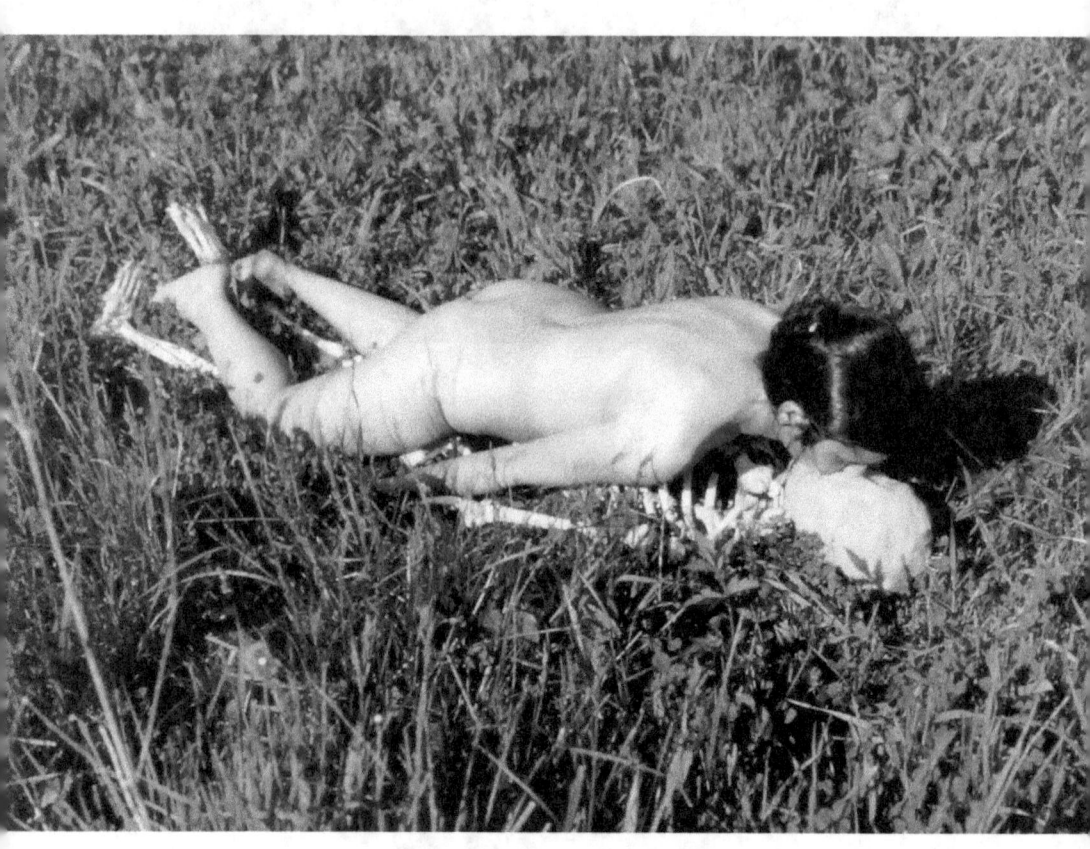

Anna Mendieta, On Giving Life, 1975

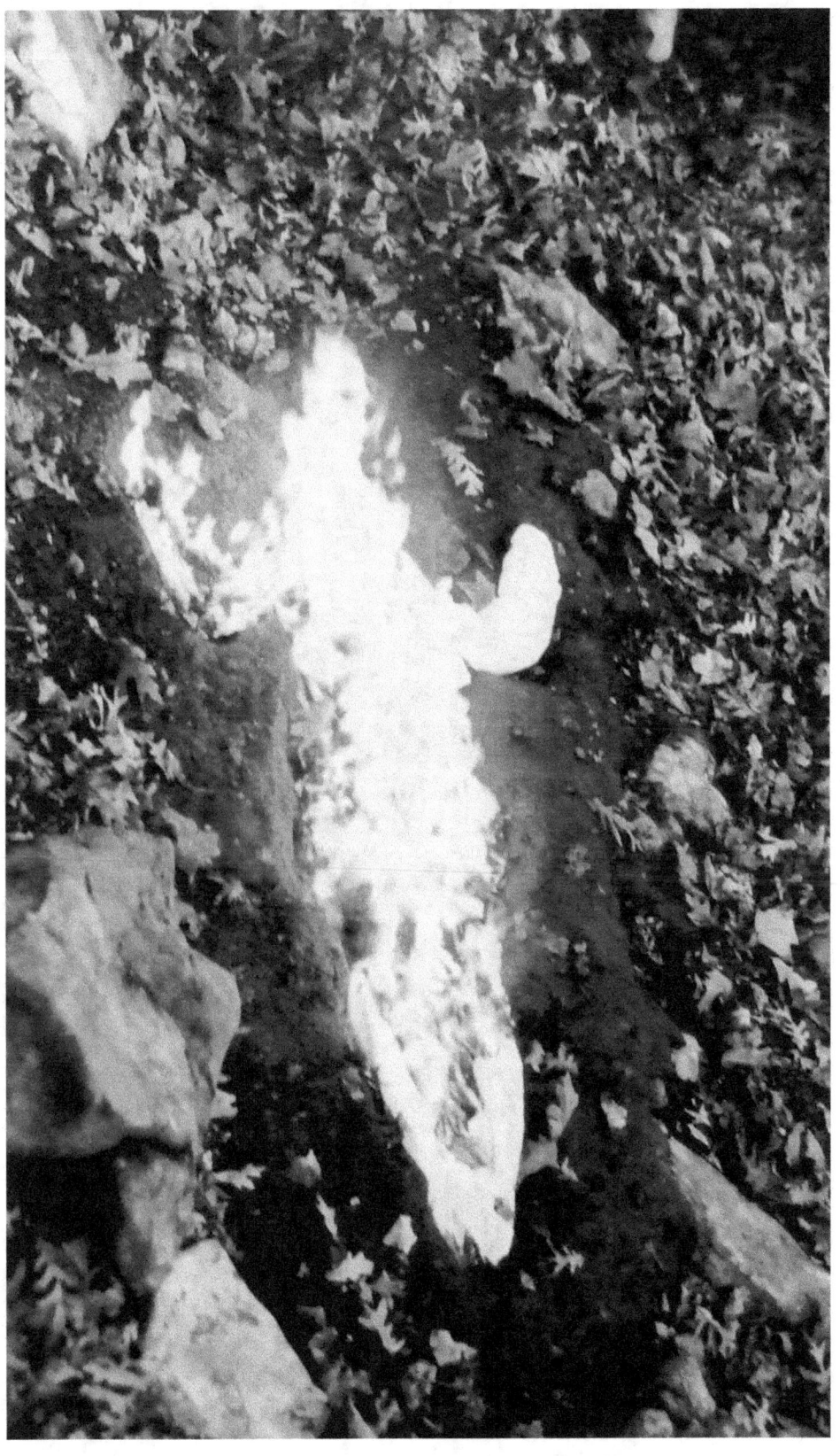

Ana Mendieta, Soul Silhouette On Fire, 1975

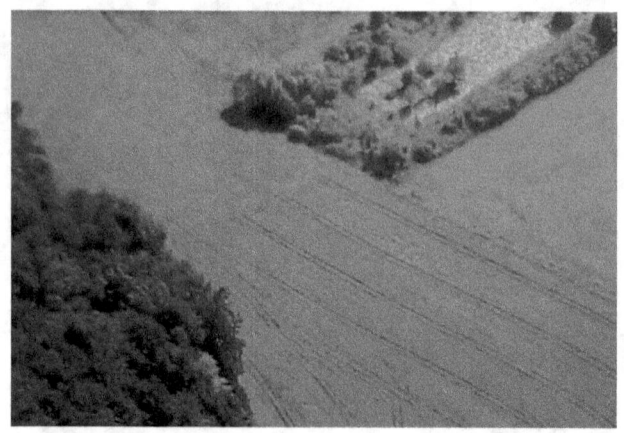

Hermann de Vries, Field

PART THREE

EUROPEAN LAND ARTISTS
IN AMERICA

17

Andy Goldsworthy in America

Andy Goldsworthy (b. 1956) has created land art in Grise Fiord, the North Pole, in Japan, upstate New York, California, Castres, Digne, La Rochelle and Sidobre in France, the Australian outback, and in Haarlem, Holland.

Goldsworthy continues to work in countries such as Japan, Australia, Canada, North America and France, but his home ground of Dumfriesshire in Scotland remains (at) the heart of his work. (From the mid-Nineties, Goldsworthy worked increasingly frequently at Digne in South France; it became one of the most valuable places for the sculptor outside of his home in Scotland, and was the site of a major commission, *Réfuges d'Art* [*Time*, 82]).

Around the world, Goldsworthy has concentrated on Westernized territories: on America, of course (it's the centre of land art), Western Europe, Australia and Japan (with the odd excursion to exotic spots, such as the North Pole). Goldsworthy has not made much art in Eastern Europe, in Russia, in mainland China, in India, in Africa or South America. (Goldsworthy did visit Russia in 1991, but 'administration difficulties' prevented the intended work in Siberia [*Time*, 193]). Visits to India, Africa, China and so on will probably come.

In the 1990s, Andy Goldsworthy's art began to rise in popularity: the glossy coffee table book *Stone* became a bestseller (bear in mind it was priced at 35 pounds or about 55 dollars). In 1994 Goldsworthy took over some London galleries with a large one-man show, *Stone* (this included *Herd of Arches*, also made for the Hathill Sculpture Foundation at Goodwood in Sussex, and ultimately finding a permanent home in Cornwall).[1] In 1995 he took part in an intriguing group show, *Time Machine: Ancient Egypt and Contemporary Art,* at the British Museum in London and Museo Egizio, Turin, creating sculptures, along with Richard Deacon, Peter Randall-Page and others, in amongst the monumental statuary of the famous Egyptian Hall. Also in 1995, Goldsworthy designed a set of Royal Mail stamps. As well as commissions, installations, TV and radio programmes, and books, Goldsworthy has also produced limited edition prints (the pictures of cairns were made with Eyestorm, in editions of 500, priced at $720 each).

Andy Goldsworthy's presence in America grew steadily with a series of exhibitions beginning with the Storm King *Wall* and show at the end of the millennium: Cornell University in 2000; the *Three Cairns* show and installations in 2002-03; Austin Museum in 2003; the *Garden of Stone* and *Stone Houses* in New York City in 2003-04; and *Roof* in Washington in 2005.

At 2,278 feet long, another wall, the *Storm King Wall* in upstate New York, was not only Goldsworthy's biggest wall, it was one of Goldsworthy's most significant works. Other artists who had work at the Storm King Art Center included Richard Serra, Louise Nevelson, David Smith, Mark di Suvero, Isamu Noguchi, Alice Aycock and Alexander Calder.

Andy Goldsworthy has built many arches: it has become one of his most distinctive motifs. No other land artist had employed the arch so often as a key structure in their *œuvre*. Goldsworthy's arch sculptures include the offshoot of the *Sheepfolds* project, the *Arch* project of 1996-97; a number of 'herds' of stone arches (such as *Herd of Arches* and *A Clearing of Arches*); arches exhibited in Montréal (1998); a private commission made near the Storm King Art Center, *Eleven Arches* (1997); and some large commissioned arches: a stone arch sited in Montréal (1999) and Rainscombe Park, Oare, Wiltshire (2000), both constructed from red Scottish sandstone. Of the *Montréal Arch*, commissioned by Cirque du Soleil for its HQ, Goldsworthy remarked: '[t]he arch is heavy and strong, expressing permanence, but it is in fact about change, movement and journey' (*Time*, 60).

Other Goldsworthy shows and projects of the 1990s and after included *Mid Winter Muster* in Australia (1991), various wall commissions (such as in New York, 1993, 1996 and 1997); various *Cones* (New York and Oxford, 1995); *Fieldgate* (New York, 1993); clay holes and throws at Runnymede Sculpture Farm, California (1992); *Two Autumns* in Japan (1994); *Breath of Earth* at San Jose Museum of Art (1995); a clay installation (a hole) in L.A. (at the Getty Center for the Arts, 1997; later destroyed by a burst pipe); another wall at Storm King (*Folded Wall*, 1999); *Snowballs in Summer* in London (2000); *Garden of Stone*, a memorial for victims and survivors of the Holocaust, sited in Manhattan (2003); and a show at Yorkshire Sculpture Park in 2007.

Andy Goldsworthy works with the natural world, and within nature. He uses natural materials in (apparently) natural shapes and forms set in natural contexts. Goldsworthy takes his cue from nature: as Jan Dibbets put it in 1969: 'I realized that if you want to use nature, you have to derive the appropriate structure from nature too'.[2] Andy Goldsworthy seems to be a particularly gentle and sensitive artist, compared to many sculptors and land artists: he stitches together leaves to forms lines (which're often placed in water, or over branches), or makes circular slabs of snow, or entwines twigs in an arc. He creates a delicate spiral of chestnut leaves, called *Autumn Horn* (1986); he pins bright yellow dandelions on willowherb stalks in a circle, on bluebells (1987); he makes lines and cairns of pebbles; a horizontal line of red sumach leaves was pinned to a willow (at Storm King in 1998); he rubs red stones to stain rockpools; he pins leaves to tree trunks; he makes hollow, circular structures, recalling igloos, from slate, leaves, driftwood and bracken; he makes long wavy ridges in Arizonan and Australian desert sand; he throws sand and sticks in the air and photographs the moment; he makes arches, globes, hollow spheres, slabs, spires, spirals and star-shapes out of snow and ice. Very impressive it all is. The sculptures made of sticks, for instance, stuck together in an arch, or a line, reflected in the mirror-like water of Derwent Water in Cumbria in 1988, are indeed wonderful. The sculptures exude tranquillity, an early morning calm (quite the opposite of another water work, Klaus Rinke's *Water Sculpture*, where a water canon blasted water over visitors as they approached a gallery, or Jim Sanborn's 1995 *Coastline*, which employs a wave generator to simulate waves in a Maryland garden).

Goldsworthy, like Turrell, Aycock and Smithson, has made some huge pieces, such as the long 'snake' and the 'pool' or maze, in Country Durham, large works which take up a lot of space, and certainly dominate the surrounding landscape. Goldsworthy's large-scale outdoor works often use the serpent coil as a fundamental form. Goldsworthy maintained, however, that his 'snake-like' or serpent-shaped sculptures does not refer directly to snakes.[3] Instead, he preferred to call one of his favourite motifs a 'river of earth', or a tree root, or a river.[4]

Other large-scale Goldsworthy works include installations *Slate Wall* and *Clay Wall* (1998, Edinburgh), *Clay Wall* (1996, San Francisco) and *Clay Wall* (2000, London). The *Fall Creek* installation, at the Herbert F. Johnson Museum of Art at Cornell University (in 2000), comprised a group of low holed mounds fashioned from hundreds of branches on the floor. Goldsworthy has worked at Cornell a number of times: the university has a long history of land art links: one of the important land exhibitions, *Earth Art*, took place in 1969 (it featured Long, Oppenheim, Smithson, Morris and Heizer).

GARDEN OF STONE (2003)

One of the most important of Andy Goldsworthy's later commissions was the installation *Garden of Stone* (2003) at the Museum of Jewish Heritage in Lower Manhattan. *Garden of Stone: A Living Memorial* was a group of 18 hollowed Vermont granite glacial boulders, with an oak tree inside (dwarf oaks, which only grow very slowly). The trees were planted at the top of each stone, with the hollow space below for the roots. The largest boulders weighed 13 tons. *Garden of Stone* was situated on the second floor garden, overlooking the river, with socio-political icons such as the Statue of Liberty and Ellis Island easily visible beyond. *Garden of Stone* cost a million dollars (the Public Art fund collaborated with the museum), making it easily Goldsworthy's most expensive commission to date. Jacob Ehrenberg was project manager.

The glacial granite boulders were taken from Vermont (near Barre). They were then transported to a Connecticut quarry (Stony Creek) where Ed Monti, a guy in his seventies, hollowed them using a cutting torch. The bases were flattened so that the rocks would sit properly on the ground (Goldsworthy said that in trimming the stones, he aimed to retain as much height to each stone as possible). Goldsworthy allowed the marks made on the boulders by their journeys and hollowing to remain. That was part of his preference for retaining evidence of the transformations materials undergo. It was part of the social project of Goldsworthy's art: it was important for the artist where the stones came from; the source was part of the overall sculpture. Hence the boulders were collected from fields and the landscape, rather than quarries (the more obvious place to shop for stones): 'how the sculpture is made and the journey of both the ideas and material are also important' (*Passage*, 65).

Goldsworthy also wanted to maintain the integrity of his garden of trees and stones, and was concerned about the planting the Jewish Museum planned for the borders of the site. Goldsworthy said he hoped to retain the 'sense of barrenness' of just the stones and the trees, and the introduction of other plants would compromise his sculpture, as well as the look of the building (*Passage*, 69). Originally, Goldsworthy planned to have all of the stones roughly the same size, but the idea developed to having a range of sizes, with the larger ones acting as 'guardians or leaders in the group' (*Passage*, 67).

Garden of Stone was made as a memorial for the victims and survivors of the Holocaust. Goldsworthy was an unusual choice, perhaps, for an artist to tackle such a massive political and ideological issue. Goldsworthy has not been known for addressing issues such as the Holocaust in his art. Certainly he could not be described as a high profile political artist. He has also not had much of a connection with Jewish culture or history.

A group of Holocaust survivors were invited at the opening of the exhibit (September 16, 2003) to plant the saplings in the stones. (Goldsworthy's mother Muriel also planted a tree). *Garden of Stone* brought together two of Goldsworthy's favourite materials, trees and stones, and obvious (but no less noble) themes of change, growth, transformation, burial and rebirth.

STONE HOUSES (2004)

Stone Houses (2004) was a prestigious commission from the Metropolitan Museum of Art in Gotham, for its roof garden. The rocks were taken from Glenluce Bay in Scotland and transported to the US, but the wood (white cedar) for the *Stone Houses* was from New England. The roof garden overlooked Central Park and the formidable skyline of Manhattan, so the sculptures had plenty to contend with visually. This setting certainly wasn't the undulating hills around Penpont or the windswept beaches of Scotland or California, but one of the most famous cityscapes in the world.

The two columns of granite stones were about thirteen feet high. They were fashioned in the familiar Goldsworthy form of a tapering column, decreasing in size so that the topmost stone was a pebble. Around the columns of stones Goldsworthy constructed an octagonal 'house' – basically a domed-shaped shelter structure which enclosed the columns (they were eighteen feet tall). The cedar wood had been split into rails, with each end overlapping.

Andy Goldsworthy continued his series of prestigious exhibitions in the United States of America with *Roof* (2005), at the National Gallery of Art in the nation's capital. *Roof* consisted of several slate domes which were basically very large versions of a form Goldsworthy had developed years ago: low, hollow domes of pieces of slate stacked on top of each other, with circular holes at the top. Goldsworthy related the dome shape of *Roof* to the famous domes of downtown Washington, including the

West Building of the National Gallery, the U.S. Capitol, the National Museum of Natural History and the Jefferson Memorial. For the *Roof* project, Goldsworthy used stone (Buckingham slate) from the same source as the materials for the domes of the Smithsonian Castle and Ford's Theater. Goldsworthy had begun the commission by visiting Government Island, Stafford, Virginia, in 2003, where he made some ephemeral sculptures.

TOUCHING NORTH (1989)

Andrew Goldsworthy's most dramatic work to date is probably *Touching North* (1989), four circular arches made of snow. It is dramatic mainly due to its location, that space so thoroughly a masculine 'wild zone', the place of macho adventures, colonization and courage: the North Pole. The *Touching North* project was organized by the Fabian Carlsson Gallery, London (one of Goldsworthy's dealers at the time), and overseen by Fabian Carlsson. In March and April, 1989, the expedition visited Montréal, Resolute, Grise Fjord, Camp Hazen and the North Pole, and the show travelled to London, Edinburgh and L.A. through 1989.

Goldsworthy's intention with the grandeur of *Touching North* was 'to follow North to its source'. He had already encountered 'North' in 'the cold shadow of a mountain', he said, meaning he had already found the extreme cold associated with the North Pole in Scotland or Northern Britain. But there was a practical reason for going all the way North to the North Pole, and that was so that Goldsworthy could enjoy 'the luxury of constant freezing' (in Britain, snow comes and goes: it does not stay for months on end as it does in the North Pole). As Goldsworthy wrote: 'so much that I have made in ice has been frustrated by a rise in temperature. I have held ice seemingly for ages waiting for it to freeze only to let go and see it drop off.'[5] Yeah, we all know that feeling.

Although the four circular walls were the centrepiece of the *Touching North* project, Goldsworthy made other snowworks at the time. *Snow Spires* was two little groups of pyramid forms between five and seven feet tall (1989, Ellesmere Island), while *Snow Slabs* was a long line of slabs, recalling the lines of prehistoric stones at

Carnac in France. Other works in *Touching North* included a wall constructed from narrow slabs of snow balanced on top of each other; flat wedges of snow piled on top of each other to form a low bridge; a series of free-standing arches placed in a row, recalling the nave of a Gothic cathedral; a cairn made from circular slabs of snow; a low wall of snow with arrow-shaped slits carved in it; another wall consisting of chevrons placed end-to-end. There were also various narrow walls of snow with slits carved in them: one in the shape of a star; another in a Goldsworthyan serpent; another with parallel zigzag lines.

THREE CAIRNS (2000-02)

Some of Andy Goldsworthy's earliest works (of the 1970s) were tidal, beachbound sculptures which relied very much on the power and majesty of the sea to make them work. Some were sculptures which required the action of the tide to complete them. They were fabricated specifically so that the sea would cover them up. They involved Goldsworthy working very fast, usually arriving at a beach site at lowest tide, to give him the most time to complete a sculpture (it was thus best when low tide coincided with early morning). Beaches were often good places for materials, too (always an important consideration for an artist): sand and stones aplenty, and wood, and flotsam and jetsam. Building the sculpture was only half of the work, though: Goldsworthy always stayed around for the moment when the tide came in, photographing the sculpture throughout its immersion. The moment of collapse was particularly important for Goldsworthy, and he was disappointed if he didn't witness it.

Although the tidal works are dealing with big themes, of time, change, decay, the sea, nature, lunar power, and so on, there is also something undeniably childlike about such sculptures. They're reminiscent of children (and adults) who build castles, boats and walls from sand below the high tideline, so they can watch them (or stand in them) when the waves approach. Thus, Goldsworthy's tidal works are some of his most fun art: they can be regarded as serious explorations of nature and time, or larking about on a beach, building stuff then watching it disintegrate.

Later tidal works included *Eleven Arches* (1992, Carrick Bay), *Sand Stones* (1992, California), *Beach Holes* (1990, Morecambe), *Balanced Rocks* (1993, Porth Ceiriad, Wales), *Sand Holes* (1997, Rockcliffe), *Cairn* and *Stick Dome Hole* (both 1999, Nova Scotia), and the *Three Cairns* project (2001-02). In Collieston (Aberdeenshire) in 2000 Goldsworthy produced a group of ephemeral beachworks: a rock covered with smooth sand, or ridges of sand, or a negative circle of sand. Each sand work was washed away by the tide. Goldsworthy's very early works were consciously irregular and 'organic' in shape and form, rather than the more geometric forms he later adopted (such as circles, spirals and lines).

Many (land) artists have worked with the tide apart from Andy Goldsworthy: Barry Flanagan, Christo, Dennis Oppenheim, Michael McCafferty, Michelle Oka Doner, Chris Drury and Jan Dibbets. Jan Dibbets had a tractor plough the sand on a beach which would then be covered by the tide, in a film made for television (in 1969), for a *Land Art* exhibition.

Three Cairns (2000-02) was an important large-scale commission to construct three cairns in the United States of America: one on the West Coast (in California), one on the East Coast (in New York state), and one in the Mid-West (at Des Moines, Iowa). *Three Cairns* was a collaboration with three cultural institutions: Des Moines Art Center, Neuberger Museum of Art, Purchase, New York, and La Jolla Museum in San Diego. In the event, Goldsworthy built six cairns: apart from the three permanent pieces, there were three ephemeral sculptures: two were tidal, on the East and West coasts, and the third, in Iowa, was built on the prairie, which was set alight (with fire replacing water as the natural force which engulfed the sculpture. However, the stone cairn survived the fire).

The project had a conceptual basis, with the cairns linked up. They wouldn't be able to be viewed at the same time, in the same space, and thus part of *Three Cairns* 'will to an extent always exist only as an idea', as Goldsworthy put it (*Passage*, 118). Goldsworthy defined the cairn for him again: '[t]he cairn is a marker to the flow of change, life, growth, decay, death and renewal of the prairie landscape' (*Passage*, 94).

The *Prairie Cairn* was constructed especially for the burn (the cairn and burn was managed in collaboration with Grinnell College and Faulconer Gallery). Goldsworthy has often combined stones and heat – he's fired stones in stoves, for instance, and was fascinated by the process of hollowing out the glacial boulders for *Garden of Stones* with a cutting torch. In the event, the burning of *Prairie Cairn* was hot enough to melt part of Goldsworthy's camera, and he didn't get the shots he wanted of the prairie on fire around the cairn. Goldsworthy also failed to capture the collapse of the tidal cairn in the West, so the series of ephemeral US cairns was in some way a failure. 'The series remains one of my strongest achievements and yet contains great failures' (*Passage*, 95).

The *West Coast Sea Cairn* was constructed at Half Moon Bay in California in August, 2001. The tidal process was central to the cairn, as with all of Goldsworthy's sculptures made on the seaboard. It was built to collapse with the next tide, and, as ever, capturing the moment of the downfall photographically was crucial. It was a paradox that something as solid and enduring as stone could be so ephemeral. That was part of the conception of the stone cairns built on beaches: stone and water, the permanent and the impermanent, solidity and fragility.

As with his *Réfuges d'Art* sculptures in Digne in South France, and the walls built at Clougha Pike in Lancashire (1999-2001), Goldsworthy constructed some limestone walls with hollowed-out spaces, which surrounded the permanent *Midwest Cairn* at Des Moines Art Center. At Digne and Lancashire, Goldsworthy had built walls with vertical elliptical cavities, large enough for a person to stand in (there was a step just below the space to help the visitor up). In Iowa, Goldsworthy turned the elliptical hollows into cairn-shaped spaces. Now each wall had a recess in the middle of it shaped roughly like half an egg. The limestone walls were grouped around the central cairn in the familiar Goldsworthyan guise of guardians or sentinels

Each cairn-shaped cavity related directly to the exact shape of the three cairns, as if the cairns from the East and West coasts could be brought to Iowa and slotted into the walls, as if the coastal cairns had a womb-like resting place waiting for them in perpetuity in Iowa, as if the cairns on the coasts had travelled outwards, away from Iowa, and the Iowa walls were 'home'.

The *East Coast Cairn* (2001), built at the Neuberger Museum of Art, took on personal associations for Goldsworthy, because his father had died recently (in October, 2001). The cairn, constructed under a large tree, became something of a memorial for his father (Goldsworthy also discussed the events of September 11, 2001 in relation to the work – *East Coast Cairn* was created a couple of months after the attacks on New York and Washington [*Passage*, 112, 115]).

The *West Coast Cairn* was built outside the Museum of Contemporary Art in San Diego in early 2002. The California cairn was constructed under another tree: Goldsworthy spoke of the tree in his usual terms of sheltering and guardianship

(*Passage*, 118). Scale was always an important consideration in siting a sculpture beside a tree: the tree shouldn't dominate the sculpture, and the sculpture should be able to assert itself.

Some of the poetic links artists make in the course of their work are sometimes obscure. Goldsworthy liked the fact that the San Diego cairn was made of limestone, which was created, geologically, on the seabed, and the cairn was near the ocean (*Passage*, 117). It's a connection an artist can discover over time, because s/he's working on the piece for hours or days, but one wonders how many visitors to the Museum of Contemporary Art would make the link between limestone and the nearby Pacific.

18

Christo in America

Christo (b. 1935) is perhaps most well-known land artist working today. He makes huge, very public gestures: tarpaulin and plastic shrouded buildings, the wrapped Pont Neuf and Reichstag, and curtains hanging across Colorado valleys. His art is not 'invisible' like Walter de Maria's kilometre-long brass rod which only reveals a brass disc on the ground, or Hamish Fulton's walks, which are only memories or text pieces.

Christo's first large-scale wrapping was to cover the Museum of Contemporary Art in Chicago with 10,000 square feet of brown tarpaulin. Christo's wrapping of the museum made it the focus of attention in the neighbourhood – some people hadn't realized the museum was there until it had been wrapped. The museum's director reckoned Christo had parodied 'all the associations a museum evokes: a mausoleum, a repository for precious contents, an intent to wrap up all of art history'.[1] Inside the museum was the *Wrapped Floor*, consisting of 2,000 square feet of rented drop cloths.

Valley Curtain (1972), at Rifle Pass in Colorado, did not last so long. It was blown down. The huge bright orange curtain hung across the valley, providing a passageway as well as a visual block to what was beyond.

> When I was doing *Valley Curtain* everybody knew that this is a huge curtain crossing a valley. Now everybody knew what it is that is behind the valley. The thing that is behind is not so important… only that motion, the passing through.[2]

The use of orange, as with the pink in *Surrounded Islands*, gave *Valley Curtain* a new æsthetic, more attuned to Henri Matisse and Claude Monet, quite different from the dull brown tarpaulin of the *Wrapped Museum*. Christo would continue to use such colours throughout his career on his major wrappings.

Many of Christo's large-scale wrapped works were situated next to water: *Running Fence* plunged into the sea; *Wrapped Coast* was submerged by the tides; *Surrounded Islands* floated on the ocean; *Pont-Neuf* stretched over the River Seine. *Surrounded Islands* (1980-83) was one of Christo's largest works. Not a wrapping this time, but still involving masses of fabric (6 million ft^2 of it). With a budget of $3.5 million, 4 engineers, 2 ornithologists, a marine biologist, 2 attorneys and 430 helpers, Christo surrounded 11 little islands for 2 weeks in May, 1983. The choice of brilliant pink meant the enclosed islands stood out vividly against the green sea at Biscayne Bay in Florida. The pink-enclosed islands looked like flowers floating on the sea, recalling the Japanese Buddhist ceremony of setting flowers afloat. Or, more in tune with Western art history, evoking Claude Monet's waterlilies.

Running Fence (1972-76) comprised 2,050 18 foot panels of white nylon attached to steel poles, running across Marin and Sonoma counties and 12 roads in California. As with Christo's other mammoth projects, there was much opposition to *Running Fence*. A committee designed to 'stop Running Fence' brought the subject to the Superior Court of the State of California 3 times. The subsequent report on the environmental impact of the *Running Fence* project found that there were no endangered species in the region, except for the Brown Pelican, and virtually no wildlife would be affected by it. *Running Fence* went ahead, and stayed up for two weeks in September, 1976.[3] When it was taken down, nothing remained of it in the area: the holes were filled in, and bare parts of soil were reseeded. As with other Christo projects, when it was taken away some locals were dismayed, the work had helped them realize the beauty of the area. Christo says his art is

> about displacement. Basically even today I am a displaced person. And this is why I make art that does not last. Of course, it will stay for ever in the minds of people.[4]

Christo here espouses the fundamental Romanticism in land art: that it will live on in the memories of people. Christo's large-scale projects – *Running Fence, Surrounded Islands, Wrapped Coast* – were spectacular works, part of the land art tradition which moved towards the sublime in landscape art (which has affinities with the Abstract Expressionism of Mark Rothko, Barnett Newman and Robert Motherwell). The ocean end of *Running Fence* was particularly impressive: at Bodega Bay the *Fence* extended gracefully into the Pacific, 558 feet, descending from a height of 18 feet on land to 2 feet at the section which was anchored to the bottom of the sea. The *Umbrellas* stretched for 12 miles in Japan and 18 miles in California.

Christo's large-scale works are expensive: *Running Fence* cost over $3 million, *Surrounded Islands* cost $3.5 million, and *The Umbrellas* in Japan and California cost $26,000,000. Denigrators of Christo's work have noted the expense of the projects, but Christo pays for them himself, by selling photos, drawings, collages, models, lithographs and plans and other works, and by collaborating with industry.

19

Richard Long In the United States

The central fact and act of Richard Long's (b. 1945) art is walking. His work is founded on the art of walking, the act of walking, the actuality of walking, and on walking as art, as act, as experience. His walks become 'artwalks', artwalks which become artworks. As he walks he works. Art-walking and art-working become interchangeable. 'I have met with but one or two persons in the course of my life who understood the art of Walking, that is, of taking walks – who had a genius, so to speak, for *sauntering*', wrote Henry David Thoreau.[1]

Richard Long has had one-man shows at most of the major Western galleries, including many in the US: Museum of Modern Art, New York (1972), Fogg Art Museum, Cambridge, MA (1980), National Gallery of Canada, Ottawa (1982), Guggenheim, New York (1986), La Jolla Museum of Contemporary Art (1989), Philadelphia Museum of Art (1994), Sao Paolo Biennale (1994), Contemporary Arts Museum, Houston (1996), Modern Art Museum, Fort Worth (1996), Milwaukee Art Museum (2001), and Stommein Synagoge (2004).

Some of Richard Long's group shows include many in the United States, such as the *Earth Art* exhibition at the White Museum at Cornell University in 1969 (an important land art show), the Conceptual art show *Information* at MOMA in Gotham in 1970, the Guggenheim International in 1971, a show with Andre (and Le Va) in Washington in 1976, *Probing the Earth: Contemporary Land Projects* at the Hirshhorn in Washington 1977 (another important land art exhibition, which travelled to La Jolla and Seattle), and *A Quiet Revolution: British Sculpture Since 1965* in Chicago and San Francisco in 1987.

Richard Long is associated with the American land, Minimal, Process, Conceptual and postmodern artists (such as Lawrence Weiner, Michael Heizer, Dennis Oppenheim, Nancy Holt, Alice Aycock, Donald Judd, Robert Smithson, Tony Smith, Sol LeWitt, and especially Carl Andre), and with European Arte Povera and Minimal/ Conceptual artists (Hans Haacke, Christo, Jannis Kounellis, Alberto Burri, Daniel Buren, Giovanni Anselmo, Mario Merz and Jan Dibbets). Other key names one might link with Richard Long include John Cage, Jackson Pollock, Joseph Beuys, Yves Klein, Constantin Brancusi, Joseph Kosuth, Bruce Nauman, Barnett Newman, and Anthony Caro.

Richard Long has tended to concentrate on favourite sites for making walkworks (most walkers have their special places). The Longian territories include America, Scotland, England, Ireland, Italy, Portugal, Tanzania, Turkey, Holland, Japan, Lappland, Nepal, India, the Sahara, Argentina, Malawi, Bolivia, Ecuador, Canada, Korea, Finland,

Mongolia, Mexico, Patagonia, Iceland and Peru. That's a pretty big number of territories for anyone to visit, let alone an artist (artists often being poor). But Long hasn't made walkworks absolutely everywhere on the planet. On the European mainland, for instance, Long hasn't made as much art as one would expect in Switzerland, Norway, Finland, Denmark or Sweden, Belgium, Spain, the former Yugoslavia, Hungary, Austria, Germany, Romania, Bulgaria, Albania, Turkey, the Czech Republic and Greece. Many of those countries contain landscapes Long favours.

One of the distinctive Richard Long artforms is the stone circle. *Red Slate Circle* (1980) in the Fogg Art Museum in Cambridge (MA), or *Sandstone Spiral* (1983) in the National Gallery of Canada, or the *Puget Sound Driftwood Circle* (1996) in Houston, or *Forte de Vinadio Circle* (Italy, 2001), or *13th Street Ellipse* (2004, New York City) are set on museum floors, in the clean, sparse gallery environment, and look Minimal and sophisticated and not obviously 'Romantic'. What concerns Richard Long is that '[e]ach work is appropriate to its place and context', and the wilderness works and the museum pieces are 'equal and complementary'. What counts, Long says, is the feelings that the work, whether inside or outside, arouses: 'my ambition is basically with the emotional power of the work, in both idea and image' (1994a). Walking, nature and the landscape are at the heart of Long's work (1994c, 8), but Long knows, as any professional artist must know, that the art world conducts its business indoors (and in cities – and the international art scene where Long works and trades is concentrated in a few major cities). The art may be 'natural' or about the natural landscape, but the art world in which artists operate is distinctly urban, sophisticated, wealthy, highly educated and high culture. The *content* of Long's art is walking in the natural world, but the *context* is as urban as Keith Haring, Jean-Michel Basquiat, Frank Gehry or anonymous graffiti artists tagging the New York subway.

The slate, stick, wood and footprint circles of Richard Long look like late 20th century artworks, not 'Romantic', but Minimal, Conceptual and Arte Povera, like Carl Andre's copper and zinc plate squares or Donald Judd's Plexiglas and steel stacks and boxes. They have a coolness and clarity that one associates with Dan Flavin's fluorescent tubes, Anne Truitt's rectilinear slabs, Tony Smith's cubes and the white open boxes of Sol LeWitt. Long's stone circles make sense to the viewer partly because of a grounding in the discourses of contemporary art. Without assimilating the circularity of signs that flow around contemporary art, the spectator might not know how to make full sense of Long's circles. True, the circle as a shape has been around for eons, but only in the contemporary era have circles been made out of bits of the landscape, in galleries and in landscape settings in this particular way.

> I think circles have belonged in some way or other to all peoples at all times
> [remarked Long]. They are universal and timeless, like the image of a human
> hand. For me, that is part of their emotional power, although there is nothing
> symbolic or mystical in my work. They are also easy to make. (1995a)

Take Richard Long's *Tarahumara Circle* (Mexico, 1987): it's what seems at first
to be a simple shape. But it's not 'simple'. It's a 'negative circle', a circle made into a
circle by the ring of rocks around it (like *Walking a Circle In Ladakh*, 1984). The line of
rocks marks out the circle, but not evenly. Some of the rocks are piled deeper on one
side of the circle. Hardly anyone will have seen this circle intact, in its situation, so it's
known only from a photograph. The seemingly straightforward approach of Long's
photography has made a few æsthetic decisions, which shape the viewer's
perception of this artwork. For instance, the viewer sees the stone circle in the centre
of the frame, in the lower third, in the sort of classical composition that was taught in
the fine art academies of yore. Behind the circle the trees and hills of Mexico are
glimpsed. Long's photograph thus 'captures' the stone ring amidst the Mexican
landscape, placing it firmly within a wilderness landscape. The setting is impressive
and it is meant to be. With its wooded slopes and hills receding into the blue haze, the
photograph is worthy of the æerial effects described by Leonardo da Vinci in his
treatise of Renaissance painting. The composition of *Tarahumara Circle*, the more one
studies it, becomes increasingly 'classical' and carefully controlled: there are even
two small trees either side of the stone circle, in the foreground, framing the circle, a
compositional device favoured by J.M.W. Turner, Thomas Girtin, John Sell Cotman
and other late 18th century landscapists.

So *Tarahumara Circle* is actually a complex cultural artefact. The elements in
Tarahumara Circle that could be called 'natural' or 'organic' (the landscape setting,
the material used for the circle) are actually the last aspects of the work to be
considered. Sure, for the artist, they may be the most important, but they're just one
component in a highly sophisticated manifestation of 'high culture'.

Red Slate Ring (1986) was installed for the 1986 show at the Guggenheim
Museum: pieces of slate of a roughly similar size were overlaid to produce a wide
open circle, each piece of slate covering the ones below so that no part of the floor
showed through. *Stone Lake* (1988) was a large solid circle of stone slabs made in a
field of long grass in Schloss Crottorf. *Chisos Circle* (1990) was a medium-sized open

circle drawn in the stones in Texas. For the Haunch of Venison show (2003), Long produced irregular, curved rows of stones (*Cornwall State Lines*, 2003), and a *Norfolk Ellipse* (2003).

In the late Nineties, Richard Long started to fashion floor-based stone circles using different coloured stones: black, white, purple, green, and blue rocks. Each circle comprised coloured stones which were grouped together in single colour. Thus, in *Black White Green Pink Purple Circle* (1998, Galerie Tschudi, Glarus), about half the circle is green stone, a sixth segment is white, a smaller chevron-shaped part is black, a slightly larger zigzag section is pink stone, with purple placed along a third of the circumference. *Mohawk* (2002, Florida) was an ellipse made from white and grey stones, the grey placed in a wide zigzag through the middle. At *OPENASIA 2004: The East Meets the West*, Long showed a *Blue Sky Circle* (2002) comprising different coloured stones.

As one can see from the above examples of Richard Long's stone circles, Long has probably made more circles in land art than any other artist. It's hard to think of any artist who has created more circles out of stone, wood, snow, mud and slate than Richard Long.

New shapes appeared in Long's floor-standing sculptures in the 1990s: solid ellipses (as in *Spring Ellipse* [Salisbury, 1999], *Basalt Ellipse* [2001, Kleve], *Trento Ellipse* [Trento, 2000], and *White Quartz Ellipse* [New York, 2000]); open ellipses (as in *Periphery Stones* [1999], *Porfido Ellipse* and *Red Mud Ellipse*, Italy, 1998), and a wheel (as in *Circle of Life*, 1997.

And in the wall and mud drawings, Long developed new forms: the arc (*Gulf of Mexico Arc* [Houston, 1996], *River Avon Mud Arc* [Bilbao, 2000], and *Fast Hand Mud Arc* [Athens, 1999]); the open ellipse (*River Avon Mud Ellipse* [London, 2000]), and the demi-circle (*From One To Another* [Houston, 1996], or *Seminole* [2004], a half-circle shown at Seminole, Florida). One of the largest of the upside-down arcs was made at the new Guggenheim museum in Bilbao (2000).

Richard Long also utilizes quotations from pop music, from artists such as Bob Dylan, John Barleycorn, Johnny Cash (in *Reflections In Little Pigeon River, Great Smokey Mountains, Tennessee*, 1970), and country singer Nanci Griffith. His 1994 work in Orkney had a verse from a Bob Dylan song printed with it which ended: '[b]ut we still ain't going nowhere'.2 The Johnny Cash song which accompanies the photo work *Reflections in the Little Pigeon River, Great Smokey Mountains, Tennessee* ends: '[b]ecause you're mine / I walk the line' (in *Old World, New World*, 56). Music, Long feels, is another way of dealing with the emotions of a work. It expresses something in a work which words and photographs cannot.3 Music is something important for Long – he refers to it a number of times in his works (it is one of the phrases he used to sum up his work in his 1997 Japan lecture). The kind of music Long uses in his art is generally American, country and western or folk or soft rock. Long's favourite time and place in music would probably be the late 1960s in America.

In 1994, Long commented: 'I couldn't imagine life without music. I think it is really a fantastically emotional feel-good kind of art form' (1994b). When he visited art schools to give lectures and slide shows, Long said he used to play a piece of music to accompany just one slide, so the students had to look at one image for the duration of the song. (Andy Goldsworthy recalled a visit from Long to his art college in Northern Britain in the 1970s: how Long played Country and Western music during his 'lecture', but refused to answer questions from the students.)

> But the one piece of music that always got the most rapt attention, where you could almost hear a pin drop, was Roisin Dubhn, the slow air played on a tin whistle, with people looking at the circle in Ireland. That was always the most moving piece in the slide show. (1994b)

Roisin Dubh ('a slow air') was cited in the photowork A Thousand Stones (1974).

20

Other European Land Artists in America

CHRIS DRURY

Chris Drury (b. 1948) is one of the most intriguing British land artists and has made many works in the United States. Drury's art is instantly recognizable and distinctive. His cairns and shelters are among his most well-known pieces. Drury has treated his cairns in different ways: many of the stone cairns have had fires lit inside them, such as *Midsummer Fire Cairn* (1989), *Falling Water Fire Cairn* (1997, Norway), *Fire Cairn* (1993, Ireland), *Fire Mountain Cairn* (1996, Japan), and *Fire Cairn* (1989, Colorado). Some cairns have been enclosed with basket weaving, such as *Basket Cairn* (1991) and *Covered Cairn* (1993, Denmark).

Like much of US land art, Chris Drury's stone cairns are usually erected in wilderness or spectacular scenery: Norway (1988), New Mexico (1993), Lappland (1988), Ladakh (1997) and Colorado (1989). For Drury, the cairns are about commemorating a particular moment in a special place: 'they're just saying, 'this is an extraordinary place. Grab a few rocks, put them up before the moment's gone and photograph it'' (2002, 79). If the shelters were the stopping-places on a journey, the cairns were the 'markers of highpoints/ moments of exhilaration along the way' (1998, 58).

Another favourite Drury motif is the shelter: low, squat structures, some like teepees or witches' hats, some like prehistoric beehive huts. The shelters were often made from stone (but also in chalk, turf, ice, wood, plants and coal. Some of these materials, such as turf, coal and chalk, are unexpected, and give Drury's shelters a very particular quality). The shelters are usually (but not always) constructed at human scale. That is, in the correct scale for someone to enter them bodily.

Chris Drury's shelters have all sorts of connotations, stretching back thousands of years (shelters must have been one of the first structures that humans ever built – shelter being one of the primal human needs). 'Shelter is a basic human need and a manifestation of human presence', remarked Drury (1998, 20). Drury's shelters have obvious affinities (with Celtic and Bronze Age huts and houses in Britain, for example), but they are also about 'organic' forms, forms which repeat endlessly, and geometrically, like crystals. They are stopping and resting places, and also enclosing spaces. 'I like the way this interior space draws you inside yourself, enclosing, protecting, just as mountains pull you outside yourself, pushing mind and body beyond their usual confines', said Drury (ibid.).

Some of Drury's most appealing sculptures are 'cloud chambers', developments of his shelter form: these are basically circular stone or wooden shelters with holes and mirrors in the roof which act as lenses and reflectors. In these *camera obscuras*, the spectator can observe the sky above projected onto the floor below. The cloud chambers (constructed in many areas) articulate classic land art concerns: the dialectic between inner and outer, indoor and outdoor, stillness and movement, nature and culture. Drury's cloud chambers include *Coppice Cloud Chamber* (1998, Kent), *Cedar Log Sky Chamber* (1996, Japan), *Cloud Chamber* (1990, Belgium), and *Cloud Chamber For the Trees and Sky* (2003, North Carolina). The cloud chambers are 'still, silent, meditative and mysterious places', Chris Drury wrote on his website.

HANS HAACKE

The German artist Hans Haacke (b. 1936) has produced some of the most intriguing land artworks (although Haacke is more usually linked with Arte Povera, Conceptual and Process art, than land art). Many of Haacke's early works explored natural or organic systems. Later, Haacke moved on to social, economic and political systems (what Haacke called 'real-time systems'). Haacke's 1965 artistic statements included: 'make something that lives in time and makes the "spectator" experience time... articulate something natural'.[1] One of Haacke's tenets was 'the simpler the better'.

Grass Grows (1966 and 1969) was a mound of soil with grass growing out of it. Haacke later fashioned a row of beans growing along string suspended at an angle, in soil mounted on glass on the gallery floor (*Directed Growth*, 1972), and in tropical plants growing on a circular area of soil, *Rye in the Tropics* (1972). *Condensation Cube* (1963-65) was a Plexiglas cube (a metre on each side) with water inside which condensed on the clear sides of the box, an exploration of process. 'It is changing freely, bound only by statistical limits', remarked Haacke of his 'Weather Box'.

In *Sky Line* (1967) Haacke released white helium balloons over Central Park. Hans Haacke commented that

> in spite of my environmental and monumental thinking I am still fascinated by the nearly magic, self-contained quality of objects. My water levels, waves and condensation boxes are unthinkable without this physical separation from their

surroundings.[2]

Many of Hans Haacke's most compelling artworks were made to explore the ephemeral qualities of ice, snow, fog, steam, smoke and water. *Fog, Flooding, Erosion* (1969) employed a sprinkler system to turn a lawn in Seattle, Washington, into mud. *Fog Dripping From or Freezing On Exposed Surfaces* (Boston, 1971) and *Spray of Ithaca: Falls Freezing and Melting On Rope* (1969) explored water and fog freezing on waterfalls and trees.

One of Haacke's air and wind constructions comprised a fan blowing a seven by seven foot chiffon sail hung parallel to the gallery floor. Another air sculpture was a balloon balanced above an air jet (a favourite display with science and natural history museums). He had proposals for monumental-sized windmills and sails, all naturally powered by the winds. Haacke preferred to use unmechanical sources of energy.

Hans Haacke later considered economic systems in works such as *Shapolsky et al, Manhattan Real Estate Holdings, a Real-Time Social System* (1971). For the *Information* show at Gotham's MOMA (in 1971), Haacke exhibited a poll about Governor Rockerfeller running for election, inviting visitors to vote. Haacke took on cultural institutions such as museums, landlords, and politicians such as President Reagan and British PM, Margaret Thatcher. On a few occasions Haacke's proposals were negated by the authorities of the Guggenheim, Wallraf-Richartz and Metropolitan museums, with works and shows being cancelled as a result. Other artists (such as Daniel Buren) protested in support of Haacke.

PETER HUTCHINSON

Peter Hutchinson was born in England (in 1930), but spent most of his artistic career in the US (based in Massachusetts). He collaborated with Dennis Oppenheim on a series of underwater works: fruit, vegetables and bread were packed in plastic bags and suspended from a fishing line in the West Indes (1969). Hutchinson also planted flowers in the sand underwater, and made a dam from sand bags in Tobago (*Underwater Dam,* 1969). Along the rim of a volcano (Paricutin, 1970), Hutchinson sited a 76 metre line of white bread wrapped in plastic. Hutchinson recorded the growth of mould and decomposition. Later works include *Ice Sandwich* (1994), a Brancusi-like tower of slabs of wood interlaced with blocks of ice, and 'thrown ropes' of flowers planted in the ground in the shape of a rope that Hutchinson threw (1996). Hutchinson preferred works that combined his love of horticulture, science, art and botany.[3]

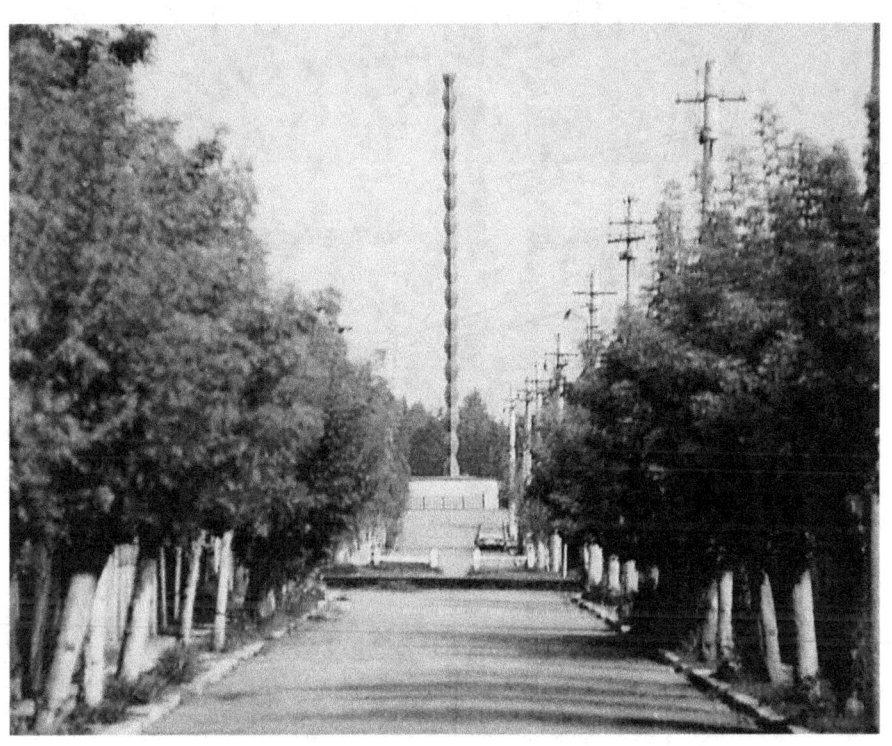

Constantin Brancusi, Endless Column

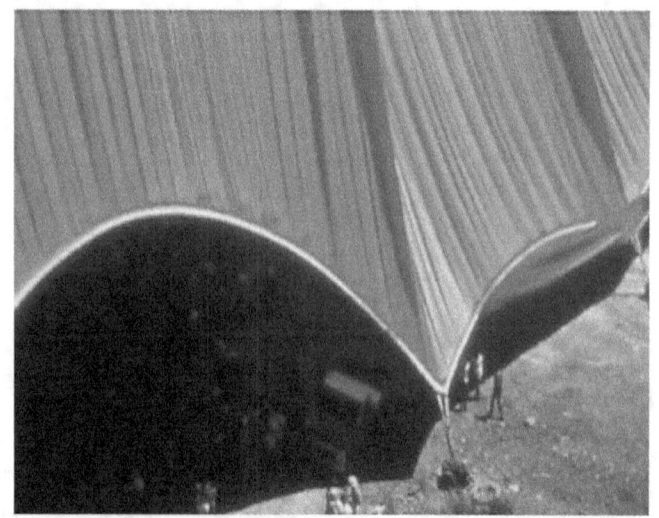

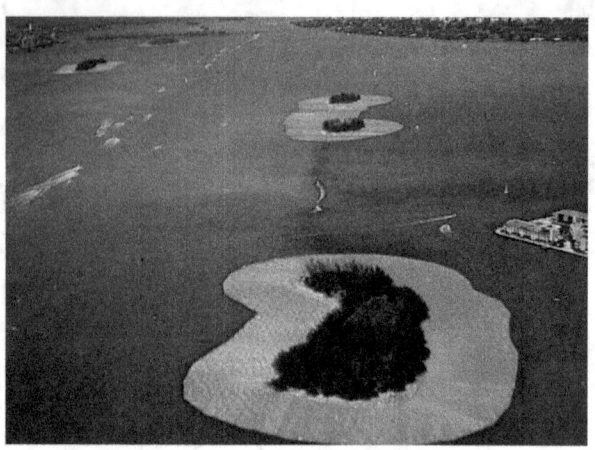

The Christos in the U.S. of A.: in Colorado (top);
in Florida (middle);
and in the Golden State (bottom).

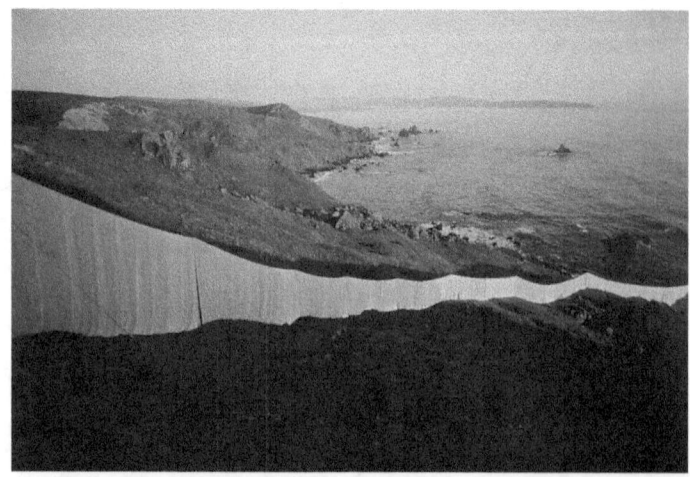

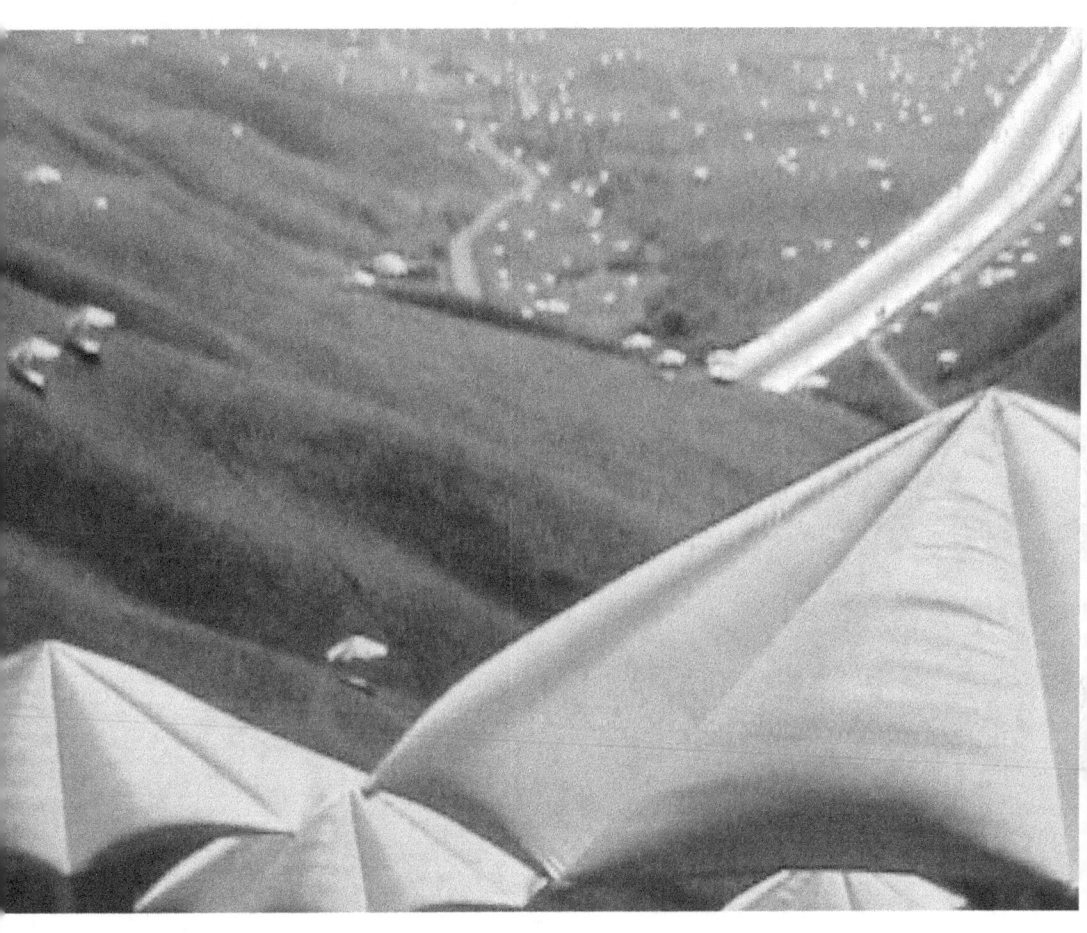

Christo, Umbrellas, 1976

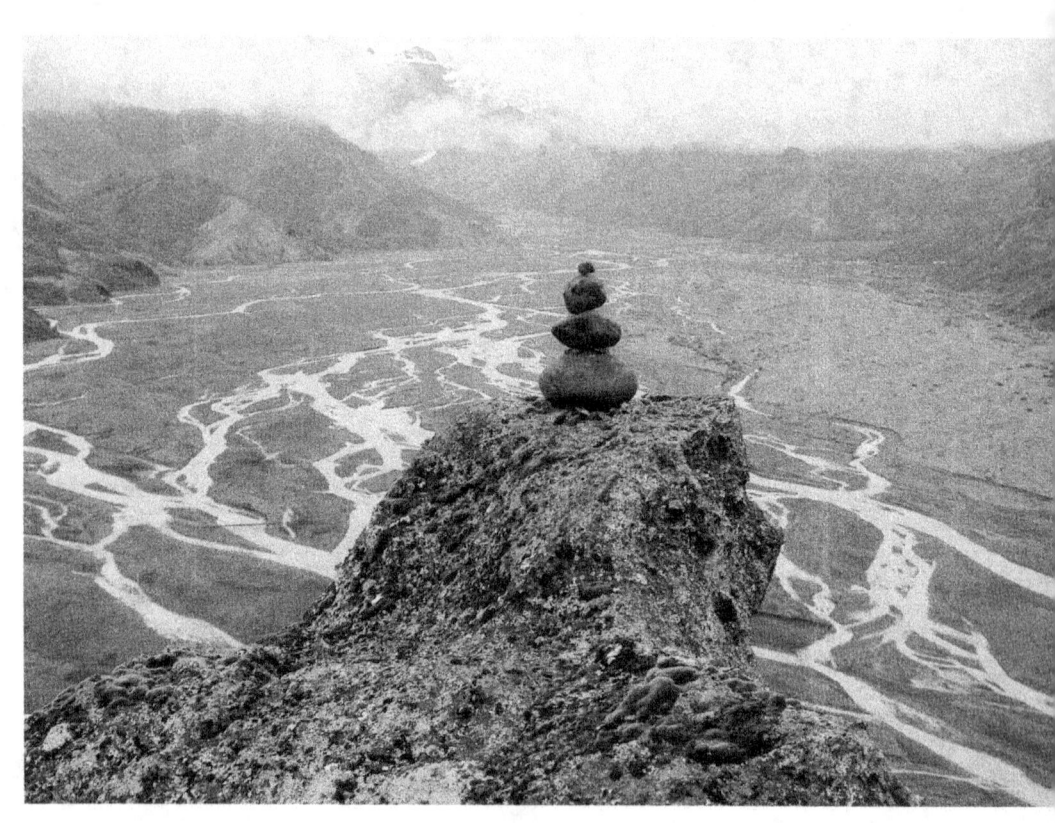

Chris Drury, Cairn

Hamish Fulton, No Talking For Seven Days, Scotland, 1993

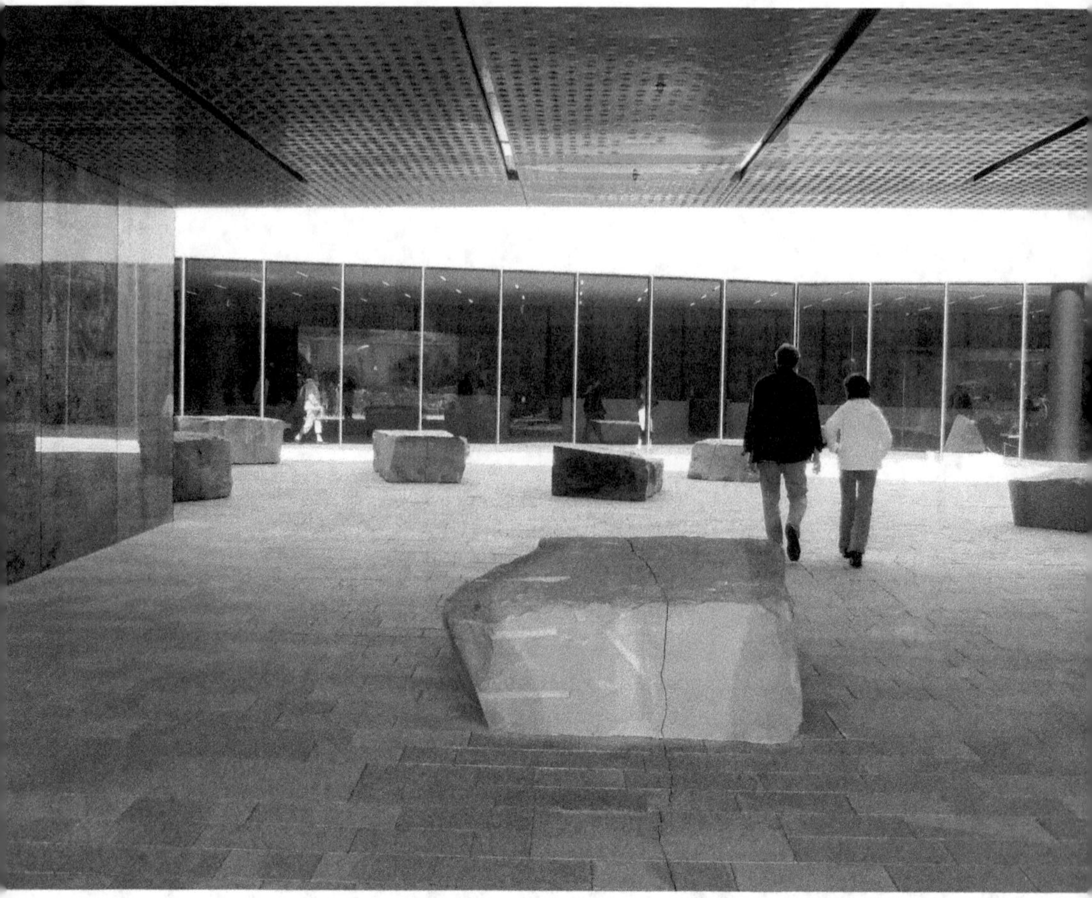

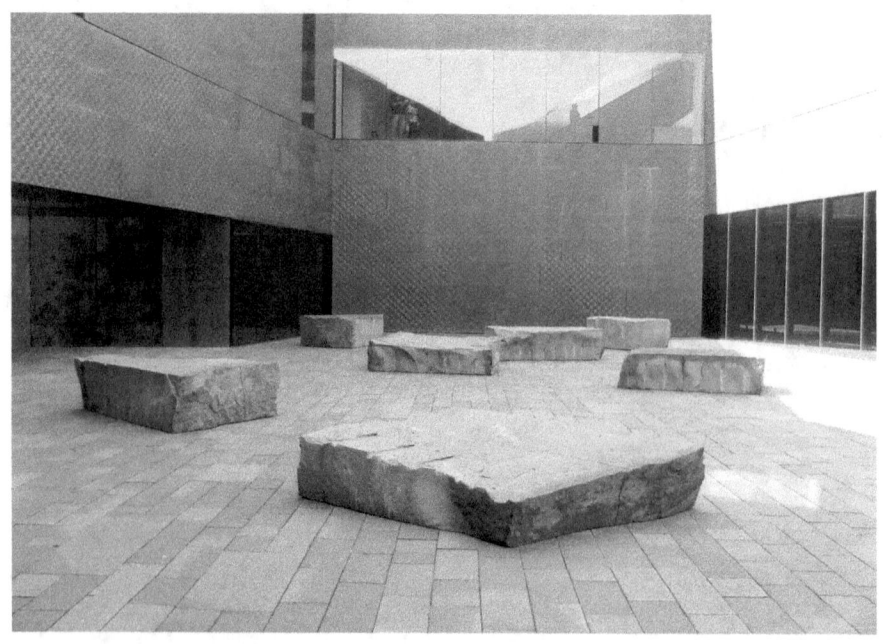

Andy Goldsworthy in San Francisco, at the de Young in 2008

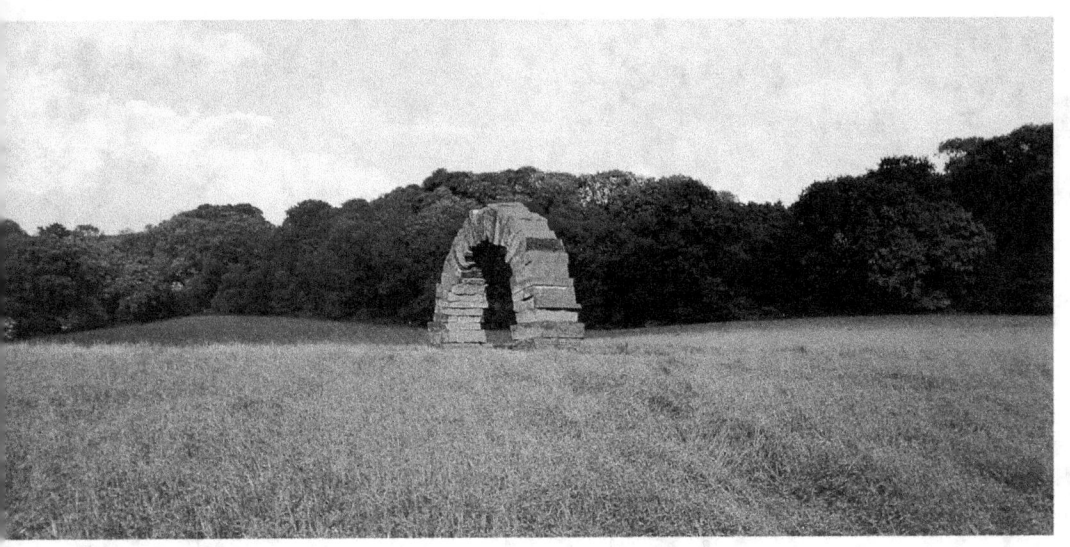

Andy Goldsworthy, Locharbriggs Sandstone Arch, 2000, Wiltshire

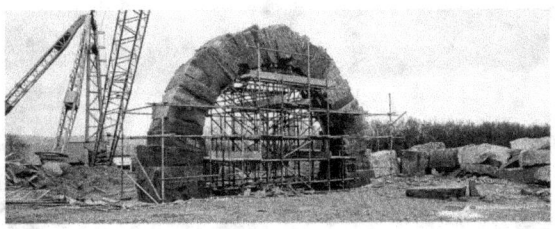

Andy Goldsworthy, Montréal Arch under construction, 1998

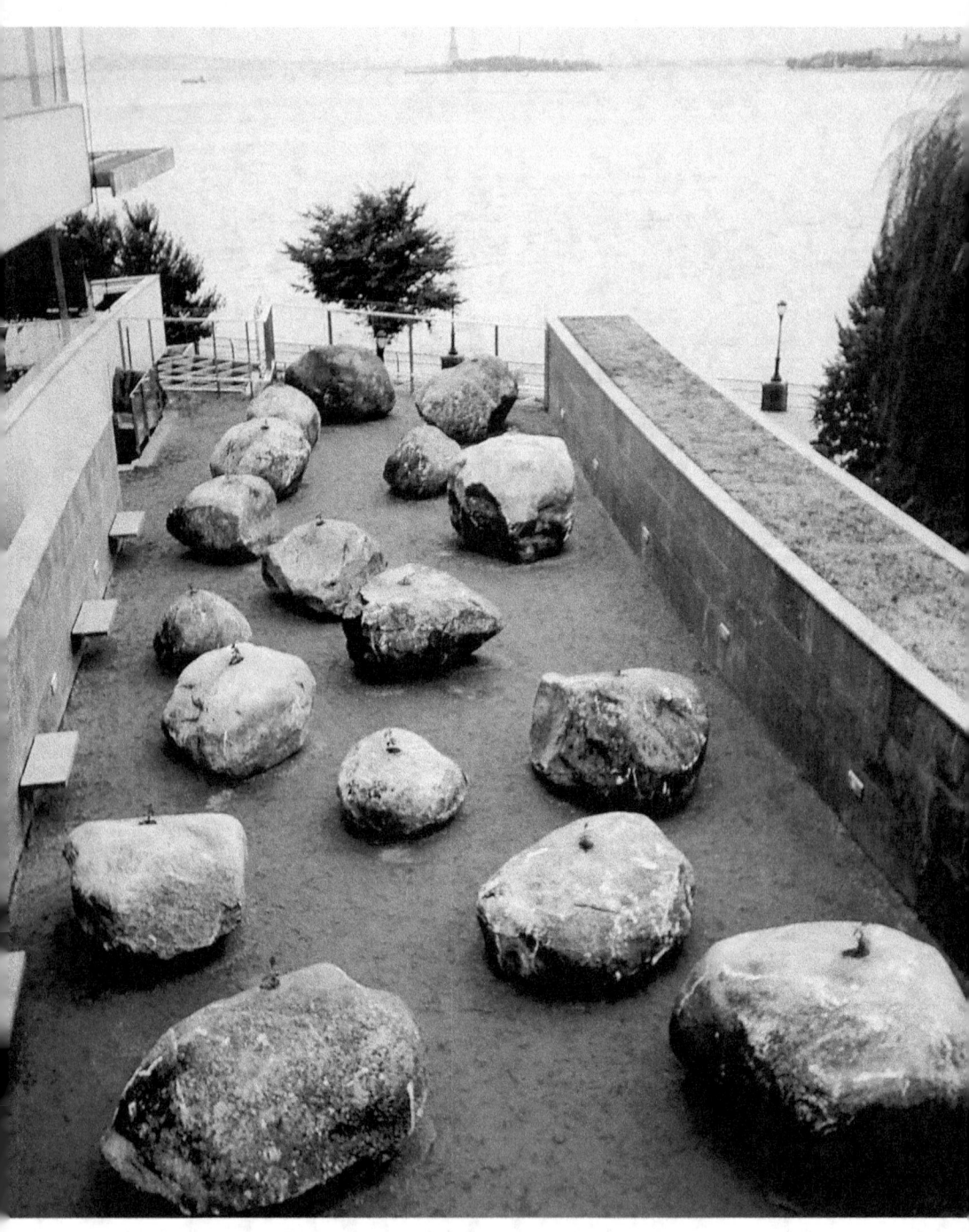

Andy Goldsworthy, Garden of Stones, New York City, 2003

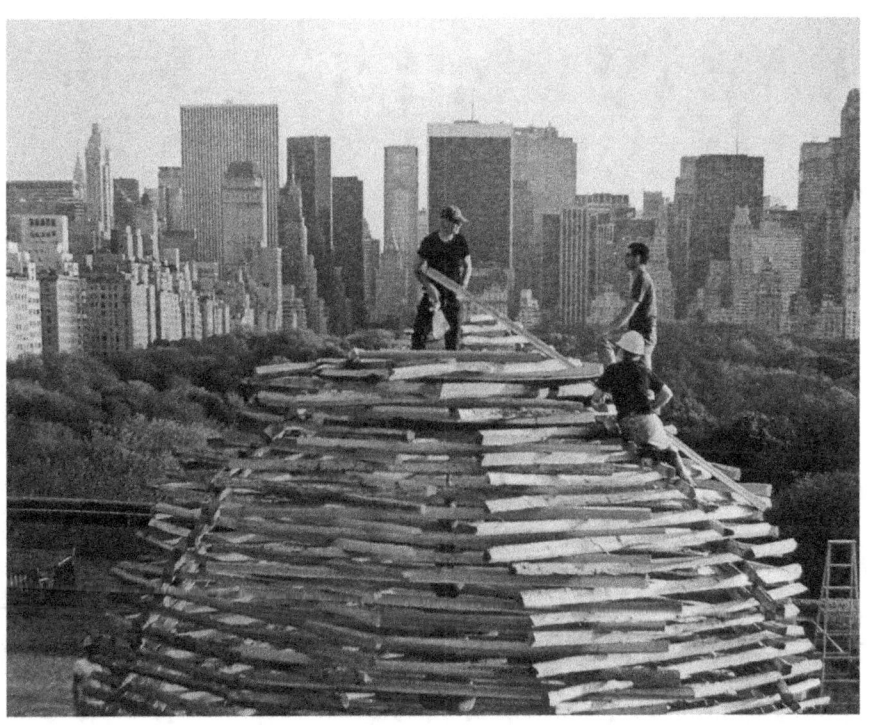

Andy Goldsworthy, Garden of Stones, New York City, 2003

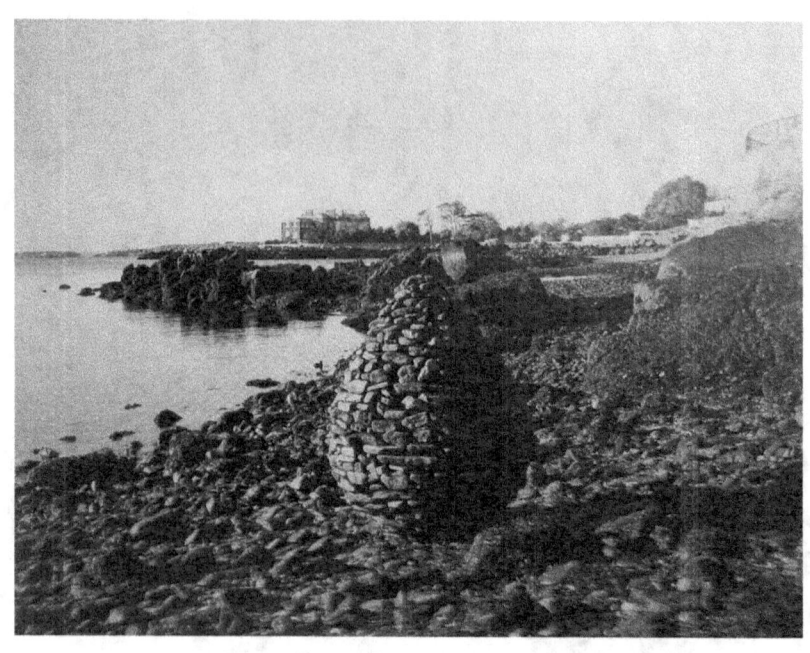

Andy Goldsworthy, East Coast Sea Cairn, New York, 2001

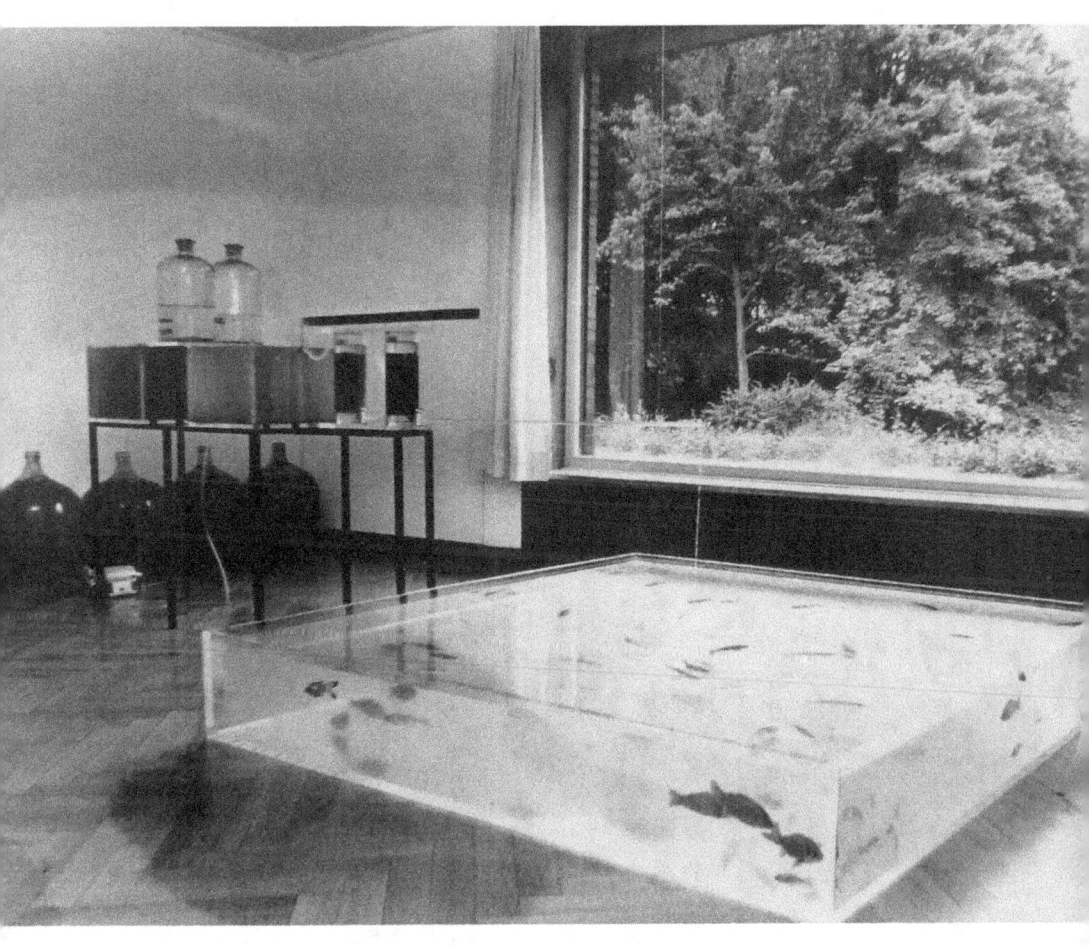

Hans Haacke, Rhine-Water Purification Plant, 1972

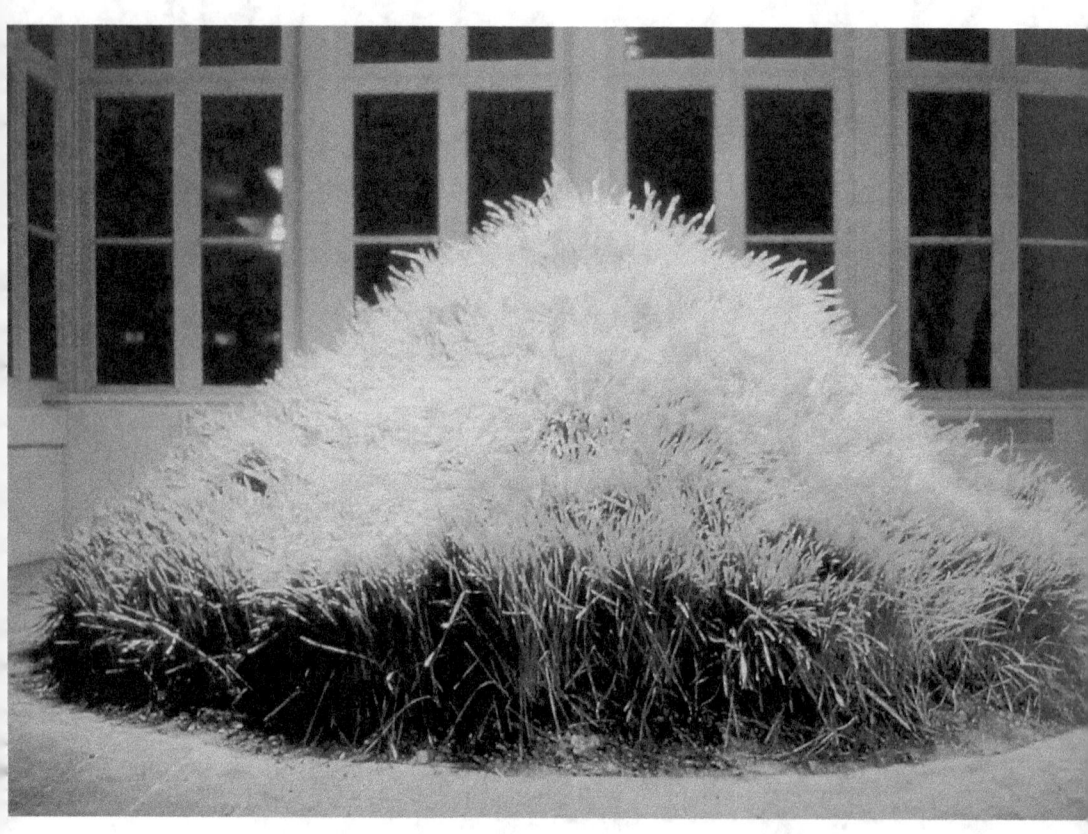

Hans Haacke, Grass Grows, 1969

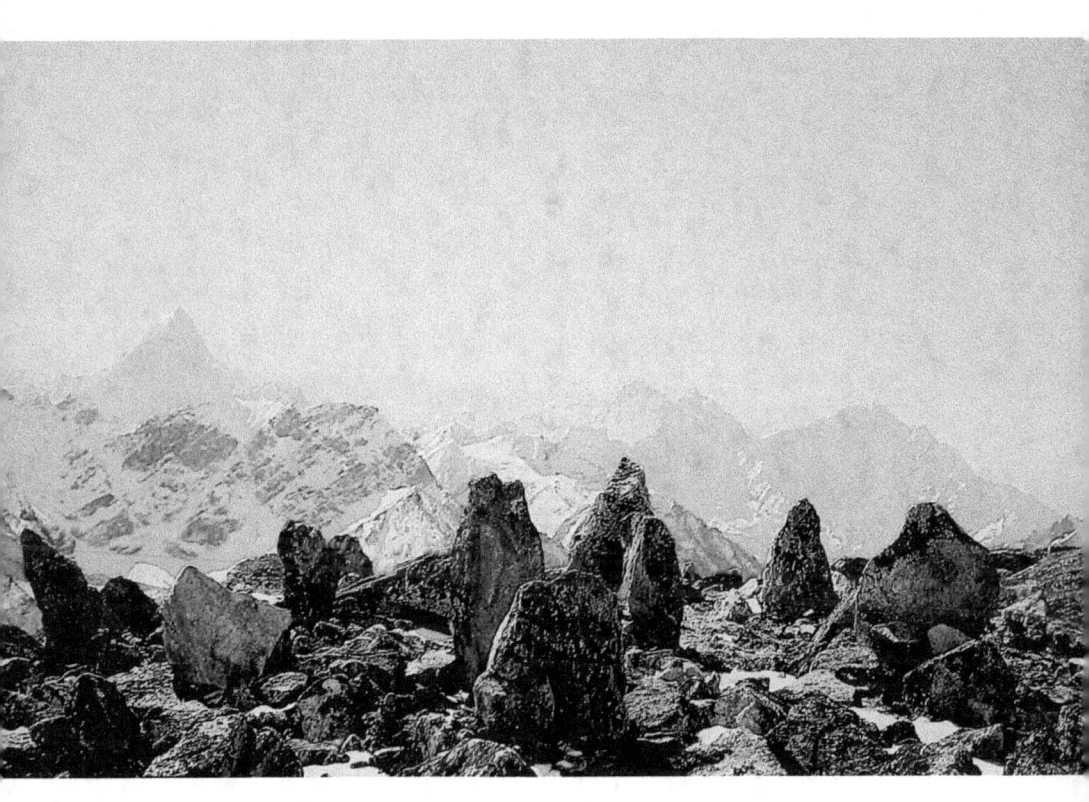

Richard Long, Nepal

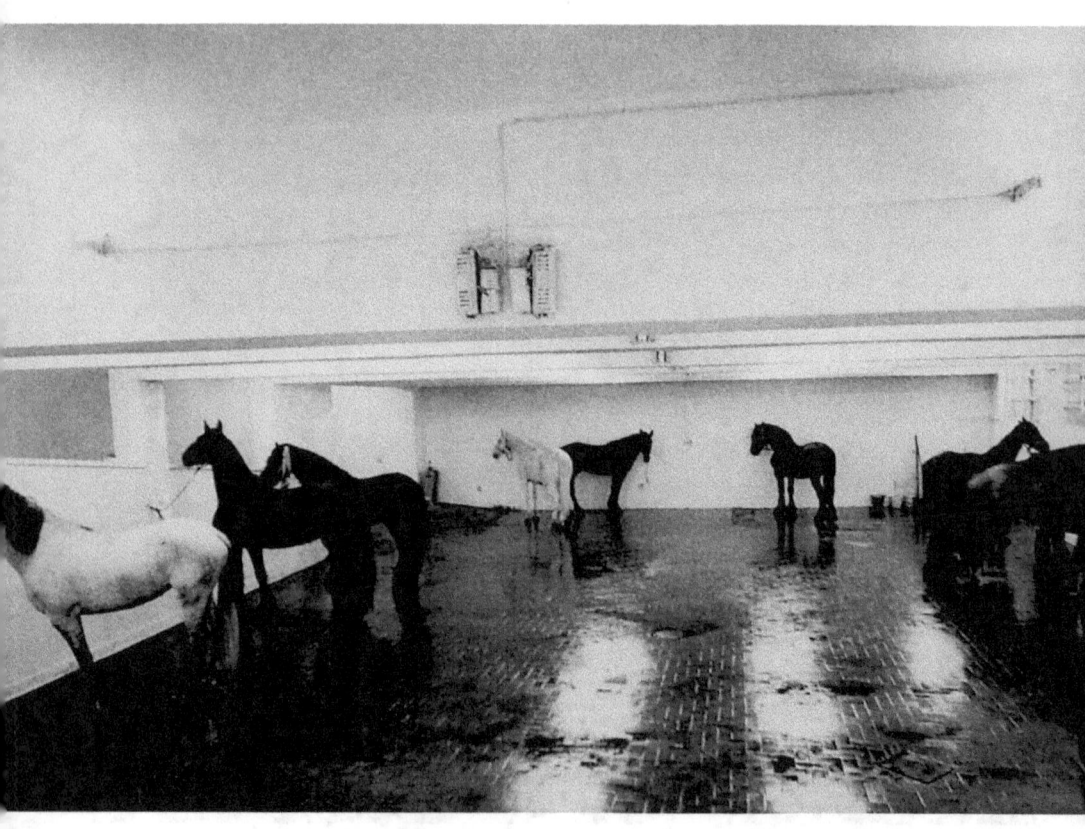

Of this Italian horse piece, Jannis Kounellis said the aim was
to increase awareness of the 'basic nature of a gallery, of its
bourgeois origin', its economic and ideological aspects.

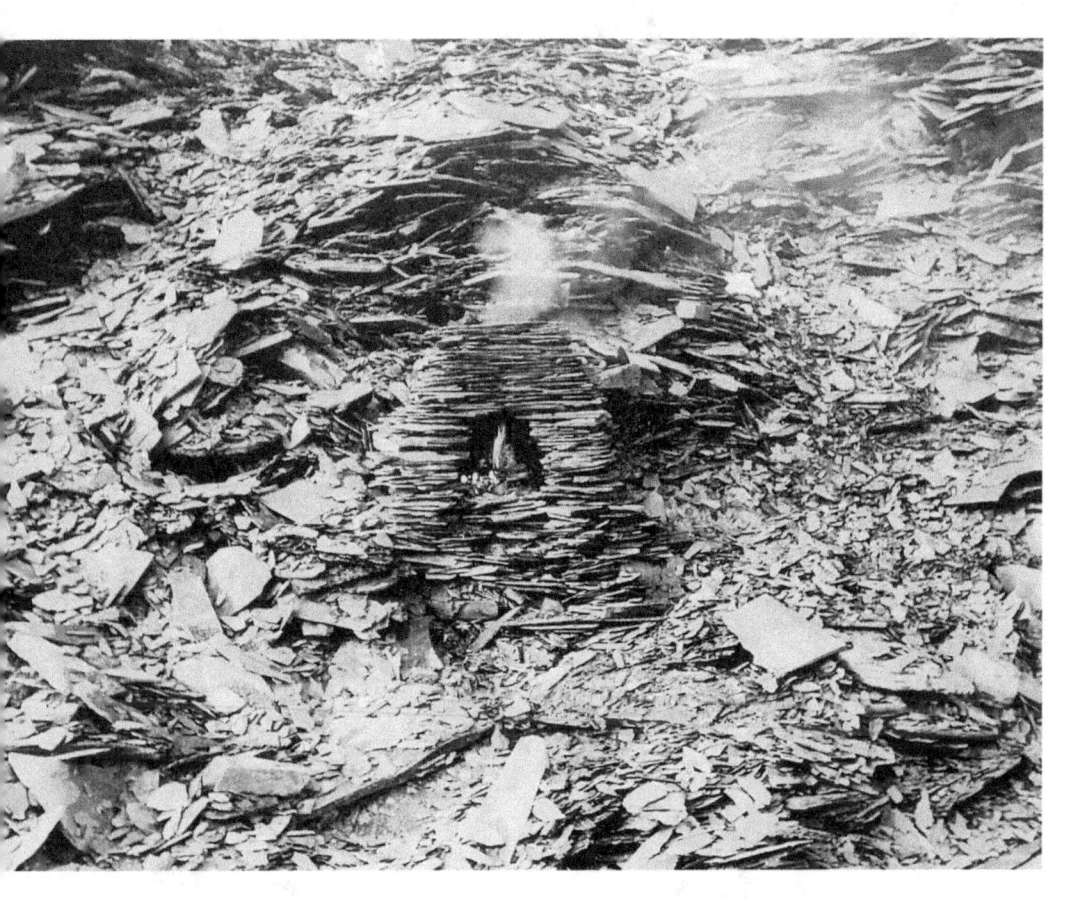

David Nash

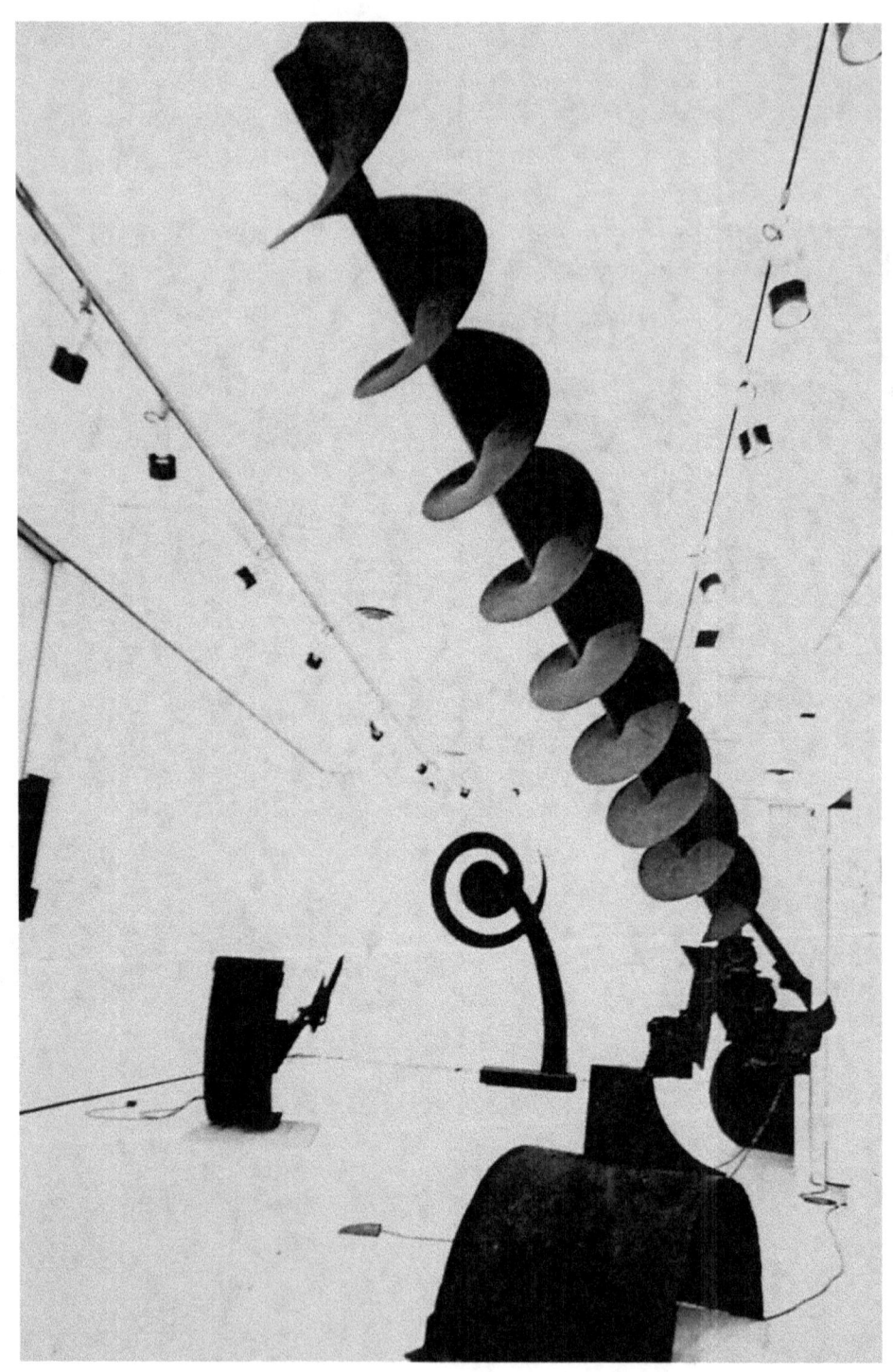

Jean Tinguely

Notes

1   INTRODUCTION

1. R. Krauss, "Sculpture in the Expanded Field", *October*, 8, Spring, 1978.

2   THE ALCHEMY OF MATTER

SPIRIT OF PLACE: LAND ART, NATURE POETRY AND NATURE MYSTICISM

1. In B. Redhead, 24-25.

THE LAND ART SUBLIME: LAND ART AND ROMANTICISM

1. R. Hughes, 1991, 386.
2. There is eroticism in Tony Cragg's steel vessels, or Anne and Patrick Poirier's long, elegant *Archæological Model*, or Jannis Kounellis' *Cotton Sculpture*, a mass of cotton stuffed into a large steel container – a sculpture of contrasts between the softness of the cotton and the rigidity of the steel, or Jackie Winsor's *Burnt Piece*, a 3 ft cube made of concrete, wire and burnt wood. Tony Cragg has spoken of having 'an erotic response to the external world', something which, it seems, all artists have, or have to have, to be truly 'great' artists (quoted in D. Wheeler, 1991, 324). See also T. Neff, 1967; Jones, 1977, 16; L. Ponti, 50-51; Lamaitre, 1985, 7-11; G. Celant, 40-46.
3. W. Laib, in A. Benjamin, 91.

LAND ART AND GARDENS

1. S. Ross, 1993, 161.
2. S. Ross, 1998, 23.

3. R. Smithson, paraphrased by Lucy Lippard (1983).

'TRUE CAPITALIST ART'?: THE COST OF LAND ART

1. A. Henri, *Total Art*, 81-82.
2. Richard Long, quoted in S. Gablik: *Has Modernism Failed?*, Thames & Hudson, London, 1984, 44.
3. 'I make art in the capitalist system which in itself is a political statement (selling art for the next walk)', remarked Hamish Fulton (1995).
4. In A. Haden-Guest, 40.

LAND ART AND PHOTOGRAPHY

1. S. Mills: "Special Kaye [Tony Kaye]", *Sunday Times Magazine*, June 12, 1994, 55.
2. In N. Hedges, 77.
3. E. Hesse, in *Eva Hesse*, Guggenheim, New York 1972.
4. J. Dibbets, 1970.
5. R. Long, Santa Fe interview.
6. R. Long, in W. Malpas, 1995.
7. R. Long, 1985, 1, 1.
8. R. Smithson, in C. Robins, 1984, 78.

INSIDE—OUTSIDE

1. Robert Smithson reckoned that a 'work of art when placed in a gallery loses its charge and becomes a portable object or surface disengaged from the outside world.' (*Selected Writings*, 132).
2. D. Oppenheim, 1992.
3. In A. McPherson, 30.
4. In M. Heizer, 1970.
5. In ib.
6. L. Weiner, in *Avalanche*, Spring, 1972, 67.
7. A. Goldsworthy, *Time,* 11.

CHANGES, CYCLES, SEASONS

1. J. Beuys, in *Documenta 7*, 2, Documenta, Kassel, 1982.
2. R. Smithson: *Writings*, 56-57; C. Robins, 1984, 80.
3. R. Long, 1986, 1, 9.
4. R. Long, in *Words After the Fact*, in R. Fuchs, 1986, 236.
5. 'Goldsworthy's pieces dig at the roots of our relationship with nature, he is conducting an interrogative process with the fundamentals of our world – water, stone, earth, growing things and – latterly, in his work with volcanic rock and 'fired' stones – fire', commented P. Whitaker (1995, 109).
6. In B. Redhead, 19.

7. See J. Burnham, 1971.

8. Quoted in G. Baro, 1969, 122; see C. Harrison, 1968, 266-8; J. Kirshner: "Barry Flanagan", *Artforum*, 23, 10, Summer, 1985, 112.

TREES

1. Writers on the symbolic and religious aspects of trees include Mircea Eliade (*Patterns of Comparative Religion*), Robert Graves (*The White Goddess*), James G. Frazer (*The Golden Bough*), and J.R.R. Tolkien, among others.

HOLES

1. C. Koelb: "Castration Envy", in P. Burgard, 1994, 79.

STONE CIRCLES: LAND ART AND PREHISTORIC ART

1. See M. Berger, 1989.

2. Quoted in L. Lippard, 1967c, 26.

3. The allusions to prehistory would be quite different if Richard Long had stuck a picture of the Cerne Giant next to himself instead of the Wilmington Man, for the Cerne Giant has the biggest penis in public (or any) art (at least in the United Kingdom).

4. R. Long, 1972, in *Fragments of a Conversation I-VI*, in *Walking in Circles*, 38.

LAND ART AND CONSTANTIN BRANCUSI

1. H. Moore, in *The Listener*, 1937, quoted in H. Chipp, 595.

2. A. Goldsworthy, *Refuges d'art*, 85.

3. A. Goldsworthy, *Sheepfolds,* 22-23.

LIGHT AND SPACE

1. Quoted in J. Butterfield, 161.

3   THE BIRTH OF LAND IN 1960S CULTURE

THE PRESENCE OF THE OBJECT: LAND ART, MINIMAL ART AND 'OBJECTHOOD'

1. C. Andre, 1978, 31.

2. See J. Yoshihara, in B. Bertozzi & K. Wolbert: *Gutai: Japanese Avant-Garde*, Darmstadt, 1991.

3. R. Morris, 1966, in G. Battock, 1995, 224.

4. R. Morris, 1966, 20-23. See also: P. Patton, 1983.

MINIMAL ART, POSTMINIMAL ART AND LAND ART

1. B. Rose, 1964, 41.
2. D. Judd: "Questions to Stella and Judd", in G. Battock, 1995, 159.

LAND ART AND CONCEPTUAL ART

1. "Mel Bochner on Malevich", 1974, 62.
2. R. Serra, in *Richard Serra, Interviews,* Hudson River Museum, New York, NY, 1980, 37.
3. D. Oppenheim, in 1992.
4. B. Flanagan, 1969.
5. J. Beuys, in *Documenta 7*, 2, Documenta, Kassel, 1982.
6. L. Weiner, in E. Lucie-Smith, 1987, 117.
7. L. Weiner: *Billowing Clouds…,* 1986, 86.2 x 17.5 in, Anthony d'Offay Gallery, London.
8. R. Long, 1985, 2, 24.

4   LAND ART, GENDER, SEXUALITY AND THE BODY

GENDER AND SCALE IN LAND ART

1. In A. Benjamin, 47.
2. "Donald Judd", *The New York Times*, Apl 1, 1977, C20.
3. L. Lippard, 1968, 42.
4. L. Lippard, 1979, 88.
5. See L. Anderson, 1973; *Mary Miss: Interior Works*, Bell Gallery, University of Rhode Island, Autumn, 1981.
6. See N. Holt, 1975, 1977; T. Castle, 1982.
7. See D. Judd, 1975; W. Agee, 1975, 40-49; P. Carlson, 1984, 114-8; D. Kuspit: "Donald Judd", 1985; B. Haskell, 1988; B. Smith, 1975.
8. Such as Tony Smith: *Die*, 1962, 72 x 72 x 72 in, Paula Cooper Gallery, New York, NY. See L. Lippard, 1972a; G. Baro, 1967; E. Greene: "Morphology of Tony Smith's Work", *Artforum*, April, 1974.
9. Such as Dan Flavin: *Untitled (to the "innovator" of Wheeling Peach-blow)*, 1968, Museum of Modern Art, New York; *Untitled*, 1976, pink, blue, green fluorescent light, Saatchi Collection, London. See I. Licht, 1968, W. Wilson: "Dan Flavin: Fiat Lux", *Art News*, Jan, 1970; J. Burnham, 1969.
10. Such as Richard Serra: *Clara-Clara*, 1983, Cor-Ten steel, installation, Jardin des Tuileries, Paris; *Prop*, 1968, 96in high, sheet 60 x 60 in, Whitney Museum of Art, New York See R. Krauss, 1972, D. Crimp: "Richard Serra: Sculpture Exceeded", *October*, Fall, 1981.
11. See K. Baker, 1980, 88-94; D. Waldman, Oct, 1970, 60-62, 75-79; P. Tuchman, 1978, 29-33; E. Develing, 1969.

WOMEN SCULPTORS AND LAND ARTISTS

1. Other artists who have worked in postmodern, feminist modes include Cindy Sherman, Mary Kelly, Marie Yates, Yves Lomax, Martha Rosler, Sutapa Biswas, Mitra Tabrizian, Zarina Bhimji, Mona Hatoum, Lubaina Himid, Barbara Kruger, Jenny Holzer, Rose Garrard, Susan Hiller, Nancy Spero, Rosa Lee and Rachel Whiteread.

2. In C. Nemser, 62.

3. See B. Barrette: *Eva Hesse's Sculpture*: Catalogue Raisonné, New York, NY, 1989; R. Krauss & E. Hesse, 1979; C. Nemser, 1973, 12-13.

4. A. Chave, in H. Cooper, ed. *Eva Hesse*, Yale University Press, New Haven, CT, 1992, 100f.

5. In L. Lippard, 1976.

6. Quoted in L. Lippard, ib., 6.

5   LAND ART AND RELIGION

1. Basho, *The Narrow Road to the Deep North and Other Travel Sketches*, tr. N. Yuasa, Penguin, London, 1966, 33.

2. M. Ueda: *Matsuo Basho*, Twayne, New York, NY, 1970, 167.

3. C. Andre, in *Carl Andre: Sculpture*, 1984.

4. M. Heizer, 1970.

5. Richard Long, 1985, part 1, 14.

6. P. Redgrove, letter to the author, Apl 20, 1994.

7. R. Long, interview with R. Cork, in D. Sylvester.

8. Mircea Eliade, 1984, 136.

9. M. Fried, "Art And Objecthood", 1967, in G. Battock, 1995, 28.

10. M. Eliade, 1984, 185.

11. M. Eliade: "Sacred Architecture and Symbolism", in *Eliade*, ed. C. Tacou, L'Herne, Paris, 1978, and in M. Eliade, 1988, 107.

12. A. Goldsworthy, *Stone*, 6.

13. A. Goldsworthy, *Hand to Earth*, 58.

14. A. Goldsworthy, sketchbook no. 22, 1988, *Hand To Earth*, 150.

6   ROBERT SMITHSON

1. In C. Robins, 78.

2. Robert Smithson, in *Selected Writings*, 20, hereafter indicated as RS.

3. R. Hobbs, 12.

4. J.G. Ballard, in R. Smithson, 1997.

5. Smithson labelled pre-existing sites land artworks, non-sites, such as the pipes, boxes and walkways of an industrial zone in *Monuments of Passaic* (1967)

6. J.G. Ballard, in R. Smithson, 1997.

7. R. Smithson, "A Sedimentation of the Mind: Earth Projects", in *Selected Writings*,

85.

8. R. Smithson, "Discussion with Heizer, Oppenheim, Smithson", *Avalanche*, 1970, and in E. Johnson, 1982, 182.

9. C. Robins, 1984, 82.

10. In L. Lippard, 1973, 88.

11. J. Kounellis, in W. Sharp, 1972.

12. See M. Gimbutas, 1989.

13. R. Smithson: "The Spiral Jetty", unpublished MS, quoted in R. Krauss, 282. See R. Hobbs, 1981.

14. I. Sandler, 1990, 60.

15. *Selected Writings*, 37.

16. J. Coplans: "Robert Smithson: The Amarillo Ramp", in R. Hobbs, 53.

17. In R. Hobbs, 212.

7   CARL ANDRE

1. C. Andre, quoted in D. Bourdon: "The Razed Sites of Carl Andre", in G. Battock, 1995, 103.

2. ib., 104.

3. L. Lippard, 1973, 157.

4. C. Andre, in *Carl Andre: Sculpture*, 1984

5. L. Lippard, 1965, 58.

6. C. Andre, 1970, 61.

7. In ib., 107.

8. D. Bourdon, 1978, 56. See M. Bochner, 1967, 39-43.

9. D. Bourdon, in G. Battock, 1995, 107.

10. R. Krauss, 1977, 271f.

11. M. Bochner, in G. Battock, 1995, 94.

12. C. Tomkins, 1989, 155.

13. C. Andre, in L. Lippard, 1970, 7.

14. Carl Andre, *Joint*, 1968, 183 units, each 14 x 18 x 36 in, installation at Windham College, Putney, Vermont.

15. A. Goldsworthy, *Time*, 180.

16. C. Andre, quoted in D. Bourdon, in G. Battock, 1995, 108.

17. T. Smith, quoted in M. Fried, 1967, in G. Battock, 1995, 131.

18. ib., 131.

19. David Lee said that 'Andre repeats one thing in each piece; Smithson repeats one thing but increases its size' (1967, 44).

8   JAMES TURRELL

1. Dia Foundation, the McArthur Foundation, the National Endowment for the Arts, the Lannan Foundation, the Canon Company, the Bohen Foundation, the Martin

Bucksbaum Family Foundation, Count Guiseppe Panza di Buimo, Dr Pentti Kouri, Jean Stein, plus other donors.

2. J. Turrell, in A. Benjamin, 47.

3. J. Turrell, 1987.

9   DENNIS OPPENHEIM

1. In D. Oppenheim, 1992.

2. L. Lippard, 1983, 52.

3. In M. Heizer, 1970.

4. D. Oppenheim, in M. Heizer, 1970.

5. In D. Oppenheim, 1978.

10   ROBERT MORRIS

1. J. Perreault, 1995, 259.

2. R. Morris, quoted in M. Fried, 1967, in G. Battock, 1995, 126.

3. M. Friedman, 1966, 23.

4. D. Factor, 1966, 13.

5. In M. Compton, 1971, 16.

6. R. Morris, "Notes on Sculpture", 4, 51.

7. In D. Wheeler, 1991, 221.

8. B. Rose, 1965.

11   NANCY HOLT

1. N. Holt, "Sun Tunnels", 1977, 34.

2. In T. Castle, 1982, 88.

3. See N. Holt, 1975, 1977; T. Castle, 1982.

4. C. Robins, 1984, 10.

12   ALICE AYCOCK

1. H. Risatti, 37.

2. A. Aycock, quoted in E. Johnson, 1982, 223.

3. R. Smith, 1975, 68.

4. Aycock, quoted in N. Rosen: "A Sense of Place: Five American Artists", *International Sculpture*, Merriewold West, 1975.

5. E. Johnson, 1982, 221.

6. A. Aycock, 1977.

13   MARY MISS

1. R. Onoratio, 1978, 32. See also Onoratio, 1979; K. Linker: "Mary Miss", *Mary Miss*, ICA, 1983.
2. See L. Anderson, 1973; M. Miss, 1981.

14   MICHAEL HEIZER

1. M. Heizer, 1970.
2. See A. Sonfist, 1983; J. Beardsley, 1984.
3. Sol LeWitt was sceptical of enormity: '[i]f it's so big that you can't really comprehend it except by its emotive force then I don't want it' (in F. Colpitt, 77). And Robert Morris wrote that 'beyond a certain size the object can overwhelm and the gigantic scale becomes the loaded term' (1966, 21).
4. See J. Brown, 1984; G. Müller, 42-45.
5. In H. Smagula, 1983, 286.
6. M. Heizer, in J. Bell: "Positive and Negative", *Arts Magazine*, Nov, 1974, 55.
7. R. Hughes, 1997, 571.
8. M. Miss, 1981, 6-7.
9. R. Hughes, 1991, 386.

15   WALTER DE MARIA

1. Walter de Maria proposed another shaft, *Olympic Mountain Project* (1970) – never made – which would have been 400 ft deep and 3 ft wide.
2. Quoted in H. Smagula, 289.
3. R. Smith, 1978, 104.
4. H. Rosenberg, 1972, 36.
5. See D. Bourdon, 1968, 39-43, 72; M. Winton, 1970, 18-19; R. Smith, 1978, 102-5.
6. K. Baker, 1988, 125-7.
7. W. de Maria, 1980.
8. See P. Redgrove: *The Black Goddess and the Sixth Sense*, Bloomsbury, London, 1987; *The Cyclopean Mistress*, Bloodaxe, Newcstle, 1993.
9. H. Smagula, 290. De Maria himself thought that a lightning strike is a 'false climax' to the work, which really needs to be seen over a period of time to appreciate its qualities.

16   OTHER AMERICAN LAND ARTISTS

1. G. Matta-Clark, "Interview With *Avalanche*", *Avalanche*, Dec, 1974.
2. See L. Lippard, 1983, 49.

3. T. Murak. in B. Nemitz, 94.
4. D. Hollis, in B. Oakes, 107.

17   ANDY GOLDSWORTHY

1. Many of the big names in British sculpture have exhibited works at Goodwood, including Elisabeth Frink, David Mach, Phillip King, David Nash, Eduardo Paolozzi, Bill Woodrow, Tony Cragg, Ian Hamilton Finlay, Stephen Dilworth, Anthony Caro and Anthony Gormley.
2. J. Dibbets, in D. Ashton, ed. *20th Century Artists on Art,* Pantheon, New York, NY, 1985, 174.
3. 'Some works have qualities of snaking but are not snakes. The form is shaped through a similar response to environment', said Goldsworthy (AG).
4. *Réfuges d'Art*, 113.
5. A. Goldsworthy, *Touching North*, 1989, and in HE, 75.

18   CHRISTO

1. J. Marck: *Wrapped Museum*, Museum of Contemporary Art, Chicago, 1969.
2. Christo, quoted in E. Johnson, 1982, 198.
3. See W. Spies: *The Running Fence Project, Christo*, Abrams, New York, NY, 1977.
4. Christo, in A. Haden-Guest, 40.

19   RICHARD LONG

1. H. Thoreau. in *Walking*, 1861, in *The Portable Thoreau*, ed. C. Bode, Viking, New York, NY, 1980, 592.
2. R. Long, Orkney, 1994.
3. *Richard Long: In Conversation*, Parts 1 & 2, MW Press, Noordwijk, Holland, 1985-86, 2, 15.

20   OTHER EUROPEAN LAND ARTISTS IN AMERICA

1. H. Haacke, in J. Burnham, 1967.
2. H. Haacke, in ib.
3. B. Nemitz, 78.

Bibliography

S. Adams & A. Robins, eds. *Gendering Landscape Art*, Manchester University Press, Manchester, 2000

C. Adcock. *James Turrell*, University of California Press, Berkeley, CA, 1990

W. C. Agee. "Unit, Series, Site: A Judd Lexicon", *Art in America*, May, 1975

L. Alloway. *Christo*, Abrams, New York, NY, 1969

—. "Robert Smithson", *Artforum*, 11, Nov, 1972

L. Anderson. "Mary Miss", *Artforum*, Nov, 1973

C. Andre. "Frank Stella: Preface to Stripe Painting", in D. Miller, 1959

—. "An Interview with Carl Andre", P. Tuchman, *Artforum*, 8, 10, June, 1970

—. *Carl Andre, Sculpture, 1958-1974*, Kunsthalle, Bern, 1975

—. "Object v Phenomenon", *Sculpture Today*, The International Sculpture Center, Toronto, 1978

—. *Carl Andre: Sculpture*, State University of New York Press, Albany, NY, 1984

—. *Carl-Andre: works on land*, Exhibitions International, 2001

J. Andrews. *The Sculpture of David Nash*, Lund Humphries, London, 1999

E. de Antonio & Mitch Tuchman. *Painters Painting*, Abbeville Press, New York, NY, 1984

M. Auping. *Common Ground*, John and Mable Ringling Museum of Art, Sarasota, 1982

—. "Hamish Fulton", *Art in America*, 71, Feb, 1983

A. Aycock. "Work", "Maze", 1975, in A. Sondheim, 1977

J. Baal-Teshuva, ed. *Christo: The Reichstag and Urban Projects,* Prestel Verlag, Munich, 1993

K. Baker. "Andre in Retrospect", *Art in America*, Apl, 1980a

—. "Reckoning with Notation: The Drawings of Pollock, Newman, and Louis", *Artforum*, 18, 10, Summer, 1980b

—. *Minimalism: Art of Circumstance*, Abbeville, New York, NY, 1988

S. Bann & W. Allen, eds. *Interpreting Contemporary Art*, Reaktion Books, London, 1991

G. Baro. "Toward Speculation in Pure Form", *Art International*, Summer, 1967

—. "American Sculpture", *Studio International*, 172, 896, 1968

G. Battock, ed. *The New Art*, Dutton, New York, NY, 1966

—. ed. *Minimal Art: A Critical Anthology*, University of California Press, Berkeley, CA, 1995

J. Beardsley. *Probing the Earth: Contemporary Land Projects*, Smithsonian Press, Washington DC, 1977

—. *Art in Public Spaces*, Partners For Liveable Places, Washington DC, 1981

—. *Earthworks and Beyond: Contemporary Art in the Landscape*, Abbeville Press, New York, NY, 1984/ 1998

M.R. Beaumont. "Romantic Sculpture", in A. Papadakis, 1988

—. "Andy Goldsworthy", *Arts Review*, July 14, 1989

A. Benjamin, ed. *Installation Art, Art & Design*, 30, 1993

L. Bennett. *The Life and Work of Andy Goldsworthy*, Heinemann, London, 2005

N. Bennett, ed. *The British Art Show: Old Allegiances and New Directions, 1979-1984*, Arts Council/ Orbis, London, 1984

M. Berger. *Labyrinths: Robert Morris, Minimalism, and the 1960s*, Harper & Row, New York, NY, 1989

M. Bloem, ed. *Lawrence Weiner*, Stedelijk Museum, Amsterdam, 1989

M. Bochner. "Art in Process – Structures", *Arts Magazine*, 40, 9, 1966a

—. "Primary Structures", *Arts*, June, 1966b

—. "Systematic", *Arts Magazine*, 41, 1, Nov, 1966c

—. "Serial Art Systems: Solipsism", *Arts Magazine*, 41, 8, Summer, 1967

—. "Mel Bochner on Malevich", interview with J. Coplans, *Artforum*, June, 1974

S. Boettger. *Earthworks*, University of California Press, Berkeley, CA, 2002

D. Bourdon. "The Razed Sites of Carl Andre", *Artforum*, 5, 2, Oct, 1966

—. "Walter de Maria: The Singular Experience", *Art International*, Dec 20, 1968

—"The Mini-Conceptual Age", *Village Voice*, Oct 17, 1974

—. "You Can't Tell a Painter By His Colors", *Village Voice*, Mch 24, 1975

—. *Carl Andre: Sculpture, 1959-1977*, Jaap Rietman, New York, NY, 1978

C. Brown. "Natural arts", *The Magazine*, July, 1987

D. Brown. "New British sculpture in Normandy", *Arts Review*, Feb 10, 1989

J. Brown *et al. Michael Heizer: Sculpture in Reverse*, see M. Heizer, 1984

—. ed. *Occluding Front: James Turrell*, Lapis Press, Larkspur Landing, CA, 1985

D. Bruckner. "Earth works", *New York Times Book Review*, Jan, 1996

P. J. Burgard, ed. *Nietzsche and the Feminine*, University Press of Virginia, Charlottesville, VI, 1994

J. Burnham. *Beyond Modern Sculpture*, Braziller, New York, NY, 1968

—. "A Dan Flavin Retrospective in Ottawa", *Artforum*, 8, 4, Dec, 1969

—. "Robert Morris", *Artforum*, 8, 7, 1970

—. "Haacke's Cancelled Show at the Guggenheim", *Artforum*, June, 1971

—. *Great Western Salt Works*, Brazillier, New York, NY, 1974

—. "Hans Haacke: Wind and Water Sculpture", 1967, in A. Sonfist, 1983

K. Bussman & F. Matzner, eds. *Hans Haacke*, Cantz, Stuttgart, 1993

J. Butterfield. *The Art of Light and Space*, Abbeville Press, New York, NY, 1993

D. Cameron. "When is a door not a door?", *XLIII esposizione Internazionale d'Arte La Biennale di Venezia*, Edizioni La Biennale, Venice, 1988

—. "Art for the new year: who's worth catching?", *Art & Auction*, Jan, 1994

J. Campbell. *The Power of Myth*, with B. Moyers, ed. B. Flowers, Doubleday, New York, NY, 1988

P. Carlson. "Donald Judd's Equivocal Objects", *Art in America*, Jan, 1984

T. Castle. "Nancy Holt, Siteseer", *Art in America*, Mch, 1982

A. Causey. "Space and Time in British Land Art", *Studio International*, 193, 98, Feb, 1977

—. *Nature as Material: An Exhibition of Sculpture and Photographs Purchased For the Arts Council Collection,* Arts Council, London, 1980

—. "Environmental Sculptures", in A. Goldsworthy, *Hand to Earth*, 1990

—. *Sculpture Since 1945*, Oxford University Press, Oxford, 1998

G. Celant. "Introduction", *Arte Povera*, Praeger, New York, NY, 1969

—. *Conceptual Art, Arte Povera, Land Art,* Galeria Civica d'Arte Moderna, Turin, 1970

—. *Dennis Oppenheim*, Edizioni Charta Srl, 1997

A. Chave: "Minimalism and the Rhetoric of Power", *Arts*, Jan, 1990

H.B. Chipp, ed. *Theories of Modern Art,* University Press of California, LA, CA, 1968

M. Church. "A shower of stones, a flash in the river", *The Sunday Telegraph*, 10 April, 1994, 6

F. Colpitt. *Minimal Art: The Critical Perspective,* University of Washington Press, Seattle, WA, 1990

M. Compton. *Some Notes on the Work of Richard Long*, British Council, London, 1976

—. & D. Sylvester. *Robert Morris*, Tate Gallery, London, 1971

Concept Art, Minimal Art, Land Art, Edition Cantz, Stuttgart, 1990

L. Cooke. "Richard Long replies to a critic", *Art Monthly*, 68, July, 1983

—. "Between Image and Object: The "New British Sculpture"", in T. Neff, 1987

J. Coplans. "Serial Imagery", *Artforum*, 7, 2, Oct, 1968

—. "Robert Smithson", *Artforum,* Apl, 1974

T. Cragg. *Writings*, Editions Isy Brachot, Brussels, 1992

—. *Sculptures on the Page*, Henry Moore Institute, Leeds, Yorkshire, 1997

D. Crane. *The Transformation of the Avant Garde: The New York Art World, 1940-1985*, University of Chicago Press, Chicago, IL, 1987

P. Crowther, ed, *The Contemporary Sublime, Art & Design*, 40, 1995

A. Davies. "Richard Long and Hamish Fulton", *Art Monthly*, 25, April, 1979

H. Davies *et al. Blurring the Boundaries: Installation Art 1969-1996*, Museum of Contemporary Art, San Diego, CA, 1997

R. Davies & T. Knipe, eds. *A Sense of Place: Sculpture in Landscape*, London, 1984

W. de Maria. "The Lightning Field", *Artforum,* 18, 8, Apl, 1980

P. de Monchaux *et al*, eds. *The Sculpture Show*, Arts Council of Great Britain, London, 1983

N. de Oliveira *et al. Installation Art*, Thames & Hudson, London, 1994

—. *et al*, eds. *Installation Art in the New Millennium*, Thames & Hudson, London, 2003

R. Deutsche *et al. Hans Haacke*, MIT Press, Cambridge, MA, 1986

E. Develing. *Carl Andre*, Gemeentenmeuseum, The Hague, 1969

—. & L. Lippard. *Minimal Art*, Stadtische Kunsthalle, Dusseldorf, 1969

J. Dibbets, in L. Bear & W. Sharp: "DIBBETTS", *Avalanche*, 1, Autumn, 1970.

R. Donnell. *Double Vision: Perspectives On Gender and the Visual Arts*, Farleigh Dickinson University Press, Rutherford, NJ, 1995

L. Dougherty. "Art in nature: a new site for sculpture in Denmark", *Maquette*, Sept, 1994

C. Drury. *Shelters and Baskets*, Orchard Gallery, 1988

—. *Stones and Bundles*, Rebecca Hossack Gallery, London, 1995

—. *Silent Spaces*, Thames & Hudson, London, 1998/ 2004

—. interview with W. Furlong, in M. Gooding, 2002
—. *Defying Gravity*, North Carolina Museum of Art, NC, 2003
—. *Heart of Stone*, Aberystwyth Art Gallery, Wales, 2003
M. Duncan. "On site: straddling the great divide", *Art in America*. 83, 3, Mch 1995
—. "Live from the Getty", *Art in America*, 86, 5, May, 1998
A. Dyson. *Richard Long: Sao Paulo Biennial 1994*, The British Council, 1994
J.C. Eade, ed. *Projecting the Landscape*, Humanities Research Centre, Canberra, 1987
M. Eliade. *Ordeal by Labyrinth*, University of Chicago Press, Chicago, IL, 1984
—. *Symbolism, the Sacred and the Arts*, Crossroad, New York, NY, 1985
D. Factor. "Los Angeles", *Artforum*, 4, 9, May, 1966
S. Farr. "Andy Goldsworthy: stone works in America", *Reflex*, 8, 6, Dec, 1995
S. Field. "Touching the Earth", *Art and Artists*, 8, Apl, 1973
J. Fineberg: *Art Since 1940: Strategies of Being*, Laurence King, London, 1995
A. Fisher & G. Gerster. *The Art of the Maze*, Weidenfeld & Nicholson, London, 1990
—. & J. Saward. *The British Maze Guide*, Minotaur Designs, London, 1991
—. & D. Kingham. *Mazes*, Shire Pulications, London, 1991
J. Fisher. "Richard Long", *Aspects*, 14, Spring, 1981
B. Flanagan. "Sculpture made visible: Barry Flanagan in discussion with Gene Baro",
    Studio International, 178, 915, Oct, 1969
S. Foley. *Unitary Forms: Minimal Structures by Carl Andre, Donald Judd, John
    McCracken, Tony Smith*, Museum of Modern Art, San Francisco, CA, 1970
N. Foote. "Long Walks", *Artforum*, 18, Summer, 1980
M. Fried. "Shape as Form: Frank Stella's New Paintings", *Artforum*, 5, 3, Nov, 1966
—. "Art and Objecthood", *Artforum*, 5, Summer, 1967
M. Friedman. "Robert Morris: Polemics and Cubes", *Art International*, 10, 10, Dec,
    1966
—. *14 Sculptors*, Walker Art Center, Minneapolis, MN, 1969
E. Fry. *Alice Aycock*, University of South Florida Art Galleries, Tampa, FL, 1981
—. "The Poetic Machines of Alice Aycock", *Portfolio*, Nov, 1981
—. *et al. Robert Morris*, Museum of Contemporary Art, Chicago, IL, 1986
R.H. Fuchs. "Memories of Passing: A Note on Richard Long", *Studio International*, 187,
    965, Apl, 1974
—. *Carl Andre*, Van Abenmuseum, Eindhoven, 1978
—. *Richard Long*, text, in R. Long, 1986
T. Fulgate-Wilcox. "Force Art: a New Direction", *Arts Magazine*, Mch, 1971
P. Fuller. *Peter Fuller's Modern Painters: Reflections on British Art*, ed. J. McDonald,
    Methuen, London, 1993
H. Fulton. *Hamish Fulton: Selected Walks, 1969-89*, Albright-Knox Art Gallery, Buffalo,
    New York, NY, 1990
—. "Into a Walk Into Nature", *Thirty One Horrors*, Lenbachhaus, Munich, 1995
—. *Walking Artist*, Annely Juda, London, 1998
S. Gardiner. "Their medium is nature", *Landscape Architecture*, 80, Feb, 1990
M. Garlake. "Andy Goldsworthy", *Art Monthly*, 93, Feb, 1986
J. Gear. "Andy Goldsworthy", *Review*, Dec. 1, 1996
J. Giovannini. *Mary Miss*, Architectural Association, London, 1987
T. Godfrey, Tony. "Richard Wilson's watertable, Andy Goldsworthy", *Burlington
    Magazine*, 136, 1096, July, 1994
—. *Conceptual Art*, Phaidon, London, 1998
E. Goheen. *Wrapped Walk Ways*, Abrams, New York, NY, 1978

A. Goldsworthy & J. Fowles. *Winter Harvest*, Scottish Arts Council, 1987
—. *Mountain and Coast: Autumn Into Winter: Japan 1987*, Art Data, 1988
—. *Parkland*, Yorkshire Sculpture Park, West Bretton, 1988
—. *Touching North*, Fabian Carlsson, London, 1989
—. *Snowballs in Summer Installation*, Old Museum of Transport, Glasgow, 1989
—. *Leaves*, Common Ground, London, 1989
—. *Andy Goldsworthy*, Viking, London, 1990
—. *Hand to Earth: Andy Goldsworthy, Sculpture, 1976-1990*, Henry Moore Centre for Sculpture, Leeds, Yorkshire, 1990
—. interview, *Third Ear*, BBC Radio 3, June 30, 1989, in 1990
—. *Sand Leaves*, Arts Club of Chicago, IL, 1991
—. *Ice and Snow Drawings*, Fruitmarket Gallery, Edinburgh, 1992
—. *Andy Goldsworthy: Breakdown*, Rose Art Museum, 1992
—. *Stone*, Viking, London, 1994
—. *Black Stones, Red Pools*, Pro Arte Foundation, 1995
—. *Wood*, Viking, London, 1996
—. *Sheepfolds*, Michael Hue-Williams Gallery, London, 1996
—. *Végètal*, Ballet Atlantique-Regine Chopinot, La Rochelle, France, 1996
—. *Alaska Works*, Anchorage Museum of History and Art, Anchorage, AK, 1996
—. *Andy Goldsworthy: A Collaboration With Nature*, Abrams, NY, 1996
—. *Andy Goldsworthy: Jack's Fold*, ed. Judy Glasman, University of Hertfordshire, 1996
—. *Hand to Earth: Andy Goldsworthy Sculpture,* T. Friedman, Thames and Hudson, London, 1997 & 2004
—. *Arch*, with D. Craig, Thames & Hudson, London, 1999
—. *Wall,* intr. K. Baker, Thames & Hudson, London, 2000
—. *Time,* Thames & Hudson, London, 2000
—. *Midsummer Snowballs*, intr. J. Collins, Abrams, New York, NY, 2001
—. *Andy Goldsworthy – Réfuges D'Art,* Editions Artha, 2002
—. *Passage,* Thames & Hudson, London, 2004
—. *Enclosure*, Thames & Hudson, London, 2007
M. Gooding & W. Furlong. *Song of the Earth,* Thames and Hudson, London, 2002
A. Gopnik. "Basic Stuff: Robert Smithson, Myth, Science and Primitivism", *Art Magazine*, Mch, 1983
J. Grande. *Balance: art and nature*, Black Rose Books, Montréal, 1994
—. "Back to nature?", *Sculpture*, 13, 4 July/ Aug, 1994
—. *Art Nature Dialogues*, State University of New York Press, NY, 2004
N. Graydon. "Magic in the field", *Ritz*, 133, 1989
B. Graziani. "Robert Smithson's Picturable Situation", *Critical Inquiry*, 20, 3, Spring, 1994
C. Greenberg. *Art and Culture,* Beacon Press, Boston, MA, 1961
G. Greig. "Circular Tours In the Name of Art", *Sunday Times*, June 16, 1991
H. Gresty & D. Reason. *Landscape*, Kettle's Yard, Cambridge, 1986
H. Haacke. *Framing and Being Framed*, New York University Press, New York, NY, 1975
A. Haden-Guest. "The King of Wrap", *The Sunday Times Magazine*, Jan, 1994
O. Hahn & P. Restany. *Christo*, Editioni Apollinaire, Milan, 1966
J. Haldane. *A Road From the Past To the Future*, Crawford Arts Centre, St Andrews, 1997

C. Hall. "Shared earth", *Arts Review*, 43, June 14, 1991
—. "Site lines", *Arts Review*, 46, Oct, 1994
A.M. Hammacher. *The Sculpture of Barbara Hepworth*, Abrams, New York, NY, 1968
—. *The Evolution of Modern Sculpture: Tradition and Innovation*, Abrams, New York, NY, 1969
C. Harrison. "Barry Flanagan's Sculpture", *Studio International*, 175, 900, May, 1968
B. Haskell. *BLAM! The Explosion of Pop, Minimalism, and Performance, 1958-64*, Whitney Museum of American Art, New York, NY, 1984
—. *Donald Judd*, Whitney Museum of American Art, New York, NY, 1988
N. Hedges. "Growth, decay and the movement of change", *World Magazine*, 45, Jan, 1991
M. Heizer, D. Oppenheim & R. Smithson. "Discussion", *Avalanche*, 1, Autumn, 1970
—. *Sculpture in Reverse*, Museum of Contemporary Art, LA, CA, 1984
A. Henri. *Environments and Happenings*, Thames & Hudson, London, 1974
—. *Total Art*, Praeger, New York, NY, 1974
J. Heslewood. *The History of Western Sculpture: A Young Person's Guide*, Belitha Press, London, 1994
A. Hess. "Technology Exposed", *Landscape Architecture*, May, 1992
Galerie Max Hetzler. *Carl Andre, Gunther Forg, Hubert Kiecol, Richard Long, Meuser, Reinhard Mucha, Bruce Nauman and Ulrich Ruckreim*, Cologne, 1985
G. Hilty. *Recent British Sculpture*, Arts Council, London, 1993
R. Hobbs. *Robert Smithson: Sculpture,* Cornell University Press, Ithaca, NY, 1981
—. "Earthworks", *Art Journal*, 42, Fall, 1982
N. Hodges ed. *Art and the Natural Environment, Art & Design,* 36, 1994
—. ed. *The Contemporary Sublime, Art & Design,* 40, 1995
N. Holt. "Amarillo Ramp", *Avalanche*, Fall, 1973
—. "Hydra's Head", *Arts Magazine,* Jan, 1975
—. "Sun Tunnels", *Artforum,* Apl, 1977
K. Honnef. *Concept Art*, Phaidon, Oxford, 1971
P. Hovdenakk. *Christo: Complete Editions*, Schellman & Klüser, Munich, 1982
S. Hubbard, intr. *Sculpture At Goodwood: A Vision For 21st Century British Sculpture*, Sculpture At Goodwood, Sussex, 2002
R. Hughes. *The Shock of the New*, Thames & Hudson, London, 1991
—. *Nothing If Not Critical: Selected Essays on Art and Artists*, Collins Harvill, London, 1990
—. *American Visions: The Epic History of Art In America*, Knopf, New York, NY, 1997
L. Iizawa. "Earth work", *Studio Voice*, Mch, 1988
P. Inch. "Andy Goldsworthy", *Arts Review*, 42, July 13, 1990
R. Ingleby. "Visual arts: Andy Goldsworthy", *The Independent*, Nov 8, 1996
In Praise of Trees, Salisbury Festival, Wilts., 2002
G. Jeppson. *Richard Long*, Harvard College, Cambridge, MA, 1980
E.H. Johnson, *Modern Art and the Object*, Harper & Row, New York, NY, 1976
—. ed. *American Artist on Art*, Harper & Row, New York, NY, 1982
B. Jones. "A New Wave in Sculpture", *Artscribe*, 8, Sept, 1977
D. Judd. "Frank Stella", *Arts Magazine,* 36, Sept, 1962
—. "In the Galleries", *Arts Magazine*, 37, 10, Sept, 1963
—. "Local History", *Arts Yearbook 7*, 1964
—. "Black, White and Gray", *Arts Magazine*, 38, 6, Mch, 1964
—. "Specific Objects", *Arts Yearbook*, 8, Art Digest, New York, NY, 1965

—. "Barnett Newman", *Studio International*, 179, 919, Feb, 1970
—. *Complete Writings, 1959-1975*, Nova Scotia College of Art and Design, Halifax, Canada, 1975
—. *Complete Writings, 1975-1986*, Van Abbemuseum, Netherlands, 1987
E. Juncosa. "Landscape as experience", *Lapiz*, 61 Oct, 1989
D. Karshan. *Conceptual Art and Conceptual Aspects,* Farleigh Dickinson University, 1970
J. Kastner, ed. *Land and Environmental Art,* Phaidon, London, 1998
S. Kemal & I. Gaskell, eds. *Landscape, natural beauty and the arts,* Cambridge University Press, Cambridge, 1993
G. Kepes, ed. *Arts of the Environment,* Brazillier, New York, NY, 1972
P. King *et al.* "Colour in Sculpture", *Studio International*, 177, 907, 1969
R.E. Krauss. "Richard Serra: Sculpture Redrawn", *Artforum*, May, 1972
—. "Sense and Sensibility: Reflection on Post '60s Sculpture", *Artforum*, 12, Nov, 1973
—. *Passages in Modern Sculpture,* Thames & Hudson, London, 1977
—. "Sculpture in the Expanded Field", *October*, 8, Spring, 1979
—. *Eva Hesse*, Whitechapel Art Gallery, London, 1979
—. *et al. Robert Morris*, Abrams, New York, NY, 1994
Z. Kraus, ed. *From Nature to Art, From Art to Nature*, Venice Biennale, Milan, 1978
D. Kuspit. "Robert Smithson's Drunken Boat", *Arts Magazine*, Oct, 1981
—. "Aycock's Dream Houses", *Art in America*, Sept, 1985
—. "Donald Judd", *Artforum*, 23, 5, Feb, 1985
I. Lamaitre. "Interview with Tony Cragg", *Artefactum*, 2, Dec, 1985
T. Lang. "News from the imagination", *Issues in Architecture, Art & Design,* 3, 1, 1993
Land Marks, Edith C. Blum Art Institute, Bard College, Annadale-on-Hudson, 1984
D. Laporte. *Christo*, Pantheon Books, New York, NY, 1985
B. Laws. "Where Art and Nature Meet", *The Telegraph Weekly*, Nov 12, 1988
D. Loo. "Serial Rights", *Art News*, 66, 8, Dec, 1967
—. "London Ecology Centre, Exhibit", *Arts Review*, 38, Jan 17, 1986
—. "Great art of the outdoors: bio-degrading sculptures", *Country Life*, 181, 35, Aug 27, 1987
—. "Pure, ephemeral spires", *The Times*, June 26, 1989
—. "Opinion: Richard Long and Hamish Fulton", *Arts Review*, July 26, 1991
—. "In profile: Goldsworthy", *Arts Review*, 47, Feb 1995
A. Legg, ed. *Sol LeWitt*, Museum of Modern Art, New York, NY, 1978
P. Leider. "For Robert Smithson", *Art in America*, Nov, 1973
K. Levin. "Robert Smithson", *Art News*, Sept, 1982
—. "Reflections on Robert Smithson's *Spiral Jetty*", *Arts Magazine*, May, 1978
F. Licht: *Sculpture, 19th and 20th Centuries*, Michael Joseph, London, 1967
—. "Dan Flavin", *Artscanada*, Dec, 1968
L. Lippard. "New York Letter: Apl-June, 1965", *Art International*, 9, 6, 1965
—. "New York Letter: Recent Sculpture as Escape", *Art International*, Feb, 1966a
—. "An Impure Situation", *Art International*, May 20, 1966b
—. "The Silent Art", *Art in America*, 55, 1, Jan-Feb, 1967a
—. "Sol LeWitt: Non-Visual Structures", *Artforum*, Apl, 1967b
—. "Tony Smith", *Art International*, Summer, 1967c
— "Rebelliously Romantic?", *New York Times*, June 4, 1967d
—. "Escalataion in Washington", *Art International*, 12, 1, Jan, 1968

—. ed. *Surrealists on Art*, Prentice-Hall, Englewood Cliffs, NJ, 1970

—. *Tony Smith*, Thames & Hudson, London, 1972a

—. *Grids*, Philadelphia Institute of Contemporary Art, PA, 1972b

—. *Six Years: The Dematerialization of the Art Object from 1966 to 1972*, Praeger, New York, NY, 1973

—. *From the Center: feminist essays on women's art*, Dutton, New York, NY, 1976

—. *Eva Hesse*, New York University Press, New York, NY, 1976

—. "Complexities: Architectural Sculpture in Nature", *Art in America*, Feb, 1979

—. *Overlay*, Pantheon, New York, NY, 1983

C. Loeffier, ed. *Performance Anthology*, Contemporary Art Press, San Francisco, CA, 1979

R. Long. *Richard Long: In Conversation*, Parts 1 & 2, MW Press, Noordwijk, Holland, 1985-86

—. *Richard Long*, text by R.H. Fuchs, Thames & Hudson, London, 1986

—. *Old World New World*, Anthony d'Offay, London, 1988

—. *Richard Long: Walking in Circles*, Hayward Gallery/ Thames & Hudson, London, 1992

—. *Kicking Stones*, Antony d'Offay Gallery, London, 1990

—. *Richard Long: Mountains and Water*, Anthony d'Offay, London, 1992

—. *An Interview with Richard Long*, Santa Fe. 1994a

—. *No Where*, interview with C. Kirkpatrick, Piers Arts Centre, Orkney, 1994b

—. Interview with Richard Long, 1994; in *Mirage*, 1998 (1994c)

—. *Circles, Cycles, Mud*, D. Friis-Hansen, Contemporary Arts Museum, 1996

—. *From Time to Time*, DAP, 1997

—. *Richard Long*, Hatje Cantz, 1997

—. *Mirage*, Phaidon, London, 1998

—. *Richard Long: a Moving World,* Tate Publishing, London, 2002

—. *Richard Long – Walking the Line,* Thames and Hudson, London, 2002

E. Lucie-Smith: *Sculpture Since 1945*, Phaidon, Oxford, 1987

N. Lynton. *David Nash: Sculpture, 1971-90*, Serpentine Gallery, London, 1990

R. Mabey. "Art and ecology", *Modern Painters*, 3, 4, Winter, 1990

D. Macmillan. "David Nash: Brancusi Joins the Garden Gang", *Art Monthly*, 65, Apl, 1983

L. MacRitchie. "Ancient Egypt", *Financial Times*, Dec 12, 1994

—. "Residency on earth", *Art in America*, 83, 4, Apl 1995

S. Madoff. "Andy Goldsworthy", *Garden Design*, 13, June, 1994

W. Malpas. *Richard Long: The Art of Walking*, Crescent Moon, 2007

—. *Andy Goldsworthy*, Crescent Moon, 2004

—. *The Art of Andy Goldsworthy*, Crescent Moon, 2004

A.T. Mann. *Sacred Architecture*, Element Books, Shaftesbury, Dorset, 1993

J. van der Marck. *Wrapped Museum*, Museum of Contemporary Art, Chicago, IL, 1969

—. *Herbert Bayer*, Dartmouth College Museum, Hanover, NH, 1977

M. Marmer. "James Turrell", *Art in America*, 69, May, 1981

R. Martin. *The Sculpted Forest: Sculpture in the Forest of Dean*, Redcliff, Bristol, 1990

B. Matilsky. *Fragile Economies*, Rizzoli, New York, NY, 1992

W.H. Matthews. *Mazes and Labyrinths*, Dover, New York, NY, 1970

J. May. "Landscape Fired by Ice", *Landscape*, Dec, 1987

B. McAvera. "Public art: site sensitivities", *Art Monthly*, 215, Apl, 1998

A. McPherson. "David Nash: interviewed by Allan McPherson", *Artscribe*, 12, June,

1978
K. McShine. *Primary Structures*, Jewish Museum, New York, NY, 1966
—. *Information*, Museum of Modern Art, New York, NY, 1970
—. *An International Survey of Recent Painting and Sculpture*, MOMA, New York, NY, 1984
H.C. Merillat: *Modern Sculpture: The New Old Masters*, Dod, Mead & Co, New York, NY, 1974
U. Meyer. *Conceptual Art*, Dutton, New York, NY, 1972
D.C. Miller, ed. *Sixteen Americans*, Museum of Modern Art, New York, NY, 1959
M. Miller. *The Garden as an Art*, State University of New York Press, Albany, NY, 1993
M. Miss. *Mary Miss: Interior Works*, Bell Gallery, University of Rhode Island, Autumn, 1981
J. Morland. *New Milestones: Sculpture, Community and the Land*, Common Ground, 1988
H. Morphy & M. Boles, eds. *Art from the Land*, University of Washington Press, 2000
R. Morris. "Notes on Sculpture", *Artforum,* Feb, 1966, Oct, 1966, June, 1967, Apl, 1969
—. "Aligned with Nazca", *Artforum*, Oct, 1975
—. *Robert Morris: Mirror Works, 1961-1978*, Leo Castelli Gallery, New York, NY, 1979
—. *et al. Earthworks*, Seattle Art Museum, Seattle, WA, 1979
—. *Selected Works*, Contemporary Arts Museum, Houston, TX, 1981
—. *Continuous Project Altered Daily*, MIT Press, Cambridge, MA, 1993
S. Morris. "A Rhetoric of Silence: Redefinitions of Sculpture in the 1960s and 1970s", in S. Nairne, 1981
J. Morland. *New Milestones: Sculpture, Community and the Land*, Common Ground, London, 1988
H. Morphy & M. Boles, eds. *Art from the Land*, University of Washington Press, 2000
S. Morris. "A Rhetoric of Silence: Redefinitions of Sculpture in the 1960s and 1970s", In S. Nairno, 1981
J. Morrison. "Landmatters", *British Journal of Photography*, 133, June 6, 1986
A. Morgan. "Maze and labyrinth", *Sculpture*, 14, 4, July/ Aug, 1995
D. Morse. "At Runnymede Farm, the crop is sculptures", *San Francisco Examiner*, May 2, 1997
M. Mosser & G. Teyssot, eds. *The History of Garden Design*, Thames & Hudson, London, 1991
A. Moszynska. *Abstract Art*, Thames & Hudson, London, 1990
G. Müller. "Michael Heizer", *Arts Magazine*, Dec, 1969
—. "The Earth, Subjected To Cataclysms, Is a Cruel Master", *Arts Magazine*, Nov, 1971
S. Nairne & N. Serota. *British Sculpture in the Twentieth Century*, Whitechapel Art Gallery, London, 1981
—. *State of the Art: Ideas & Images in the 1980s*, Chatto, London, 1987
H. Nakamura. "Andy Goldsworthy and Anthony Green", *Ikebana Ryusei*, 38, Apl, 1988
D. Nash. *Fletched Over Ash*, AIR Gallery, 1978
—. "David Nash", *Aspects*, 10, Spring, 1980
—. *Stoves and Hearths*, Duke Street Gallery, London, 1982
T.A. Neff, ed. *A Quiet Revolution: British Sculpture Since 1965*, Thames & Hudson, London, 1987
B. Nemitz. *Trans Plant: Living Vegetation in Contemporary Art*, Hatje Cantz, 2000

C. Nemser. "An interview with Eva Hesse", *Artforum*, May, 1970
—. "My Memories of Eva Hesse", *Feminist Art Journal*, Winter, 1973
P. Nesbitt. "At Home with Nature: Andy Goldsworthy in Scotland", *Alba*, Spring, 1989
—. "A Landscape Touched by Gold", in G. Hughes, 1990
M. Newman. "New Sculpture in Britain", *Art in America*, Sept, 1982
I. Noguchi. *A Sculptor's World*, Harper & Row, New York, NY, 1968
A. Le Normand-Romain *et al. Sculpture: The Adventure of Modern Sculpture in the Nineteenth and Twentieth Centuries*, Skira, Geneva, 1986
J. Norrie. "Andy Goldsworthy", *Arts Review*, 3 July, 1987
B. Oakes, ed. *Sculpting the Environment*, Van Nostrand Reinhold, New York, NY, 1995
P. Oakes. "The Incomparable Andy Goldsworthy", *Country Living*, 48, Dec, 1989
R. Onoratio. "Illusive Spaces: The Art of Mary Miss", *Artforum*, Dec, 1978
—. *Mary Miss – Perimeters/ Pavilions/ Decoys*, Nassau County Museum, 1979
D. Oppenheim. *Dennis Oppenheim*, Musée d'Art Contemporain, Montréal, 1978.
—. *Selected Works, 1967-1990*, Abrams, New York, NY, 1992
P. Osborne, ed. *Conceptual Art*, Phaidon, London, 2002
E. Osaka. *Andy Goldsworthy: Mountain and Coast: Autumn Into Winter*, Gallery Takagi, Nagoya, 1987
W. Packer. "Andy Goldsworthy's Transient Touch", *Sculpture*, July, 1989
—. "Sculpture from the countryside", *Financial Times*, July 7, 1987
A.C. Papadakis, ed. *The New Romantics, Art & Design*, 4, 11/12, Academy Group, 1988
—. *et al*, eds. *New Art*, Academy Group, London, 1991
R. Parker & G. Pollock. *Framing Feminism*, Pandora Press, London, 1987
D. Parr. "City focus: St. Louis: 'a different kind of energy'", Art News. 95, 3, Mch, 1996
J. Partridge. "Forest work", *Craft*, 81, July/ Aug, 1986
A. Patrizio. "Cube garden: sculpture at the Edinburgh Festival 1990", *Arts Review*, 42, July 27, 1990
P. Patton. "Robert Morris and the Fire Next Time", *Art News,* 82, 10, Dec, 1983
E. Pavese, ed. *Christo: Surrounded Islands*, Abrams, New York, NY, 1986
N. Pennick. *Mazes and Labyrinths*, Hale, London, 1990
J. Perreault. "A Minimal Future? Union-Made: Report on a Phenomenon", *Arts Magazine*, 41, Mch, 1967
J. Perrone. "Seeing Through Boxes", *Artforum*, 15, Nov, 1976
R. Pincus-Witten. *Postminimalism*, Out of London, New York, NY, 1977
—. *Post-Minimalism into Maximalism*, UMI Research Press, Ann Arbor, MI, 1987
J. Poetter. *Donald Judd*, Cantz, Stuttgart, 1989
L. Ponti. "Tony Cragg", *Domus*, 611, Nov, 1980
J.C. Powys. *Wolf Solent*, Penguin, London, 1964
—. *Autobiography*, Macdonald, London, 1967
A. Price. "A Conversation With Alice Aycock", *Architectural Design*, Apl, 1980
G. Prince. "With mud on their hands, growth, decay and the movement of change", *World Magazine,* Jan, 1991
E. Rankin. "Popularising public sculpture in Britain: from landscape gardens to forest trails", *de Arte*, 53, Apl 1996
C. Ratcliff. "The Compleat Smithson", *Art in America*, Jan, 1980
B. Redhead. *The Inspiration of Landscape: Artists in National Parks*, Phaidon, Oxford, 1989
H. Risatti. "The Sculpture of Alice Aycock", *Woman's Art Journal*, Summer, 1985
J. Roberts. *Postmodernism, Politics and Art,* Manchester University Press,

Manchester, 1990

C. Robins. *The Pluralist Era: American Art, 1968-1981*, Harper & Row, New York, NY, 1984

W. Romey. "The artist as geographer: Richard Long's Earth Art", *Professional Geographer*, 39, 4, 1987

B. Rose. "New York Letter", *Art International*, Feb 15, 1964

—. "Looking at American Sculpture", *Artforum*, 3, Feb, 1965a

—. "ABC Art", *Art in America*, 53, 5, Nov, 1965b

—. *Robert Morris*, Corcoran Gallery, Washington, DC, 1990

H. Rosenberg. *The De-Definition of Art*, Horizon Press, New York, NY, 1972

—. *The Tradition of the New*, Da Capo Press, New York, NY, 1994

R. Rosenblum. *Modern Painting and the Northern Romantic Tradition*, Thames & Hudson, London, 1978

—. *Jasper Johns' Paintings and Sculptures, 1954-1974,* Ann Arbor, Michigan, MI, 1985

—. "Romanticism and Retrospective: An Interview with Robert Rosenblum", in A. Papadakis, 1988

C. Ross. *Star Axis*, University of New Mexico Press, Albuqerque, NM, 1992

S. Ross. "Gardens, earthworks, and environmental art", in S. Kemal, 1993

—. *What Gardens Mean*, University of Chicago Press, Chicago, IL, 1998

M. Roth. "Robert Smithson on Duchamp", *Artforum*, Oct, 1969

—. ed. *The Amazing Decade: Women and Performance Art in America 1970-80*, Astro Artz, Los Angeles, CA, 1983

A. Saalfield. *Mary Miss*, Fogg Art Museum, Cambridge, MA, 1980

I. Sandler. *American Art of the 1960s*, Harper & Row, New York, NY, 1988

—. *Art of the Postmodern Era: From the 1960s to the Early 1990s*, HarperCollins, London, 1997

P. Schjeldahl. *Art in Our Time: The Saatchi Collection*, Lund Humphries, London, 1984

P. Schuck. "Interview: Earth, Water, Wind", *Contemporanea*, Apl, 1990

D. Schwartz. *Lawrence Weiner*, König, Cologne, 1989

W. Seitz. *The Art of Assemblage*, MOMA, New York, NY, 1961

P. Selz. *Directions in Kinetic Sculpture*, University of California Press, Berkeley, CA, 1966

—. *Art in Our Times: A Pictorial History 1890-1980*, Thames & Hudson, London, 1982

A. Seymour. "Walking in Circles", in R. Long, *Walking in Circles*

—. "Old World New World", in R. Long, *Old World New World*

G. Shapiro. *Earthworks: Robert Smithson and After Babel*, University of California Press, Berkeley, CA, 1995

W. Sharp *et al. Earth Art*, Andrew Dickson White Museum of Art, Cornell University, Ithaca, NY, 1969

—. "Structure and Sensibility", *Avalanche*, 5, Summer, 1972

N. Shulman. "Monday at the North Pole", *Arts Review*, June 2, 1989

P. Sims. *From Minimalism to Expressionism*, New York, NY, 1963

N. Sinden. "Interview: Art in Nature: Andy Goldsworthy", *Resurgence*, 129, Aug, 1988

H.J. Smagula. *Currents: Contemporary Directions in the Visual Arts*, Prentice-Hall, Englewood Cliffs, NJ, 1983

D. Smith. *Sculpture and Drawings*, ed. J. Merkert, Prestel-Verlag, Munich, 1986

R. Smith. "Review", *Artforum*, Dec, 1975

—. "De Maria: Elements", *Art in America*, May, 1978

R. Smithson. "Entropy and the New Monuments", *Artforum*, 4, 10, June, 1966
—. "Incidents of Mirror-Travel in the Yucatan", *Artforum*, Sept, 1967
—. The Monuments of Passaic", *Artforum*, Dec, 1967
—. "Toward the Development of an Air Terminal Site", *Artforum*, Summer, 1967
—. "A Museum of Language in the Vicinity of Art", *Art International*, 12, 3, Mch, 1968
—. *The Writings of Robert Smithson*, ed. N. Holt, New York University Press, New York, NY, 1979
—. *Robert Smithson*, ed. J. Flam, University of California Press, Berkeley, CA, 1996
—. *Robert Smithson: A Collection of Writings*, Pierogi Galery New York, NY, 1997
T. Sokolowski *et al. Robert Morris*, New York University Press, New York, NY, 1989
A. Sondheim, ed. *Post-Movement Art in America*, Dutton, New York, NY, 1977
A. Sonfist. *Alan Sonfist*, Neuberger Museum, New York, NY, 1978
—. ed. *Art in the Land: A Critical Anthology of Environmental Art*, Dutton, New York, NY, 1983
W. Spies. *The Running Fence Project, Christo*, Abrams, New York, NY, 1977
J. Stathatos. "Andy Goldsworthy's Evidences", *Creative Camera*, 255, Mch, 1986
F. Stella. *Working Space*, Harvard University Press, Cambridge, MA, 1986
—. *Frank Stella*, Madrid, 1995
N. Stewart. "Richard Long, Lines of Thought: A Conversation with Nick Stewart", *Circa*, Nov, 1984
K. Stiles & P. Selz, eds. *Theories & Documents of Contemporary Art: A Sourcebook of Artists' Writings*, University of California Press, Berkeley, CA, 1996
S.L. Stoops. *Andy Goldsworthy: Breakdown*, Rose Art Museum, 1992
W.J. Strachan. *Towards Sculpture: Maquettes and Sketches from Rodin to Oldenburg*, Thames & Hudson, London, 1976
G. Sutton. "Land art", *Landskab*, Dec, 1989
D. Sylvester. *About Modern Art*, Chatto & Windus, London, 1996
G. Tiberghien. *Land Art*, Art Data, London, 1995
S. Tillim. "Earthworks and the New Picturesque", *Artforum*, Dec, 1968
C. Tomkins. *Post- to Neo-: The Art World of the 1980s*, Penguin, London, 1989
M. Treib. "Frame, moment and sequence: the photographic book and the designed landscape", *Journal of Garden History*, 15, 2, Summer, 1995
E. Tsai. *Robert Smithson Unearthed*, Columbia University Press, New York, NY, 1991
M. Tuchman. *American Sculpture of the Sixties*, Los Angeles County Museum of Art, CA, 1967
P. Tuchman. "Background of a Minimalist: Carl Andre", *Artforum*, Mch, 1978
J. Turrell. *Mapping Spaces*, Peter Blum, New York, NY, 1987.
—. interview, in B. Oakes, 1995
G. de Vries, ed. *On Art: Artists' Writings on the Changed Notion of Art After 1965*, Cologne, 1974
D. Waldman. *Carl Andre*, Guggenheim, New York, NY, 1970a
—. "Holding the Floor", *Art News*, Oct, 1970b
J. Watkins. "In the artist's studio: Andy Goldsworthy: touching North", *Art International*, 9 Winter, 1989
—. "Andy Goldsworthy: Touching North", *Art International*, Winter, 1989
M. Webster. "Andy Goldsworthy at San Jose Museum of Art", *ArtWeek*. 26, 4, Apl, 1995
U. Weilacher *et al. Between Landscape Architecture and Land Art*, Birkhauser Verlag AG, 1999

L. Weiner. *Lawrence Weiner, Works,* Anatol AV und Film-produktion Hamburg, 1977
Welsh Sculpture Trust. *Sculpture in a Country Park*, Welsh Sculpture Trust, 1983
C. West. "From genesis to box", *Modern Painters*, 5, 4, Winter, 1992
D. Wheeler. *Art Since Mid-Century: 1945 to the Present*, Thames & Hudson, London, 1991
J. White. *The Birth and Rebirth of Pictorial Space*, Faber, London, 1981
O. Wick *et al. James Turrell*, Turske & Turske Gallery, Zurich, 1990
A. Wildermuth. *Richard Long*, Galerie Buchmann, Basel, 1985
A. Wilding: *Alison Wilding*, with M. Tooby, Tate Gallery, St Ives, Cornwall, 1994
C. van Winkel. "The Crooked Path, Patterns of Kinetic Energy", *Parkett*, 33, 1992
M. Winton. "Sculptures That Blow Away", *Ark*, Spring, 1970
S. Wrede & W. Adams. *Denatured Visions: Landscape and Culture in the 20th Century*, Abrams, New York, NY, 1991
S. Yard. *Christo: Oceanfront*, Princeton University Press, Princeton, NJ, 1975
—. *Sitings*, La Jolla Museum of Contemporary Art, La Jolla, CA, 1986
M. Yule. "Andy Goldsworthy, a Lake District photowork", *National Art-Collections Fund Review*, 88, 1992
du Zeitschrift für kultur, *Walking Into Existence*, no. 756, 2005
L. Zelevansky. "Richard Long", *Art News*, 83, 8, Oct, 1984

WEBSITES

Robert Smithson <www.robertsmithson.com>
Walter de Maria <www.lightningfield.org>
Christo <www.christojeanneclaude.net>
James Turrell <www.rodencrater.org>
Mary Miss <www.marymiss.com>
Hamish Fulton <www.hamish-fulton.com>
Chris Drury <www.chrisdrury.co.uk>
Donald Judd <www.chinati.org>
Andy Goldsworthy, Sheepfolds site: <www.sheepfolds.org>
Andy Goldsworthy, *Rivers and Tides* DVD <www.skyline.uk.com/riversandtides>
Richard Long <www.richardlong.org>
Richard Long Newsletter <therichardlongnewsletter.org>

Earthworks <www.earthworks.org>
The Artists: <www.the-artists.org>
Sculpture at Goodwood, CASS: <www.sculpture.org.uk>
Crescent Moon Publishing: <www.crescentmoon.org.uk>